THE OBJECT PRIMER

THIRD EDITION

Scott Ambler, award-winning author of *Building Object Applications That Work*, *Process Patterns*, and *More Process Patterns*, has revised his acclaimed first book, *The Object Primer*. Long prized in its original edition by both students and professionals as the best introduction to object-oriented technology, this book is now completely up-to-date, with all modeling notation rewritten in the just-released UML 2.0. All chapters have been revised to take advantage of Agile Modeling (AM), which is presented in the new Chapter 2 along with other important new modeling techniques.

Review questions at the end of each chapter allow readers to test their newly acquired knowledge. In addition, the author takes time to reflect on the lessons learned over the past few years by discussing the proven benefits and drawbacks of the technology. This is the perfect book for any software development professional or student seeking an introduction to the concepts and terminology of object technology.

Scott W. Ambler is a senior consultant of Ronin International, Inc., a software services consulting firm that specializes in software process mentoring, Agile Modeling (AM), and object/component-based software architecture and development. He is also founder and thought leader of the AM methodology. He is a popular international speaker, a regular columnist for *Software Development* magazine, and the award-winning author of several books, including *The Elements of UML Style*.

THE OBJECT PRIMER

THIRD EDITION

AGILE MODEL–DRIVEN DEVELOPMENT WITH UML 2.0

SCOTT W. AMBLER
Ronin International, Inc.

CAMBRIDGE
UNIVERSITY PRESS

CAMBRIDGE UNIVERSITY PRESS
Cambridge, New York, Melbourne, Madrid, Cape Town, Singapore, São Paulo

Cambridge University Press
32 Avenue of the Americas, New York, NY 10013-2473, USA

www.cambridge.org
Information on this title: www.cambridge.org/9780521540186

First published 2004
Reprinted 2005 (twice), 2007

Printed in the United States of America

A catalogue record for this publication is available from the British Library.

Library of Congress Cataloguing in Publication data

Ambler, Scott W., 1966–
The object primer : agile modeling-driven development with UML 2 /
Scott W. Ambler – 3rd ed.
p.   cm.
Includes bibliographical references and index.
ISBN 0-521-54018-6 (pbk.)
1. Object-oriented methods (Computer science)   2. UML (Computer science)   I. Title.
QA76.64.A494   2004
005.1'17– dc22   2004040400

ISBN   978-0-521-54018-6 paperback

*T*o everyone
*T*hat includes you

Contents

Chapter 2
Understanding the Basics–Object-Oriented Concepts   23

Chapter 5
Usage Modeling   **134**

Acknowledgments

Special thanks to the people who provided insightful comments and questions that led to significant improvements in this book: Kevin Alcock, Trond Andersen, Brad Appleton, Phillipe Back, Steven Baynes, James Beliak, Chris Britton, Larry Brunelle, Francois Coallier, Mike Colbert, Rick Fisher, Martin Gainty, Adam Geras, Mark Graybill, Tom Gullion, Terry Halpin, Ron Jeffries, Jesper Rugaard Jensen, Andrew Johnston, Jon Kern, Bob Lee, Ashley McNeile, Alexey Meledin, Randy Miller, David Mulcihy, Les Munday, John Nalbone, Paul Oldfield, Neil Pitman, Chris Roffler, Doug Rosenberg, Felix Ruessel, Phil Sims, Jim Standley, Tim Tuxworth, Michael Vizdos, Stephen Webb, Ashin Wima, Yuji Yamano, and the staff at Cambridge University Press and TechBooks.

Foreword

Agile software development has moved from the fringes of the software development community to the mainstream. This movement is driven by the need to produce better software faster, which is integral to developing competitive advantage in the global software community. From North America to Asia and everywhere in between, the ability to deliver software that delights the customer has become a critical success factor. The agile community particularly focuses on that customer and ensures that he or she receives maximum value.

Much of the way that we traditionally built software was based on the constraints posed by the systems of old. The amount of time needed to compile these systems was large and software development processes were built around this activity. Getting the code right the first time was important to maximize productivity in this environment. However, many of today's integrated development environments (IDEs) no longer require us to compile the whole system to add some new functionality. In fact, newer compilers often help us get the syntax of our programs correct as we are writing it.

The agile software development movement is taking advantage of the lifting of these constraints. All agile software development processes focus on creating small increments of functionality using an iterative approach. This new approach is in contrast to the "big bang" or waterfall approach where the software is delivered all at one time. Again, today's technology and software development processes allow us to lift another constraint.

The most widely known agile software development process is eXtreme Programming (XP). XP has challenged some additional thoughts on the way in which we create software. For example, XP requires the customer to be on site and to be available to work with the project. In other words, the customer is part of the project instead of being a spec writer or an afterthought.

This idea of having developers work directly with the customer is rapidly gaining traction in other areas of software development. In the service-oriented architecture community, business process experts and software developers are working together to examine new ways in which to automate business processes. Business process fusion, merging two separate business processes, has emerged as a result. Much of this activity was not possible in the past due to the barriers between these organizations.

The agile software development movement has certainly changed the way that we build software. This movement works to maximize productivity by decreasing the elements that sap motivation or detract from the overall goal, delivering software. There is no one better than Scott Ambler to get you started on this road. Scott Ambler, inventor of Agile Modeling and Agile Database Design, creates and presents a roadmap to agile software development in this edition of *The Object Primer*.

In this book, you will find a survey of the latest software development techniques and a wealth of knowledge to get you started on the road to agile. Those new to this community will find an overview of the critical areas of the agile software movement. This book will help you become more productive. The agile principles inside will change the way that you view software development and, ultimately, the way you build software.

Those who are familiar with the agile movement will find nuggets based upon Scott's diverse experience. From his full lifecycle object-oriented testing (FLOOT) to agile requirements and architecture, the new edition of *The Object Primer* puts it all together in one place. There truly is something for everyone here. Not only is it complete, but it is highly readable as well.

The agile software development movement requires that we understand the whole lifecycle. It requires that we can not only write code but also interact with customers and other teams. We work with these other people not through contracts but through relationships. The result is a fluid and highly productive team that delivers software that the customer wants.

Being agile is about removing the constraints on our teams and on ourselves. The road to agile software development requires us to develop many new skills that span the entire software lifecycle. This new edition of *The Object Primer* is an excellent place to learn these skills and start on the continuing road to agile software development.

–Granville Miller

Preface

----

*T*he *Object Primer* is a straightforward, easy-to-understand introduction to agile software development (ASD) using object-oriented (OO) and relational database technologies. It covers the fundamental concepts of ASD and OO and describes how to take an agile approach to requirements, analysis, and design techniques applying the techniques of the unified modeling language (UML) 2 as well as other leading-edge techniques, including agile model–driven development (AMDD) and test-driven development (TDD) approaches. During the 1990s OO superceded the structured paradigm as the primary technology paradigm for software development. Now during the 2000s ASD is superceding traditional, prescriptive approaches to software development. While OO and ASD are often used to develop complex systems, learning them does not need to be complicated. This book is different from many other introductory books about these topics—it is written from the point of view of a real-world developer, someone who has lived through the difficulty of learning these concepts.

WHO SHOULD READ *The Object Primer?*

This book is aimed at two primary audiences—existing developers and university/college students who want to gain the fundamental skills required to succeed on modern software development projects. Throughout this book I use the term "developer" broadly: a developer is anyone involved in the development of a software application. This includes programmers, analysts, designers, business stakeholders, database administrators, support engineers, and so on. While many people would not include business stakeholders in

---

ADVANTAGES OF THIS BOOK

- It is concise, straightforward, and to the point—it does not waste your time.
- It presents the full development lifecycle—there is more to agile software development than just programming!
- It takes complicated concepts and makes them simple—it will shorten your learning curve.
- It is written in the language of developers, not academics—you can understand it.
- It uses real-world examples and case studies—it describes realistic applications.
- It relates new techniques with your current practices—you can see where ASD and OO fit in.
- It provides a smooth transition to these new techniques—your first project can succeed.

---

this, my experience is that active business stakeholder involvement is often the key determinant to the success of a software project. Business stakeholders can actively participate in requirements engineering, analysis, and sometimes, in design—it is clear to me that they should be considered developers. Call me a radical.

WHY READ *The Object Primer*?

By reading *The Object Primer*, you will gain a solid understanding of agile software development, object-oriented, testing, and modeling concepts and techniques. These are the fundamental skills needed to develop object-oriented applications, particularly C# and Java-based software. Furthermore, these skills are put into the context of a running example—you see how these skills can be applied in the real world.

WHY READ THIS BOOK SERIES?

The Object Primer is the first in a four-volume series describing OO techniques and ASD. These are the books:

The Object Primer	Introduction to OO and ASD concepts and techniques
Building Object Applications That Work	Intermediate OO modeling, programming, testing, patterns, metrics, user-interface design, and persistence

The Elements of Java Style	Tips and techniques for writing high-quality Java source code
The Elements of UML Style	Tips and techniques for drawing readable UML diagrams

WHY A THIRD EDITION?

When I wrote the first edition of *The Object Primer*, in the autumn of 1994, the object industry was in relative chaos. The notation wars were raging—there were seven or eight well-known modeling notations and more than 30 less-popular ones—but there was not a clear winner yet. In the winter of 1999/2000 I rewrote the book to use the UML 1.x standard, usage-centered design techniques, Java, and relational technology. This edition now covers the UML 2.x standard and agile software development techniques.

HOW TO READ THIS BOOK

Programmers, Designers, and Project Managers

Read the entire book, cover to cover.

Business Analysts and User Representatives

Chapters 4 through 9 are written specifically for you, describing in detail the techniques for gathering and validating the user requirements for an OO application. Business analysts should also read Chapter 2, which describes the fundamental concepts of object orientation, and Chapter 10, which describes architecture techniques.

Students

Like the first group of people, you should also read this book cover to cover. Furthermore, you should read this book two or three weeks before your midterm test on object orientation, and not the night before the exam. This stuff takes a while to sink in (actually it takes much longer than a few weeks, but there is only so much time in a school term).

About the Author

ScottAmbler is an instance of an **OO Consultant** for **roninInternational** (http://www.ronin-intl.com) based in **denverColorado**. roninInternational implements **architectureConsulting()**, **processMentoring()**, and **softwareDevelopment()** operations. Instances of **HumanoidLifeForm** can send e-mail messages to him at **scott.ambler@ronin-intl.com**. scottAmbler is a versatile object that will polymorphically change type to meet the needs of **roninInternational** clients. For example, he often becomes an **OOMentor**, **OOArchitect**, **OODeveloper**, or **softwareProcessMentor** object. Scott has been an instance of an **OOConsultant** since 1991. He used to be a **MastersStudent** object, having received an instance of an **InformationScienceDegree** from the **universityOfToronto**. As a **MastersStudent**, scottAmbler did a lot of work in OO CASE and instantiated a **ThesisPaper** object in computer-supported cooperative work (an academic alias used to describe groupware). The only message his instance of **ThesisPaper** responds to is **sitOnShelfAndGatherDust**, which scottAmbler finds disappointing but predictable. **scottAmbler** has worked at a variety of organizations, including instances of **Bank**, **InsuranceCompany**, **TelecommunicationsCompany**, **InternetStartup**, **ServicesOutsourcer**, **MilitaryContractor**, **Retailer**, and **ProductDistributor**.

Objects that have been declared as friends of **scottAmbler** often send him the message **youTakeThisObjectStuffTooFar**, to which he responds with the text string "It's nothing compared to how far I take Star Trek." In his spare time, Scott likes to write, having instantiated several books about object technology and agile software development. He also writes regular columns for **softwareDevelopment** (http://www.sdmagazine.com) and **computingCanada** (http://www.plesman.com). **scottAmbler** is an avid watcher of instances of **StarTrek**, and intends to one day do his **doctorateDegree** at **starFleetAcademy**. In addition to the previously mentioned sites, his writings are published at http://www.agilemodeling.com, http://www.agiledata.org, http://www.modelingstyle.info, and http://www.enterpriseunifiedprocess.info.

CHAPTER 1

Leading-Edge Software Development

Modern software development requires modern ways of working.

The only constant in the information technology (IT) industry is change. To remain employable, let alone effective, software developers must continually take the time to identify and then understand the latest development approaches. The goal of this chapter is to introduce you to leading-edge technologies and techniques that enable you to succeed at developing modern business systems. I will try to steer you through the marketing hype surrounding these approaches, and in one case try to dissuade you from adopting it—just because something is new and well hyped does not mean that it has much of a future. In short, this chapter provides you with a foundation for reading the rest of this book.

This chapter discusses

- Modern development technologies;
- Modern development techniques;
- How this book is organized; and
- The case studies.

1.1 Modern Development Technologies

Effective developers understand the fundamentals of the technologies that they have available to them. The good news is that we have many technologies available to us; the bad news is that we have many technologies available to us.

Figure 1.1, which depicts a high-level architecture detailing how these technologies are used together, shows how some applications may be *n*-tiered—an approach where application logic is implemented on several (*n*) categories of computing devices (tiers)—whereas others fall into the "fat client" approach where most business logic is implemented on the client. Object technology is used to implement all types of logic, including both business and system logic. XML is used to share data between tiers, and Web services are used to access logic that resides on different tiers. Most business data are stored in relational databases, which are accessed either via structured query language (SQL) or persistence frameworks (see Chapter 14). Data are returned from the database as a collection of zero or more records and then marshaled either into objects or into XML documents. In the case of a browser-based application the XML structures are in turn converted into HTML documents, often through XSL-T (extensible stylesheet language transformations).

Although the focus of this book is the development of business systems, much of the advice is also applicable to the development of other types of software. My specialty is business software so that is what I will stick to in this book. My experience is that when it comes to building modern business systems, you are very likely to use a combination of the following:

- Object technology;
- Extensible markup language (XML);
- Relational database (RDB); and
- Web services.

1.1.1 Object Technology

The object-oriented (OO) paradigm (pronounced "para-dime") is a development strategy based on the concept that systems should be built from a collection of reusable parts called objects. Examples of OO languages and

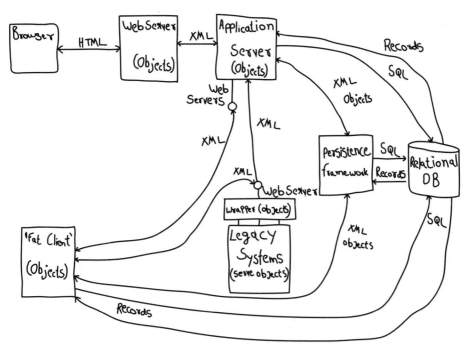

FIGURE 1.1. **High-level application architecture.**

technologies include the Java, C#, and C++ programming languages and the Enterprise JavaBeans (EJB) framework. The original motivation of the object paradigm was that objects were meant to be abstractions of real-world concepts, such as students in a university, seminars that students attend, and transcripts that they receive. This was absolutely true of business objects, but as you will see throughout this book, business objects are only one part of the picture—you also need user interface objects to enable your users to work with your system, process objects that implement logic that works with several business concepts, system objects that provide technical features such as security and messaging, and potentially some form of data objects that persists your business objects.

The use of object technology can be in fact quite robust. In fat client applications object technology is typically used on client machines, such as personal computers or personal digital assistants (PDAs), to implement both user interface code and complex business logic. In thin-client or *n*-tier applications object technology is often used to implement business logic on application

TABLE 1.1. Evaluating Object Technology

Advantages	Disadvantages
<ul><li>Enables development of complex software</li><li>Wide industry acceptance</li><li>Mature, proven technology</li><li>Wide range of development languages and tools to choose from</li><li>Very easy to find people with object experience</li></ul>	<ul><li>Significant skillset is required</li><li>No single language dominates the landscape (although Java, C#, C++, and arguably Visual Basic are clearly popular and here to stay)</li><li>Not all IT professionals, in particular some within the data community, accept it</li><li>Technical "impedance mismatch" with structured technologies and RDBs</li></ul>

servers and sometimes even on other nodes such as database servers, security servers, or business rule servers. Table 1.1 summarizes the strengths and weaknesses of object technology for business system development.

It is useful to contrast these concepts with the structured paradigm and structured technology. The structured paradigm is a development strategy based on the concept that a system should be separated into two parts: data (modeled using a data model) and functionality (modeled using a process model). Following the structured approach, you develop applications in which data are separate from behavior both in the design model and in the system implementation (that is, the program). Examples of structured technologies include the COBOL and FORTRAN programming languages. The main concept behind the object-oriented paradigm is that instead of defining systems as two separate parts (data and functionality), you now define systems as a collection of interacting objects. Objects do things (that is, they have functionality) and they know things (they have data). While this sounds similar to the structured paradigm, in practice it actually is quite different.

However, it is equally important to recognize that structured techniques and technologies still have their place. As you will see later in Section 1.1.4, it is quite common to transform legacy systems, typically implemented with structured technologies, and then wrap them with Web services to reuse their functionality. Furthermore, in coming chapters you will discover that structured

```
<office>
  <name>Ronin International, Inc. HQ</office:name>
  <state>
    <name>Colorado</state:name>
    <area>North West</state:area>
  </state>
  <country>United States of America</country>
</office>
```

FIGURE **1.2. An example of an XML document.**

modeling techniques such as data flow diagrams (DFDs) and data models are still critical to your success.

1.1.2 Extensible Markup Language (XML)

XML is a subset of standard generalized markup language (SGML), the same parent of hypertext markup language (HTML). The critical standards are described in detail at the World Wide Web Consortium Web site (http://www.w3c.org). XML is simply a standardized approach to representing text-based data in a hierarchical manner and for defining metadata about the data. From a programmer's point of view XML is a data representation, backed by metadata, plus a collection of standardized technologies for parsing that data. The data are stored in structures called XML documents and the metadata are contained in document-type definitions (DTDs) and XML schema definitions. Figure 1.2 provides an example of a simple XML document and Table 1.2 overviews the advantages and disadvantages of XML.

XML is often used to transfer data within an application when that application has been deployed across several physical servers. It is also used in enterprise application integration (EAI) as a primary means of sharing data between applications. You will also see XML used for permanent storage in data files; it is quite common to use XML for configuration files in both J2EE and .NET applications, and sometimes even in databases. Chapter 14 discusses database issues in more detail, and you will see at that point that it is often better to "shred" an XML document into individual columns instead of saving it as a single column when storing data in a relational database.

TABLE 1.2. Evaluating XML Technology	
Advantages	Disadvantages
<ul><li>XML is widely accepted</li><li>XML is cross platform</li><li>(Small) XML documents are potentially human readable</li><li>XML is standards based; the World Wide Web Consortium defines and promotes technical standards for XML and XML.org (http://www.xml.org) promotes vertical XML standards within specific industries</li><li>XML separates content from presentation</li></ul>	<ul><li>XML documents are very bulky, causing performance problems</li><li>XML requires marshaling (conversion of XML to objects and vice versa), causing performance problems</li><li>XML standards are still evolving</li><li>XML is overhyped, resulting in unrealistic expectations</li><li>XML business standards will prove elusive because most businesses compete and do not collaborate with their industry peers</li></ul>

1.1.3 Relational Database (RDB) Technology

A relational database is a persistent storage mechanism that stores data as rows in tables. Most relational databases enable you to implement functionality in them as stored procedures, triggers, and even full-fledged Java objects. Although other alternatives to RDBs exist—object-oriented database management systems (OODBMSs), XML databases (XDBs), and object-relational databases (ORDBs)—the fact is that RDBs are the database technology of choice for the vast majority of organizations. Table 1.3 summarizes the pros and cons of using RDBs for modern business applications.

It is important to understand that there is a technical impedance mismatch between RDBs and other common implementation technologies. When it comes to RDBs and objects, RDBs are based on mathematical principles, whereas objects are based on software engineering principles (Ambler 2003a). The end result is that you need to learn how to map your objects into RDBs as well as how to use the two technologies together, the topic of Chapter 14. Similarly, there is a difference between XML and RDBs—XML structures are hierarchical trees, whereas RDB table structures are "bushier" in nature.

TABLE 1.3. Evaluating RDB Technology	
Advantages	Disadvantages
• Wide industry acceptance • Very easy to find RDB expertise • Mature industry dominated by several strong vendors (Oracle, IBM, Sybase, Microsoft) • Open source databases, for example, MySQL, are available • Wide range of development tools • Sophisticated and flexible data processing are supported	• Impedance mismatch with other common technologies, in particular objects and XML

This requires you either to write marshaling code that maps individual XML elements to table columns, degrading performance, or to simply store XML documents in a single column, negating many of the benefits of RDBs.

1.1.4 Web Services

According to the World Wide Web Consortium, a Web service is "a software application identified by a Uniform Resource Identifier (URI), whose interface and bindings are capable of being identified, described, and discovered by XML artifacts and supports direct interactions with other software applications using XML-based messages via Internet-based protocols." Whew! An easier definition is that a Web service is a function that is accessible using standard Web technologies in accordance to standards (McGovern et al. 2003). The Web Services Interoperability Organization (WS-I, http://www.ws-i.org) is a consortium of mostly vendor companies that focus on Web services standards.

Web services are being used to implement functionality that is accessible via Internet technologies, often following an approach referred to as utility computing where the use of a computing service is charged for by the vendor on a usage basis much as electricity or water is charged for. It is far more common to use Web services "behind the firewall" to implement reusable functionality or to wrap legacy systems, including both programs and databases, so that they may be reused by other applications. Internal Web services such as this

TABLE 1.4. Evaluating Web Service Technology	
Advantages	Disadvantages
<ul><li>Promotes reusability through a standardized approach</li><li>Supports location transparency through a UDDI server</li><li>Contains scaleable architecture</li><li>Enables you to reduce dependency on vendors</li></ul>	<ul><li>Searching for services via UDDI is time consuming</li><li>Overhead of XML detracts from performance</li><li>Does not yet support transaction control (this is coming)</li><li>Does not yet support security (this is coming)</li></ul>

are often managed within an internal UDDI (universal description, discovery, and integration) registry or better yet a reuse repository such as Flashline (http://www.flashline.com). A system built from a collection of cohesive services has a service-oriented architecture (SOA). Table 1.4 summarizes the advantages and disadvantages of Web services.

1.2 MODERN DEVELOPMENT TECHNIQUES

Now that we understand the fundamentals of modern technologies, we should now consider modern development techniques. The IT industry is currently undergoing what I consider to be a significant shift—a move from prescriptive development techniques to agile techniques. Until just recently management often bemoaned the fact that developers did not want to follow a process, not understanding what was wrong with the 3,000 pages of procedures they expected everyone to follow. Along came agile software processes such as extreme programming (XP) (Beck 2000), feature-driven development (FDD) (Palmer and Felsing 2002), and agile modeling (Ambler 2002) and developers embraced them. Unfortunately many managers are still leery of agile techniques and fight adoption of them. This is a truly ironic situation—developers are now demanding to follow proven software processes yet are not being allowed to do so. Sigh.

In this section I briefly explore four important development techniques that all developers should be familiar with:

- Agile software development;
- Unified modeling language (UML);
- The unified process; and
- Model-driven architecture (MDA).

1.2.1 Agile Software Development

Over the years several challenges have been discovered with prescriptive software development processes, such as the waterfall lifecycle characterized by the ISO 12207 standard (http://www.ieee.org), the Object-Oriented Software Process (OOSP) (Ambler 1998b, 1999), and the Rational Unified Process (RUP) (Kruchten 2000). First, the Chaos report published by the Standish Group (http://www.standishgroup.com) still shows a significant failure rate within the industry, indicating that prescriptive processes simply are not fulfilling their promise. Second, most developers do not want to adopt prescriptive processes and will find ways to undermine any efforts to adopt them, either consciously or subconsciously. Third, the "big design up front" (BDUF) approaches to software development, particularly those followed by ISO 12207, are incredibly risky due to the fact that they do not easily support change or feedback. This risk is often ignored, if it is recognized at all, by the people promoting these approaches. Fourth, most prescriptive processes promote activities only slightly related to the actual development of software. In short, the bureaucrats have taken over.

To address these challenges a group of 17 methodologists formed the Agile Software Development Alliance (http://www.agilealliance.org), often referred to simply as the Agile Alliance, in February 2001. An interesting thing about this group is that they all came from different backgrounds, and yet they were able to come to an agreement on issues that methodologists typically do not agree upon. They concluded that to succeed at software development you need to focus on people-oriented issues and follow development techniques that readily support change. In fact, they wrote a manifesto (Agile Alliance 2001a) defining four values for encouraging better ways of developing software:

1. **Individuals and interactions** *over* **processes and tools.** The most important factors that you need to consider are the people and how they work together because if you do not get that right the best tools and processes will not be of any use.

2. **Working software** *over* **comprehensive documentation.** The primary goal of software development is to create software, not documents—otherwise it would be called documentation development. Documentation has its place; written properly it is a valuable guide for people's understanding of how and why a system is built and how to work with the system.

3. **Customer collaboration** *over* **contract negotiation.** Only your customer can tell you what they want. They likely do not have the skills to exactly specify the system, they likely will not get it right at first, and they will likely change their minds. Working together with your customers is hard, but that is the reality of the job. Having a contract with your customers is important, but a contract is not a substitute for communication.

4. **Responding to change** *over* **following a plan.** Change is a reality of software development, a reality that your software process must reflect. People change their priorities for a variety of reasons, their understanding of the problem domain changes as they see your work, and the business environment changes, as does technology. Although you need a project plan, it must be malleable and it can be in fact very simple (unlike many of the Gantt charts you may have seen in the past).

The important thing to understand is that while you should value the concepts on the right-hand side you should value the things on the left-hand side even more. A good way to think about the manifesto is that it defines preferences, not alternatives, encouraging a focus on certain areas but not eliminating others.

The Agile Alliance also defines a collection of twelve principles (Agile Alliance 2001b), based on the four values:

1. Our highest priority is to satisfy the customer through early and continuous delivery of valuable software.
2. Welcome changing requirements, even late in development. Agile processes harness change for the customer's competitive advantage.
3. Deliver working software frequently, from a couple of weeks to a couple of months, with a preference to the shorter time scale.
4. Business people and developers must work together daily throughout the project.
5. Build projects around motivated individuals. Give them the environment and support they need, and trust them to get the job done.
6. The most efficient and effective method of conveying information to and within a development team is face-to-face conversation.

TABLE 1.5. Evaluating Agile Software Development	
Advantages	Disadvantages
• Strong anecdotal and some research evidence that it works • Wide acceptance amongst object developers • Several methodologies to choose from • Focuses on working together effectively to deliver working software on a regular basis • Works well for small and large teams	• New to many traditional developers and managers • Explicitly requires active stakeholder participation • Still in early phases of the adoption curve • Significant misunderstandings about agile processes exist; for example, "you don't model" or "you don't write documentation"

7. Working software is the primary measure of progress.
8. Agile processes promote sustainable development. The sponsors, developers, and users should be able to maintain a constant pace indefinitely.
9. Continuous attention to technical excellence and good design enhances agility.
10. Simplicity, the art of maximizing the amount of work not done, is essential.
11. The best architectures, requirements, and designs emerge from self-organizing teams.
12. At regular intervals, the team reflects on how to become more effective and then tunes and adjusts its behavior accordingly.

These principles form a foundation of common sense upon which you can base successful software development efforts. These principles are reflected throughout this book; in particular an agile modeling–driven development (AMDD) approach (described in Chapter 4) supported by a test-driven development (TDD) approach (discussed in Chapter 13) to implementation is described. Table 1.5 summarizes the pros and cons of agile software development.

1.2.2 Unified Modeling Language (UML)

The unified modeling language defines the industry standard notation and semantics for properly applying that notation for software built using

TABLE 1.6. Evaluating the UML

Advantages	Disadvantages
• Wide industry acceptance • Wide range of tool support • Consistent modeling notation	• Modeling tools do not fully support it, and sometimes get the notation wrong when they do • Not yet complete • Many developers only understand UML notations, often because most books and modeling tools do not go beyond the UML to address user interface modeling, data modeling, or even business rules • The full notation is overkill for most projects; most efforts only need a small subset of the notation

object-oriented (OO) or component-based technology (Object Management Group 2003). The UML is currently in release 2.0, and it provides a common and consistent notation with which to describe OO and component software systems. The UML potentially decreases the learning curve for developers because they only need to learn the one modeling language, although as you'll see in this book this isn't completely accurate because the UML is not yet complete.

The UML is clearly a step in the right direction: we are no longer fighting the "notation wars" of the mid-1990s, but it is not perfect. For example, most business applications include user interfaces, yet at the time of this writing the UML does not include a standard way to model user interfaces. Most business applications store data in some sort of database, often a relational one, yet the UML does not include a standard way to model data schemas. The implication is that as long as you are building business software that does not include a user interface, or a database, then the UML *might* be sufficient for your needs. Personally, I have never built a system that was so narrowly constrained. My philosophy is that the UML defines a collection of models that form an important part of your modeling core, but as you will see in coming chapters you need to go beyond the UML if you are to succeed. Table 1.6 summarizes the pros and cons of the UML.

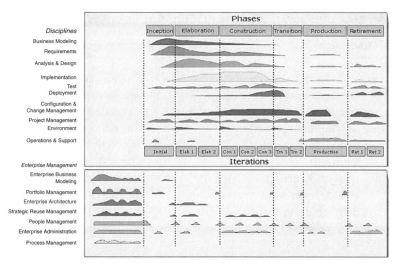

FIGURE 1.3. The lifecycle of the EUP. (Permission to use granted by Ronin International, Inc.)

1.2.3 The Unified Process (UP)

The unified process (Jacobson, Booch, and Rumbaugh 1999) is a frame-work from which software development processes are instantiated. Two such instantiations are the RUP and the enterprise unified process (EUP, http://www.enterpriseunifiedprocess.info). The RUP is a four-phase (inception, elaboration, construction, transition), prescriptive process whose scope is software development. The EUP extends the RUP to make it a full-fledged IT process. As you see in Fig. 1.3 the EUP adds two phases, production and retirement. Not only do you need to develop systems, you also need to run them in production and potentially even remove them from production at some point. The EUP adds an operations and support discipline as well as a collection of enterprise management disciplines (Nalbone, Vizdos, and Ambler 2003) that focus on cross-system issues.

In my opinion the RUP is clearly the market leader among prescriptive processes. It is well documented; you can purchase a comprehensive HTML-based definition of it from IBM's Rational Software division (http://www.rational.com). More important, it has Rational's marketing muscle behind it, ensuring that senior managers have heard about it. Although there are still some problems with the RUP, it clearly is not complete; they luckily can be addressed via extensions such as the EUP and "RUP plug-ins"

TABLE 1.7. Evaluating the UP

Advantages	Disadvantages
• Wide industry acceptance • Management seems to like it • The RUP defines comprehensive development procedures • Supports an evolutionary approach to development, increasing the chance (over serial processes) of delivering software	• Not well accepted by developers, increasing the chance that they will not actually follow it • The RUP is not (yet) complete • The EUP requires significant maturity and understanding of the RUP for organizations to succeed at it

available from Rational and some of its partners. Table 1.7 summarizes the pros and cons of the UP.

My experience is that most successful organizations either are taking an agile approach to software development or are following the RUP/EUP. Some are even trying to take an agile approach to the RUP, although in my opinion this is very hard to accomplish in practice. There simply is a lot of material in the RUP, making it very difficult to cut it down into something agile. If you want to follow an agile process, adopt something along the lines of XP or FDD.

1.2.4 Model-Driven Architecture (MDA)

The model-driven architecture is a framework for software development, defined by the Object Management Group (OMG) (http://www.omg.org), where development efforts are driven by modeling (Kleppe, Warmer, and Bast 2003). The models that you create following an MDA approach are formal; they are highly detailed and developed using sophisticated modeling tools. There are three models core to the MDA:

• **Platform-independent model (PIM).** A model that is independent of implementation technology that is also at a high level of complexity. A PIM is similar in concept to logical models from structured development

(Gane and Sarson 1979) or essential models (Constantine and Lockwood 1999).

- **Platform-specific model (PSM).** A model created by transforming a PIM tailored to specify your system in terms of implementation constructs available in one specific technology. For systems built using several technologies you will need at least one PSM for each.
- **Code.** Code is generated by the transformation of PSMs.

A critical concept of the MDA is that models are transformed by computer-based tools, not by hand. It is quite common to see PSMs transformed into code; for example, Together CC (http://www.borland.com) generates Java code from object models and ERWin (http://www.ca.com) database definition language (DDL) from physical data models (PDMs). The generation of PSMs from PIMs is what is new with the MDA, something that we are starting to see in tools such as Project Technology's Bridgepoint Development Suite (http://www.projtech.com); however, few other tools are this sophisticated. Table 1.8 summarizes the pros and cons of the MDA.

The MDA is a very sophisticated and complex approach to modeling, one that only a very small minority of elite developers will be able to adopt. For the rest of use I suspect that the AMDD approach described in this book is more along the lines of a sketching approach to modeling, one that the vast majority of developers can realistically hope to follow. My experience is that it is hard enough to get developers to create sketches before they code; getting them to produce blueprints is often too much to ask.

Where will the MDA succeed? I suspect that it will become an enabling technology for system integration/interfacing efforts. The people involved with these efforts are often highly skilled and typically lean towards modeling-intense approaches.

1.2.5 Using Them Together

Being the person behind the AM methodology, I can safely say that you can take an agile approach to apply the UML on software projects and in fact you can do so (and should) with non-UML models too. I have also successfully applied AM on RUP/EUP projects (Ambler 2002), so I can safely say that those two processes work together, although it does require you to be far more agile with the RUP than some people are comfortable with.

TABLE 1.8. Evaluating the MDA	
Advantages	Disadvantages
• Modeling tool vendors back the MDA • Provides one strategy for taking a modeling-driven approach to development • Offers potential for developing truly portable systems • Potentially increases system portability by minimizing platform-specific coding • Potentially increases system interoperability through generation of bridges between PSMs • Provides sophisticated documentation, in the form of highly detailed models • Code does not get out of sync with the models because (in ideal situations) it is generated from them • Potential to avoid platform vendor lock-in through generation of code	• Mainstream modeling tools that truly support the MDA will prove elusive • Requires developers to have a sophisticated modeling skillset, something that is not very common • Vendors are unlikely to build tools that will work well together, negating many of the potential benefits • Increases chance of tool vendor lock-in—even though MDA is a standard, it is implemented differently with each tool vendor

1.3 THE ORGANIZATION OF THIS BOOK

The Object Primer covers leading-edge development techniques and concepts that have been proven in the development of real-world applications. It describes how to apply agile software development techniques such as TDD and AMDD. It covers in detail supporting techniques, including both testing and modeling techniques that work on real-world projects. Because you can and should do more than just unit test your code, the techniques of the full lifecycle object-oriented testing (FLOOT) methodology are described. With respect to modeling, a wide range of techniques are described, including those

TABLE **1.9. Chapters in This Book**	
Chapter	Description
2. Object-Oriented Concepts	An overview of the fundamental concepts that you require to work effectively with object technology.
3. Full Lifecycle Object-Oriented Testing (FLOOT)	A description of a collection of techniques that can be used throughout the entire software development lifecycle (SDLC), including unit testing techniques that you can apply as part of your TDD efforts (Chapter 13).
4. Agile Modeling–Driven Development (AMDD)	An overview of AMDD, an evolutionary approach to development where you create agile models to understand what it is that you are building before you code it. You will discover that your modeling and documentation efforts can in fact be incredibly effective when you are following an agile approach.
5. Usage Modeling	A summary of usage modeling techniques such as use cases, user stories, and features that enable you to explore how your stakeholders work with your system.
6. User Interface Development	The user interface is the system to your users; therefore all software developers need to understand the basics of user interface development.
7. Supplementary Requirements	This chapter describes a wide range of modeling techniques, such as business rules and technical requirements, that you can use to supplement other forms of requirements.
8. Conceptual Domain Modeling	An overview of techniques that enable you to explore entities within your problem domain, such as orders and order items within an online order system, and the relationships between these entities.

(continued)

TABLE 1.9 *(continued)*	
Chapter	Description
9. Process Modeling	An overview of techniques that enable you to explore business and technical processes. These techniques supplement, and potentially replace, usage modeling techniques.
10. Agile Architecture	This chapter describes an agile approach to architecture, as well as several modeling techniques that you can apply to explore the high-level design of your system.
11. Dynamic Object Modeling	An overview of modeling techniques that explore the behavioral aspects of software built using object technology.
12. Detailed Structural Design	This chapter describes techniques such as UML class modeling and physical data modeling, which enable you to define the structure of the software that you are building.
13. Agile Object Programming Techniques	An overview of techniques for agile programming, including TDD and refactoring. It also shows how to move from detailed design to Java source code and presents a collection of programming tips and techniques.
14. Agile Database Development Techniques	This chapter presents an evolutionary approach to database development, overviewing development techniques such as database refactoring and the fundamentals of mapping objects to relational databases. It also describes a collection of implementation techniques for working with object and relational technology effectively.
15. Where to Go From Here	This chapter briefly summarizes the book and provides advice for your next steps in learning about modern software development.

defined by the UML as well as non-UML artifacts—as you will see in the modeling chapters the UML is not complete. Table 1.9 describes the other chapters within this book.

It is interesting to note that Table 1.9 does not include chapters for requirements gathering, analysis, and design as the previous edition of this book did. That is because the industry appears, at least to me, to be moving beyond these antiquated concepts. Don't get me wrong, it still makes sense to consider these three issues—you will always want to ask what your stakeholders want (requirements), explore the details of the requirements (analysis), and determine how you're going to fulfill those requirements (design). What does not make sense is to consider them as development phases, the result of traditional/serial thinking, because modern development has moved beyond that approach. Furthermore, it may not even make sense to even consider them as iterative disciplines as you saw with the Unified Process (Section 1.2.3) because the terms can be confusing for traditionalists making the switch to evolutionary techniques and because the concepts are too broad in scope.

My experience is that it is better to consider modeling categories instead of modeling phases/disciplines. Figure 1.4 depicts this idea, indicating that there are eight different modeling categories (each of which is described in detail by a corresponding book chapter) and that there are several potential models within each category. Important concepts to understand include the following:

- You don't need to create every single model in each category.
- You don't need to create a model for each category, although you should at least consider the issues which each category addresses.
- Modeling is iterative, depicted by the starburst arrow connecting the category boxes.
- Effective developers understand a wide range of models (each model listed in Fig. 1.4 is described in this book).
- There are many other modeling artifacts available to you. The ones described in this book are simply the most common ones.

1.4 THE CASE STUDIES

Throughout this book I will use three case studies—a university information system and an online ordering system, which I will use throughout, although the focus will be on the university system, and a banking case study, which

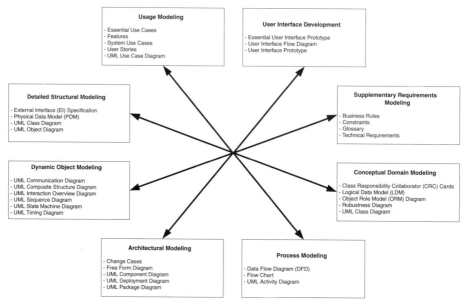

FIGURE 1.4. A modern look at modeling.

I will ask you to work on throughout the book. As I present examples from the university and online ordering systems I will explain them as needed. The bank case study, however, is described in detail here.

1.4.1 The Bank Case Study

The Archon Bank of Cardassia (ABC) would like to develop an information system for handling accounts. The following is a summary of interviews with employees and customers of the bank.

The bank has many different types of accounts. The basic type of account is called a savings account. Savings account customers do not get a monthly account statement. Instead, they have a passbook, which gets updated when they come in. Each passbook page has enough room to have up to ten transactions and, everytime the book is updated, the next transaction is printed immediately after the last one in the book. The bank already has the passbook printers and printing software in place (we bought it from a third-party vendor).

Customers are able to open and close accounts. They can withdraw or deposit money, or get the current balance. The current balance is displayed on an account update screen, which will be part of the teller's information system. This screen displays the account number, the customer's name, and the current balance of the account. An account is associated with a specific branch. Although we now support multibranch banking, every account is still assumed to have a "home" branch.

A checking account is just like a savings account, except customers can also write checks on it. We sell checks for $30 for a box of 100. Once a customer uses 75 checks, or check #90 comes in, we send them a notice in the mail asking them if they want to purchase more checks. Account statements are sent out every month. Checking accounts do not have passbooks, and savings accounts do not have account statements.

We charge $1,200 a year for private banking accounts (PBAs). PBAs are just like checking accounts. PBAs entitle customers to investment counselling services, as well as to other services unavailable to other clients. A PBA account can be held by only one customer, although a customer may have more than one PBA account. This is exactly like savings accounts. Checking accounts, however, can be joint. This means a checking account can be accessed by one or more customers (perhaps a husband and a wife).

A current account is for our corporate customers. It works like a checking account, with a few extra features. For example, a quarterly account statement (which is exactly the same as a monthly account statement, except it is done for an entire quarter) is sent out, in addition to the regular monthly statements. The quarterly statement is sent in the same envelope as the statement for that month. Corporate customers also get to choose the number of checks they are sent (100, 250, 500, or 1,000) at a time. Current accounts are not joint and they cannot be accessed through an ATM. Furthermore, because of the different service needs of our corporate customers, we deal with them at special branches called "corporate branches." Corporate branches serve only corporate customers. They do not serve our retail (normal) customers. Corporate customers can be served at "retail branches," although they rarely do because the tellers in a retail branch do not have the necessary background to meet their special needs.

More than one account can be accessible from a bank card. We currently give cards out to any customer who wants them. Customers access their accounts using two different methods: at an automated teller machine (ATM) or at a bank branch. ATMs enable customers to deposit to, withdraw from, and get balances from their accounts. They can also pay bills (this is basically a withdrawal) and transfer money between accounts (this is basically withdrawing from one account and depositing into another).

Everything that can be done at a bank machine can also be done by a real live teller in a branch. The teller will have an information system that provides the screens to perform all of these functions. Additionally, tellers can also help customers to open and close their accounts, as well as print out account statements for the customer. The account statements are just like the monthly/quarterly statements, except they can be for any time period. For example, a customer could request a statement from the 15th of August to the 23rd of September, and we should be able to print that out on the spot.

Monthly and quarterly account statements are normally printed out on the first Saturday of the following month. This is done by an automated batch job.

Because we have started to put ATMs into variety stores and restaurants (in the past, we only had ATMs in branches), we now consider every ATM, including those in our "brick and mortar" branches, to be a branch as well. This means ATMs have branch IDs and addresses, just like a normal branch does.

To manage the bank effectively, we split it up into collections of branches called "areas." An area is a group of between 10 and 30 branches. A branch is part of only one area, and all branches are in an area. Each area has a unique name and is managed by an "area manager." Area managers receive weekly transaction summary reports every Monday before 9 in the morning. This report summarizes the number and total amounts of all withdrawals, deposits, and bill payments performed at each branch (including ATMs) for the previous week. For brick and mortar branches, there is also an indication of how many accounts in total were at that branch at the beginning of the week, how many accounts were opened during the week, how many accounts were closed during the week, and how many accounts there are now. Finally, all these figures are summarized and outputted for the entire area.

1.5 WHAT YOU HAVE LEARNED

This chapter summarized modern software technologies (object technology, relational databases, XML, and Web services), discussed the trade-offs of each technology, and described how to use them together. It also summarized modern software techniques (agile software development, the Unified Process, the UML, and the MDA) and also discussed their trade-offs and how to use them together.

CHAPTER 2

Understanding the Basics–Object-Oriented Concepts

Object-oriented concepts seem simple.
Don't be deceived.

You need to understand object-oriented (OO) concepts before you can successfully apply them to systems development. Because OO techniques grew, in part, out of the disciplines of software engineering, artificial intelligence, and information modeling, many of them will seem familiar to you. Do not let this make you complacent—you also need to understand several new concepts.

This chapter explores the following:

- A brief overview of OO concepts;
- OO concepts from a structured point of view;
- The diagrams of the unified modeling language (UML 2);
- Objects and classes;
- Attributes and operations;
- Abstraction, encapsulation, and information hiding;
- Inheritance;

- Persistence;
- Relationships;
- Collaboration;
- Polymorphism;
- Interfaces;
- Components; and
- Patterns.

2.1 A Brief Overview of OO Concepts

This chapter discusses the concepts that make up the foundation of OO development techniques. People experienced with structured technologies such as COBOL and FORTRAN will have seen some of these concepts before, and some will be new to you. For example, many concepts that go to the heart of OO—encapsulation, coupling, and cohesion—come from software engineering. These concepts are important because they underpin good design regardless of the technology you are working with. The main point to be made here is you do not want to deceive yourself: just because you have seen some of these concepts before, it does not mean you were doing OO; it just means you were doing good design. While good design is a big part of object orientation, there is a lot more to it than that.

OO concepts appear deceptively simple. Do not be fooled. The underlying concepts of structured techniques also seemed simple, yet we all know structured development was actually quite difficult. Just as there was more to the structured paradigm than a few simple concepts, there is also more to the OO paradigm. Just as it took time to get truly good at structured development it will also take time to get good at OO development. To give you a taste for what this chapter is about, the concepts and the terms I describe are briefly summarized in Table 2.1.

TIP
Keep a List of Common Terms at Hand
You should consider making a photocopy of Table 2.1 and keeping it handy while learning object orientation, particularly if you are attending a class on this topic. You are being inundated with new ideas and techniques, and it certainly would not hurt to have a "cheat sheet" close at hand to help you understand OO concepts.

TABLE 2.1. A Summary of Object-Oriented Concepts and Terms

Term	Description
Abstract class	A class that does not have objects instantiated from it
Abstraction	The essential characteristics of an item (perhaps a class or operation)
Aggregation	Relationships between two classes or components defined as "is part of"
Aggregation hierarchy	A set of classes related through aggregation
Association	A relationship between two classes or objects
Attribute	Something a class knows (data/information)
Cardinality	The concept of "how many?"
Class	A software abstraction of similar objects, a template from which objects are created
Classifier	A UML term that refers to a collection of instances that have something in common. This includes classes, components, data types, and use cases.
Cohesion	The degree of relatedness of an encapsulated unit (such as a component or a class)
Collaboration	Classes work together (collaborate) to fulfill their responsibilities
Component	A cohesive unit of functionality that can be independently developed, delivered, and composed with other components to build a larger unit
Composition	A strong form of aggregation in which the "whole" is completely responsible for its parts and each "part" object is only associated to one "whole" object
Concrete class	A class that has objects instantiated from it
Coupling	The degree of dependence between two items
Encapsulation	The grouping of related concepts into one item, such as a class or a component
Information hiding	The restriction of external access to attributes
Inheritance	Relationships defined as "is a" and "is like"
Inheritance hierarchy	A set of classes related through inheritance
Instance	An object that is an example of a particular class

(*continued*)

TABLE 2.1 (continued)

Term	Description
Instantiate	To create objects from class definitions
Interface	A collection of one or more operation signatures that defines a cohesive set of behaviors
Message	A request either for information or to perform an action
Messaging	The process of collaboration between objects by sending messages to each other
Method	A process implemented by a class that performs an action of value (similar to a function in structured programming)
Multiple inheritance	The direct inheritance from more than one class
Object	A person, place, thing, event, concept, screen, or report, based on a class definition
Optionality	The concept of "do you need to have it?"
Override	To redefine attributes and/or methods in subclasses so that they are different from the definition in the superclass
Pattern	A reusable solution to a common problem taking relevant forces into account
Persistence	The storing of objects to permanent storage, for example, files, databases, etc.
Persistent object	An object saved to permanent storage
Polymorphism	The ability of different objects to respond to the same message in different ways, enabling objects to interact with one another without knowing their exact type
Property	In UML 2, a named value, for example, attributes and associations, including composition, denoting a characteristic of an element (such as a class or component). In C# the combination of an attribute with its getter and setter.
Single inheritance	The direct inheritance from only one class
Stereotype	A common usage of a modeling element
Subclass	A class that inherits from another class
Superclass	A class from which another class inherits
Transitory object	An object not saved to permanent storage

2.2 OO CONCEPTS FROM A STRUCTURED POINT OF VIEW

Chances are pretty good that you were overwhelmed by the list of concepts presented in Table 2.1. If you are studying for a test, I suppose the list will be useful to you. Most of us are looking for a way to learn OO concepts easily. Before I get into detailed explanations, I want to describe the four basic OO concepts quickly, in language that may be familiar to you: structured terminology.

- **Class.** A class is a software abstraction of an object, effectively, a template from which objects are created. If you have database experience, you can start thinking of a class as a table, although there is much more to classes than this, as we shall see later. The definition of a table describes the layout of the records to be stored in it. The definition of a class describes the layout, including both the data and the functionality, of the objects to be created from it. Notice how I said both data and functionality. Unlike a table, which defines only data, a class defines both data (attributes) and code (operations/methods). For now, a good way to think about a class is that it is the combination of a table definition and the definition of the source code that accesses the data. Unfortunately this is a very data-oriented view of objects as it ignores the main strength of objects, i.e., the ability to respond to requests to do things. But it is a good enough start for now.

- **Object.** An object is a software construct that mirrors a concept in the real world, e.g., a person, place, thing, event, concept, screen, or report. Objects are typically (but not always) nouns. If a class can be thought of as a table, an object can be thought of as a record occurrence. Again, this is a very data-oriented approach to objects. For example, a student object can do many of the things that a "real" student could, e.g., provide its name, compute how old it is, and request to enroll in a seminar. In a structured application, each student would be represented as a record in the *Student* data table. In an object-oriented application, each student would be represented as an object in memory. The main difference is that where student records only have data, student objects have both data (attributes) and functionality (methods). More on this later.

- **Attribute.** An attribute is equivalent to a data element in a record. From a programming point of view, it also makes sense to think of an attribute as a local variable applicable only to a single object.

- **Method.** A method can be thought of as either a function or procedure. Methods access and modify the attributes of an object. Better yet, methods can do a whole bunch of stuff that has nothing to do with attributes. Some methods return a value (like a function), whereas other methods cause side effects, like printing and persisting data. A useful method should either return a value or have a meaningful side effect.

While you are reading this book, you may find the need to come back to these definitions occasionally. Do not worry, that is normal. Object orientation introduces several new concepts and terms that can easily overwhelm you. So take your time and reread this chapter a few times. That is the only way you're going to learn this stuff.

2.3 THE DIAGRAMS OF UML 2

Understanding the thirteen diagrams of UML 2.x, summarized in Table 2.2, is an important part of understanding OO development. Although there is far more to modeling than just the UML, as you will see throughout this book, the reality is that the UML defines the standard modeling artifacts when it comes to object technology.

There are three classifications of UML diagrams:

- **Behavior diagrams.** This is a type of diagram that depicts behavioral features of a system or business process. This includes activity, state machine, and use case diagrams as well as the four interaction diagrams.

- **Interaction diagrams.** This is a subset of behavior diagrams that emphasize object interactions. This includes communication, interaction overview, sequence, and timing diagrams.

- **Structure diagrams.** This is a type of diagram that depicts the static elements of a specification that are irrespective of time. This includes class, composite structure, component, deployment, object, and package diagrams.

2.4 OBJECTS AND CLASSES

The OO paradigm is based on building systems from items called objects. An object is any person, place, thing, event, concept, screen, or report. A

TABLE 2.2. The Diagrams of UML 2	
Diagram	Description
Activity diagram	Depicts high-level business processes, including data flow, or to model the complex logic within a system. See Chapter 9.
Class diagram	Shows a collection of static model elements such as classes and types, their contents, and their relationships. See Chapters 8 and 12.
Communication diagram	Shows instances of classes, their interrelationships, and the message flow between them, and typically focuses on the structural organization of objects that send and receive messages; called a collaboration diagram in UML 1.x. See Chapter 11.
Component diagram	Depicts the components, including their interrelationships, interactions, and public interfaces, that compose an application, system, or enterprise. See Chapter 10.
Composite structure diagram	Depicts the internal structure of a classifier (such as a class, component, or use case), including the interaction points of the classifier to other parts of the system. See Chapter 8.
Deployment diagram	Shows the execution architecture of systems, including nodes, either hardware or software execution environments, and the middleware connecting them. See Chapter 12.
Interaction overview diagram	A variant of an activity diagram, which overviews the control flow within a system or business process,whereby each node/ activity within the diagram can represent another interaction diagram. See Chapter 11.
Object diagram	Depicts objects and their relationships at a point in time, typically a special case of either a class diagram or a communication diagram. See Chapter 12.

(continued)

TABLE 2.2 *(continued)*	
Diagram	Description
Package diagram	Shows how model elements are organized into packages as well as the dependencies between packages. See Chapter 10.
Sequence diagram	Models sequential logic, in effect the time ordering of messages between classifiers. See Chapter 11.
State machine diagram	Describes the states an object or interaction may be in, as well as the transitions between states; formerly referred to as a state diagram, state chart diagram, or a state-transition diagram. See Chapter 11.
Timing diagram	Depicts the change in state or condition of a classifier instance or role over time, and typically used to show the change in state of an object over time in response to external events. See Chapter 11.
Use Case Diagram	Shows use cases, actors, and their relationships. See Chapter 5.

class generalizes/represents a collection of similar objects and is effectively a template from which to create objects. In a university system, Sarah is a student object, she attends several seminar objects, and she is working on a degree object. In a banking system, Sarah is a customer object. She has a checking account object from which she bounces rubber-check objects. In an inventory control system, every inventory item is an object, every delivery is an object, and every customer is an object.

In the real world, you have objects; therefore, you need them as a concept to reflect your problem space accurately. However, in the real world, objects are often similar to other kinds of objects. Students share similar qualities (they do the same sort of things; they are described in the same sort of way), courses share similar qualities, inventory items share similar qualities, bank accounts share similar qualities, and so on. While you could model (and program) every object, that is a lot of work. I prefer to define what it is to be a student once, define course once, define inventory item once, define bank account once, and so on. That is why you need the concept of a class.

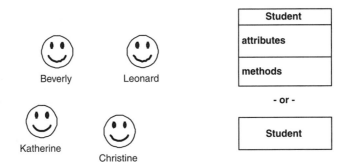

Some Student Objects   **The Student Class**

FIGURE **2.1. Student objects in the real world and two ways to model the class *Student*.**

Figure 2.1 depicts how we have student objects and how we model the class *Student*. It also shows the standard notations to model a class using the UML. Classes are typically modeled in one of two ways: as either a rectangle that lists its attributes and methods or as just a rectangle (in fact a class box can have as many sections as needed, but one or three sections are the norm). There are reasons for modeling classes either way. On the one hand, listing the attributes and methods can be quite helpful. It enables readers of your class models to gain a better understanding of your design at a single glance. On the other hand, listing the attributes and methods can clutter your diagrams and obscure readability. In this book, I use both techniques, listing the methods and attributes only where appropriate.

Class names are typically singular nouns. The name of a class should be one or two words, usually a noun, and should accurately describe the class using common business terminology. If you are having trouble naming a class, either you need to understand it better or it might be several classes you have mistakenly combined. You should model classes with names like *Student, Professor*, and *Course*, not *Students, People Who Teach Seminars*, and *CLS32A*. Think of it like this: in the real world, you would say "I am a student," not "I am a students."

Class can also represent concepts that are not nouns, like the process of checking out a book from a library. More on this concept can be found in Chapter 12.

When object-oriented software is running, objects are instantiated (created/defined) from classes. We say an object is an instance of a class and we instantiate those objects from classes.

2.5 ATTRIBUTES AND OPERATIONS/METHODS

Classes have responsibilities, the things they know and do. Attributes are the things classes know; methods are the things classes do. The object-oriented paradigm is based on the concepts that systems should be built out of objects, and that objects have both data and functionality. Attributes define the data, while methods define the functionality.

When you define a class, you must define the attributes it has, as well as its methods. In UML 2 an attribute is a type of property, discussed in Section 2.9.4, as are relationships such as association and composition. The definition of an attribute is straightforward. You define its name, perhaps its type (whether it is a number, a string, or a date, and so forth). Weakly typed languages like Smalltalk enable you to use attributes any way you want and, therefore, do not require you to define their type. Strongly typed languages like Java and C++, however, insist you define the type of an attribute before you actually use it. You may also choose to indicate any business rules or constraints applicable to the attribute, such as the valid values the attribute may have.

The definition of a method is simpler: you define the logic for it, just as you would code for a function or a procedure. I am using the term "method" differently than the UML does—what I am really showing are the operations of the class, and methods are the implementation of those operations. I used to program a fair bit in Smalltalk and Smalltalk uses the term method, and that has stuck with me. Do not worry about it; object terminology is notorious for its inexactness. In future chapters I elaborate on object-oriented modeling and object-oriented programming; moreover, I go into further detail regarding the specification of methods. When I cover the concept of collaboration in Section 2.10 you will see that collaborations are fulfilled by methods. For now, an important implication is that methods do one of two things: either they return a value and/or they do something of value; that is, they have a side effect.

In Fig. 2.2, you see two different types of objects: a *student* and a *seminar*. Both objects know and do certain things, and you want to make sure you record this in your models, as you see in Fig. 2.3. I am using the three-section class notation in this case: the top section for the name, the middle section to list the attributes, and the bottom section to list the methods.

Figure 2.3 depicts two types of attributes: instance attributes, which are applicable to a single object, and static attributes, which are applicable to all instances of a single class. Static attributes are underlined, instance attributes are not. For example, *name* is an instance attribute of the class *Student*. Each

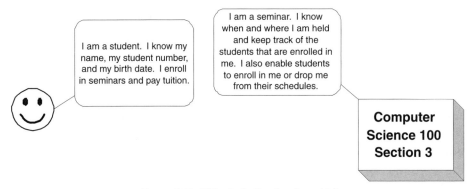

FIGURE 2.2. Objects in the "real world."

individual student has a name; for example, one student may have the name "Smith, John," whereas another student may have the name "Jones, Sally." It could even happen that two individual students may have the same name, such as "Smith, John" although they are, in fact, two different people.

On the other hand, *nextStudentNumber* is a static attribute (also referred to as a class attribute) that is applicable to the class *Student*, not specifically to individual instances. This attribute is used to store the value of the next student number to be assigned to a student: when a new student joins the school, his or her student number is set to the current value of *nextStudentNumber*, which is then incremented to ensure all students have unique student numbers.

Similarly, there is the concept of instance methods and static/class methods: instance methods operate on a single instance, whereas static methods operate potentially on all instances of a single class. In Fig. 2.3, you see that *Student* has instance methods called *enrollInSeminar* and *dropSeminar*, things an individual student would do. It also has the static method *findByName*, which supports the behavior of searching for students whose names

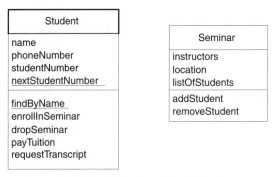

FIGURE 2.3. The *Student* and *Seminar* classes.

meet specified search criteria, a method that operates on all instances of the class.

2.6 ABSTRACTION, ENCAPSULATION, AND INFORMATION HIDING

Instead of saying we determined what a class knows and does, we say we "abstracted" the class. Instead of saying we designed how the class will accomplish these things, we say we "encapsulated" them. Instead of saying we designed the class well by restricting access to its attributes, we say we have "hidden" the information.

2.6.1 Abstraction

The world is a complicated place. To deal with that complexity we form abstractions of the things in it. For example, consider the abstraction of a person. From the point of view of a university, it needs to know the person's name, address, telephone number, social security number, and educational background. From the point of view of the police, they need to know a person's name, address, phone number, weight, height, hair color, eye color, and so on. It is still the same person, just a different abstraction, depending on the application at hand.

    Abstraction is an analysis issue that deals with what a class knows or does. Your abstraction should include the responsibilities, the attributes, and the methods of interest to your application—and ignore the rest. That is why the abstraction of a student would include the person's name and address, but probably not his or her height and weight. OO systems abstract only what they need to solve the problem at hand. People often say abstraction is the act of painting a clear box around something: you are identifying what it does and does not do. Some people will also say that abstraction is the act of defining the interface to something. Either way, you are defining what the class knows and does.

2.6.2 Encapsulation

Although the act of abstraction tells us that we need to store a student's name and address, as well as be able to enroll students in seminars, it does not tell us how we are going to do this. Encapsulation deals with the issue of how you intend to modularize the features of a system. In the object-oriented world, you modularize systems into classes, which, in turn, are modularized into methods and attributes. We say that we encapsulate behavior into a class or we encapsulate functionality into a method.

Encapsulation is a design issue that deals with how functionality is compartmentalized within a system. You should not have to know how something is implemented to be able to use it. The implication of encapsulation is that you can build anything anyway you want, and then you can later change the implementation and it will not affect other components within the system (as long as the interface to that component did not change).

People often say encapsulation is the act of painting the box black: you are defining how something is going to be done, but you are not telling the rest of the world how you are going to do it. In other words you are hiding the details of the implementation of an item from the users of that item. For example, consider your bank. How does it keep track of your account information, on a mainframe, a mini, or a PC? What database does it use? What operating system? It does not matter, because it has encapsulated the way in which it performs account services. You just walk up to a teller and initiate whatever transactions you want. By hiding the details of the way it has implemented accounts, your bank is free to change that implementation at any time, and it should not affect the way services are provided to you.

2.6.3 Information Hiding

To make your applications maintainable, you want to restrict access to data attributes and some methods. The basic idea is this: if one class wants information about another class, it should have to ask for it, instead of taking it. When you think about it, this is exactly the way the real world works. If you want to learn somebody's name, what would you do? Would you ask the person for his name, or would you steal his wallet and look at his ID? By restricting access to attributes, you prevent other programmers from writing highly coupled code. When code is highly coupled, a change in one part of the code forces you to make a change in another, and then another, and so on. Coupling is described in detail in Section 2.11.

2.6.4 An Example

Figure 2.4 depicts the driver's interface for a car. The abstraction is how you work with the wheel, pedals, and gearshift to drive a car. Encapsulation allows

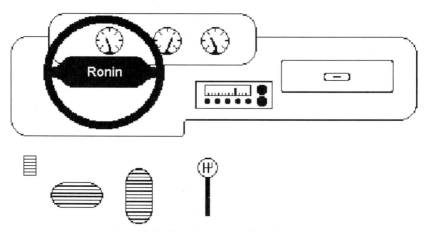

FIGURE **2.4. The driver's interface for a car.**

various carmakers to provide a consistent interface, although each brand of car is built differently. Information hiding is represented by the fact that although the oil is kept at a specific pressure within the engine the driver does not know what the exact pressure is. In other words, information about the oil is hidden from the user.

Remember how I said it was up to you how you implement things and that you should be able to change the way you implemented it at any time? This was called encapsulation. Encapsulation absolutely requires information hiding. For example, say the programmer for class *Student* knows the attribute *listOfStudents* in the class *Seminar* was implemented as an array. The programmer decides to have the instance of *Student* add itself in the first available array element. A few months later, somebody else comes along and decides to reimplement *listOfStudents* as a linked list to use memory more efficiently. This is a reasonable and likely change. Unfortunately, the second programmer does not know the first programmer was directly updating the array of students; consequently, the university information system crashes.

Had access to the attribute *listOfStudents* been restricted, the programmer of *Student* would not have been able to update its value directly. Therefore, the programmer would have had to write code to ask seminar objects to add a student object into its list. If this had been the case, when *listOfStudents* was changed into a linked list, a problem would not have occurred (when the second programmer changed the implementation of the attribute, she would also have modified any methods of *Seminar* that accessed it). By hiding the information (the seminar list) and encapsulating how students are enrolled in courses, you are able to keep the abstraction the same.

2.7 INHERITANCE

Similarities often exist between different classes. Two or more classes often share the same attributes and/or the same methods. Because you do not want to have to write the same code repeatedly, you want a mechanism that takes advantage of these similarities. Inheritance is that mechanism. Inheritance models "is a", "is kind of", and "is like" relationships, enabling you to reuse existing data and code easily.

For example, students have names, addresses, and telephone numbers, and they drive vehicles. At the same time, professors also have names, addresses, and telephone numbers, and they drive vehicles. Without a doubt, you could develop the classes for student and professor and get them both running. In fact, you could even develop the class *Student* first and, once it is running, make a copy of it, call it *Professor*, and make the necessary modifications. While this is straightforward to do, it is not perfect. What if there was an error in the original code for student? Now you must fix the error in two places, which is twice the work. What would happen if you needed to change the way you handled names (say, you go from a length of 30 to a length of 40)? Now you would have to make the same change in two places again, which is a lot of dull, boring, tedious work (and costly). Would it not be nice if you had only one copy of the code to develop and maintain?

This is exactly what inheritance is all about. With inheritance, you define a new class that encapsulates the similarities between students and professors. This new class would have the attributes *name*, *address*, and *phoneNumber*, and the method *driveVehicle*. Because you need to name all our classes, you need to ask yourself what this collection of data and functionality describes. In this case, I think the name *Person* is fitting.

Once you have the class *Person* defined, you then make *Student* and *Professor* inherit from it. You would say *Person* is the superclass of both *Student* and *Professor*, and *Student* and *Professor* are the subclasses of *Person*. Everything that a superclass knows or does, the subclass knows or does free without writing extra code. Actually, for this example, you would need to write two lines of code, one saying *Student* is a subclass of *Person*, and another saying *Professor* is a subclass of *Person*; therefore, it is almost free. Because *Person*

> **TIP**
>
> **Place Subclasses below Superclasses**
>
> When you are drawing a class model, such as that in Fig. 2.6, common practice is to show a subclass below its superclass(es). Although this is not always possible, it is a good practice to follow because it increases the consistency within your diagrams, making them easier to read.

has a name, address, and telephone number, both *Student* and *Professor* also have those attributes. Because *Person* has the ability to drive a vehicle, so do the classes *Student* and *Professor*.

2.7.1 Modeling Inheritance

Figure 2.5 depicts the UML modeling notation for inheritance, a line with a closed arrowhead. The way you would read the diagram is "*B* inherits from *A*." In other words, *B* is a direct subclass of *A* and *A* is the direct superclass of *B* (I discuss the concept of indirect subclasses and superclasses later in Section 2.7.3).

Figure 2.6 presents how you would model the *Person* inheritance class hierarchy, often simply called a class hierarchy. Notice how the name of the *Person* class is in italics, indicating it is abstract, whereas *Professor* and *Student* are concrete classes. Abstract and concrete classes are discussed in Section 2.7.4. For now, simply take note of the way to indicate classes in the UML.

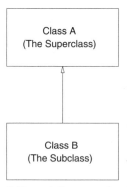

FIGURE 2.5. The UML modeling notation for inheritance.

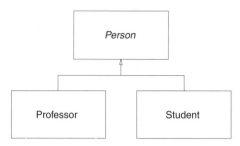

FIGURE 2.6. Modeling the concept that *Professor* and *Student* inherit from *Person*.

2.7.2 Inheritance Tips and Techniques

The following tips and techniques should help you to apply inheritance effectively.

1. **Look for similarities.** Whenever you have similarities between or among two or more classes, either similar attributes or similar methods, then you probably have an opportunity for inheritance.

2. **Look for existing classes.** When you identify a new class, you might already have an existing class to which it is similar. Sometimes you can directly inherit from an existing class, and just code the differences of the new class. For example, assume your university information system also needed to support university administrators. The *Person* class already has many of the features an *Administrator* class needs so you should consider having *Administrator* inherit from *Person*.

3. **Follow the sentence rule.** One of the following sentences should make sense: "A subclass *is a kind of* superclass" or "A subclass *is like a* superclass." For example, it makes sense to say a student is a kind of person and a dragon is like a bird. It does not make sense to say a student is a kind of vehicle or is like a vehicle, so the class *Student* likely should not inherit from *Vehicle*. If one of the sentences does not make sense, then you have likely found either a composition relationship or an association (I describe both of these concepts later in this chapter).

4. **Avoid implementation inheritance.** Developers new to object orientation have a tendency to misapply inheritance, often in an effort to reuse as much as they possibly can (a good motive). Inheritance often is arguably the most exciting concept in their object repertoire, so they want to use it as much as possible. Usually the problem is something called implementation or

convenience inheritance: the application of inheritance when the sentence rule does not apply and the only justification is the subclass needed one or more of the features of the superclass, the application of inheritance being more convenient than refactoring your classes. A good rule of thumb is to reconsider "is like a" applications of inheritance because this is a weaker justification.

5. **Inherit everything**. The subclass should inherit everything from the superclass, a concept called pure inheritance. If it does not, the code becomes harder to understand and maintain. For example, say Class B inherits from A. To understand B, you need to understand what A is all about, plus all the features B adds on. If you start removing functionality, you also need to understand what B **is not**. This is a lot of work and becomes a maintenance nightmare.

2.7.3 Single and Multiple Inheritance

When a class inherits from only one other class, we call this single inheritance. When a class inherits from two or more other classes, we call this multiple inheritance. Remember this: the subclass inherits all the attributes and methods of its superclass(es).

Not all languages support multiple inheritance. C++ is one of the few languages that does, whereas languages such as Java, Smalltalk, and C# do not. The point to be made is if your target implementation language does not support multiple inheritance, then you should not use it when you are modeling.

In Fig. 2.7, you see several similarities between airplanes and cars. They both have a number of passengers, a maximum fuel level, and they can either increase or decrease their speed. To take advantage of these similarities, you could create a new class called *Vehicle* and have *Airplane* and *Car* inherit from it. We say the classes *Vehicle*, *Airplane*, and *Car* form an inheritance hierarchy,

> ### TIP
> #### You Do Not Need to Indicate Inherited Things
> Notice how the attributes and methods of the superclass are not listed in the subclasses (they have been inherited). The only time you would model an attribute or method in both a subclass and a superclass is when the subclass overrides its definition.

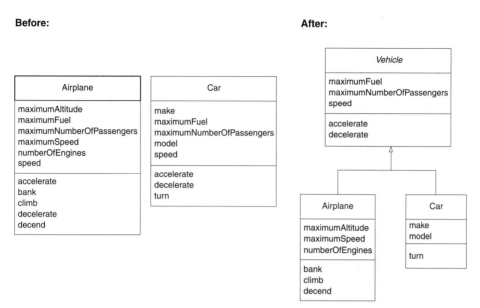

After:

FIGURE **2.7. Creating the vehicle class hierarchy.**

also called a class hierarchy. The topmost class in a class hierarchy (in this case *Vehicle*) is called the root or root class.

Notice how there is the method *Turn* for *Car* and *Bank* for *Airplane*. Turning and banking are exactly the same thing. You could have defined a *Turn* method in *Vehicle*, and had *Airplane* and *Car* inherit it (then you would remove *Bank* and *Turn* from the subclasses). This would imply that you would require users of airplanes (probably pilots) to change the terminology they use to work with airplanes. Realistically, this would not work. A better solution would be to define *Turn* in *Vehicle* and have the method *Bank* invoke it as needed.

In the before picture of Fig. 2.8, you want to create a new class called *Dragon*. You already have the classes *Bird* and *Lizard*. A dragon is like a bird because they both fly. A dragon is also like a lizard because they both have claws and scales. Because dragons have the features of both birds and lizards, in the after picture I have the class *Dragon* inheriting from both *Bird* and *Lizard*. This is an example of an "is like" relationship: a dragon *is like* a bird and a dragon *is* (also) *like* a lizard.

It is important to realize that the sentence rule is not perfect. For example, it makes sense to say that a redwood tree *is like* a skyscraper in that they both are tall, rooted to the ground, and sway in the breeze. They should not share an inheritance relationship, however. It also makes sense to say that a black

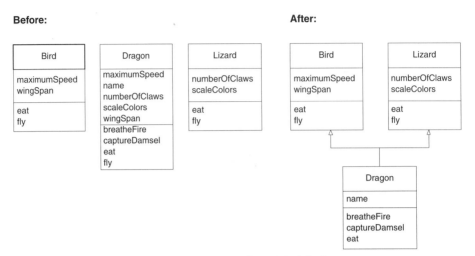

FIGURE 2.8. An example of multiple inheritance.

belt is a martial artist, yet it does not make sense to have the *Clothing* class inherit from the *Person* class.

Notice how I listed the method *eat* for *Dragon*. Although all three types of creatures eat, they all eat in different ways. Birds eat bird seed, lizards eat bugs, and dragons eat knights in shining armor. Because the way dragons eat is different than the way either birds or lizards eat, I needed to redefine, or override, the definition of the *eat* method. The general idea is a subclass will need to override the definition of either an attribute (occasionally) or a method whenever it uses that data, or performs that method in a manner different than that of its superclass.

TIP

Multiple Inheritance Rarely Occurs in the Real World

Unless you're a game designer, the example in Figure 2.8 likely does not apply to your problem domain. In fact, it is one of the few non-business examples in this book for the simple reason that, in my experience, multiple inheritance rarely occurs in the real world. In over ten years of object development I have only seen one example where the use of multiple inheritance was truly required (granted, I have seen many times where it was incredibly convenient). In the early 1990s, there was a great debate regarding the value of multiple inheritance. I suspect this debate still rages on occasionally at local pubs after work, although the designers of Java and C# choose not to include it in the language (and still do not) although it was a well-understood concept at the time.

2.7.4 Abstract and Concrete Classes

In Fig. 2.7, the class *Vehicle* is marked as abstract (the name is in italics; in previous versions of the UML you could also indicate with the constraint {abstract}), whereas *Airplane* and *Car* are not. We say *Vehicle* is an abstract class, whereas *Airplane* and *Car* are both concrete classes. The main difference between abstract classes and concrete classes is that objects are instantiated (created) from concrete classes, but not from abstract classes. For example, in your problem domain, you have airplanes and cars, but you do not have anything that is just a vehicle (if something is not an airplane or a car, you are not interested in it). This means your software will instantiate airplane and car objects, but will never create vehicle objects. Abstract classes are modeled when you need to create a class that implements common features from two or more classes.

I am not all that worried about whether a class is abstract while I am modeling, as I assume that I will do the right thing when it comes time to implement the class, which on an agile project team could be minutes after modeling it. Using italics to indicate that a class is abstract is an unfortunate choice made by the folks at the OMG. As Fowler (2004) points out, when you are modeling on a white board or paper (remember the agile modeling practice: *use the simplest tools*) you need to apply the older notation of {abstract} to get the point across. If you truly intend for a class to be strictly abstract, most OO programming languages allow you to designate a class as abstract so that it can never be instantiated.

2.8 PERSISTENCE

Persistence focuses on the issue of how to make objects available for future use of your software. In other words, how to save objects to permanent storage. To make an object persistent, you must save the values of its attributes to permanent storage (such as a relational database or a file) as well as any information needed to maintain the relationships (aggregation, inheritance, and association) with which it is involved. In other words you need to save the appropriate properties to permanent storage. In addition to saving objects, persistence is also concerned with their retrieval and deletion. Chapter 14 discusses agile database issues (Ambler 2003a) in detail.

From a development point of view, there are two types of objects: persistent objects that stick around and transient objects that do not. For example, a

Customer is a persistent class. You want to save *customer* objects into some sort of permanent storage so you can work with them again in the future. A customer editing screen, however, is a transient object. Your application creates the *customer-editing screen* object, displays it, and then gets rid of it once the user is done editing the data for the customer with whom he or she is currently dealing.

The following tips and techniques should help you to understand and apply persistence concepts better:

1. **Business/domain classes are usually persistent.** You are naturally going to need to keep a permanent (persistent) record of the instances of real-world classes like *Student, Professor,* and *Course.*

2. **User-interface classes are usually transitory.** User-interface classes (screens and reports) are usually transitory. Screens are created and displayed when needed, and then once they are no longer in use, they are destroyed (removed from memory). Report classes are created, they gather the data they need, manipulate the data, and then output the data. Once this is done, the report object is usually destroyed as well. Note that sometimes you might need to maintain a log of when you printed a report and who/what you sent it to, making the report log persistent.

3. **You need to store both attributes and associations.** When an object is written to disk, you obviously need to store the value of its attributes. However, you must also store information about any relationships/associations with which the object is involved. For example, Alyssa is taking the courses Bio-Medicine 101 and Nursing 301, so you want to ensure that when you store the Alyssa object to disk that the software records the information that she is enrolled in those two courses.

2.9 RELATIONSHIPS

In the real world, objects have relationships with other objects. The relationships between objects are important because they help us to define how they interact with each other. For example, students *take* courses, professors *teach* courses, criminals *rob* banks, politicians *kiss* babies, and captains *command* starships. Take, teach, rob, kiss, and command are all verbs that define associations between objects. You want to identify and potentially document these relationships; therefore, you can gain a better understanding as to how objects interact with one another.

TIP

Consider Optionality and Cardinality Separately

My experience is that significant value exists in considering the two concepts in isolation: for each direction of an association there is value in asking whether the association must exist (optionality) and how many could possibly exist (cardinality)? For example, consider the "teaches" association between professors and seminars. I would ask the following:

- Must a professor teach a seminar, or is it possible that some professors do not do any teaching?
- How many seminars could a single professor teach?
- Must a seminar be taught by a professor, or is it possible that someone who is not a professor could teach a course?
- Can more than one professor teach a single seminar? How many?
- Are there seminars that require more than one professor to teach them?

Not only must you identify what the relationship(s) are between classes, you must also describe the relationship. For example, it is not enough to know that students take seminars. How many seminars can students take? None, one, or several? Furthermore, relationships are two-way streets: not only do students take seminars, but also seminars are taken by students. This leads to questions like how many students can be enrolled in any given seminar and is it possible to have a seminar with no one in it? The implication is that you also need to identify the cardinality and optionality of a relationship. Cardinality represents the concept of "how many," whereas optionality represents the concept of "whether you must have something." It is important to note that the UML chooses to combine the concepts of optionality and cardinality into the single concept of multiplicity.

2.9.1 Associations

An association is a persistent relationship between two or more classes or objects. When you model associations in UML class diagrams, you show them as a thin line connecting two classes, as you see in Fig. 2.9. Associations

Figure 2.9. Notation overview for modeling associations on UML class diagrams.

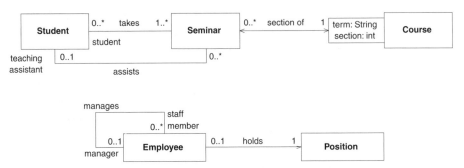

FIGURE 2.10. Several examples of association.

can become quite complex; consequently, you can depict several things about them on your diagrams. Figure 2.9 shows the common items to model for an association:

- **Directionality.** The open arrowheads indicate the directionality of the association. When there is one arrowhead the association is unidirectional: it can be traversed in one direction only (in the direction of the arrow). When there is either zero or two arrowheads the association is bi-directional: it can be traversed in both directions. Although you should indicate both arrowheads it is common practice to drop the arrowheads from bi-directional associations. Examples of both ways to notate bi-directional associations appear in Fig. 2.10. Throughout this book I will follow the agile modeling practice—*depict models simply*—and drop the arrowheads from bi-directional associations. My advice is to choose one approach and stick to it.

- **Label.** The label, which is optional, is typically one or two words describing the association. Reading one class, the label, and then the other class should produce a sentence fragment that describes the relationship, e.g., *Professor teaches Seminars*. Avoid generic labels like "has" or "communicates with" as much as possible.

- **Multiplicity.** The multiplicity of the association is labeled on either end of the line, one multiplicity indicator for each direction (Table 2.3 summarizes the potential multiplicity indicators you can use).

- **Role.** The role—the context that an object takes within the association—may also be indicated at each end of the association.

- **Qualifier.** A qualifier is a value that selects an object from the set of related objects across an association. For example, in Fig. 2.10 the *section of*

TABLE 2.3 UML Multiplicity Indicators	
Indicator	Meaning
0..1	Zero or one
1	One only
0..*	Zero or more
1..*	One or more
n	Only n (where $n > 1$)
0..n	Zero to n (where $n > 1$)
1..n	One to n (where $n > 1$)

association from *Seminar* to *Course* is qualified by the combination of the *term* and the *section* attributes (potentially implemented by *Seminar*). Qualifiers are optional and in practice are rarely modeled.

Consider the class diagram depicted in Fig. 2.10, which shows several classes and the associations between them. First, here is how you would read the associations:

• A student takes one or more seminars;
• A seminar is taken by zero or more students;
• A student, as a teaching assistant, may assist in zero or more seminars;
• A seminar may have zero or one student who acts as a teaching assistant;
• A seminar is a section of one course;
• A course has zero or more sections;
• An employee holds one position;
• A position may be held by one employee (some positions go unfilled);
• An employee may be managed by one other employee, their manager (the company president is the only one without a manager); and
• An employee manages zero or more employees (some employees do not have any staff members).

Second, several important lessons are contained in Fig. 2.10. First, you see it is possible to have more than one association between two classes: the classes *Student* and *Seminar* have the *takes* and *assists* associations between them. You are interested in two relationships between these two classes for your university information system; therefore, you need to model both associations.

Second, it is valid that the same class may be involved with both ends of an association; something called a recursive association or a self association (Fowler 2004). A perfect example of this is the *manages* association that the *Employee* class has with itself. The way you read this association is that any given employee may have several other employees he or she manages, and that one other employee may, in turn, manage them.

Third, sometimes the direction of an association is one way, as you see in Fig. 2.10, with the *holds* association between *Employee* and *Position*. The implication is employee objects know the position object they hold, but the position object does not need to know what employee holds it. This is called a unidirectional association, an association that is traversed in only one direction. If you do not have a requirement to traverse an association in both directions, for example, position objects do not have a need to collaborate with employee objects, then you should use a unidirectional association. You will see in Section 2.9.3 that unidirectional associations require less work to implement.

2.9.2 Modeling the Unknown

No matter how good a job you do, you are almost guaranteed to have missed the full details about object relationships. So what do you do: make something up and hope for the best? Of course not. You would go back to your users and ask them what the real situation is, wouldn't you? The problem is remembering to go back to your users. The solution: mark it as "currently unknown" by putting a question mark beside the part of the relationship of which you are unsure. For example, in Fig. 2.11, you believe zero or more employees hold a position. You know it is possible for a position not to be currently filled, but what you are not sure of is whether you can have one or several persons holding the same position. Is job sharing going on in the organization? Are there generic positions, such as Janitor, that are held by many people? Or is it really one person to one position, as we currently show now? Because you do not know for sure yet, you mark the relationship with a question mark, indicating you must go back later and verify your "educated guess." Note, the UML does not include question marks as part of the notation, yet it is just a technique I have found to work well in practice—ideally you should not guess or make assumptions without speaking with your stakeholders, but if you must, then mark the assumption on your work and strive to resolve the issue quickly.

FIGURE **2.11. Indicating the unknown.**

2.9.3 How Associations Are Implemented

Associations are maintained through the combination of attributes and methods. The attributes store the information necessary to maintain the relationship and methods keep the attributes current. For example, the *Student* class of Fig. 2.10 would potentially have an attribute called *takes*, perhaps an array, which is used to keep track of the *Seminar* objects the student is currently taking. The *Student* class might also have methods such as *addSeminar* and *removeSeminar* to add and remove seminar objects into the array. The *Seminar* class would have a corresponding attribute called *students* and methods called *addStudent* and *removeStudent* to maintain the association in the opposite direction. All of this has a significant implication: because attributes and methods are inherited, associations are, too. You will see why this is important in Chapter 12.

In Fig. 2.10, the unidirectional association *holds* between *Employee* and *Position* would be easier to implement because you only need to traverse it in one direction: from *Employee* to *Position*. Therefore, *Employee* would have an attribute called *position* and methods, called something like *setPosition()* and *getPosition()*, to maintain the association. There would be nothing added to *Position* because there is no need for position objects to collaborate with employee objects; therefore, there is no added code to maintain the association in that direction.

TIP

Do Not Show the Attributes and Methods to Maintain Associations

It is common style is to assume the attributes and methods exist to maintain associations (you do not need to show them on your diagrams). You should consider setting naming conventions for these attributes and methods. I typically use the role name or the class name for the attribute name and method names, such as *addAttributeName* and *removeAttributeName* for many associations, and *setAttributeName* and *getAttributeName* for single associations when I am writing the source code, the topic of Chapter 13.

2.9.4 Properties

In UML 2 a property is a named value denoting a characteristic of an element (such as a class or component). Attributes and associations, including composition, are properties. For example, the name of a student is an important property of the *Student* class. The fact that students take seminars is also an important property of the *Student* class. Does it make sense that both attributes and relationships be considered properties of a class? I think so—in Section 2.9.3 relationships are implemented in part via attributes.

2.9.5 Aggregation and Composition

Sometimes an object is made up of other objects. For example, an airplane is made up of a fuselage, wings, engines, landing gear, flaps, and so on. A delivery shipment contains one or more packages. A project team consists of two or more employees. These are all examples of the concept of aggregation, which represents "is part of" relationships. An engine is part of a plane, a package is part of a shipment, and an employee is part of a team.

Composition is a strong form of aggregation in which the "whole" is completely responsible for its parts and each "part" object is only associated to the one whole object. For example, at any given time, an engine is part of one and only one airplane (otherwise, you have a serious problem). Furthermore, no object other than the airplane will directly collaborate with an engine object; for example, passenger objects on the airplane cannot directly request that an engine increase its speed.

In UML 1.x you could model both aggregation and composition, but in UML 2.x the notation for aggregation has been dropped. Although this may sound like a good idea because many people got the two concepts confused I suspect that we are going to see aggregation used on UML class diagrams for some time to come because it has been in common practice since 1997 when the UML was first popularized. Figure 2.12 shows examples of both—aggregation was depicted in UML 1.x as a hollow diamond and composition is depicted in both UML 1.x and UML 2.x as a filled diamond. The diamond is connected to the whole class. Aggregation is simply a type of association; therefore, you still need to model the multiplicity and roles, just as you would with associations. Not indicating the multiplicity of the whole end of an aggregation association is permissible although I consider it bad style (Ambler

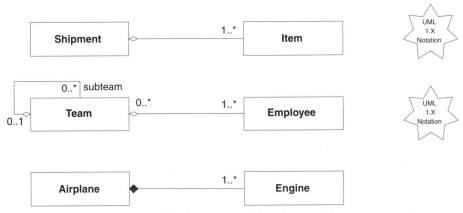

FIGURE **2.12. Several examples of aggregation.**

2003c). For example, in Fig. 2.12, multiplicity is not indicated for either shipments or airplanes; in these cases it is assumed the multiplicity is 1.

Just as associations are two-way streets, so is aggregation. Furthermore, the aggregation/composition associations depicted in Fig. 2.12 are read in a similar manner:

- An item is part of one and only one shipment;
- A shipment is composed of one or more items;
- An engine is part of one and only one airplane;
- An airplane has one or more engines;
- An employee may be part of one or more teams;
- A team is made up of one or more employees;
- Any given team may be part of a larger team; and
- A team may be made up of smaller subteams.

It is important to be aware of the older notation for aggregation although I will not use it again in this book.

The following tips and techniques should help you to model composition effectively:

1. **Apply the sentence rule.** The first test is that it should make sense to say "the part *is part of* the whole." For example, it makes sense to say an engine is part of an airplane. However, it does not make sense to say an employee is part of a position or a position is part of an employee, which

is why association is appropriate in the example depicted in Fig. 2.10. If the sentence does not make sense, then composition is most likely not appropriate. Either inheritance (Section 2.7) or association (Section 2.9.1) is what you need.

2. **The whole should manage the part.** The second test, assuming the sentence rule passes, is whether the whole manages the part. For example, an airplane should manage its engines; you would not want a passenger on the plane to be able to manipulate the engines.

3. **You should be interested in the part.** An object may actually be a part in the real world, but if you are not interested in keeping track of it, then do not model it. For example, an airplane maintenance system would be interested in keeping track of engines because it needs to record maintenance information about each engine. On the other hand, an air-traffic control system is not interested in tracking engines, just airplanes. Therefore, an engine would not appear as a class in an air-traffic control system.

4. **Show multiplicity and roles.** Just as you show the multiplicity and roles for an association, you need to do the same for a composition association.

5. **Composition is inherited.** Composition associations, like ordinary associations, are maintained by a combination of attributes and methods that can be inherited.

2.9.6 Dependencies

Two types of object relationships exist: persistent and transitory. The main difference is persistent associations must be saved, whereas transitory relationships are only temporary in nature and, thus, are not saved.

Persistent relationships are those that are permanent or, at least semipermanent, in nature. An object relationship is persistent if information to maintain it is saved to permanent storage. For example, the *take* relationship between students and courses is persistent. This is important business information that must be stored to disk. The *teach* relationship between professors and courses is persistent for the same reason. All of the associations we have dealt with so far in this book have been persistent.

Transitory associations are temporary in nature. They are not saved to permanent storage. Transitory relationships usually (but not always) involve at least one transitory object, such as a screen or report. The reason for this

FIGURE 2.13. A dependency between two classes.

is simple: if you are not persisting the object, then you likely are not going to be persisting any of the associations it was involved with either.

Transitory relationships exist between objects for one reason only—so they may collaborate with one another. For an object to collaborate with another object it needs to know about it. This means there must be either an object relationship or a part-of relationship between the two objects. When a persistent association does not exist between two objects, but they need to collaborate with one another, you model a dependency relationship between the two classes.

In Fig. 2.13, you see there is a dependency relationship—modeled as a dashed line with an open arrowhead—between the classes *Student* and *Student Editing Screen*, representing the transitory relationship between a student-editing screen object as it updates the student object. The editing screen obtains the current information from the student object, displays it in editing mode, and then updates the student object with the new information once it is finished. The transitory relationship between the editing screen object and the student object exists as long as the student information is displayed on

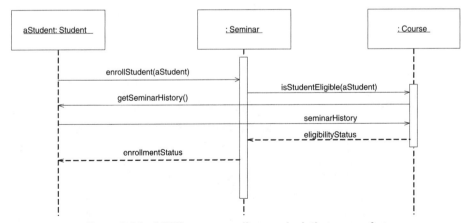

FIGURE 2.14. A UML sequence diagram depicting messaging.

the screen. Once the screen is closed, the relationship no longer exists (the screen likely does not exist either) and the transient objects are most likely destroyed.

Transitory associations can also occur between two persistent objects. For example, in Fig. 2.14, an implied transitory association[1] exists between the student object and the course object (student is passed as a parameter to the course, which then asks it for its prerequisites).

2.10 COLLABORATION

Classes often need to work together to fulfill their responsibilities. Actually, it is typically the objects and the instances of the classes that are working together. Collaboration occurs between objects when one object asks another for information or to do something. For example, an airplane collaborates with its engines to fly. For the plane to go faster, the engines must go faster. When the plane needs to slow down, the engines must slow down. If the airplane did not collaborate with its engines, it would be unable to fly.

Objects collaborate with one another by sending each other messages. A message is either a request to do something or a request for information. Messages are modeled in UML sequence diagrams and UML communication diagrams (formerly called collaboration diagrams in UML 1.x). Figure 2.14 depicts a simple sequence diagram (see Chapter 11 for a detailed description of sequence diagrams and their use). You see how a student object requests to be enrolled in a seminar; the seminar object, in turn, sends a message to the course object to which it is associated because it needs to know whether the student object is qualified to enroll in the course (for example, the student has the prerequisites for the course). Figure 2.15 shows the same example as a communication diagram. Communication diagrams are described in detail in Chapter 11.

Although sequence diagrams are described in detail in Chapter 11, I will take this opportunity to present a quick overview of them. The boxes across the top of the diagram represent classifiers, in this case objects. The dashed lines hanging from them are called lifelines, which represent the life span of the object during the scenario being modeled. Objects have labels in the format *name: class* where *name* is optional (objects that have not been given a name on the diagram are called anonymous objects). The instance of *Student*

---

[1] This association was not modeled in Fig. 2.10 because the concept had not been introduced at that point. For consistency purposes, however, it normally would have been modeled.

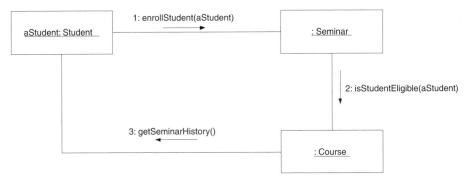

FIGURE 2.15. A UML communication diagram depicting messaging.

was given a name because it is used as a parameter in a message, whereas the instances of *Seminar* and *Course* did not need to be referenced anywhere else in the diagram and, thus, could be anonymous. Messages are indicated as labeled arrows, the label being the signature of the method. Return values are optionally indicated using a dashed arrow with a label indicating the return value. Return values were indicated in Fig. 2.14, but not in Fig. 2.16. My preference is to keep the diagrams simple and assume that the return value comes back. The sequencing of the messages is implied by the order of the messages themselves, starting at the top-left corner of the diagram.

Communication diagrams have a similar notation to sequence diagrams. Objects are indicated in the same sort of manner, although they are connected via unlabeled association lines unlike sequence diagrams. Messages are indicated with arrows again, although they are not connected to the objects (there are no lifelines on collaboration diagrams). The sequence of the messages is

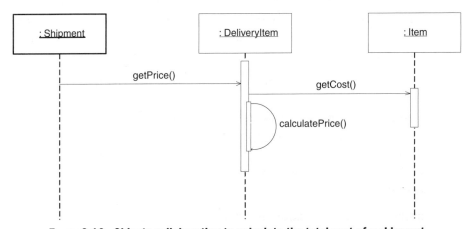

FIGURE 2.16. Objects collaborating to calculate the total cost of a shipment.

optionally indicated by putting a number in front of the message name. In Fig. 2.15, the same messaging sequence is indicated as in the sequence diagram of Fig. 2.14.

The following tips and techniques should help you to model collaborations effectively:

1. **There must be some sort of relationship.** The only way an object can send a message to another object is if it knows about it in the first place. In the real world, you cannot ask anyone for help unless you know how to get in contact with them. The same principle applies to objects. There must be an association, or an aggregation association, between the two classes for their instances (objects) to be able to collaborate.

2. **There must be a corresponding method in the target object.** Collaborations are implemented as method invocations, implying the method must exist in the target for it to be invoked. If an object is asked for information, it must have a method that returns this information. For example, in Figure 2.14, the message *isStudentEligible()* is sent to the course object; therefore, there must be a corresponding method implemented in the *Course* class called *isStudentEligible()*. If an object is asked to do something, it must have a method to do it. Similarly, in Fig. 2.14, you see the message *enrollStudent()* is sent to seminar objects; therefore, the *Seminar* class must have a method *enrollStudent()*.

3. **There might be a return value.** If the collaboration is a request for information, then there must be a return value (the requested information). This fact should be included in the documentation for the method and will, optionally, be indicated on the sequence diagram as a dashed line. Return values typically are not modeled on collaboration diagrams because they tend to clutter the diagrams.

4. **There may or may not be parameters.** Some messages have parameters and some do not. Remember that a message is effectively a method (function) call. Just as functions may take parameters, so do methods. For example, in Fig. 2.14, a student object passes itself as a parameter when it invokes the *enrollStudent()* message on the seminar object. In Fig. 2.16, the shipment object does not need to pass any parameters when it asks the item object for its cost.

5. **Messages show collaboration, not data flows.** Messages are requests. That is it. They are not data flows. Process diagrams (data flow diagrams) from

the structured world show data flows, which are movements of data from one part of the system to another. These are discussed in detail in Chapter 9.

6. **Sometimes the target needs to collaborate.** The receiver of a message may be unable to fulfill the request by itself completely and may need to collaborate with other objects to fulfill its responsibility. For example, in Fig. 2.14, the seminar object needed to interact with the course object of which it is a section to enroll a student into it. That is perfectly fine.

7. **Each method should do something.** It is important that each object being collaborated with should always do something—not just forward the message to another object, something called a passthrough. Passthroughs often result in "spaghetti code" that can be difficult to maintain. Sometimes delegation makes sense, but when you are starting out you are better off to avoid it.

8. **An object can collaborate with itself.** Objects will often send themselves messages to obtain information and/or to have itself get something done. This is the same as a function calling another function in a procedural language such as C. In Fig. 2.16, the *DeliveryItem* object sends itself a message to calculate the price (presumably the cost of the *Item* object multiplied by the number of items to be delivered).

2.11 COUPLING

Coupling is a measure of how two items, such as classes or methods, are interrelated. When one class depends on another class, we say they are coupled. When one class interacts with another class, but does not know any of the implementation details of the other class, we say they are loosely coupled. When one class relies on the implementation (that is, it directly accesses the data attributes of the other), we say they are tightly coupled.

Previously I discussed the example of how *Student* could implement the *enroll* method: it could directly access the attribute *listOfStudents* in *Seminar*, or it could send *Seminar* objects a message asking it to enroll the student in the seminar. Directly accessing and updating the attribute *listOfStudents* might save a few CPU cycles and run a little quicker, but as soon as the implementation of that attribute changes, you would need to modify the code in *Student*. As you saw, this was not very good. The basic problem is when two classes are tightly coupled; a change in one often requires a change in the other. This, in turn, could require a change in another class, and then another, and then another, and so on. Tight coupling is one of the main reasons such a large maintenance burden exists. What should be a simple maintenance change can often create months of work, if it can be done at all. It is amazing how much code is out there that nobody is willing to touch because they are afraid of breaking it. Remember Y2K!

Every so often, developers are seduced by the dark side of the force and decide to write code that is tightly coupled. This approach only makes sense when you are truly desperate to cut down on the processing overhead in your system. For example, database drivers are often tightly coupled to the file system of the operating system on which the database runs. If you can save a few milliseconds accessing data, it quickly adds up when you are accessing hundreds of thousands of objects.

2.12 COHESION

Cohesion is a measure of how much an item, such as a class or method, makes sense. A good measure of the cohesiveness of something is how long it takes to describe it in one sentence: the longer it takes, the less cohesive it likely is. You want to design methods and classes that are highly cohesive. In other words, it should be very clear what a method or class is all about.

A method is highly cohesive if it does one thing and one thing only. For example, in the class *Student* you would have methods to enroll a student in a seminar and to drop a student from a seminar. Both of these methods do one thing and one thing only. You could write one method to do both these functions, perhaps called *changeSeminarStatus*. The problem with this solution is the code for this method would be more complex than the code for the separate *enrollInSeminar* or *dropSeminar* methods. This means your software would be harder to understand and, hence, harder to maintain. Remember that you want to reduce the maintenance burden, not increase it.

TIP

Method Names Often Indicate Their Cohesiveness

The name of a method often indicates how cohesive it is. Whenever you see a strong verb/noun combination used for the name of the method, very often it is highly cohesive. For example, consider methods like *getName, printName, enrollInSeminar*, and *dropSeminar*. Verbs such as get, print, enroll, and drop are all very strong. Now consider *changeSeminarStatus*. Is change as strong or as explicit as the words enroll and drop? I do not think so.

A highly cohesive class represents one type of object and only one type of object. For example, for the university information system we model professors, not employees. While a professor is, indeed, an employee, they are very different from other kinds of employees. For example, professors do different things than do janitors, who do different things than do secretaries, who do different things than do registrars, and so on. We could easily write a generic *Employee* class that is able to handle all the functionality performed by every type of employee working for the university. However, this class would quickly become cumbersome and difficult to maintain. A better solution would be to define an inheritance hierarchy made up of the classes *Professor, Janitor, Secretary, Registrar*, and so on. Because many similarities exist between these classes, you would create a new abstract class called *Employee*, which would inherit from *Person*. The other classes, including *Professor*, would now inherit from *Employee*. The advantage of this is each class represents one type of object. If there are ever any changes that need to be made with respect to janitors, you can go right to the class *Janitor* and make them. You do not need to worry about affecting the code for professors. In fact, you do not even need to know anything about professors at all.

2.13 POLYMORPHISM

An individual object may be one of several types. For example, a John Smith object may be a student, a registrar, or even a professor. Should it matter to other objects in the system what type of person John is? It would significantly reduce the development effort if other objects in the system could treat people objects the same way and not need to have separate sections of code for each type. The concept of polymorphism says you can treat instances of various classes the same way within your system. The implication is you can send a message to an object without first knowing what type it is and the object will still do "the right thing," at least from its point of view.

2.13.1 An Example: The Poker Game

Consider an example. A poker game had been going on for hours, and it was Slick Scotty's turn to deal. One of the players turns to him and asks, "So what'll it be, partner?" Thinking about it, Slick Scotty replies, "Draw." Suddenly, everyone goes wild. The artist who was sitting across the table from Slick Scotty suddenly pulls out a pad of paper and a pencil and starts drawing.

The professional card player to Scotty's right gets ready to play draw poker. To Scotty's alarm, the gunfighter to his left goes for his guns. *This always happens whenever I say "draw." Darn polymorphism*, thinks Slick Scotty to himself.

You can learn several interesting lessons from this experience. First, the polymorphism is in the way the dealer interacts with the players. The dealer did not care what types of people objects he had at the table; he treated them all the same way, even though the message "draw" meant one thing to an artist, another thing to a poker player, and yet another thing to a gunslinger. As far as the dealer is concerned, they are only people. Polymorphism is the concept that permits this to happen.

Second, the different objects responded to the message in their own way. In this scenario, Slick Scotty sends out the *draw* message to each person at the table. The artist object responded to the message by drawing a picture. The professional card player object responded to the message by starting to play draw poker. The gunfighter object responded to the message by drawing his guns. The same message went out to different objects and each one did something different (actually, a better way to look at it is that, from their point of view, they each did the appropriate thing). The interesting thing to note is that Slick Scotty did not have to send different messages to each object (for example, *drawPicture, playDrawPoker,* and *drawYourGuns*), he just had to send *draw*.

Third, there is still work to be done. Although each type of object responds to *draw* in an appropriate manner, somebody still must implement each version of that method.

2.13.2 Polymorphism at the University

Consider a slightly more realistic example of polymorphism by exploring the design of how the university handles the hiring of new staff, depicted in Fig. 2.17. There is a standard process for hiring staff at the university: once a person is hired, she is added to the university pension plan and an employee card is created for her. When a professor is hired at the university, the same process is followed, with the addition of a parking space assigned to her (if there is no parking space, the professor is added to the waiting list).

If the *hire* method has been implemented in the *Employee* class, it would implement the behavior needed to add the person into the university pension plan and print an employee card for them. The *hire* method has been overridden in the *Professor* class. Presumably, it would invoke the *hire* method in the *Employee* class because that behavior is still applicable for professors, plus it

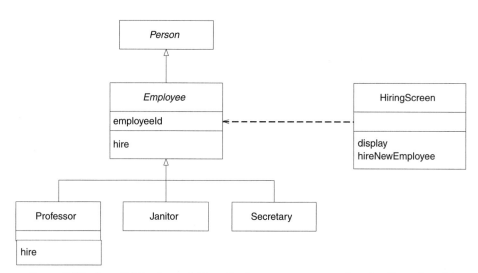

FIGURE 2.17. A partial implementation of a human resources system for the university.

would add the functionality needed to reserve a parking space (or place the professor on the waiting list).

By being able to send the message *hire* to any kind of employee, there is not the need for a complicated set of IF or CASE statements in the *hireNewEmployee* method of the screen object. This method does not need to send a *hireProfessor* message to professor objects, *hireJanitor* to janitor objects, and so on. It just sends *hire* to any type of employee and the object will do the right thing. As a result, you can add new types of employees (perhaps *Registrar*) and you do not need to change the screen object at all. In other words, the class is loosely coupled to the employee class hierarchy, enabling you to extend your system easily.

It is important to mention that Fig. 2.17 is not a very good design. A better approach would be to rework this hierarchy into that presented in Fig. 2.18. This is an application of the *Roles Played* analysis pattern (Coad 1992;

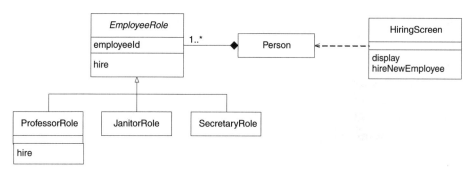

FIGURE 2.18. Refactored class model.

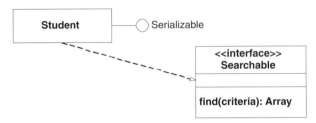

FIGURE 2.19. The two UML notations for interfaces.

Ambler 1998a) described in greater detail in Chapter 8. This pattern separates the concept of someone being a person and the role(s) that they play at work.

2.14 INTERFACES

An interface is the definition of a collection of one or more methods, and zero or more attributes. Interfaces ideally define a cohesive set of behaviors. Interfaces are implemented by classes and components. To implement an interface, a class or component must include the methods defined by the interface. For example, Fig. 2.19 indicates the class *Student* implements the *Serializable* interface and the *Searchable* interface. To implement the *Searchable* interface, *Student* must include a method called *find*, which takes criteria as a parameter. In Chapters 8 and 12, I describe operation signatures in greater detail. Any given class or component may implement zero or more interfaces, and one or more classes or components can implement any given interface. Interfaces are used to promote consistency within your models and source code.

Interfaces are a powerful method for ensuring loose coupling. They allow a class to participate in a common set of functionality without another class having to know anything about it except that it supports that interface. A GUI object, for example, could present a list of students that meet a set of criteria without knowing anything about the *Student* class except that it implements the *Searchable* interface and the name of a single method to get a presentation name, which could perhaps be part of a *Description* interface. That same GUI could perform the exact same action with professors if the *Professor* class also implemented those two interfaces. If the *Seminar* class implemented those interfaces, the GUI could display them, too, and anything else that implemented those interfaces. The GUI knows nothing about these classes except that they implement two interfaces; this promotes loose coupling between the GUI and those classes.

In languages such as Java and C# interfaces provide a typing mechanism. In other words the *Student* class of Fig. 2.19 has three at least types–*Student, Serializable,* and *Searchable.* It would also have any other types of its super-classes. For example, if *Student* inherits from *Person* and it implements the *Printable* interface then student objects also are type *Person* and *Printable* as well. The typing mechanism(s) of your implementation language will affect the extent to which polymorphism is supported.

Also notice in Fig. 2.19 that there are two ways to indicate something implements an interface: the lollipop notation used for the *Serializable* interface and the box notation used for the *Searchable* interface. The lollipop notation has the advantage that it is visually compact, whereas the box notation provides details about the interface itself. The *Searchable* interface box is the same notation as a class, with the addition of the stereotype of *interface.* Stereotypes are a mechanism for defining common and consistent extensions to the UML notation. The dashed arrow from *Student* to *Searchable* is a UML *realizes* relationship, indicating that *Student* implements (realizes) the *Searchable* interface.

2.15 COMPONENTS

A component is a modular, extensible unit of independent deployment that has contractually specified interface(s) and explicitly defined dependencies, if any. Ideally, components should be modular, extensible, and open. Modularity implies a component contains everything it needs to fulfill its responsibilities; extensibility implies a component can be enhanced to fulfill more responsibilities than it was originally intended to, and open implies it can operate on several platforms and interact with other components through a single programming interface.

Components, like classes, implement interfaces. A component's interfaces define its access points. Components are typically implemented as collections of classes, ideally classes that form a cohesive subset of your overall systems. Components are typically heavyweights and could even be thought of as large classes or even subsystems. For example, a database could be a component or the collection of business/domain classes that implement the behaviors required to implement people within your application could be a component.

Component diagrams (Object Management Group 2003) show the software components that make up a larger piece of software, their interfaces, and their interrelationships. For the sake of our discussion, a component may be any

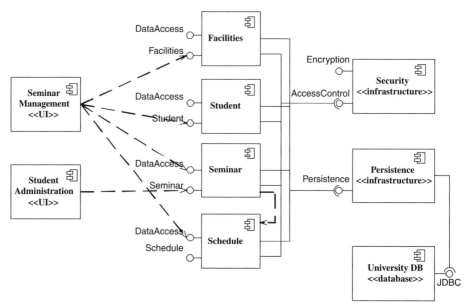

FIGURE 2.20. A UML 2.0 component diagram.

large-grain item—such as a common subsystem, a commercial off-the-shelf (COTS) system, an OO application, or a wrapped legacy application—used in the daily operations of your business. In many ways, a component diagram is simply a class diagram at a larger, albeit less-detailed, scale.

Figure 2.20 shows an example of a component diagram being used to model the business architecture for the university. The boxes represent components—in this case either the user interfaces that people use to interact with the university systems, business components such as *Facility*, or technical components such as the *Security* component or the database. Component diagrams are described in detail in Chapter 10.

In the figure you see that the UI components have dependencies on the interfaces of the business components. By making them dependent on the interfaces and not the components themselves you make it possible to replace the components with different implementations as long as the new version implements the given interfaces. This reduces coupling. Similarly it is possible for business components to be dependent on each other; for example, the *Seminar* component is coupled to the *Schedule* component.

An interesting new notation in UML 2 is the use of sockets. A socket is the semicircle around the interface lollipop symbol, as you see with the *AccessControl* and *Persistence* interfaces with the *Security* and *Persistence* components respectively. This symbol is used to indicate that something requires the existence of an interface. For example, the four business components (*Facilities, Student, Seminar*, and *Schedule*) all require the existence of something that implements the *AccessControl* interface.

You may notice the consistency of the notation between class diagrams and component diagrams: they use exactly the same notation for dependency relationships, as you saw in Fig. 2.13. This is a good feature of the UML: its notation is consistent. There are a few details of the UML that are not consistent but, for the most part, each concept is modeled the same way across the various diagrams of the UML.

2.16 PATTERNS

Doesn't it always seem as if you are solving the same problems repeatedly? If you personally have not solved a given problem before, then chances are pretty good you could find somebody who had tackled the same or, at least, a similar problem in the past. Sometimes the problem you are working on is simple, sometimes it is complex, but usually it has been worked on before. Wouldn't it be nice to be able to find a solution easily, or at least a partial solution, to your problem? Think how much time and effort could be saved if you had access to a library of solutions to common system development problems. This is what patterns are all about.

A pattern is a solution to a common problem taking relevant forces into account, effectively supporting the reuse of proven techniques and approaches of other developers. Several flavors of patterns exist, including analysis patterns, design patterns, and process patterns. Analysis patterns describe a solution to common problems found in the analysis/business domain of an application, design patterns describe a solution to common problems found in the design of systems, and process patterns address software process-related issues. Analysis patterns are discussed in Chapter 9 and design patterns in Chapter 12. See the books *Process Patterns* (Ambler 1998b) and *More Process Patterns* (Ambler 1999) for a more detailed description of process patterns.

For example, it is common to discover classes in your application that should only have one instance. Perhaps there should only be one instance of a certain editing screen open at any given time, perhaps you have configuration information you want to store in one place only, or perhaps you have one or more constant values you need to maintain somewhere. In all these examples,

Singleton
singleInstance
create()

FIGURE **2.21. The Singleton design pattern.**

you need to have a single instance of the class in question—a single instance of the dialog box, a single instance of the configuration information, and a single instance of the constants. This problem is resolved by the *Singleton* pattern (Gamma et al. 1995), a design pattern that shows how to ensure that only one single instance of a class exists at any one time. In Fig. 2.21, you see a class diagram describing the *Singleton* design pattern. A static attribute exists that keeps track of the single instance and a static method that creates the instance if it does not already exist. Although *Singleton* is a simple pattern, I suspect it is one you will use over and over again when developing OO applications.

There are some very complicated patterns out there; in fact most design patterns are based on three or more classes. The primary challenge with patterns is that when you first learn about them everything seems to be a pattern, and sometimes that is even true. The danger is that you can dramatically over-build your software, increasing your maintenance burden while at the same time reducing the amount of time that you can spend implementing actual requirements. To avoid this problem, Chapter 4 shows that agile modeling (AM) includes the practice *apply patterns gently* where you ease into the pattern by refactoring your design slowly over time instead of simply applying the pattern when you think you might need it.

2.17 WHAT YOU HAVE LEARNED

In this chapter, you discovered the main concepts of the object-oriented paradigm and were presented with the basic UML 2.0 notations to model them. Object-oriented concepts are quite numerous as well as complex. Do not worry; it is common to feel a little overwhelmed at first, but with a little practice you will soon learn this material.

2.18 REVIEW QUESTIONS

1. Discuss the difference between inheritance and composition. What are the advantages and disadvantages of each? Can you implement one with the other?
2. How is a class similar to a database table? How is it different? How do these similarities and differences justify the need for class models and for data models? Or do they?
3. Discuss the difference between association and composition. What are the advantages and disadvantages of each?
4. When would you apply inheritance? When would you not? Provide examples of when inheritance is appropriate and when it is not, discussing each.
5. Compare and contrast the concepts of coupling and cohesion. How do they relate, if at all, to one another?
6. Describe the relationship between polymorphism and typing.
7. Via the Internet, research common database technologies including relational databases, object databases, object-relational databases, XML databases, network databases, and hierarchical databases. Provide at least one example of each. Compare and contrast each technology, listing the advantages, disadvantages, and an indication of when you would use each.
8. How do interfaces reduce coupling in OO systems? In what ways might they increase it? Why?

CHAPTER 3

Full Lifecycle Object-Oriented Testing (FLOOT)

Anything worth building is worth testing.
You build a wide variety of artifacts, including models, documents, and source code.

Software development is a complex endeavor. You create a variety of artifacts throughout a project, some of which you keep and some you do not. Regardless of whether you keep the artifact, the reason why you create it (I hope) is because it adds some sort of value. Perhaps you create a model in order to explore a business rule, a model that may then be used to drive your coding efforts. If the model is wrong then your code will be wrong too. If it is a complex business rule, one that requires a significant amount of time to implement, you might be motivated to validate your model before you act on it. If it's a simple business rule you might instead trust that your code-testing efforts will be sufficient. You will also find that many artifacts, such as user manuals and operations manuals, never become code yet still need to be validated. The point is that you will need testing techniques that enable you to validate the wide range of artifacts that you create during software development.

In this chapter I explore the following:

- The cost of change;
- Testing philosophies;
- The FLOOT methodology;
- Regression testing;
- Quality assurance;
- Techniques for validating models;
- Techniques for testing code;
- Techniques for system testing;
- Techniques for user-based testing; and
- Test-driven development (TDD).

3.1 THE COST OF CHANGE

A critical concept that motivates full-lifecycle testing is the cost of change. Figure 3.1 depicts the traditional cost of change curve (McConnell 1996; Ambler 1998a, b) for the single release of a project following a serial (waterfall) process. It shows the relative cost of addressing a changed requirement, because it was either missed or misunderstood, throughout the lifecycle. As you can see, the cost of fixing errors increases exponentially the later they are detected in the development lifecycle because the artifacts within a serial process build on each other. For example, if you make a requirements error and find it during the requirements phase it is relatively inexpensive to fix. You merely change a portion of your requirements model. A change of this scope is on the order of $1 (you do a little bit of retyping/remodeling). If you do not find it until the design stage, it is more expensive to fix. Not only do you have to change your analysis, you also must reevaluate and potentially modify the sections of your design based on the faulty analysis. This change is on the order of $10 (you do a little more retyping/remodeling). If you do not find the problem until programming, you need to update your analysis, design, and potentially scrap portions of your code, all because of a missed or misunderstood user requirement. This error is on the order of $100, because of all the wasted development time based on the faulty requirement. Furthermore, if you find the error during the traditional testing stage, it is on the order of $1,000 to fix (you need to update your documentation and scrap/rewrite large portions of code). Finally, if the error gets past you into

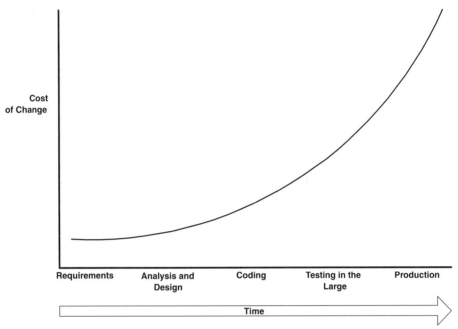

FIGURE 3.1. Traditional cost of change curve.

production, you are looking at a repair cost on the order of $10,000+ to fix (you need to send out update disks, fix the database, restore old data, and rewrite/reprint manuals).

It is clear from Fig. 3.1 that you want to test often and test early. By reducing the feedback loop, the time between creating something and validating it, you will clearly reduce the cost of change. In fact, Kent Beck (2000) argues that in extreme programming (XP) the cost of change curve is flat, more along the lines of what is presented in Fig. 3.2. Heresy, you say! Not at all. Beck's curve reflects the exact same fundamental rules that Fig. 3.1 does. Once again, heresy, you say! Not at all. The difference is that the feedback loop is dramatically reduced in XP. One way that you do so is to take a test-driven development (TDD) approach (Astels 2003; Beck 2003) as described in Section 3.10. With a TDD approach the feedback loop is effectively reduced to minutes—instead of the days, weeks, or even months, which is the norm for serial processes—and as a result there is not an opportunity for the cost of change to get out of hand.

Many people have questioned Beck's claim, a claim based on his own anecdotal evidence and initially presented as a metaphor to help people to rethink

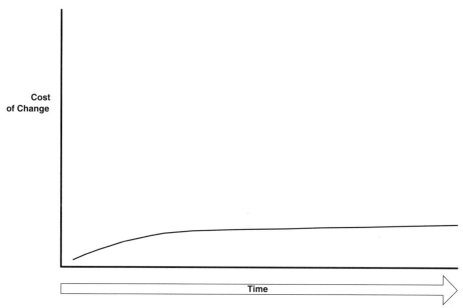

FIGURE **3.2. Kent Beck's cost of change curve.**

some of their beliefs regarding development. Frankly all he has done is found a way to do what software engineering has recommended for a long time now, to test as early as possible—testing first is about as early are you are going to get. To be fair, there is more to this than simply TDD. With XP you reduce the feedback loop through pair programming (Williams and Kessler 2002) as well as by working closely with your customers (project stakeholders). One advantage of working closely with stakeholders is that they are available to explain their requirements to you, increasing the chance that you do not misunderstand them, and you can show them your work to get feedback from them, which enables you to quickly determine whether you have built the right thing. The cost of change is also reduced by an explicit focus on writing high-quality code and by keeping it good through refactoring (Fowler 1999; Ambler 2003a), a technique where you improve the design of your code without adding functionality to it. By traveling light, in other words by retaining the minimum amount of project artifacts required to support the project, there is less to update when a change does occur.

Figure 3.3 presents a cost of change curve that I think you can safely expect for agile software development projects. As you can see the curve does not

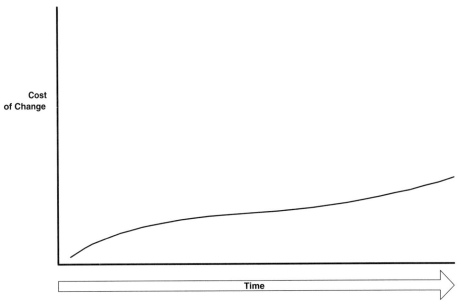

FIGURE **3.3. A more realistic cost of change curve.**

completely flatten but in fact rises gently over time. There are several reasons
for this:

- **You travel heavier over time.** Minimally your business code and your test
  code bases will grow over time, increasing the chance that any change that
  does occur will touch more things later in the project.

- **Noncode artifacts are not as flexible as code.** Not only will your code
  base increase over time, so will your noncode base. There will be documents
  such as user manuals, operations manuals, and system overview documents
  that you will need to update. There are models, perhaps a requirements or
  architectural model, that you will also need to update over time. Taking an
  agile modeling–driven development (AMDD) approach (see Chapter 4),
  will help to reduce the cost of this but will not fully eliminate it.

- **Deployment issues may increase your costs.** Expensive deployment
  strategies (perhaps you distribute CDs instead of releasing software electronically to shared servers) motivate you to follow more conservative procedures such as holding reviews. This both increases your cost and reduces
  your development velocity.

- **You may not be perfectly agile.** Many agile software development teams find themselves in very nonagile environments and as a result are forced to follow procedures, such as additional paperwork or technical reviews that increase their overall costs. These procedures not only increase the feedback loop but also are very often not conducive to supporting change.

An important thing to understand about all three cost curves is that they represent the costs of change for a single, production release of software. Over time, as your system is released over and over you should expect your cost of change to rise over time. This is due to the fact that as the system grows you simply have more code, models, documents, and so on to work with, increasing that chance that your team will need to work with artifacts that they have not touched for awhile. Although unfamiliarity will make it harder to work with and change an artifact, if you actively keep your artifacts of high quality they will be easier to change.

Another important concept concerning all three curves is that their scope is the development of a single, major release of a system. Following the traditional approach some systems are released once and then bug fixes are applied over time via patches. Interim patches are problematic because you need to retest and redeploy the application each time—something that can be expensive, particularly when it is unexpected and high priority. Other times an incremental approach is taken where major releases are developed and deployed every year or two. With an agile approach an incremental approach is typically taken although the release timeframe is often shorter—for example, releases once a quarter or once every six months are common; the important thing is that your release schedule reflects the needs of your users. Once the release of your system is in production the cost of change curve can change. Fixing errors in production is often expensive because the cost of change can become dominated by different issues. First, the costs to recover from a problem can be substantial if the error, which could very well be the result of a misunderstood requirement, corrupts a large amount of data. Or in the case of commercial software, or at least "customer facing" software used by the customers of your organization, the public humiliation of faulty software could be substantial (customers no longer trust you, for example). Second, the cost to redeploy your system, as noted above, can be very large in some situations. Third, your strategy for dealing with errors affects the costs. If you decide to simply treat the change as a new requirement for a future release of the system, then the cost of change curve remains the same because you are now within the scope of a new release. However, some production defects need to be addressed right away, forcing you to do an interim patch, which clearly can be expensive. When you include the cost of interim patches into the curves my expectation is that Fig. 3.1 will flatten out at the high level that it has reached and that both Fig. 3.2 and Fig. 3.3 will potentially have jumps in them, depending on your situation.

What is the implication? Although it may not be possible to reduce the feedback loop for noncode artifacts so dramatically, it seems clear that it is worth your while to find techniques that allow you to validate your development artifacts as early as possible.

3.2 Testing Philosophies

To help set a foundation for the rest of the chapter, I would like to share a few of my personal philosophies with regards to testing:

1. **The goal is to find defects.** The primary purpose of testing is to validate the correctness of whatever it is that you are testing. In other words, successful tests find bugs.

2. **You can validate all artifacts.** As you will see in this chapter, you can test all your artifacts, not just your source code. At a minimum you can review models and documents and therefore find and fix defects long before they get into your code.

3. **Test often and early.** As you saw in Section 3.1 the potential for the cost of change to rise exponentially motivates you to test as early as possible.

4. **Testing builds confidence.** Many people fear making a change to their code because they are afraid that they will break it, but with a full test suite in place if you do break something you know you will detect it and then fix it. Kent Beck (2000) makes an interesting observation that when you have a full test suite, which is a collection of tests, and if you run it as often as possible, then it gives you the courage to move forward.

5. **Test to the amount of risk of the artifact.** McGregor (1997) points out that the riskier something is, the more it needs to be reviewed and tested. In other words you should invest significant effort testing in an air-traffic control system but nowhere near as much effort testing a "Hello World" application.

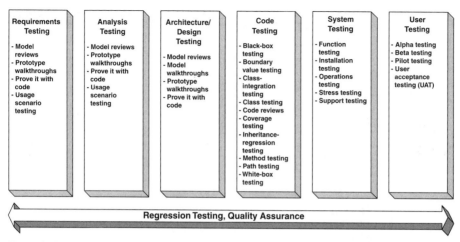

Requirements Testing	Analysis Testing	Architecture/ Design Testing	Code Testing	System Testing	User Testing
- Model reviews - Prototype walkthroughs - Prove it with code - Usage scenario testing	- Model reviews - Prototype walkthroughs - Prove it with code - Usage scenario testing	- Model reviews - Model walkthroughs - Prototype walkthroughs - Prove it with code	- Black-box testing - Boundary value testing - Class-integration testing - Class testing - Code reviews - Coverage testing - Inheritance-regression testing - Method testing - Path testing - White-box testing	- Function testing - Installation testing - Operations testing - Stress testing - Support testing	- Alpha testing - Beta testing - Pilot testing - User acceptance testing (UAT)

Regression Testing, Quality Assurance

FIGURE 3.4. The techniques of the full lifecycle object-oriented testing (FLOOT) methodology.

6. **One test is worth a thousand opinions.** You can tell me that your application works, but until you show me the test results, I will not believe you.

7. **Testing is *not* about fixing things**. Testing is about discovering defects. Correcting defects falls into other areas.

3.3 FULL LIFECYCLE OBJECT-ORIENTED TESTING (FLOOT)

The *full-lifecycle object-oriented testing* (FLOOT) methodology is a collection of testing and validation techniques for verifying and validating object-oriented software. The FLOOT lifecycle is depicted in Fig. 3.4, indicating a wide variety of techniques (described in Table 3.1) are available to you throughout all aspects of the development lifecycle. The list of techniques is not meant to be complete, as several other testing books are suggested throughout the chapter; instead the goal is to make it explicit that you have a wide range of options available to you. It is important to understand that although the FLOOT method is presented as a collection of serial phases it does not need to be so: the techniques of FLOOT can be applied with evolutionary/agile processes as well. The reason I present the FLOOT in a "traditional" manner is to make it explicit that you can in fact test throughout all aspects of software development, not just during coding.

TABLE 3.1. The Techniques of the FLOOT Methodology

FLOOT technique	Description
Black-box testing	Testing that verifies the item being tested when given the appropriate input provides the expected results.
Boundary-value testing	Testing of unusual or extreme situations that an item should be able to handle.
Class testing	The act of ensuring that a class and its instances (objects) perform as defined.
Class-integration testing	The act of ensuring that the classes, and their instances, which form a larger software entity, perform as defined.
Code inspection	A form of technical review in which the deliverable being reviewed is source code.
Component testing	The act of validating that a component works as defined.
Coverage testing	The act of ensuring that every line of code is exercised at least once.
Design review	A model review in which a design model is inspected.
Function testing	Testing by IT staff to verify that the application meets the defined needs of their users.
Inheritance-regression testing	The act of running the test cases of the superclasses, both direct and indirect, on a given subclass.
Installation testing	Testing to verify that your application can be installed successfully.
Integration testing	Testing to verify several portions of software work together.
Method testing	Testing to verify a method (member function) performs as defined.
Model review	An inspection, ranging anywhere from a formal technical review to an informal walkthrough, by others who were not directly involved with the development of the model.
Operations testing	Testing to verify that the requirements of operations personnel are met.
Path testing	The act of ensuring that all logic paths within your code are exercised at least once, a subset of coverage testing.

FLOOT technique	Description
Prototype review	A process by which your users work through a collection of use cases, using a prototype as if it were the real system. The main goal is to test whether the design of the prototype meets their needs.
Prove it with code	Determining whether a model actually reflects what is needed, or what should be built, by building software that shows that the model works.
Regression testing	The acts of ensuring that previously tested behaviors still work as expected after changes have been made to an application.
Stress testing	The act of ensuring that the system performs as expected under high volumes of transactions, users, load, and so on.
Support testing	Testing to verify that the requirements of support personnel are met.
Technical review	A quality assurance technique in which the design of your application is examined critically by a group of your peers, typically focusing on accuracy, quality, usability, and completeness. This process is often referred to as a walkthrough, an inspection, or a peer review.
Usage scenario testing	A testing technique in which one or more person(s) validate a model by acting through the logic of usage scenarios.
User interface testing	The testing of the user interface (UI) to ensure that it follows accepted UI standards and meets the requirements defined for it; often referred to as graphical user interface (GUI) testing.
White-box testing	Testing to verify that specific lines of code work as defined; also referred to as clear-box testing.

In the following sections I will explore each of the techniques depicted in Fig. 3.4.

3.4 REGRESSION TESTING

Regression testing is the act of ensuring that changes to an application have not adversely affected existing functionality. Have you ever made a small change to a program, and then put the program into production only to see it fail because the small change affected another part of the program you had completely forgotten about? Regression testing is all about avoiding problems like this. Regression testing is the first thing you should be thinking about when testing. How angry would you get if you took your car into a garage to have a new stereo system installed only to discover afterward that the new stereo works, but the headlights do not? Pretty angry. How angry do you think your users would get when a new release of an application no longer lets them fax information to other people because the new e-mail feature you just added has affected it somehow? Pretty angry.

How do you regression test? The quick answer is to run all your previous test cases against the new version of your application. When it comes to testing your code, open source tools such as JUnit (http://www.junit.org) or VBUnit (http://www.vbunit.org) help you immensely. However, there are potential challenges to regression testing. First, you may have changed part of, or even all of, the design of your application. This means you need to modify some of the previous test cases. The implication is that you want to proceed in small steps when developing, a key concept in TDD (Section 3.10). Second, if the changes you have made truly affect only a component of the system, then potentially you only need to run the test cases that affect this single component. Although this approach is a little risky because your changes may have had a greater impact than you suspect, it does help to reduce both the time and cost of regression testing. Third, it is difficult to regression test paper documents. The implication is that the more noncode artifacts that you decide to keep, the greater the effort to regression test your work and therefore the greater the risk to your project because you are more likely to skimp on your testing efforts.

It is important to recognize that incremental development makes regression testing critical. Whenever you release an application, you must ensure its previous functionality still works, and because you release applications more often when taking the incremental approach, this means regression testing becomes that much more important.

3.5 QUALITY ASSURANCE

Quality assurance (QA) is the act of reviewing and auditing the project deliverables and activities to verify that they comply with the applicable standards, guidelines, and processes adopted by your organization. Fundamentally, quality assurance attempts to answer the following questions: "Are you building the right thing?" and "Are you building it the right way?" In my opinion the first question is far more important than the second in most cases, the only exception being in highly regulated industries where noncompliance to your defined process could result in legal action or even dissolution of your organization. Perhaps a more effective question to ask would be "Can we build this a better way?" because it would provide valuable feedback that developers could use to improve the way that they work.

A key concept in quality assurance is that quality is often in the eye of the beholder, indicating many aspects exist to software quality, including the following:

- Does it meet the needs of its users?
- Does it provide value to its stakeholders?
- Does it follow relevant standards?
- Is it easy to use by its intended users?
- Is it reasonably free of defects?
- Is it easy to maintain and to enhance?
- How easy will it integrate into the current technical environment?

Quality assurance is critical to the success of a project and should be an integral part of all project stages, but only when it is done in an effective and efficient manner. However, I have seen some spectacularly dysfunctional QA efforts within IT organizations. Sometimes the effort is underfunded, other times it is far too bureaucratic. For QA professionals to be relevant within an agile world, they need to be able to work in an agile manner. This means that they need to be willing to do the following:

- Work closely with other team members (they must do more than just review the work of others);
- Work in an evolutionary manner, understanding that artifacts change over time and are never "done" until you deliver the working system; and
- Gain a wider range of skills beyond that of QA.

3.6 Testing Your Models

You saw that the earlier you detect an error, the less expensive it is to fix. Therefore, it is imperative for you attempt to test your requirements, analysis, and design artifacts as early as you can. Luckily, a collection of techniques exist that you can apply to do exactly that. As you see in Fig. 3.4 these techniques are

- Proving it with code;
- Usage scenario testing;
- Prototype walkthroughs;
- User interface testing; and
- Model reviews.

3.6.1 Proving It with Code

Everything works on a whiteboard, or on the screen of a sophisticated modeling tool, or in presentation slides. But how do you know whether it really works? You don't. The problem is that a model is an abstraction, one that should accurately reflect an aspect of whatever you are building. Until you build it, you really do not know whether it works. So build it and find out. If you have developed a screen sketch you should code it and show your users to get some feedback. If you have developed a UML sequence diagram representing the logic of a complex business rule, write the testing and business code to see whether you have gotten it right. My basic advice is to take an evolutionary approach to development. Do a little bit of modeling, a little bit of coding, and a little bit of testing. This shortens the feedback loop and increases the chance that you will find problems as early as possible.

Unfortunately there are two common impediments to this technique, both of them people oriented. First, this strategy works best when the same people are both modeling and coding, implying that agile developers need a wide range of skills. Second, many developers have a "big design up front" (BDUF) mindset that leads them to model for greater periods of time than they need to, putting off coding for awhile. This is particularly true of people following serial processes, but it is also often true of experienced developers who are new to agility.

In Chapter 4 you will see that agile modeling includes an explicit practice called *prove it with code*.

3.6.2 Usage Scenario Testing

Usage scenario testing, formerly called use-case scenario testing (Ambler 1998a), is an integral part of the object-oriented development lifecycle. It is a technique that can be used to test your domain model, which is a representation of the business/domain concepts and their interrelationships, applicable to your system. A domain model helps to establish the vocabulary for your project. Domain models are often developed using class responsibility collaborator (CRC) models (Chapter 8), logical data models (Chapter 8), or class models (Chapters 8 and 12). However, because usage scenario testing addresses both data and behavioral aspects within your domain, you will find that it works best with CRC and class models but not as well with data models (which do not address behavior).

Using a collection of usage scenarios, whereby a usage scenario is a series of steps describing how someone works with your system, you walk through your domain model and validate that it is able to support those scenarios. If it does not, you update your model appropriately. It can and should be performed in parallel with your domain modeling efforts by the same team that created your domain model, and in fact, many people consider usage scenario testing as simply an extension of CRC modeling. Fundamentally, usage scenario testing is a technique that helps to ensure that your domain model accurately reflects your business.

The steps of a usage scenario testing process are straightforward. They are

1. **Perform domain modeling.** Create a conceptual domain model, discussed in Chapter 8, representing the critical domain concepts (entities) and their interrelationships. In fact, use-case scenario testing is typically performed as a part of domain modeling.

2. **Create the usage scenarios.** A usage scenario describes a particular situation that your system may or may not be expected to handle. If you are taking a use-case driven approach to development, use cases describe a collection of steps that provides value to one or more actors, a usage scenario will comprise a single path through part or all of a use case. Some scenarios even encompass several use cases. Figure 3.5 presents an example of a usage scenario for a university information system.

3. **Assign entities/classes to your subject matter experts (SMEs).** Each SME should be assigned one or more entities that they are to represent. For now, let us assume that you are using CRC cards to create your domain model,

A student successfully enrolls in several seminars and pays partial tuition for them.

Description:
A student decides to register in three seminars, which the student has the prerequisites for and which still have seats available in them, and pays half the tuition at the time of registration.

Steps:
The student prepares to register:

- The student determines the three seminars she wants to enroll in.
- The student looks up the prerequisites for the seminars to verify she is qualified to enroll in them.
- The student verifies spots are available in each seminar.
- The student determines the seminars fit into her schedule.

The student contacts the registrar to enroll in the seminars.
The student enrolls in the seminars:

- The student indicates to the registrar she wants to enroll in the seminars.
- For each seminar:
  - The registrar verifies a spot is available in it.
  - The registrar verifies the student is qualified to take the seminar.
  - The registrar registers the student in the seminar.

A total bill for the registration is calculated and added to the student's outstanding balance (there is none).
The outstanding balance is presented to the student.
The student decides to pay half the balance immediately, and does so.
The registrar accepts the payment.
The payment is recorded.
The outstanding balance for the student is calculated and presented to the student.

FIGURE 3.5. An example usage scenario.

where each CRC card represents a single business concept such as *Student* or *Course* at a university or *Customer* and *Order* in an online ordering system. Entities have responsibilities, things they know or do; for example, students know their name and they enroll in seminars. Sometimes an entity needs to collaborate with another one to fulfill a responsibility; for example, the

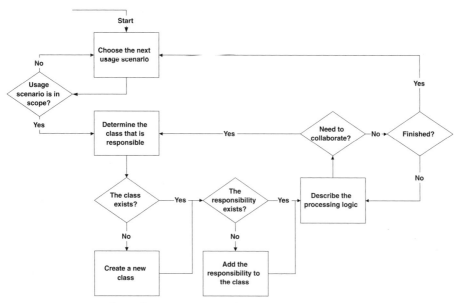

FIGURE **3.6. The process of usage scenario testing.**

Student card needs to collaborate with the *Seminar* card in order to enroll in it. Ideally the CRC cards should be distributed evenly; therefore, each SME should have roughly the same amount of responsibilities assigned. This means some SMEs will have one or two busy cards, while others may have numerous not-so-busy cards. The main goal here is to spread the functionality of the system evenly among SMEs. Additionally, it is important not to give two cards that collaborate to the same person (sometimes you cannot avoid this, but you should try). The reason for this will become apparent when you see how to act out scenarios.

4. **Describe how to act out a scenario.** The majority of work with usage scenario testing is the acting out of scenarios. If the group you are working with is new to the technique you may want to go through a few practice rounds.

5. **Act out the scenarios**. As a group, the facilitator leads the SMEs through the process of acting out the scenarios, depicted in Fig. 3.6. The basic idea is the SMEs take on the roles of the cards they were given, describing the business logic of the responsibilities that support each use-case scenario. To indicate which card is currently "processing," a soft, spongy ball is held by the person with that card. Whenever a card must collaborate with

another one, the user holding the card throws the ball to the holder of the second card. The ball helps the group to keep track of who is currently describing the business logic and also helps to make the entire process a little more interesting. You want to act the scenarios out so you gain a better understanding of the business rules/logic of the system (the scribes write this information down as the SMEs describe it) and find missing or misunderstood responsibilities and classes.

6. **Update the domain model.** As the SMEs are working through the scenarios, they will discover they are missing some responsibilities and, sometimes, even some classes. Great! This is why they are acting out the scenarios in the first place. When the group discovers the domain model is missing some information, it should be updated immediately. Once all the scenarios have been acted out, the group ends up with a robust domain model. Now there is little chance of missing information (assuming you generated a complete set of use-case scenarios) and there is little chance of misunderstood information (the group has acted out the scenarios, describing the exact business logic in detail).

7. **Save the scenarios.** Do not throw the scenarios away once you finish acting them out. The scenarios are a good start at your user-acceptance test plan and you will want them when you are documenting the requirements for the next release of your system.

3.6.3 Prototype Reviews/Walkthroughs

The user interface (UI) of an application is the portion the user directly interacts with: screens, reports, documentation, and your software support staff. A user interface prototype is a user interface that has been "mocked up" using a computer language or prototyping tool, but it does not yet implement the full system functionality.

A prototype walkthrough is a testing process in which your users work through a series of usage scenarios to verify that a user prototype meets their needs. It is basically usage scenario testing applied to a user interface prototype instead of a domain model. The basic idea is that your users pretend the prototype is the real application and try to use it to solve real business problems described by the scenarios. Granted, they need to use their imaginations to fill in the functionality the application is missing (such as reading and writing objects from/to permanent storage), but, for the most part, this is a fairly straightforward process. Your users sit down at the computer and begin to work through the use cases. Your job is to sit there and observe them, looking for places where the system is difficult to use or is missing features. In many ways, prototype walkthroughs are a lot like user-acceptance tests (Section 3.9), the only difference being you are working with the prototype instead of the real system.

3.6.4 User-Interface Testing

UI testing is the verification that the UI follows the accepted standards chosen by your organization and the UI meets the requirements defined for it. User-interface testing is often referred to as graphical user interface (GUI) testing. UI testing can be something as simple as verifying that your application "does the right thing" when subjected to a defined set of user-interface events, such as keyboard input, or something as complex as a usability study where human-factors engineers verify that the software is intuitive and easy to use.

3.6.5 Model Reviews

A model review, also called a model walkthrough or a model inspection, is a validation technique in which your modeling efforts are examined critically by a group of your peers. The basic idea is that a group of qualified people, often both technical staff and SMEs, get together in a room to evaluate a model or document. The purpose of this evaluation is to determine whether the models not only fulfill the demands of the user community but also are of sufficient quality to be easy to develop, maintain, and enhance. When model reviews are performed properly, they can have a large payoff because they often identify defects early in the project, reducing the cost of fixing them. In fact, Grady (1992) reports that where project teams take a serial (non-agile) approach, 50 to 75 percent of all design errors can be found through technical reviews.

There are different "flavors" of model review. A requirements review is a type of model review in which a group of users and/or recognized experts review your requirements artifacts. The purpose of a user requirement review is to ensure your requirements accurately reflect the needs and priorities of your user community and to ensure your understanding is sufficient from which to develop software. Similarly an architecture review focuses on reviewing architectural models and a design review focuses on reviewing design models. As you would expect the reviewers are often technical staff.

My advice is to hold a review only as a last resort. The reality is that model reviews are not very effective for agile software development. Teams co-located with an on-site customer have much less need of a review than teams not co-located. The desire to hold a review is a "process smell," an indication that you are compensating for a process-oriented mistake that you have made earlier. Typically you will have made the mistake of letting one person, or a small subset of your team, work on one artifact (e.g., the data model or a component). Agile teams work in high-communication, high-collaboration, and high-cooperation environments—when you work this way you quickly discover that you do not need to.

If you are going to hold a review, the following pointers should help you to make it effective:

1. **Get the right people in the review.** You want people, and only those people, who know what they are looking at and can provide valuable feedback. Better yet, include them in your development efforts and avoid the review in the first place.

2. **Review working software, not models.** The traditional, near-serial development approach currently favored within many organizations provides little else for project stakeholders to look at during most of a project. However, because the iterative and incremental approach of agile development techniques tightens the development cycle you will find that user-acceptance testing can replace many model review efforts. My experience is that given the choice of validating a model or validating working software, most people will choose to work with the software.

3. **Stay focused.** This is related to maximizing value: you want to keep reviews short and sweet. The purpose of the review should be clear to everyone; for example, if it is a requirements review do not start discussing database design issues. At the same time recognize that it is okay for an informal or impromptu model review to "devolve" into a modeling/working session as long as that effort remains focused on the issue at hand.

4. **Understand that quality comes from more than just reviews.** In application development, quality comes from developers who understand how to build software properly, who have learned from experience, and/or who have gained these skills from training and education. Reviews help you to identify quality deficits, but they will not help you build quality into your application from the outset. Reviews should be only a small portion of your overall testing and quality strategy.

5. **Set expectations ahead of time.** The expectations of the reviewers must be realistic if the review is to run smoothly. Issues that reviewers should be aware of are
   - The more detail a document has, the easier it is to find fault.
   - With an evolutionary approach your models are not complete until the software is ready to ship.
   - Agile developers are likely to be traveling light and therefore their documentation may not be "complete" either.
   - The more clearly defined a position on an issue, the easier it is to find fault.
   - Finding many faults may often imply a good, not a bad, job has been performed.
   - The goal is to find gaps in the work, so they can be addressed appropriately.

6. **Understand you cannot review everything.** Karl Wiegers (1999) advises that you should prioritize your artifacts on a risk basis and review those that present the highest risk to your project if they contain serious defects.

7. **Focus on communication.** Alan Shalloway (2000) points out that reviews are vehicles for knowledge transfer, that they are opportunities for people to share and discuss ideas. However, working closely with your co-workers and project stakeholders while you are actually modeling is even more effective for this purpose than reviews. This philosophy motivates agile developers to avoid formal reviews, due to their restrictions on how people are allowed to interact, in favor of other model validation techniques.

8. **Put observers to work.** People will often ask to observe a review either to become trained in the review process or to get updated on the project. These are both good reasons, but do they require the person to simply sit there and do nothing? I do not think so. If these people understand what is being reviewed and have something of value to add, then let them participate. Observers do not need to be dead weight.

3.6.6 When to Use Each Technique

My main preference is to try to prove my models with code—it is the quickest and most concrete feedback that I know of. More importantly when my models prove to be valid this practice also helps me to move forward in actual development; when my models have problems I would rather find out early as possible due to the exponential cost of change. I also find that many artifacts, such as user manuals and operations manuals, never become code yet still need to be validated.

3.7 TESTING YOUR CODE

You have a wide variety of tools and techniques to test your source code. In this section I discuss

- Testing terminology;
- Testing tools;
- Traditional code testing techniques;
- Object-oriented code testing techniques; and
- Code inspections.

3.7.1 Testing Terminology

Let us start off with some terminology applicable to code testing, system testing (Section 3.8), and user testing (Section 3.9). To perform these types of testing you need to define, and then run, a series of tests against your source code. A test case is a single test that needs to be performed. If you discover that you need to document a test case, you should describe

- Its purpose;
- The setup work you need to perform before running the test to put the item you are testing into a known state;
- The steps of the actual test; and
- The expected results of the test.

   Given the chance, I prefer to write human readable test scripts in order to implement my test cases, scripts that include the information listed above. A test script is the actual steps, sometimes either written procedures to follow or the source code, of a test. You run test scripts against your testing targets: either your source code, a portion of your system (such as a component), or the entire system itself.

   A test suite is a collection of test scripts, and a test harness is the portion of the code of a test suite that aggregates the test scripts. You run your test suite against your test target(s), producing test results that indicate the actual results of your testing efforts. If your actual test results vary from your expected test results, documented as part of each test case, then you have identified a potential defect in your test target(s).

3.7.2 Testing Tools

As you learned in Section 3.4, regression testing is critical to your success as an agile developer. Many agile software developers use the xUnit family of open source tools, such as JUnit (http://www.junit.org) and VBUnit (http://www.vbunit.org), to test their code. The advantage of these tools is that they implement a testing framework with which you can regression test all of your source code. Commercial testing tools, such Mercury Interactive (http://www-svca.mercuryinteractive.com), jTest (http://www.parasoft.com), and Rational Suite Test Studio (http://www.rational.com), are also viable options. One or more testing tools must be in your development toolkit; otherwise I just do not see how you can develop software effectively.

3.7.3 Traditional Code Testing Concepts

You saw in Chapter 1 that object technology such as Java is different from structured/procedural technology such as COBOL. The critical implication is that because the technologies are different, then some of the associated techniques must be different too. That is absolutely true. However, some structured testing techniques are still relevant for modern software development (*important life lesson*: not everything old is bad). In this section I overview a collection of techniques that are still relevant, and likely will always remain relevant, for your testing efforts.

These techniques are

- **Black-box testing.** Black-box testing, also called interface testing, is a technique in which you create test cases based only on the expected functionality of a method, class, or application without any knowledge of its internal workings. One way to define black-box testing is that given defined input *A* you should obtain the expected results *B*. The goal of black-box testing is to ensure the system can do what it should be able to do, but not how it does it. For example, if you invoke *differenceInDays(June 30 2004, July 3*

2004) the expected result should be three. The creation of black-box tests is often driven by the requirements for your system. The basic idea is you look at the user requirement and ask yourself what needs to be done to show the user requirement is met.

- **White-box testing.** White-box testing, also called clear-box testing, is based on the idea that your program code can drive the development of test cases. The basic concept is you look at your code, and then create test cases that exercise it. For example, assume you have access to the source code for *differenceInDays()*. When you look at it, you see an IF statement determines whether the two dates are in the same year. If so a simple strategy based on Julian dates is used; if not then a more complex one is used. This indicates that you need at least one test that uses dates from the same year and one from different years. By looking at the code, you are able to determine new test cases to exercise the different logic paths within it.

- **Boundary-value testing.** This is based on the knowledge that you need to test your code to ensure it can handle unusual and extreme situations. For example, boundary-value test cases *differenceInDays()* would include passing it the same date, two wildly different dates, one date on the last day of the year and the second on the first day of the following year, and one date on February 29th of a leap year. The basic idea is you want to look for limits defined either by your business rules or by common sense, and then create test cases to test attribute values in and around those values.

- **Unit testing.** This is the testing of an item, such as an operation, in isolation. For example, the tests defined so far for *differenceInDays()* are all unit tests.

- **Integration testing.** This is the testing of a collection of items to validate that they work together. In the case of the data library/class, do the various functions work together? Perhaps the *differenceInDays()* function has a side effect that causes the *dayOfWeek()* function to fail if *differenceInDays()* is called first. Integration testing looks for problems like this.

- **Coverage testing.** Coverage testing is a technique in which you create a series of test cases designed to test all the code paths in your code. In many ways, coverage testing is simply a collection of white-box test cases that together exercise every line of code in your application at least once.

- **Path testing.** Path testing is a superset of coverage testing that ensures not only have all lines of code been tested, but all paths of logic have also been tested. The main difference occurs when you have a method with more

	TABLE 3.2. Comparing Traditional Testing Techniques	
Technique	Advantages	Disadvantages
Black box	• Enables you to prove that your application fulfills the requirements defined for it.	• Does not show that the internals of your system work.
Boundary value	• Enables you to confirm that your program code is able to handle "unusual" or "extreme" cases.	• Does not find the "usual" errors.
Coverage	• Ensures that all lines of code within your application have been tested.	• Does not ensure that all combinations of the code have been tested.
Integration	• Validates that the pieces all fit together.	• Can be difficult to formulate the test cases. • Does not work well if the various pieces have not been unit tested.
Path	• Tests all combinations of your code.	• Requires significantly more effort to formulate and run the test cases. • Unrealistic in most cases because of its exponential nature.
Unit	• Tests small portions of code in isolation. • Relatively easy to formulate unit test cases because the test target is small.	• The individual portions may work on their own but may not work together. For example, a boat engine likely will not work with your car transmission.
White/clear box	• Enables you to create tests that exercise specific lines of code.	• Does not ensure that your code fulfils the actual requirements. • Testing code becomes highly coupled to your application code.

than one set of case statements or nested IF statements: to determine the number of test cases with coverage testing you would count the maximum number of paths between the sets of case/nested IF statements and, with path testing, you would multiply the number of logic paths.

As you can see in Table 3.2 each traditional testing technique has its advantages and disadvantages. The implication is that you need to use a combination of them for any given project.

3.7.4 Object-Oriented Testing Techniques

Until just recently, object-oriented testing has been a little understood topic. I wrote about it in *Building Object Applications That Work* (Ambler 1998a) in my initial discussion of FLOOT, although the books that you really want to look at for details are *The Craft of Software Testing* (Marick 1995) and *Testing Object-Oriented Systems* (Binder 1999).

When testing systems built using object technology it is important to understand that your source code is composed of several constructs, including methods (operations), classes, and inheritance relationships. These concepts are described in detail in Chapter 2. Therefore you need testing techniques that reflect the fact that you have these constructs. These techniques, compared in Table 3.3, are

1. **Method testing.** Method testing is the act of ensuring that your methods, called operations or member functions in C++ and Java, perform as defined. The closest comparison to method testing in the structured world is the unit testing of functions and procedures. Although some people argue that class testing is really the object-oriented version of unit testing, my experience has been that the creation of test cases for specific methods often proves useful and should not be ignored, hence, the need for method testing. Issues to address during method testing include the following:
   - Ensuring that your getter and setter methods manipulate the value of a single property work as intended;
   - Ensuring that each method returns the proper values, including error messages and exceptions;
   - Basic checking of the parameters being passed to each method; and
   - Ensuring that each method does what the documentation says it does.

TABLE 3.3. Comparing Object-Oriented Testing Techniques		
Technique	Advantages	Disadvantages
Class	• Validates that the operations and properties of a class work together. • Validates that a class works in isolation.	• Does not guarantee that a class will work with the other classes within your system.
Class integration	• Validates that the various classes within a component, or a system, work together.	• Can be difficult to define and develop the test cases to fully perform this level of testing.
Inheritance regression	• Ensures that new subclasses actually work.	• Requires you to rerun the test suite for the immediate superclasses.
Method	• Ensures that an operation works in isolation. • Relatively easy to do.	• Does not guarantee that you will discover unintended side effects caused by the method.

2. **Class testing.** This is both unit testing and traditional integration testing. It is unit testing because you are testing the class and its instances as single units in isolation, but it is also integration testing because you need to verify the methods and attributes of the class work together. The one assumption you need to make during class testing is that all other classes in the system work. Although this may sound like an unreasonable assumption, it is basically what separates class testing from class-integration testing. The main purpose of class testing is to test classes in isolation, something that is difficult to do if you do not assume everything else works. An important class test is to validate that the attributes of an object are initialized properly.

3. **Class-integration testing.** Also known as component testing, this technique addresses the issue of whether the classes in your system, or a component of your system, work together properly. The only way classes or, to be more accurate, the instances of classes, can work together is by sending each other messages. Therefore, some sort of relationship must

exist between those objects before they can send the message, implying that the relationships between classes can be used to drive the development of integration test cases. In other words, your strategy should be to look at the association, aggregation, and inheritance relationships that appear on your class diagram and in formulating class-integration test cases.

4. **Inheritance-regression testing.** This is the running of the class and method test cases for all the superclasses of the class being tested. The motivation behind inheritance-regression testing is simple: it is incredibly naive to expect that errors have not been introduced by a new subclass. New methods are added and existing methods are often redefined by subclasses, and these methods access and often change the value of the attributes defined in the superclass. It is possible that a subclass may change the value of the attributes in a way that was never intended in the superclass, or at least was never expected. Personally, I want to run the old test cases against my new subclass to verify that everything still works.

3.7.5 Code Inspections

Code inspections, also known as code reviews, often reveal problems that normal testing techniques do not, in particular, poor coding practices that make your application difficult to extend and maintain. Code inspections verify you built the code right and you have built code that will be easy to understand, to maintain, and to enhance. Code inspections should concentrate on quality issues, such as

- Does the code satisfy the design?
- Naming conventions for your classes, methods, and attributes.
- Code documentation standards and conventions.
  - Have you documented what a method does?
  - Have you documented what parameters must be passed?
  - Have you documented what values are returned by a method?
  - Have you documented both what and why a piece of code does what it does?
- Writing small methods that do one thing and one thing well.
- How to simplify the code.

Code inspections are a valid technique for project teams taking a traditional approach to development. They can be an effective means for training developers in software engineering skills because the inspections reveal areas that the coders need to improve. Furthermore they help to detect and fix problems as early in the coding process as possible. Writing 1,000 lines of code, reviewing it, fixing it, and moving on is better than writing 100,000 lines of code, and then finding out the code is unintelligible to everyone but the people who wrote it.

Just as model reviews are process smells, my experience is that the desire to hold a code inspection is also a process smell. Code inspections are rarely used by agile teams because they do not add value in those environments. Agile techniques such as pair programming, where two coders work together at a single computer, in combination with regularly switching pairs and collective ownership of code (Beck 2000), have a tendency to negate the need for code inspections. Following these practices there are several sets of eyes on any line of code, increasing the chance that problems will be found and fixed as a regular part of coding. Furthermore, adoption of coding standards (see Chapter 13) within the team helps to ensure that the code all looks and feels the same.

3.8 TESTING YOUR SYSTEM IN ITS ENTIRETY

System testing is a testing process in which you aim to ensure that your overall system works as defined by your requirements. System testing is typically performed at the end of an iteration, enabling you to fix known problems before your application is user tested (Section 3.9). System testing comprises the following techniques:

1. **Function testing.** When function testing, development staff verifies that their application meets the defined needs of their users. The idea is that developers, typically test engineers, work through the main functionality that the system should exhibit to assure themselves that their application is ready for user-acceptance testing (UAT) (Section 3.9). During user testing is when users confirm for themselves that the system meets their needs. In many ways, the only difference between function testing and user-acceptance testing is who does it: testers and users, respectively.

2. **Installation testing.** The goal is to determine whether your application can be installed successfully. The installation utility/process for your application is part of your overall application package and, therefore, must be tested. Several important issues should be considered:
   - Can you successfully install the application into an environment that it has not been installed into before?
   - Can you successfully install the application into an environment where it, or a previous version, already exists?
   - Is configuration information defined correctly?
   - Is previous configuration information taken into account?
   - Is online documentation installed correctly?
   - Are other applications affected by the installation of this one?
   - Are there adequate computer resources for the application? Does the installation utility detect this and act appropriately?

3. **Operations testing.** The goal of operations testing is to verify that the requirements of operations personnel are met. The main goal of operations testing is to ensure that your operations staff will be able to run your application successfully once it is installed.

4. **Stress testing.** Sometimes called volume testing, this is the process of ensuring that your application works with high numbers of users, high numbers of transactions (testing of high numbers of transactions is also called volume testing), high numbers of data transmissions, high numbers of printed reports, and so on. The goal is to find the stress points of your system under which it no longer operates, so you can gain insights into how it will perform in unusual and/or stressful situations.

5. **Support testing.** This is similar to operations testing except with a support personnel focus. Tourniaire and Farrell (1997) suggest that the needs of your support organization, in addition to those of your operations organization, be tested before your application is allowed to go into production.

3.9 TESTING BY USERS

User testing, which follows system testing, is composed of testing processes in which members of your user community perform the tests. The goal of user testing is to have the users verify that an application meets their needs.

User testing comprises the following techniques:

1. **Alpha testing.** Alpha testing is a process in which you send out software that is not quite ready for prime time to a small group of your customers to enable them work with it and report back to you the problems they encounter. Although the software is typically buggy and may not meet all their needs, they get a heads-up on what you are doing much earlier than if they waited for you to release the software formally.

2. **Beta testing.** Beta testing is basically the same process as alpha testing, except the software has many of the bugs identified during alpha testing (beta testing follows alpha testing) fixed and the software is distributed to a larger group. The main goal of both alpha and beta testing is to test run the product to identify and then fix any bugs before you release your application.

3. **Pilot testing.** Pilot testing is the "in-house" version of alpha/beta testing, the only difference being that the customers are typically internal to your organization. Companies that sell software typically alpha/beta test, whereas IT organizations that produce software for internal use will pilot test. Basically we have three different terms for effectively the same technique.

4. **User-acceptance testing (UAT).** After your system testing proves successful, your users must perform user-acceptance testing, a process in which they determine whether your application truly meets their needs. This means you have to let your users work with the software you produced. Because the only person who truly knows your own needs is you, the people involved in the user-acceptance test should be the actual users of the system—not their managers and not the vice presidents of the division they work for, but the people who will work daily with the application. Although you may have to give them some training to gain the testing skills they need, actual *users* are the only people who are qualified to do *user*-acceptance testing. The good news is, if you have function tested your application thoroughly, then the UAT process will take only a few days to a week at the most.

3.10 TEST-DRIVEN DEVELOPMENT (TDD)

Test-driven development (TDD) (Astels 2003; Beck 2003), also known as test-first programming or test-first development, is an evolutionary approach to

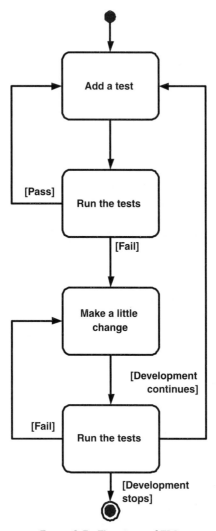

FIGURE 3.7. The steps of TDD

development where you must first write a test that fails before you write new functional code. As depicted in Fig. 3.7, the steps of TDD are these:

1. Quickly add a test, basically just enough code so that your tests now fail.
2. Run your tests, often the complete test suite, although for sake of speed you may decide to run only a subset, to ensure that the new test does in fact fail.
3. Update your functional code so that it passes the new test.

4. Run your tests again.
5. If the tests fail return to step 3.
6. Once the tests pass, the next step is to start over (you may also want to refactor any duplication out of your design as needed).

What is the primary goal of TDD? For the purposes of this book the primary goal is that TDD is an agile programming technique (Chapter 13)—as Ron Jeffries likes to say, the goal of TDD is to write clean code that works. Another view is that the goal of TDD is specification and not validation (Martin, Newkirk, and Koss 2003). In other words, it is one way to think through your design before your write your functional code. I think that there is merit in both arguments although I leave it for you to decide.

The reason I chose to overview TDD here in this chapter is to make it clear that testing and programming go hand in hand. In this case a technique that based on its name initially appears to be a testing technique really turns out to be a programming technique. The primary advantages of TDD are that it forces you to think about what new functional code should do before you write it, it ensures that you have testing code available to validate your work, and it gives you the courage to know that you can refactor your code because you know that there is a test suite in place that will detect whether you have "broken" anything as the result of the refactoring.

3.11 WHAT YOU HAVE LEARNED

One of the fundamentals of software engineering is you should test as early as possible because the cost of fixing defects increases exponentially the later they are found. Better yet, you want to test first. You then learned that a wide variety of testing techniques are available to you, encapsulated by the full lifecycle object-oriented testing methodology of Fig. 3.4. FLOOT techniques exist to test a wide range of project artifacts including, but not limited to, models, documentation, and source code.

3.12 REVIEW QUESTIONS

1. Define a collection of test cases for the *differenceInDays(date1, date2)* function. Assume that valid dates are being passed as parameters.

2. Compare and contrast black-box testing and white-box testing. Provide examples for how would you use these two techniques in combination with each of method testing, class testing, and class-integration testing.
3. Compare and contrast "quality assurance" and "testing." What value does each activity add to the development of software? Which is more important? Why?
4. When you are inspecting source code, what other artifacts would potentially prove useful as reference material in the review? Explain how each item would be useful.
5. Compare and contrast coverage testing and path testing. Discuss the feasibility of each approach.
6. Compare and contrast the techniques of usage scenario testing, user interface walkthroughs, and model reviews. When would you use one technique over the other? Why? What factors would lead you to choose one technique over the other? Why?
7. Internet assignment: For each FLOOT testing technique try to identify open source software (OSS) tools or commercial tools that support the technique. For techniques that you cannot find supporting tools for, explain why tools apparently do not exist and suggest tools that may help.
8. Internet assignment: For each FLOOT category (e.g., requirements testing) identify one or more sites that describe best practices for it.

CHAPTER 4

Agile Model–Driven Development (AMDD)

Are you agile or are you fragile?

Modeling and documentation are critical aspects of any software project. Modeling is the act of creating an abstraction of a concept, and documentation is a permanent record of information. In traditional software processes, such as the IEEE 12207 (http://www.ieee.org), modeling is included as one or more serial phases. Modern prescriptive processes, such as the rational unified process (RUP) (Kruchten 2000) or the enterprise unified process (EUP) (http://www.enterpriseunifiedprocess.info), which describe in specific detail the activities required to develop software, include modeling disciplines that you work through in an evolutionary manner. Agile software processes, such as feature-driven development (FDD) (Palmer and Felsing 2002) and extreme programming (XP) (Beck 2000), also include evolutionary modeling efforts, although in FDD, modeling is an explicit activity, whereas in XP it is implicit. The point is that modeling and documentation are important parts of software development, so it makes sense to want to be as effective and efficient at it as possible.

This chapter describes agile model–driven design (AMDD), an approach to software development where your implementation efforts are guided by agile models that are just barely good enough. This chapter addresses the following topics:

- Modeling philosophies;
- Project stakeholders;
- What is agile modeling (AM)?;
- The values of AM;
- The principles of AM;
- The practices of AM;
- Easing into agile modeling;
- Agile model–driven development (AMDD);
- Fundamental information gathering skills;
- Agile documentation;
- Making whiteboards work for software development;
- AMDD and other agile methodologies; and
- AMDD and test-driven development (TDD).

4.1 MODELING PHILOSOPHIES

I would like to begin by sharing some of my philosophies pertinent to modeling:

1. **Models are not necessarily documents**. The reality is that the concepts of "model" and "document" are orthogonal—you can have models that are not documents and documents that are not models. A sketch on the back of a paper napkin is a model, as is a drawing on a whiteboard (see Figure 4.1), as is a low-fidelity user-interface prototype built from flip chart paper and Post-It notes. These are all valuable models, yet questionable documents.

2. **Many developers do not like modeling.** I think the biggest problem is that when many developers hear the term model they think document, and due to bad experiences in the past they think that modeling is dysfunctional. Often a developer's first exposure to modeling is during a "documentation after the fact" effort in which a system has been released into production and now management insists that the project team create all the models that they "should have" created during development. Some of these documents may in fact add value, but more often than not much of this effort is simply

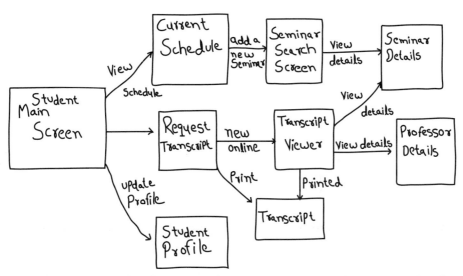

FIGURE 4.1. A user-interface flow diagram for a student services application at a university.

bureaucratic busy work. Similarly, many organizations like to take a serial, "big design up front" (BDUF) approach where large, detailed models are created early in the lifecycle, reviewed, and accepted long before coding starts. In many ways this is "documentation before the fact" and is just as problematic. Is it any wonder that many people are jaded with respect to modeling?

3. **Modeling is attractive to visual thinkers.** Many people think visually and they react well to diagrams, whereas others do not. Naturally there are the two extremes, people who only think visually and those who cannot at all, but the reality is that the vast majority of people are somewhere between these two extremes. The point is that modeling will be more effective for some people than it is for others, and that you need to understand both your cognitive preferences and those of the people you are working with to be effective.

4. **You need to think before you act.** Modeling is one way of thinking something through before you code it (writing tests along the lines of test-driven design is another way, see Chapter 13). The reality is that you are very often more productive sketching a diagram, developing a low-fidelity prototype, or creating a few index cards, in order to think something through before you code it. Productive developers model before they code. Furthermore, modeling is a great way to promote communication

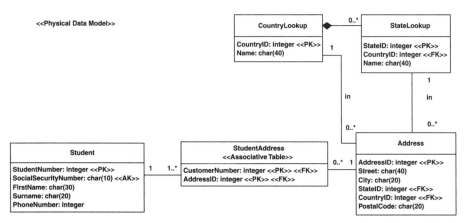

FIGURE **4.2. A partial physical data model, depicted using UML notation, for the university.**

between team members and project stakeholders because you are talking through issues, coming to a better understanding of what needs to be built and building bonds among everyone involved with the project in the process.

5. **Domain knowledge is important.** I am a firm believer that every developer should become a generalizing specialist (Chapter 15), someone with one or more specialties that also has a general understanding of development and the business domain in which they work. If you do not understand the problem domain there is very little chance that you can be effective.

6. **Each type of model has its strengths and weaknesses.** In this book you will learn about a wide range of models, including those of the unified modeling language (UML) as well as non-UML models such as user-interface flow diagrams (Figure 4.1) and data models (Figure 4.2). The implication is that no one model is right for every situation.

7. **You need a wide range of models.** The systems you are building have user interfaces; are often deployed to several hardware tiers; use object technology, relational database technology, Web services, and XML; implement complex business rules; need to work for years if not decades; and need to be responsive to change. Because you want to think before you act, because each model is good for certain purposes, and because software development is complex, this points to the need to know how to work with several types of models.

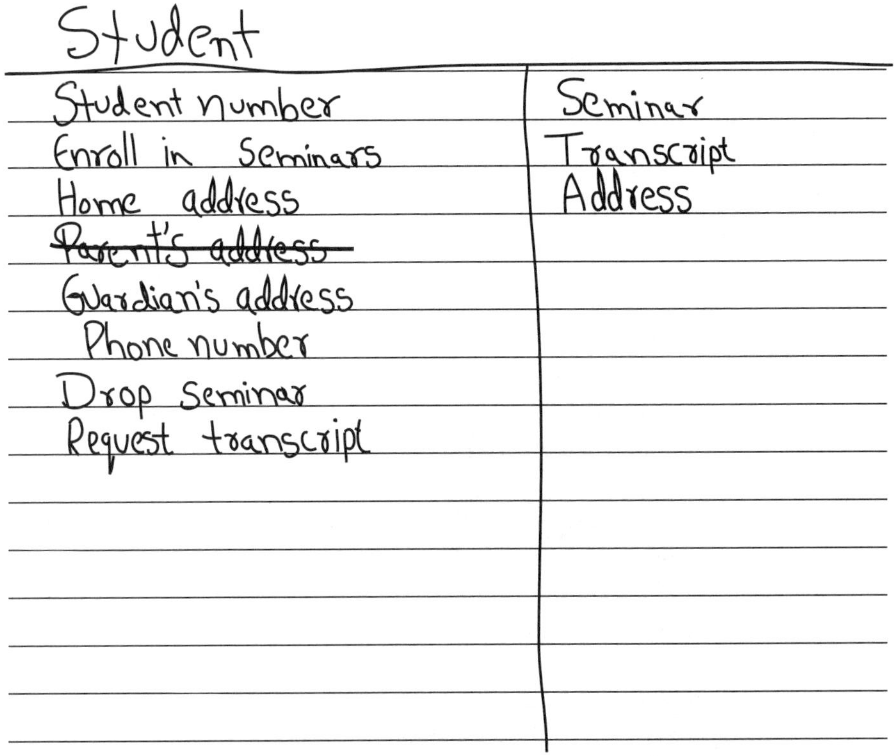

Student

Student number	Seminar
Enroll in Seminars	Transcript
Home address	Address
~~Parent's address~~	
Guardian's address	
Phone number	
Drop Seminar	
Request transcript	

FIGURE 4.3. A CRC card representing a university student.

8. **Beware "visual modeling."** "Visual modeling" is a marketing term first coined by a modeling tool vendor. Although many models are in fact visual, for example, UML class diagrams and physical data models, many are not. Class responsibility collaborator (CRC) cards (Fig. 4.3), described in Chapter 8, are text based as are business rule definitions, user stories, and technical requirements to name a few. When you start to include non-visual models in your intellectual toolkit, something you need to do if you want to work effectively with people who are not visual thinkers, you begin to realize that the term visual modeling is far too limiting. Let us leave the marketing rhetoric out of the equation.

9. **Modeling is hard**. Modeling skills are gained over years of experience and only when a developer chooses to gain them. As the agile community will tell you, people need to work together and to balance off one another's strengths. Everyone should have the humility to understand that they do not know everything and therefore they can always learn something

important from everyone else: modelers can learn details of a certain technology from a programmer and programmers can learn valuable design and architecture techniques from modelers. In short, everyone is a novice, including myself.

Now that we have set a philosophical foundation for modeling, the next step is to ask how we can be effective at modeling.

4.2 PROJECT STAKEHOLDERS

What is a project stakeholder? A project stakeholder is anyone who is a direct user, indirect user, manager of users, senior manager, operations staff member, support (help desk) staff member, developer working on other systems that integrate or interact with the one under development, or maintenance professional potentially affected by the development, upkeep, and/or deployment of a software project. There is a wide range of people potentially affected by a new system, including end users; therefore to succeed you must understand and then synthesize their requirements into a cohesive vision. This is one of the things that makes software development hard—each project stakeholder will have their own requirements, their own vision, and their own priorities—but it also makes software development fun.

Aren't developers also stakeholders? Of course they are, but I do not include them in this definition because I want convenient terms to distinguish the two roles; I really do not like terms such as "developer stakeholder" and "non-developer stakeholder."

I cannot say this enough—requirements come from your project stakeholders. As a developer you cannot make up new requirements on your own and simply add it to the list of what needs to be built. Instead you can, and should, suggest the requirement to your project stakeholder(s), explain it to them, and then respect their prioritization of that requirement. If your requirement is a good idea, and you make your case sufficiently, then it will be given a high priority and will likely be implemented. If not then that is the way it is. Agile software developers have the humility to respect the decisions of their stakeholders, even when they do not agree with those decisions. Although you may have hundreds or even thousands of stakeholders, you only need a handful to actively work with your team. Good candidates exhibit the following qualities:

1. **They know the business, or at least a portion of it.** They understand one or more aspects of the problem domain. They are the subject matter experts (SMEs) after all.

2. **They think (reasonably) logically.** Not only do stakeholders need to understand the business, they must also be able to describe what they do systematically in a logical manner.

3. **They can communicate well.** Stakeholders must have good people and communication skills to help them work closely with developers.

4. **They are willing to invest the time in software development.** Stakeholders typically have other things to do than work on a software project. Your job is to convince the stakeholders it is worth their while to invest their time providing expertise to your team. It is important to understand that many stakeholders have had bad experiences in the past with broken promises from the systems department and may be unwilling to take the time out of their busy schedules. You will need to convince them to have faith in you, then justify that faith by successfully delivering working software.

5. **They are not too narrowly focused.** People who believe it is all about them or their respective part of their organization, who only understand how it is done today, who are unwilling or unable to consider new approaches, or who are unable to prioritize their needs seldom make good stakeholders. They need to be able to understand overall priorities!

6. **They understand their role in the software development process.** Stakeholders (and developers) must have an understanding of how important it is that they perform their respective roles correctly. If they shirk their responsibilities, they jeopardize the entire effort.

4.3 WHAT IS AGILE MODELING (AM)?

AM (Ambler 2002a) is a chaordic, practice-based methodology for effective modeling and documentation of software-based systems. The AM methodology is a collection of practices, guided by principles and values, which are meant to be applied by software professionals on a day-to-day basis. AM is not prescriptive, it does not define detailed procedures for how to create a given type of model, but instead provides advice for how to be effective as a modeler. AM is chaordic (Hock 2000) in that it blends the "chaos" of simple modeling practices with the "order" inherent in software modeling artifacts.

AM has three main goals:

1. To define and show how to put into practice a collection of values, principles, and practices for effective, lightweight modeling.
2. To describe how to apply modeling techniques on agile software projects teams.
3. To describe how you can improve your modeling activities following a "near-agile" approach to software development, in particular, project teams following the RUP or EUP.

A model is an abstraction that describes one or more aspects of a problem or a potential solution to a problem. Traditionally, models are thought of as zero or more diagrams plus any corresponding documentation. However, non-visual artifacts such as collections of CRC cards, a textual description of one or more business rules, or the structured English description of a business process are also models. An agile model is a model that is just barely good enough. But how do you know when a model is good enough? Agile models are just barely good enough when they exhibit the following traits:

- Agile models fulfill their purpose;
- Agile models are understandable by their intended audience;
- Agile models are sufficiently accurate;
- Agile models are sufficiently consistent;
- Agile models are sufficiently detailed;
- Agile models provide positive value; and
- Agile models are as simple as possible.

4.4 THE VALUES OF AM

The five values of AM, the first four of which are adopted from XP (Beck 2000), provide a philosophical foundation upon which its principles are based, providing the primary motivation for the method. AM's values include those of XP. Briefly, those values are

1. **Communication.** It is critical to have effective communication within your development team as well as with and among all project stakeholders.

2. **Simplicity.** Strive to develop the simplest solution possible that meets all of your needs.

3. **Feedback.** Obtain feedback regarding your efforts often and early.

4. **Courage.** Have the courage to try new techniques and to make and then stick to your decisions.

5. **Humility.** You need to have the humility to admit that you may not know everything, that others have value to add to your project efforts.

4.5 THE PRINCIPLES OF AM

The values of AM provide a foundation for its principles, several of which are adopted from XP. There are eleven core principles, described in Table 4.1, that you must adopt in order to be able to claim that you are "doing AM." To reflect the fact that every project team finds itself in a unique situation, AM includes seven supplementary principles described in Table 4.2 that you can optionally tailor into forming a version of AM that best fits your environment. You will see these principles applied throughout this book.

4.6 THE PRACTICES OF AM

The practices of AM were formulated from its principles. There are thirteen core practices, described in Table 4.3, that you must adopt to be able to accurately claim that you are doing AM—if you like, you can still adopt only a subset of them, and benefit from doing so, but you are just not fully doing AM until you adopt at least the entire core. There are eight supplementary practices, described in Table 4.4, that you can tailor into your process to meet your unique needs. You will see these practices applied throughout this book.

4.7 EASING INTO AGILE MODELING

The first published description of AM appeared in the November 2000 issue of *Software Development* (http://www.sdmagazine.com) under the name extreme modeling (XM). I then led the evolution of the technique, for the most part via the Web although also at the XP 2001 conference held in Italy in May of that year. AM started out fairly complex and it grew a bit into its current form.

TABLE 4.1. The Core Principles of AM	
Principle	Description
Model with a purpose	If you cannot identify why and for whom you are creating a model then why are you bothering to work on it at all?
Maximize stakeholder investment	Your project stakeholders are investing resources—time, money, facilities, and so on—to have software developed that meets their needs. Stakeholders deserve to invest their resources the best way possible and to not have them frittered away by your team. For example, I could have invested several hours cleaning up the sketch in Fig. 4.1 by redrawing it using a sophisticated drawing tool, but the sketch is good enough to get the idea across. Furthermore, stakeholders deserve to have the final say in how those resources are invested or not invested. If it was your money, would you want it any other way?
Embrace change	Change happens—new requirements are discovered, people's understanding of what they need improves as they see the system evolve, and their priorities change. This is perfectly normal.
Incremental change	To embrace change you need to take an incremental approach to your own development efforts, to change your system a small portion at a time instead of trying to get everything accomplished in one big release. You can make a big change as a series of small, incremental changes.
Multiple models	You have a wide range of modeling artifacts available to you, as you will see in later chapters. Take the opportunity to expand upon your intellectual toolkit and learn new techniques whenever you can.
Travel light	Traveling light means that you create just enough models and documentation to get by.

Principle	Description
Software is your primary goal	The primary goal of software development is to produce high-quality software that meets the needs of your project stakeholders in an effective manner.
Enabling the next effort is your secondary goal	Your project can still be considered a failure even when your team delivers a working system to your users—part of fulfilling the needs of your project stakeholders is to ensure that your system is robust enough so that it can be extended over time. The implication is that you may also need to deliver supporting documentation along with your working software. As Alistair Cockburn (2002) likes to say, when you are playing the software development game your secondary goal is to set up to play the next game.
Quality work	Agile developers understand that they should invest the effort to make permanent artifacts, such as source code, user documentation, and technical system documentation of sufficient quality. It does not have to be perfect—just good enough.
Rapid feedback	Because the time between an action and the feedback on that action is critical, agile modelers prefer rapid feedback over delayed feedback whenever possible.
Assume simplicity	Assume that the simplest solution is the best solution.

In the time since then I have been applying AM to projects, mentoring people in its techniques, teaching AM courses, and speaking about AM at a variety of conferences. The one thing that I have noticed is that many people struggle with its plethora of concepts—five values, eleven core principles, seven supplementary principles, thirteen core practices, and eight supplementary practices—so it should not be any surprise that some people find AM complex. Sigh.

TABLE 4.2. The Supplementary Principles of AM	
Principle	Description
Content is more important than representation	Any given model could have several ways to represent it. For example, a UI specification could be created using Post-It notes on a large sheet of paper (an essential or low-fidelity prototype), as a sketch on paper or a whiteboard, as a "traditional" prototype built using a prototyping tool or programming language, or as a formal document including both a visual representation and a textual description of the UI.
Open and honest communication	People need to be free, and to perceive that they are free, to offer suggestions. Open and honest communication enables people to make better decisions because the quality of the information that they are basing them on is more accurate. Actions speak highly here.
Everyone can learn from everyone else	Agile modelers have the humility to recognize that they can never truly master something; there is always opportunity to learn more and to extend your knowledge. They take the opportunity to work with and learn from others, to try new ways of doing things, and to reflect on what seems to work and what does not.
Know your models	Because you have multiple models that you can apply as an agile modeler you need to know their strengths and weaknesses to be effective in their use. You are not expected to be an expert with all modeling techniques, but you should know about them and be willing to learn more over time.
Local adaptation	It is doubtful that you will be able to "apply AM out of the box"; instead you will need to modify it to reflect your environment, including the nature of your organization, your co-workers, your project stakeholders, and your project itself.
Work with people's instincts	As you gain experience at developing software your instincts become sharper, and what your instincts are telling you subconsciously can often be an important input into your modeling efforts.

TABLE 4.3. The Core Practices of AM	
Practice	**Description**
Active stakeholder participation	Project success often requires a significant level of involvement by project stakeholders—your team must work with senior management to gain their public and private support, with operations and support staff to ensure that your system is ready for production, with other system teams to integrate/interface with their systems, and with maintenance developers so they become adept at the technologies and techniques used by your system.
Use the simplest tools	The vast majority of models can be drawn on a whiteboard, on paper or even the back of a napkin. Note that AM has nothing against CASE tools—if investing in a CASE tool is the most effective use of your resources then by all means do so and then use it to the best of its ability.
Model with others	Software development is a lot like swimming: it is very dangerous to do it alone; it is also best to swim with people who know how to swim (they should at least know how to stay afloat).
Prove it with code	A model is an abstraction, one that should accurately reflect an aspect of whatever you are building. To determine whether it will actually work you should validate that your model works by writing the corresponding code.
Apply the right artifact(s)	This practice is AM's equivalent of the adage "use the right tool for the job"; in this case you want to create the right model(s) to get the job done. Each artifact—such as a UML state chart, an essential use case, source code, or data flow diagram (DFD)—has its own specific strengths and weaknesses, and therefore is appropriate for some situations but not for others.

(continued)

TABLE 4.3 (continued)	
Practice	Description
Create several models in parallel	Because each type of model has its strengths and weaknesses no single model is sufficient for all your modeling needs. By working on several at once you can easily iterate back and forth between them and use each model for what it is best suited.
Iterate to another artifact	Whenever you find you are having difficulties working on one artifact, perhaps you are working on a use case and find that you are struggling to describe the business logic, then that is a sign that you should iterate to another artifact. By iterating to another artifact you immediately become "unstuck" because you are making progress working on that other artifact.
Model in small increments	With incremental development you model a little, code a little, test a little, and then deliver a little. No more big design up front (BDUF) where you invest weeks or even months creating models and documents.
Collective ownership	Everyone can work on any model, and ideally any artifact on the project, if they need to.
Create simple content	You should keep the actual content of your models—your requirements, your analysis, your architecture, or your design—as simple as you possibly can while still fulfilling the needs of your project stakeholders. The implication is that you should not add additional aspects to your models unless they are justifiable.
Depict models simply	Use a subset of the modeling notation available to you—a simple model that shows the key features that you are trying to understand; a class model depicting the primary responsibilities of classes and the relationships among them often proves to be sufficient.

Practice	Description
Display models publicly	This supports the principle of *open and honest communication* on your team because all of the current models are quickly accessible to them, as well as with your project stakeholders because you are not hiding anything from them.
Consider testability	When you are modeling you should be constantly asking yourself "How are we going to test this?" because if you cannot test the software that you are building you should not be building it.

A question that I get asked is how can people get started with AM but perhaps not fully adopt it all at once. Some organizations do not want to adopt just the core principles and practices at first, let alone some of the supplementary ones. One common situation is that the organization is very non-agile at the present moment and that adopting the entire AM core is just too much to attempt at once. It is clear that many people need a way to ease into AM slowly.

First, focus on improving communication between people. Modeling with others is critical as is active stakeholder participation. When you use simple tools it is much easier to model with others because there is not a tool learning curve to overcome, and simple tools also make it possible for your stakeholders to actively model with you. You will learn from your stakeholders.

Second, you should strive to keep things as simple as possible and to travel as light as possible. This is easy to talk about but often proves quite difficult to do in practice, at least at first. Using simple tools such as whiteboards and paper to create models is a critical first step. Simple tools also make it much less painful to discard temporary models because you have not invested as much effort in them. It is also sometimes easier to purchase the low-tech whiteboard and paper without investing in a sophisticated CASE tool.

Third, adopt techniques that enable you to work in an evolutionary (iterative and incremental) manner. Creating several models in parallel and iterating to another artifact are crucial practices, but this of course requires you to accept that you need multiple models. You may need more than one whiteboard—a roomful helps! Keeping your models small by working on

TABLE 4.4. The Supplementary Practices of AM	
Practice	Description
Formalize contract models	Contract models are often required when an external group controls an information resource that your system requires, such as a database, legacy application, or information service. A contract model is formalized between all parties (there may be more than one involved) agreeing to it and is ready to mutually change it over time if required.
Update only when it hurts	You should update an artifact such as a model or document only when you absolutely need to, when not having the model updated is more painful than the effort of updating it.
Discard temporary models	The vast majority of the models that you create are temporary/working models—design sketches, low-fidelity prototypes, index cards, potential architecture/design alternatives, and so on—models that have fulfilled their purpose but no longer add value now that they have done so.
Reuse existing resources	There is a wealth of information that agile modelers can take advantage of by reusing them.
Apply modeling standards	Developers should agree to and follow a common set of modeling standards on a software project. Good sources of modeling standards and guidelines are *The Elements of UML Style* (Ambler 2003c) and http://www.modelingstyle.info.
Apply patterns gently	Effective modelers learn and then appropriately apply common architectural, design, and analysis patterns in their models. However, both Martin Fowler (2001) and Joshua Kerievsky (2001) believe that developers should consider easing into the application of a pattern, to apply it gently.

Practice	Description
Model to communicate	One reason you model is to communicate with people external to your team or to create a contract model.
Model to understand	The most important application of modeling is to explore the problem space, to identify and analyze the requirements for the system, or to compare and contrast potential design alternatives to identify the potentially simplest solution that meets the requirements.

them incrementally is also important. Together, these techniques help to break you of any BDUF habits that you may have as well as any delusions that one single model is the primary artifact that drives all your development efforts. For example it is quite common for people to insist that data models or use case models drive your projects, and this may in fact be true for a very small minority of projects, but often this attitude is the result of political ambitions more than any thing else. Proving it with code is a critical practice that supports evolutionary development because it provides the link from modeling to implementation, once again helping you to break out of a BDUF mindset— and your stakeholders will love seeing something working if they have never seen it before.

In short, to make this first step into AM you should consider adopting the following principles and practices:

- Active stakeholder participation;
- Create several models in parallel;
- Depict models simply;
- Iterate to another artifact;
- Model in small increments;
- Model with others;
- Multiple models;
- Prove it with code;
- Travel light; and
- Use the simplest tools.

Upon adopting these concepts you will discover that it is quite easy to add other ideas incrementally. For example, you will quickly discover that you are getting rapid feedback by working in an evolutionary manner, and likewise that embracing change makes sense in such an environment. Because you are working closely together to create models you will soon see that collective ownership makes things much easier for you as does displaying models publicly. As you gain more experience with the modeling techniques, something that happens quickly in an evolutionary environment, you get much better at applying the right artifacts for the situation.

In short, I think that you can see it is possible to ease into AM over time. However, I want to make it perfectly clear that to truly be "doing AM" you must adopt the five values as well as all of the core principles and practices.

4.8 AGILE MODEL–DRIVEN DEVELOPMENT (AMDD)

As the name implies, AMDD is the agile version of model-driven development (MDD). MDD is an approach to software development where extensive models are created before source code is written. A primary example of MDD is the Object Management Group's (OMG) model driven architecture (MDA) standard. With MDD a serial approach to development is often taken, MDD is quite popular with traditionalists, although as the RUP/EUP shows it is possible to take an iterative approach with MDD. The difference with AMDD is that instead of creating extensive models before writing source code you instead create agile models, which are just barely good enough.

Figure 4.4 depicts a high-level lifecycle for AMDD for the release of a system. First, let us start with how to read the diagram. Each box represents a development activity. The initial up-front modeling activity includes two main sub-activities, initial requirements modeling, and initial architecture modeling. These are done during cycle 0, cycle being another term for iteration. "Cycle 0" is an XP term for the first iteration before you start into development cycles, which are iterations one and beyond (for that release). The other activities—detailed modeling, reviews, and implementation—potentially occur during any cycle, including cycle 0. The time indicated in each box represents the length of an average session: perhaps you will model for a few minutes then code for several hours. I will discuss timing issues in more detail below.

The initial modeling effort is typically performed during the first week of a project. For short projects (perhaps several weeks in length) you may do this work in the first few hours and for long projects (perhaps on the order of twelve or more months) you may decide to invest up to two weeks in this

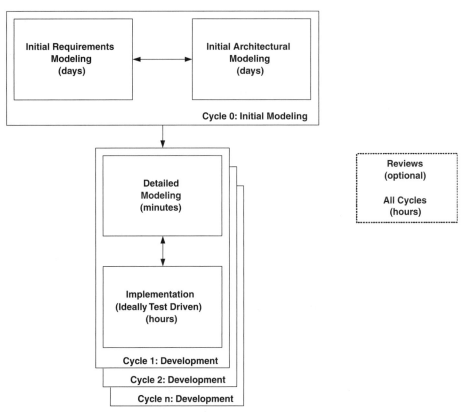

FIGURE **4.4. Taking an AMDD approach to development.**

effort. I highly suggest not investing any more time than this as you run the danger of over modeling and of modeling something that contains too many problems (two weeks without the concrete feedback that implementation provides is a long time to go at risk, in my opinion).

For the first release of a system you need to take several days to identify some high-level requirements as well as the scope of the release (what you think the system should do). The goal is to get a good gut feel what the project is all about, and very likely to gather sufficient information to provide an initial estimate for your project. The goal of the initial architecture modeling effort is to try to identify an architecture that has a good chance of working. In later cycles both your initial requirements and your initial architect models will need to evolve as you learn more, but for now the goal is to get something that is just barely good enough so that your team can get coding. In subsequent releases you may decide to shorten cycle 0 to several days, several hours, or even remove it completely as your situation dictates.

During detailed modeling you explore the requirements or design in greater detail. During the development cycles of a release your modeling efforts are often on the order of minutes. Perhaps you will get together with a stakeholder to analyze the requirement you are currently working on, create a sketch together at a whiteboard for a few minutes, and then go back to coding. Or perhaps you and several other developers will sketch out an approach to implement a requirement, once again spending several minutes doing so. Or perhaps you and your programming pair will use a modeling tool to model in detail and then generate the code for that requirement. Perhaps this will take 15 or 20 minutes.

It is important to understand that your initial requirements and architecture models will evolve through your detailed modeling and implementation efforts. That is perfectly natural. Depending on how light you are traveling, you may not even update the models if you kept them at all.

You may optionally choose to hold model reviews and even code inspections, but as I wrote in Chapter 3, these quality assurance (QA) techniques really do seem to be obsolete with agile software development.

Implementation is where your team will spend the majority of its time, something that Figure 4.4 unfortunately does not communicate well. During development it is quite common to do detailed modeling for several minutes and then code, following common coding practices such as test-driven design (TDD) and refactoring (Chapter 13), for several hours and even several days at a time. Why does this work? Because your detailed modeling efforts enable you to think through larger, cross-entity issues, whereas with TDD you think through very focused issues typically pertinent to a single entity at a time. With refactoring you evolve your design via small steps to ensure that your work remains of high quality.

In my opinion it does not make sense to have people who are just modeling specialists on your development team any more. What are they going to do, model for a few minutes and then sit around for hours or days until they are needed again? What is really needed is something I call a generalizing specialist, someone with one or more specialties as well as general skills in the entire lifecycle, who can both code and, when they need to, model. The concept of generalizing specialists is described in detail in Chapter 15.

4.8.1 How is AMDD Different?

From a design point of view the AMDD approach of Figure 4.4 is very different from traditional MDD approaches where you create a design model first then code from it. With AMDD you do a little bit of modeling and then a lot of coding, iterating back when you need to. Your design efforts are now spread out between your modeling and coding activities, with the majority of design being done as part of your implementation efforts. In many ways this was also true for many traditional projects: the developers would often do significantly different things than what was in the design models, but the designers would often blame the developers instead of question their overly serial processes.

AMDD is different from techniques such as feature-driven development (FDD) or the use case-driven development (UCDD) styles of RUP and ICONIX (Rosenberg and Scott 1999) in that it does not specify the type of model(s) to create. All AMDD suggests is that you apply the right artifact, but it does not insist on what that artifact is. For example, FDD insists that features are your primary requirements artifact, whereas UCDD insists that use cases are. AMDD works well with either a FDD or a UCDD approach because the messages are similar—all three approaches are saying that it is a good idea to model before you code.

4.9 FUNDAMENTAL INFORMATION GATHERING SKILLS

Agile modelers need a wide range of information gathering skills. Although not directly part of AM, you should strive to be adept at three fundamental information gathering skills:

- Interviewing;
- Observation; and
- Brain storming.

4.9.1 Interviewing

Although you should have one or more project stakeholders actively involved in your project, and therefore readily accessible to you, you will still find that you need to obtain information from others from time to time. A common way to do this is via interviews. When interviewing someone you have several potential goals to accomplish:

- Broaden your understanding of the business domain;
- Determine whom to invite to become active stakeholders; and
- Identify new or existing requirements directly for the application.

Interviewing is a skill that takes years to master, one that cannot possibly be taught in a few paragraphs. There are, however, a few helpful pointers to help you to improve your interviewing skills:

1. Send ahead an agenda to set expectations and thus allow your interviewee to prepare for the interview. An agenda can be something as simple as a short e-mail.
2. Verify a few hours ahead of time that the interviewee is still available because schedules may change.
3. Thank the interviewee for taking time out of their busy day.
4. Tell the interviewee what the project is about and how input is important.
5. Summarize the issues you want to discuss and verify how long the interview will take. This helps to set expectations and enables the interviewee to help you manage the time. This should mirror the agenda sent in step 1.
6. State and verify all assumptions. Do not assume that each stakeholder holds the same assumptions.
7. Ask the interviewee whether you have missed anything or whether anything should be added. This gives him a chance to voice concerns and often opens new avenues of questioning.
8. Practice active listening skills—ask open-ended questions. Do not assume you know everything, especially if you think you have already heard it before. Your stakeholders rarely have a consistent view of the world and part of the requirements definition process is to understand where everyone is coming from. If everyone has the same view on everything, that is great, but it is incredibly rare. Do not shut down your users with a comment like "I have already heard this before. . . ."
9. End the interview by summarizing the main points. Discuss any misunderstandings and clear them up at this point. This gives you a chance to review your notes and ensure you understood everything.
10. Thank the person at the end of the interview. Follow up with a thank-you note too.
11. If you formalize the interview notes, send them to the interviewee for review. This helps to put your interviewees at ease because they know the input was not taken out of context. It also helps to improve the quality of your notes because they will provide feedback.
12. Interviewing is more about listening than talking. Talking starts the process, but the information you want comes from listening to responses. Even when you ask an important question, e.g., "This system needs to be

> **TIP**
>
> **Take an Interviewing Course**
>
> Although few computer science programs offer interviewing courses, most journalism programs do. Although the focus will be on news interviewing, the fundamental skills are the same.

restricted to field reps, right?", the important part of the interview is the answer, e.g., "Yes" or "No" or "Well it's actually like this. . . ."

4.9.2 Observation

I make it a habit to spend a day or two with my direct end users simply to sit and observe what they do. One of the problems with interviewing people is they leave out important details, details that you may not know to ask about because they know their jobs so well. Another advantage of observing your users is you see the tools they use to do their jobs. Perhaps they use a key reference manual or use a notepad to write reminder notes for themselves and/or their co-workers. Often they do things differently than the official manual tells you it should be done. Taking the time to observe users doing their work can give you insight into the requirements for the application you are building.

4.9.3 Brainstorming

Brainstorming is a technique where groups of people discuss a topic and say anything that comes into their minds about it. The rules are simple; all ideas are

- Good—ideas are not judged by the group;
- Owned by the group, not by the individual; and
- Immediately public property: anybody is allowed to expand upon them.

The basic idea is that someone, referred to as a facilitator, leads the group through brainstorming. The facilitator starts by explaining the rules of brainstorming and explaining what issues are to be discussed. All people present must understand and abide by these rules. A good idea is to give everyone a copy of the brainstorming rules before a brainstorming session so they are aware of them. When someone suggests an idea, it should be immediately recorded onto a publicly visible area, such as a flip chart paper or a whiteboard.

4.10 AGILE DOCUMENTATION

Documentation is an intrinsic part of any system, even those created following agile software development techniques. Documentation can be made agile when you choose to do so—like agile models, agile documents are just barely good enough. A document is agile (Ambler 2002) when it meets the following criteria:

- **Agile documents maximize stakeholder investment.** Documentation must at least provide positive value and ideally provides the best value possible—according to the stakeholder.

- **Agile documents are concise.** An agile document is as simple as it can possibly be, containing just enough information to fulfill its purpose. One way to keep agile documents lean and mean is to follow pragmatic programming's (Hunt and Thomas 2000) "DRY" (don't repeat yourself) principle.

- **Agile documents fulfill a single purpose.** For example, it may make sense to have a user document, an operations document, and a requirements document for your system. It would be inappropriate to have a single document trying to accomplish all three goals.

- **Agile documents describe information that is less likely to change.** The greater the chance that information will change, the less value there is in investing significant time writing external documentation about it because the information will most likely change before you are finished writing and it will be difficult to maintain over time.

- **Agile documents describe "good things to know."** Agile documents capture critical information, information that is not readily obvious such as design rationale, requirements, usage procedures, or operational procedures.

- **Agile documents have a specific customer and facilitate the work efforts of that customer.** You must work closely with the customer for their documentation. When you do not, you are at risk of creating too much documentation, unnecessary documentation, or documentation that does not meet their actual needs.

- **Agile documents are sufficiently accurate, consistent, and detailed.** Agile documents do not need to be perfect; they just need to be good enough.

- **Agile documents are sufficiently indexed.** Documentation is not effective if you cannot easily find the information contained in it; therefore an index and a table of contents are important.

In addition, the following points about documentation are critical to your success:

- The fundamental issue is effective communication, not documentation.
- Documentation is as much a part of the system as the source code.
- You should actually need the documentation, not just want it.
- The investment in system documentation is a business decision, not a technical one—it is your stakeholder's money, so they are the ones that should decide whether it will be invested in documentation, not you. You will often need to educate the stakeholder about the importance of certain documentation though.
- The reader, not the writer, determines whether documentation is sufficient.

Why are people so adamant about writing significant amounts of documentation? Because it increases their comfort level with your project team. With traditional approaches to development your project stakeholders might not receive a working system until months or even years after they requested it. In these situations it was comforting for them to see a formal requirements document produced after a few months, to be followed by an architecture model, then a design model, and so on. It showed that progress was being made. With agile approaches to development the primary measure of success is the regular delivery of working software that meets the needs of its stakeholders. In my experience this is far more comforting to your stakeholders than regular delivery of extensive documentation.

4.11 MAKING WHITEBOARDS WORK FOR SOFTWARE DEVELOPMENT

Whiteboards are my favorite modeling tool, and I stand by my claim that they are the modeling tool with the greatest install base worldwide. In fact

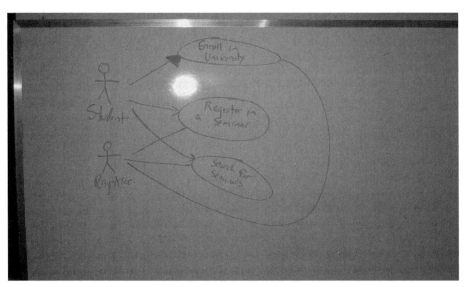

FIGURE 4.5. Digital picture of a whiteboard sketch.

throughout this book you will see many whiteboard sketches, which is nice for a book but are they acceptable for real-world development? My experience is yes. Here is how I make it work for me.

Figure 4.5 shows a digital photo taken of a whiteboard sketch of a simple use case diagram (Chapter 5), which I drew with a couple of stakeholders. We took the photo because we were afraid that we would lose the valuable information that it contains, although I am sure that we could easily reproduce this diagram in less than a minute if we ever needed to (one of the side benefits of practices such as *depict models simply*, *create simple content*, and *model in small increments* is that you create models that you can easily reproduce). Digital photos such as this prove to be useful ways to comfort people who think that you need more documentation than you actually do because with the photograph you have retained the model—it might not be pretty, but at least you haven't "lost" the information.

There are a couple of problems with Figure 4.5—the file size is relatively large and it is hard to read because it is so dark. I am not that worried about file size issues; disk storage is cheap, although large files can be a problem for people with slow network connections. The readability problem is more of an issue for me. Luckily there's a quick solution, a product called Whiteboard Photo (http://www.websterboards.com/products/wbp.html) from Polyvision, formerly Pixid. I used this product to create Figure 4.6 from the original photo, a process that took about two minutes end to end, including the time to run

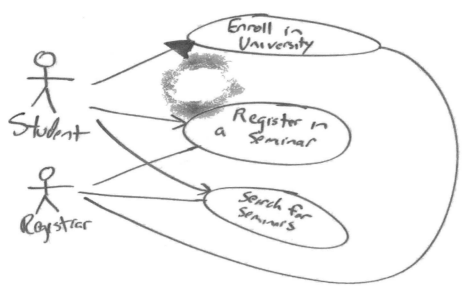

FIGURE 4.6. Automatic cleanup of the sketch.

Whiteboard Photo, open the file, clean the photo, and then save it back to disk. One feature of the product is that you can clean many photos at once, something I did not do in this case, so you can reduce the average cleaning time even further.

Figure 4.6 is not perfect, the blotch in the diagram is the reflection of the flash (the lighting in my work area could be better), but it addresses the problems with Fig. 4.5. I then invested a few minutes with a paint program to produce Fig. 4.7.

So how far should you go with whiteboard sketches? My experience is that you can safely erase 95–99 percent of all sketches that you create. Then between 95 and 99 percent of the diagrams that remain can be photographed and retained that way and a few diagrams I will transcribe into a sophisticated software-based modeling tool. These percentages seem to be true for teams familiar with AMDD; teams with people new to this approach will find that they want to keep more diagrams because it comforts them. Over time, experience will teach them to have greater courage and to travel even lighter than they think that they need to, but it takes time to wean people off their "documentation habit." Digital photos of whiteboards are a radical step for many experienced IT professionals.

Of the photos that I do take, I will either stick with the raw photo as you see in Fig. 4.5 or the automatically cleaned-up version in Fig. 4.6. It is

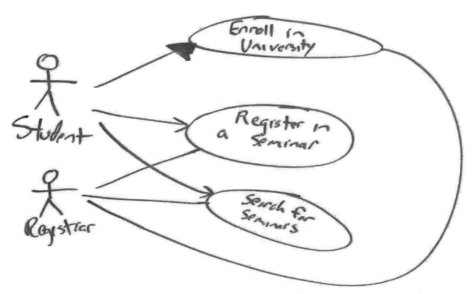

FIGURE **4.7. Hand-crafted cleanup of the sketch.**

important to understand that you are still investing time, albeit a short time, when using Whiteboard Photo to clean up your diagrams. Remember the AM principle to *maximize stakeholder investment* and only do this work if it adds value, and very often it does. The only time that I will clean up the diagram further, as you see in Fig. 4.7, is when the diagram is included in some sort of official document such as a presentation to management, a system overview document, or in this case a book. This cleanup step can often be avoided if you work in brightly lit rooms and/or get good at aiming the camera so that the flash appears off to the side of your photo.

The primary advantages of modeling on whiteboards are that it is an easy and inclusive approach because practically anyone can use a whiteboard. The primary disadvantages are that whiteboard sketches are not permanent, something that you can easily address by taking a digital photo and cleaning it up as appropriate.

The primary disadvantages are that it is hard to update a digital image of a whiteboard photo; you typically have to redraw it if you happened to have erased it from the board, and you cannot do sophisticated things such as generate code from a static, hand-drawn image. Another issue is that whiteboards are only a viable option when your team is colocated, something that I highly recommend. When this is not the case you will need to consider other modeling tools.

4.12 AMDD AND OTHER AGILE METHODOLOGIES

AM is not a complete software process; its focus is on effective modeling and documentation. That is it. It does not include programming activities (although it insists that you prove your models with code) nor does it include testing activities (although it suggests that you consider testability as you model). Furthermore, AM does not cover project management, system deployment, system operations, system support, or a myriad of other issues. The implication is that you need to use AM with another software process such as XP or RUP, tailoring AM into it to form your own process that reflects your unique needs. Table 4.5 lists several modern software processes, indicating when to apply each process as well as how AM can be used with it.

4.13 AGILE MODELING AND TEST-DRIVEN DEVELOPMENT (TDD)

As you saw in Figure 4.4 AM fits in very well with implementation efforts. As you will see in Chapter 13, TDD is an implementation technique. A primary benefit of both modeling and TDD is that they promote a "think before you act" approach to development. Just because they offer the same type of benefit does not mean that they are incompatible with one another. Instead experience shows that you can and should model on a project taking a TDD approach.

Creating agile models can help your TDD efforts because they can reveal the need for some tests. As an agile modeler sketches a diagram they will always be thinking "how can I test this" in the back of their minds because they will be following the practice *consider testability*. TDD can also improve your AM efforts. Following a test-first approach agile developers quickly discover whether their ideas actually work—the tests either validate their models or not—providing rapid feedback regarding the ideas captured within the models. This fits in perfectly with AM's practice of *prove it with code*. The bottom line is that the most effective developers have a wide range of techniques in their intellectual toolboxes, and AM and TDD should be among those techniques.

TABLE 4.5. Tailoring AM into Other Software Development Methodologies

Method	Description	When to Use It	Agile Modeling
Dynamic system development method (DSDM)	This is an agile methodology that has received ISO 9001 certification. In many ways it is a formalization of the rapid application development (RAD) methodologies of the 1980s (Stapleton 2003).	Development of a user-interface intensive system. Development of a complex business application.	Apply AM when developing the functional prototype, the design prototype, and the actual system itself.
Extreme programming (XP)	An agile development methodology that focuses on the critical activities required to build software.	Small, colocated project teams (4–10 people although more is possible). Requirements are uncertain. Project stakeholders are willing to actively participate as project team members.	AM practices can be applied when identifying user stories and the architectural metaphor/strategy and during architectural spikes. During quick design sessions AM can be applied to develop simple models such as class responsibility collaborator (CRC) cards and whiteboard sketches.

Feature-driven development (FDD)	An agile development methodology that includes explicit modeling activities.	Small project team (4–20 people). Requirements are uncertain. Team willing to follow a modeling-driven approach.	AM can be used early in an FDD project to develop the initial domain class/object model and features. During development cycles AM can also be applied in the creation of other detailed models such as UML sequence and class diagrams.
ICONIX	A simple, modeling-driven methodology that can be instantiated as an improvement to the RUP or as an agile method in its own right.	Small to medium-sized project teams (4–20 people). Business application development.	ICONIX focuses on four main models—use case models, robustness diagrams, UML sequence diagrams, and UML class models—and AM practices can clearly be used to create each of them.
Rational unified process (RUP)	A rigorous, four-phase software development process that is iterative and incremental. The RUP is rarely instantiated as an agile process although it is possible. The RUP can be extended with the enterprise unified process (EUP) (http://www.enterpriseuni fiedprocess.info).	Medium to large project teams (10+ people).	RUP is modeling intensive, and AM principles and practices can be applied to make these efforts far more effective (Ambler 2002).

4.14 WHAT YOU HAVE LEARNED

This chapter introduced you to agile modeling, a methodology that describes values, principles, and practices that enable effective modeling and documentation. AM not only streamlines your modeling and documentation efforts it is also an enabling technique for evolutionary development, the preferred approach for modern software development. You then learned about AMDD, a realistic alternative to the theoretical musings encapsulated within the OMG's model-driven architecture. Modeling before you code is a good idea; you just need to model in an effective manner. Taking an AMDD approach is exactly that.

4.15 REVIEW QUESTIONS

1. Is it actually more effective, for you, to draw a few sketches to think something through before you code. Why or why not?
2. What are the trade-offs of modeling with others? In what situations would you be faster or slower? Get a better result? Learn something new?
3. Discuss the advantages and disadvantages of working closely with your business stakeholders. Who would you consider a stakeholder and why?
4. How long would you keep a sketch for? Why? In what situations would you keep it for a long time? Clean it up and put it into a sophisticated modeling tool? Discard it completely?
5. What are the advantages and disadvantages of traveling light, of producing just barely enough documentation for your system? Consider three scenarios: the original development team stays on to continue working on the system; the original development team changes slowly over time with some people leaving and some new people coming on to the team; and the original development team disperses and the system is assigned to another team to maintain and support. How light can you travel in each of these situations?
6. Discuss the trade-offs between a "big design up front" approach to modeling versus an evolutionary approach. What are the advantages and disadvantages of each? What type of skillset would be required for each? Why?
7. Search the Web for software modeling tools. Identify ten features that you believe are important to have in a modeling tool, describe why each feature

is important, and then rate three of those tools against those features. Which one "wins"—and why?

8. Search the Web for information about the model-driven architecture. What are the advantages and disadvantages of this approach? How realistic is the MDA? Does this seem like a viable strategy to you? Why or why not?

9. Compare and contrast small development groups of three or four people versus larger development groups of ten to twenty people. Take into consideration management issues, communication issues, logistical issues, decision-making ability, group dynamics, skills, and knowledge. What do you believe is the ideal size for a development team? Why.

10. Is it important for the stakeholders to be co-located with a development team? Why or why not?

CHAPTER 5

Usage Modeling

You need to understand how people will work with your system.

An important part of software development is to explore the requirements for your system. Usage modeling explores how people work with a system, vital information that you require if you are going to successfully build something that meets their actual needs. You cannot successfully build a system if you do not know what it should do, and a critical aspect of this is exploring how people will actually use the system.

Table 5.1 overviews five common usage modeling artifacts, which are described in detail within this chapter. The table also provides a brief overview of each artifact as well as an indication of when you might want to create it.

This chapter is organized into the following sections:

- Use case modeling;
- User stories;
- Features;
- What you have learned; and
- Review questions.

5.1 USE CASE MODELING

An important goal of requirements modeling is to come to an understanding of the business problem that your system is to address in order to understand

TABLE 5.1. Usage Modeling Techniques	
Technique	Description
Essential use cases	A use case describes something of value to an actor (often a person or organization). An essential use case is a use case that is technology independent—it describes the fundamental business task without bringing technological issues into account. Essential use cases are often used to explore usage-based requirements.
System use cases	System use cases are use cases that bring technological concerns into account. System use cases are the primary requirements artifact for the rational unified process (RUP) (Kruchten 2000), although they are arguably analysis and perhaps even design artifacts.
UML use case diagram	UML use case diagrams provide an overview of the use cases and actors pertinent to your business domain.
User story	User story is a fine-grained requirement that provides just enough information from which developers can estimate the effort to implement it and project stakeholders can prioritize it. User stories are a primary development artifact of extreme programming (XP) (Beck 2000).
Feature	Features are very fine-grained requirements that can often be implemented in several hours. Features are the primary requirements artifact for feature-driven development (FDD) (Palmer and Felsing 2002).

its usage requirements. Use case models focus on exactly this issue. A use case model comprises zero or more use case diagrams, although most have at least one diagram, and one or more use case specifications (often simply called use cases). Use case diagrams are one of the standard Unified Modeling Language (UML) artifacts (Object Management Group 2003). When you are following processes such as the Rational Unified Process (RUP), the enterprise unified process (http://www.enterpriseunifiedprocess.info), or ICONIX (Rosenberg

---

TIP

Use Case Modeling Reference

The best use case book that I know of is *Writing Effective Use Cases* by Alistair Cockburn (2001a). *Advanced Use Case Modeling* by Armour and Miller (2001) is also quite good.

---

and Scott 1999), a primary requirements artifact is a use case model (Jacobson et al. 1992; Cockburn 2001a) to describe your behavioral requirements.

There are two basic flavors of use case models: essential use case models and system use case models. An essential use case model—often referred to as a task case model or an abstract use case model—models a technology-independent view of your behavioral requirements. System use case models, also known as concrete use case models or detailed use case models, model your analysis of your behavioral requirements, describing in detail how users will work with your system, including references to its user-interface aspects.

Essential modeling is a fundamental aspect of usage-centered designs, an approach to software development detailed in the book *Software for Use* (Constantine and Lockwood 1999). Essential models are intended to capture the essence of problems through technology-free, idealized, and abstract descriptions. The resulting design models are more flexible, leaving open more options and more readily accommodating changes in technology. Essential models are more robust than concrete representations, simply because they are more likely to remain valid in the face of both changing requirements and changes in the technology of implementation. Essential models of usage highlight purpose, what it is users are trying to accomplish, and why they are doing it. In short, essential models are ideal artifacts to capture the requirements for your system. When you are essential use case modeling, you develop a use case diagram, identify essential use cases, and identify potential actors/roles that interact with your system.

To explain how to use case model I am going to start out with a discussion of how to create a use case model in an agile manner, then I will explore the individual aspects of essential use case modeling one at a time.

5.1.1 Starting Agile

Although use cases can be a very effective modeling technique it is quite common for use case modeling efforts to go awry. As you will see in this

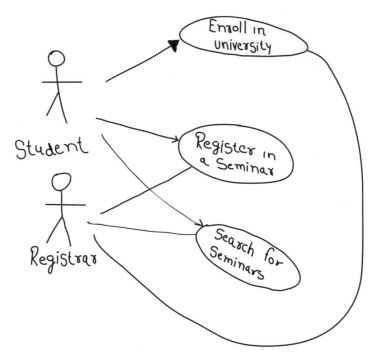

FIGURE **5.1. Initial whiteboard sketch of a use case diagram.**

book both use case diagrams and use cases can become quite large, which at first appears to go against agile modeling's (AM) practice of *model in small increments.* There is nothing wrong with large models per se, as long as they add value to your overall effort; the real issue is how they are created. The fact is that you may eventually create a very large model describing the requirements for your system, and that model may include a large use case model, but it will have been created over months or years of evolutionary work. It should not be created all up front before you start coding.

So how can you keep use case modeling agile? First, focus on keeping it as simple as possible. Use simple, flexible tools to model with. I will typically create use case diagrams on a whiteboard, as you see in Fig. 5.1, which is an example of an initial diagram that I would draw with my project stakeholders. AM tells us that *content is more important than representation* so it is not a big issue that the diagram is hand drawn; it is just barely good enough and that is all that we need. It is also perfectly okay that the diagram is not complete—there is clearly more to a university than what is depicted—because we can always modify the diagram as we need to.

> **TIP**
>
> **Requirements Gathering Is So Important That You Should Do It Every Day**
>
> With an evolutionary approach, requirements is not a phase in your project that you do at the beginning; instead it is a critical activity that you will need to do on a daily basis.

In parallel to creating the sketch I would also write a very brief description of each use case, often on a whiteboard as well, along the lines of what is shown in Figure 5.2. The goal is to record just enough information about the use case so that we understand what it is all about. If we need more details we can always add them later.

When you take an AMDD approach, see Chapter 4, during "cycle 0" you want to first develop an initial requirements model that reflects the overall scope of the system. To do this you may decide to expand the diagram of Fig. 5.1 to depict more actors and use cases, and then briefly describe those use cases as you see in Fig. 5.2. You will likely discover that you need to identify initial versions of other types of requirements, such as business rules and technical requirements (both of which are described in Chapter 7), in parallel to your use cases in order to explore different facets of your effort.

It is interesting to note that after drawing a few diagrams or use cases such as this that your stakeholders will quickly learn how to do it themselves. This is an important side effect of agile modeling's *model with others* practice—everyone quickly learns skills from the people that they are working with. Furthermore, when your team follows the practices of *active stakeholder participation* and *use the simplest tools* your stakeholders also learn the modeling

---

Enroll Student in Seminar

Student has to be enrolled in the university
Need to provide them with a list of available seminars
Need to check for prerequisites
Enroll the student in the seminar if there is a seat available, otherwise put them on the waiting list

---

FIGURE 5.2. Initial version of a use case.

> ### TIP
> ### Requirements Only Need to Be Good Enough
>
> Just good enough, not perfect? But you will build the wrong thing! Agile software developers do not need a perfect requirements specification, nor do they need a complete one, because they have access to their project stakeholders. Not sure what a requirement means, because there is not enough detail? Talk with a stakeholder and have them explain it; if they cannot explain it—keep talking.

techniques employed by the team. You never know: today's project stakeholder could become tomorrow's developer.

I think that you can see that by keeping your models simple at first that you could easily create a use case model encompassing between 50 to 100 use cases in a two- or three-day period. Then, during each development cycle/iteration you merely need to flesh out the subset of requirements that you need to for that period of time. You can in fact be quite effective modeling in small increments, just as the AM methodology claims.

5.1.2 Essential Use Case Diagrams

Now let us see what the simple diagram of Fig. 5.1 could potentially evolve to. The use case diagram in Fig. 5.3 provides an example of an UML use case diagram. Use case diagrams depict:

- **Use cases.** A use case describes a sequence of actions that provide something of measurable value to an actor and is drawn as a horizontal ellipse.

- **Actors.** An actor is a person, organization, or external system that plays a role in one or more interactions with your system. Actors are drawn as stick figures.

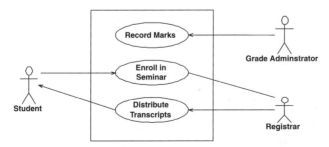

FIGURE 5.3. A simple use case diagram for a university.

- **Associations.** Associations between actors and use cases are indicated in use case diagrams by solid lines. An association exists whenever an actor is involved with an interaction described by a use case. Associations can also exist between use cases and even between actors, although this is typically an issue for system use case models (Section 5.1.6). Associations are modeled as lines connecting use cases and actors to one another, with an optional arrowhead on one end of the line. The arrowhead is often used to indicate the direction of the initial invocation of the relationship and/or to indicate the primary actor within the use case. The arrowheads are typically confused with data flow and as a result I avoid their use.

- **System boundary boxes (optional).** You can draw a rectangle around the use cases, called the system boundary box, to indicate the scope of your system. Anything within the box represents functionality that is in scope, and anything outside the box is not. System boundary boxes are rarely used, although on occasion I have used them to identify which use cases will be delivered in each major release of a system (Ambler 2003a).

- **Packages (optional).** Packages are UML constructs that enable you to organize model elements (such as use cases) into groups. Packages are depicted as file folders and can be used on any of the UML diagrams, including both use case diagrams and class diagrams. Figure 5.3 does not include a package because of the narrow scope of the diagram: I use packages only when my diagrams become unwieldy, which generally implies they cannot be printed on a single page, to organize a large diagram into smaller ones. The use of packages is discussed in Section 5.1.12.

In the example depicted in Fig. 5.3 students are enrolling in courses with the potential help of registrars. Professors input the marks students earn on assignments and registrars authorize the distribution of transcripts (report cards) to students. Note how for some use cases there is more than one actor involved. Moreover, note how some associations have arrowheads—any given use case association will have a zero or one arrowhead. The association between *Student* and *Enroll in Seminar* indicates this use case is initially invoked by a student and not by a registrar (the *Registrar* actor is also involved with this use case). Understanding that associations do not represent flows of information is important; they merely indicate an actor is somehow involved with a use case. Information is flowing back and forth between the actor and the use case; for example, students would need to indicate which seminars

TIP
Display Models Publicly
Models are important communication channels, but they work only if people can actually see and understand them. I am a firm believer in putting models, even if they are just sketches or collections of index cards, in public view where everyone can access and work on them.

they want to enroll in and the system would need to indicate to the students whether they have been enrolled. However, use case diagrams do not model this sort of information. Information flow can be modeled using UML activity diagrams, covered in Chapter 9. The line between the *Enroll in Seminar* use case and the *Registrar* actor has no arrowhead, indicating it is not clear how the interaction between the system and registrars start. Perhaps a registrar may notice a student needs help and offers assistance, whereas other times, the student may request help from the registrar, important information that would be documented in the description of the use case. Actors are always involved with at least one use case and are always drawn on the outside edges of a use case diagram.

You will notice that Fig. 5.3 was drawn with a software-based drawing tool, whereas Fig. 5.1 is a whiteboard sketch. Although I prefer to use whiteboards to model I will use sophisticated modeling tools when they offer significant value, such as the generation and reverse-engineering of source code. Take my word for it when I say that this is not a realistic option with use case diagrams because they simply do not contain sufficient detail. I will also use a software-based drawing tool when I think I will not only want to keep the model as permanent documentation but also update it in the future. This might be the case with the use case diagram of Fig. 5.4 because it is fairly large—it is doubtful that I would invest the time to input my whiteboard sketch(es) into such a drawing tool until they had grown and sufficiently matured on the whiteboard. In many ways it is a lot like fishing: it is not worth your while to keep the smaller fish. The primary reason I used a drawing tool was I wanted to show you a simple example using the official notation.

Use case diagrams give you a very good overview of the requirements, but as you will see in Section 5.1.4 the true value is the use cases. You often draw a use case diagram while you are identifying use cases, actors, and the associations among them. I like to start by identifying as many actors as possible.

Figure 5.4. A more complex use case diagram for the same university.

You should ask how the actors interact with the system to identify an initial set of use cases. Then, on the diagram, you connect the actors with the use cases with which they are involved. If an actor supplies information, initiates the use case, or receives any information as a result of the use case, then there should be an association between them. I generally do not include arrowheads on the association lines because my experience is that people confuse them for indications of information flow, not initial invocation (Ambler 2003c).

The preceding paragraph describes my general use case modeling style, an "actors first" approach. Others like to start by identifying one actor and the use cases that they are involved with first and then evolve the model from there. Both approaches work. The important point is that different people take different approaches so you need to be flexible when you're following AM's practice of *model with others*.

Schneider and Winters (2001) suggest that use case diagrams should be developed from the user's point of view, *not* the developer's. Your goal is to model the behavioral requirements for your system, how your users will work with your system to fulfill their needs, not what the developers think they should build.

TIP

Software Must Be Based on Requirements

If there are no requirements then you are done because you have nothing to build. The goal of software development is to build working software that meets the needs of your project stakeholders. If you do not know what those needs are then you cannot possibly succeed.

Figure 5.4 depicts a complex use case diagram for the university. It is "essential" because it does not imply technological decisions in any way. For example, the use case *Record student marks* could be supported by a manual forms-based process, via a browser-based online system, or via some other means. The point is that you cannot tell from the diagram. Furthermore the *Registrar* actor could be implemented via a person or via a registration system: you cannot really tell.

There are several interesting things to note about the use cases of Fig. 5.4:

1. **These are just preliminary use cases.** As you continue to model, you will refactor existing use cases, break them apart, combine them, introduce new use cases, and remove ones that do not make sense. Your models evolve over time: they are never "carved in stone."

2. **No time ordering is indicated between use cases.** For example, you need to enroll in a seminar before you attend it, and you need to attend it (I would hope) before you pass it. Although this is important information, it does not belong in a use case diagram. This sort of information, which pertains to the lifecycle of a seminar, is better modeled using a UML state machine diagram (described in detail in Chapter 11). One of the strengths of the UML is it has a wide range of models, each with its own purpose, enabling you to focus on one aspect of your system at a time.

3. **Customer actors are usually involved in many use cases.** The customer of the university, in this case *Student*, is the center of much of the action in the use case diagram. This is a normal phenomenon—after all, the main goal of most organizations is to provide services to their customers. To be fair, this is also the result of our initial focus on *Student*.

4. **Use cases are not functions.** I began by listing a series of tasks/business processes that the system needed to support, and then used this information to formulate the use case diagram. There is not one-to-one mapping

of processes to use cases, however. For example, the need for an available seminar list is identified as a function, but is modeled simply as a reference in a use case statement (see Fig. 5.14). Use cases must provide something of measurable value to an actor. Failing to do so may indicate that the task/process is a step in a use case instead of a use case by itself.

5. **No arrowheads are on the associations.** As I said earlier, showing arrowheads on use case associations can be confusing for many people and, frankly, they do not add much value anyway.

6. **The diagram is too big.** I prefer small diagrams the size of Figure 5.3 over larger, more complex ones such as that in Figure 5.4. Smaller diagrams are simpler and easier to understand and are often easier to draw, allowing you to explore a subset of the requirements and then move on. Remember, when you are taking an AMDD approach to development you want to follow practices such as *depict models simply* and *model in small increments* in order to remain effective and efficient. Remember that the goal of software development is to create working software, not to create extensive documentation, and that use case modeling is only an incremental step in making this happen.

7. **Use cases should be functionally cohesive.** A use case should encapsulate one service that provides value to an actor. Accordingly, separate use cases exist for dropping a seminar and enrolling in a seminar. These are two separate services offered to students and, therefore, they should have their own use cases.

8. **Each use case should be temporally cohesive.** A use case should describe a service whose steps occur during a contiguous period of time. For example, the steps of the use case *Enroll in Seminar* would occur during a short period, likely a few minutes. It would not make sense to have a use case such as *Attend seminar* that described the enrollment process, attending classes, and passing the seminar. This is not this functionally cohesive, and it is not cohesive in a time sense either: several steps are taken to enroll, you wait a while, and then you follow several more steps to attend the seminar, and you wait some more time to discover whether you passed or failed. The length of time is not the issue; it is the starting, stopping, and starting again that is the problem. If you were to write the logic for the *Attend seminar* use case, you might find you have temporal cohesion problems.

9. **Use cases should describe something of business value.** Use cases describe something of value to one or more actors.

10. **Every actor is involved with at least one use case, and every use case is involved with at least one actor.** Remember the definition of a use case: it provides a service of value to an actor. If a use case does not provide service to an actor, then why have it? If an actor not involved in a use case exists, why model it?

11. **Repetitive actions need not be expressed within a single use case.** For example, a student will typically enroll in many seminars each semester. It is not necessary to express this fact within the use case, unless it makes sense to do so, as an actor may invoke the single *Enroll in Seminar* use case multiple times.

12. **I chose not to include a system boundary box.** System boundary boxes are optional (per the UML), so I did not include it this time to show you it is allowable. The only time you definitely should include them is if some of the use cases are out of scope for the current effort. Place them outside the system boundary box makes it explicitly clear that they are out of scope at a glance.

An interesting observation is that the use case names are inconsistent between the two figures. Figure 5.3 includes a use case named *Enroll in Seminar*; yet Fig. 5.4 calls it *Enroll in seminar*. Worse yet there is a use case *Record Marks* and *Record student marks* in each figure, respectively. Although the diagrams are inconsistent they are still good enough: you can read them and know what I am trying to get across. Yes, in an ideal world it would be nice for your models to be perfectly consistent but frankly it is not an ideal world nor does

---

TIP

Take a Breadth-First Approach

My experience is it is better to paint a wide swath at first—to try to get a feel for the bigger picture—than it is to focus narrowly on one small aspect of your system. By taking a breadth-first approach, you quickly gain an overall understanding of your system and you can still dive into the details when appropriate. In AMDD, you gain this broad understanding as part of your initial modeling efforts during cycle 0 (see Chapter 4).

it need to be. Agile models are just barely good enough, and that means that they just need to be consistent *enough* with each other to get the job done.

I typically use a subset of the UML's use case diagram notation for essential use case modeling. The reason for this is straightforward: your goal with essential modeling is to depict the essential aspects of a system, and in the case of essential use case modeling your goal is to model the essential behavioral requirements for your system. My experience is that although the UML use case diagram notation is robust, not all of it is "essential" for requirements definition.

5.1.3 Identifying Actors

An actor represents anything or anyone that interfaces with your system. This may include people (not just the end user), external systems, and other organizations. Actors are always external to the system being modeled; they are never part of the system. To help find actors in your system, you should ask yourself the following questions (Schneider and Winters 2001; Leffingwell and Widrig 2000):

- Who is the main customer of your system?
- Who obtains information from this system?
- Who provides information to the system?
- Who installs the system?
- Who operates the system?
- Who shuts down the system?
- What other systems interact with this system?
- Does anything happen automatically at a preset time?
- Who will supply, use, or remove information from the system?
- Where does the system get information?

When you are essential use case modeling, your goal is to use actors to model roles and not the physical, real-world people, organizations, or systems. For example, Fig. 5.3 shows that the *Student* and *Registrar* actors are involved with the use case *Enroll in Seminar*. Yes, it is extremely likely that students are people, but consider *Registrar*. Today, at most modern universities, people are in the role of *Registrar*. But does it really need to be like this? Consider what registrars do: they mediate the paperwork between a university and a student, they validate the information a student submits, and they provide advice to

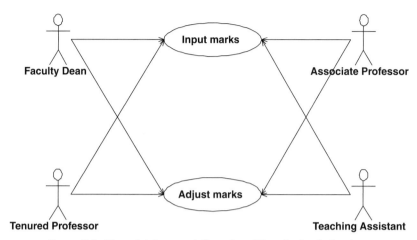

FIGURE **5.5. The mistaken modeling of positions instead of actors.**

students regarding which seminars to enroll in. The first two tasks, mediating paperwork and validating information, can obviously be automated. The third task, providing advice to students, could potentially be automated by use of an artificial intelligence (AI) expert system. The point to be made is the *Registrar* actor could be implemented via either people or systems; it could even outsource to another organization specializing in registration activities. If you assume the *Registrar* actor represents a person, then you have limited your system design opportunities, going against the grain of essential modeling. Instead, you want to describe the role of what it means to be a *Registrar* and leave design issues to your design activities.

With essential use case modeling actors represent roles. Whether the actor is a person, organization, or system should be left to your analysis and design efforts.

Note, too, this allows for the possibility that one person could fill multiple roles. For example, if the person employed as the registrar at a university is also taking courses, he or she may play the roles of both *Student* and *Registrar*. This is perfectly valid from a use case point of view.

Also important to understand is that actors do not model positions. For example, consider the use case diagram of Fig. 5.5. You see those faculty deans, tenured professors, associate professors, and teaching assistants are able both to input marks and to adjust marks (perhaps for bell-curving them). Although these people do, in fact, do these things, it is not what you want to depict on your diagram. Instead, you want to ask yourself what role these types of people are playing with respect to the use cases. In this case, the users

Name: Grade Administrator
Description: A Grade Administrator will input, update, and finalize in the system the marks that students receive on assignments, tests, and exams. Deans, professors (tenured, assistant, and associate), and teaching assistants are all potential grade administrators (see applicable business rules BR123 and BR124).
Examples: –

FIGURE 5.6. Description of the Grade Administrator actor.

appear to be taking on the role of a *Grade Administrator*, as you originally saw indicated in Fig. 5.4. The advantage of this approach is that it simplifies your diagrams and it does not tie you into the current position hierarchy within your organization: next year when the positions of tenured professor and associate professor get combined into instructor, you will not need to rework all your use case diagrams (assuming that you kept them in the first place and that the rework effort would actually add value even if you did).

To describe an actor you want to give it a name that accurately reflects its role within your model. Actor names are usually singular nouns, such as *Grade Administrator*, *Customer*, and *Payment Processor*. You also want to provide a description of the actor—a few sentences will usually do—and, if necessary, provide real-world examples of the actor. Figure 5.6 provides an example of how you might describe the *Grade Administrator* actor. Notice how the description refers to relevant business rules. Also, notice that examples were not indicated because the descriptions make it clear what a grade administrator is. Although some teams will create a separate "actor catalog" in which to

TIP

Start at Your Enterprise Business Model

Some organizations have what is called an enterprise business model that reflects their high-level business requirements. If an up-to-date enterprise requirements model exists within your organization—and it is current—then it is a perfect starting place to understand both your organization and how your system fits into the overall picture. You should be able to identify which high-level requirements your system will (perhaps partially) fulfill; otherwise, it is a clear sign that either the model is out-of-date or your system is not needed within your organization.

describe actors I have found it far easier to simply include the descriptions in the project glossary (Chapter 7) if we are maintaining one.

5.1.4 Writing an Essential Use Case

A use case is a sequence of actions that provide a measurable value to an actor. Another way to look at it is a use case describes a way in which a real-world actor interacts with the system. An essential use case (Constantine and Lockwood 1999), sometimes called a business use case, is a simplified, abstract, generalized use case that captures the intentions of a user in a technology- and implementation-independent manner. It is not quite accurate to say that an essential use case is a business use case in the RUP sense of the term, although they are very close. A business use case is often more focused on the business process and existing technology concerns are often brought into them. Think of them as somewhere in between essential and system use cases, although leaning towards the essential end of the spectrum.

Figure 5.7 presents a fully documented essential use case. Notice how brief and to the point the language is. There is not a lot of detail because you only need to get the basic idea across. The language of the application domain and of users is used, comprising a simplified, generalized, abstract, technology-free and implementation-independent description of one task or interaction. An essential use case is complete, meaningful, and well designed from the point of view of users in some role or roles in relation to a system and that embodies the purpose or intentions underlying the interaction.

Essential use cases are typically written in a two-column format: the column on the left indicating what the actors do, and the column on the right, the response to their actions. The actor(s) will do something and receive one or more responses to that action. As you can see the flow of the use case is apparent from the spacing of the actions and responses, although you may decide to number the steps to make it more apparent.

TIP

Most Requirements Should Be Technology Independent

I cringe when I hear terms such as object-oriented (OO) requirements, structured requirements, or component-based requirements. The terms OO, structured, and component are all categories of implementation technologies and therefore reflect architectural and design issues.

Enroll in Seminar
ID: UC 17
Preconditions:
• The student is enrolled in the university.
Postconditions:
• None

Actor(s)	Response
Student identifies himself	Verifies eligibility to enroll via *BR129 Determine Eligibility to Enroll.* Indicate available seminars
Choose seminar	Validate choice via *BR130 Determine Student Eligibility to Enroll in a Seminar.* Validate schedule fit via *BR143 Validate Student Seminar Schedule* Calculates fees via *BR 180 Calculate Student Fees* and *BR45 Calculate Taxes for Seminar.* Summarize fees Request confirmation
Confirm enrollment	Enroll student in seminar Add fees to student bill Provide confirmation of enrollment

FIGURE 5.7. *Enroll in Seminar* **as an essential use case.**

Constantine and Lockwood (1999) use the terms *User Actions* and *System Response* for the headings of these columns although as you can see I use *Actor(s)* and *Response*. The term *Actor(s)* is consistent with common use case terminology and the term *Response* is technology independent—*System Response* may lead some to believe that you must automate everything, which clearly is not the case. As always, find the style that works best for you.

In Fig. 5.7 I have chosen to indicate a unique identifier for the use case as well as its preconditions and postconditions. These three pieces of information are optional although very useful. I indicate an identifier whenever I need to reference an artifact somewhere else—for example, the use case itself references business rules, each of which has a unique identifier. The preconditions, if any, indicate what must be true before this use case is allowed to

---

TIP

You Cannot Be Truly System Independent

When you are essential use case modeling you can be technology independent but you will never be perfectly "system independent." You will always be bound by the scope of your effort, by the vision/goals of your project. As a result the perceived system that you are building—be it manual, automomated, or a hybrid of the two—will always affect your how you write your use cases.

---

run. The postconditions, if any, indicate what will be true once the use case finishes successfully.

A significant advantage of essential use cases is that they enable you to stand back and ask fundamental questions like "What's really going on?" and "What do we really need to do?" without letting implementation decisions get in the way. These questions often lead to critical realizations that allow you to rethink, or reengineer if you prefer that term, aspects of the overall business process.

5.1.5 Identifying Use Cases

How do you go about identifying potential use cases? Constantine and Lockwood (1999) suggest one way to identify essential use cases, or simply to identify use cases, is to identify potential services by asking your stakeholders the following questions from the point of view of the actors:

- What are users in this role trying to accomplish?
- To fulfill this role, what do users need to be able to do?
- What are the main tasks of users in this role?
- What information do users in this role need to examine, create, or change?
- What do users in this role need to be informed of by the system?
- What do users in this role need to inform the system about?

For example, from the point of view of the *Student* actor, you may discover that students

- Enroll in, attend, drop, fail, and pass seminars.
- Need a list of available seminars.

- Need to determine basic information about a seminar, such as its description and its prerequisites.
- Obtain a copy of their transcript, their course schedules, and the fees due.
- Pay fees, pay late charges, receive reimbursements for dropped and cancelled courses, receive grants, and receive student loans.
- Graduate from school or drop out of it.
- Need to be informed of changes in seminars, including room changes, time changes, and even cancellations.
- Provide fundamental information about themselves such as their name, address, and phone number.

Similarly, another way to identify use cases is to ask your stakeholders to brainstorm the various scenarios, often called usage scenarios, that your system may or may not support. A usage scenario is a description of a potential business situation that may be faced by the users of a system—the focus is on behavioral requirements issues, not technical design issues. For example, the following would be considered use case scenarios for a university information system:

- A student wants to enroll in a seminar, but the registrar informs him that he does not have the prerequisites for it.
- A student wanted to enroll in a seminar that she does have the prerequisites for and seats are still available in the seminar.
- A professor requests a seminar list for every course he teaches.
- A researcher applies for a research grant, but only receives partial funding for her project.
- A professor submits student marks to the system. These marks may be for exams, tests, or assignments.
- A student wants to drop a seminar the day after the drop date.
- A student requests a printed copy of his transcript, so he can include copies of it with his résumé.

You can take either approach, or combine the two, if you like, but the main goal is to end up with a lot of information regarding the behavioral aspects of your system. The next step is to group these aspects, by similarity, into use cases. Remember that a use case provides a service of measurable value to an actor.

Each service should be cohesive; in other words, it should do one thing that makes sense. For example, you would not want a use case called *Support Students* that does everything a student needs, such as letting them enroll in courses, drop courses, pay fees, and obtain course information. That is simply too much to handle all at once. Instead, you should identify several use cases, one for each service provided by the system.

5.1.6 System Use Case Diagrams

A system use case model is similar to an essential use case model. A system use case model is composed of a use case diagram (Object Management Group 2003) and the accompanying documentation describing the use cases, actors, and associations. The main difference between an essential use case and a system use case is that in the system use case you include high-level implementation decisions. For example, a system use case refers to specific user-interface components—such as screens, HTML pages, or reports—something you would not do in an essential use case. During your analysis efforts you make decisions regarding what will be built, information reflected in your use cases, and, arguably, even how it will be built (effectively design). Because your use cases refer to user-interface components, and because your user interface is worked on during design, inevitably design issues will creep into your use cases. For example, a design decision is whether your user interface is implemented using browser-based technology, such as HTML pages or graphical user-interface (GUI) technology such as Microsoft Windows. Because your user interface will work differently depending on the implementation technology, the logic of your system use cases, which reflect the flow of your user interface, will also be affected.

Figure 5.8 depicts the evolution of the detailed essential use case diagram of Fig. 5.4 into a system use case diagram. There are several interesting changes. First, deployment decisions are now reflected in the diagram. For example, you see that the post office is used to distribute information to students. You also see that student marks are input, instead of "recorded," implying the use of computer technology. Similarly teaching schedules are printed now instead of produced. Subtle differences, yet important ones. Relationships between some use cases have been introduced, the topic of Section 5.1.11, reflecting similarities between those use cases.

5.1.7 System Use Cases

Writing system use cases is straightforward. If you have created essential use cases then you can simply evolve them into system use cases. Often an essential

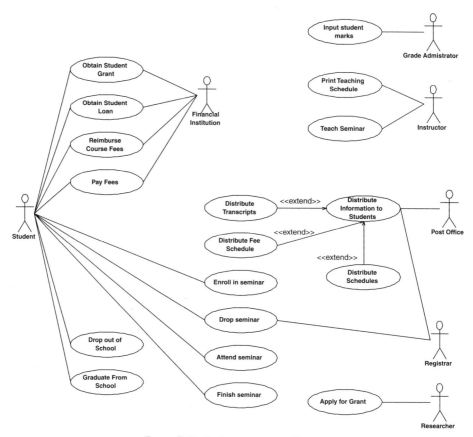

FIGURE 5.8. System use case diagram.

use case will evolve into several system use cases. A system use case considers technical considerations, such as usage issues resulting from user-interface choices that you make. For example, a registration system implemented using a GUI technology such as Microsoft Windows will work differently from a system built using browser technology, which in turn will work differently from a system built using personal digital assistant (PDA) technology. Different user-interface platforms affect the way that your users work with your system, which in turn affects the logic of your use cases.

Table 5.2 describes the potential sections you may include when documenting a use case. Although some of the sections are optional, in my opinion, they are all still a good idea.

Let us start by considering the types of use cases that you will write as part of your initial requirements gathering efforts during cycle 0 of your projects.

TABLE 5.2. The Sections of a Simple Use Case Description	
Section	Purpose
Name	The name of the use case. The name should implicitly express the user's intent or purpose of the use case.
Identifier [Optional]	A unique identifier used by other artifacts to reference this use case.
Description [Optional]	Several sentences summarizing the use case.
Goal [Optional]	The goal of this use case, i.e., the thing of measurable value that will be realized at its completion. If you cannot identify the goal you probably do not have a use case.
Preconditions [Optional]	A list of the conditions, if any, that must be met before a use case may be invoked.
Postconditions [Optional]	A list of the conditions, if any, that will be true once the use case finishes successfully.
Basic course of action	The main path of logic an actor follows through a use case. Often referred to as the "happy path," the "main success scenario," or the "main path" because it describes how the use case works when everything works as it normally should.
Alternate courses of action	The infrequently used path(s) of logic in a use case, paths that are the result of an alternate way to work, an exception, or an error condition. Sometimes called an extension.

These use cases will be either essential use cases or "informal" system use cases, an example of which is presented in Fig. 5.9. The steps are written in very brief, bullet/point-form style. They contain just enough information to get the idea across and no more. It also takes technology issues into account; for example, the text "Student inputs her name and address" implies some sort of information system. The reference to the system also implies the same. Figure 5.10 presents an alternate version of the use case, this time as a manual process involving a registrar (a person) instead of an automated system. Choosing a manual process over a software-based one is still a technical

Name: Enroll in Seminar

Identifier: UC 17

Basic Course of Action:

- Student inputs her name and student number.
- System verifies the student is eligible to enroll in seminars. If not eligible then student informed and use case ends.
- System displays list of available seminars.
- Student chooses a seminar or decides not to enroll at all.
- System validates the student is eligible to enroll in the chosen seminar. If not eligible student is asked to choose another.
- System validates the seminar fits student's schedule.
- System calculates and displays fees.
- Student verifies the cost and indicates she wants to either enroll or not enroll.
- System enrolls the student in the seminar and bills them for it.
- The system prints enrollment receipt.

FIGURE 5.9. Informal version of the *Enroll in Seminar* system use case.

Name: Enroll in Seminar

Identifier: UC 17

Basic Course of Action:

- Student inputs her name and student number.
- Registrar verifies the student is eligible to enroll in seminars. If not eligible then student informed and use case ends.
- Registrar asks student which seminar they would like to enroll in. If they do not know registrar provides student with course catalog if required.
- Student chooses a seminar or decides not to enroll at all.
- Registrar checks student record to see whether student has previously passed prerequisite courses. If not eligible student is asked to choose another.
- Registrar validates the seminar fits into student's schedule.
- Registrar calculates fees.
- Student verifies the cost and indicates she wants to either enroll or not enroll.
- Registrar enrolls the student in the seminar and bills them for it.
- The registrar writes enrollment receipt.

FIGURE 5.10. Informal version of the *Enroll in Seminar* use case for a manual system.

> **TIP**
>
> **Manual Processes Are Not Out of Scope**
>
> It is perfectly fine to have manual steps in use cases, such as working with paper forms in the use case of Fig. 5.11, and some use cases are completely manual as you see in Fig. 5.10. This happens in the real world, some things are manual and some are automated; therefore your use cases should reflect this. The manual parts may be automated at some point in the future and the automated parts may similarly be "manualized," all in the name of process improvement. It is important to realize that you still have significant implementation issues surrounding manual processes. In this case someone must define *requirements* for the form(s). Someone must *analyze and design* the forms. Someone must *implement* the forms. Someone must *test* how well those forms work. Some must *configure and change manage* the form over time. Someone must *deploy* the forms to their users. There is more to development than just the creation of software.

architecture decision, in this case a low-tech architectural decision. The differences between the two versions illuminates how system use cases are analysis and arguably even design artifacts, not requirements artifacts.

Figure 5.11 depicts a formalized version of the *Enroll in Seminar* system use case of Fig. 5.9. This version is much more detailed than the corresponding use case, and is typical of the type of use cases that people will write in documentation-intense environments. Frankly, use cases like this are overkill for many projects yet many project teams are required to write them in this manner (or something similar) because senior management is convinced that they require this level of documentation. My advice is to keep your models as simple as possible and only document them this thoroughly if it adds actual value.

It also includes alternate courses of action, i.e., infrequently used path of logic in a use case. Alternate courses are described in Section 5.1.8.

There are several interesting style issues in Fig. 5.11:

1. **I use active voice for the use case steps.** For example, the statement "The registrar informs the student of the fees" is in active voice, whereas "The student is informed of the fees by the registrar" is in passive voice. Writing in the active voice leads to succinct sentences.

2. **The basic course of action ends with a closing statement.** This is often something along the lines of "The use case ends" or "The use case ends when...," indicating that the logic for the course of action has been completely defined.

Name: Enroll in Seminar

Identifier UC 17:

Description:
Enroll an existing student in a seminar for which she is eligible.

Preconditions:
The Student is registered at the University.

Postconditions:
The Student will be enrolled in the course she wants if she is eligible and room is available.

Basic Course of Action:

1. The use case begins when a student indicates they want to enroll in a seminar.
2. The student inputs her name and student number into the system via *UI23 Security Log-in Screen*.
3. The system verifies the student is eligible to enroll in seminars at the university according to business rule *BR129 Determine Eligibility to Enroll*. [Alt Course A]
4. The system displays *UI32 Seminar Selection Screen*, which indicates the list of available seminars.
5. The student indicates the seminar in which she wants to enroll. [Alt Course B: The Student Decides Not to Enroll]
6. The system validates the student is eligible to enroll in the seminar according to the business rule *BR130 Determine Student Eligibility to Enroll in a Seminar.* [Alt Course C]
7. The system validates the seminar fits into the existing schedule of the student according to the business rule *BR143 Validate Student Seminar Schedule*.
8. The system calculates the fees for the seminar based on the fee published in the course catalog, applicable student fees, and applicable taxes. Apply business rules *BR 180 Calculate Student Fees* and *BR45 Calculate Taxes for Seminar*.
9. The system displays the fees via *UI33 Display Seminar Fees Screen*.
10. The system asks the student if she still wants to enroll in the seminar.

Figure 5.11. *Enroll in Seminar* written in narrative style.

11. The student indicates she wants to enroll in the seminar.
12. The system enrolls the student in the seminar.
13. The system informs the student the enrollment was successful via *UI88 Seminar Enrollment Summary Screen.*
14. The system bills the student for the seminar, according to business rule *BR100 Bill Student for Seminar.*
15. The system asks the student if she wants a printed statement of the enrollment.
16. The student indicates she wants a printed statement.
17. The system prints the enrollment statement *UI89 Enrollment Summary Report.*
18. The use case ends when the student takes the printed statement.

Alternate Course A: The Student is Not Eligible to Enroll in Seminars.
A.3. The registrar determines the student is not eligible to enroll in seminars.
A.4. The registrar informs the student he is not eligible to enroll.
A.5. The use case ends.

Alternate Course B: The Student Decides Not to Enroll in an Available Seminar
B.5. The student views the list of seminars and does not see one in which he wants to enroll.
B.6. The use case ends.

Alternate Course C: The Student Does Not Have the Prerequisites
C.6. The registrar determines the student is not eligible to enroll in the seminar he chose.
C.7. The registrar informs the student he does not have the prerequisites.
C.8. The registrar informs the student of the prerequisites he needs.

FIGURE 5.11. (*continued*)

3. **Pre- and postconditions can reduce functional decomposition.** Consider steps 2 and 3 of the use case of Fig. 5.11. I could just as easily have defined a precondition that the student has already logged into the system and has been verified as an eligible student. Actually, there should be two preconditions: one for being logged in and one for being eligible (that way, the preconditions are cohesive). To support the first precondition, being logged in, I would be tempted to write a *Log Into System* use case that would describe the process of logging in and validating the user,

---

TIP

Some Requirements Are Technical

It is important to recognize that some requirements, such as the technical constraints that your system must use the standard J2EE and relational database technologies used within your organization, are in fact technology dependent. Your stakeholders should understand when this is applicable, and why.

---

perhaps including alternate courses for obtaining a log-in identifier. This use case would be a candidate for inclusion in your common enterprise model because it is a feature that should belong to your organization's shared technical architecture. Cross-project issues such as this are one of the topics I cover in *Process Patterns* (Ambler 1998b) and *More Process Patterns* (Ambler 1999) as well as in the enterprise unified process (EUP) (http://www.enterpriseunifiedprocess.info). The second precondition, the one for being eligible to enroll, likely does not need its own use case, but I would still reference the appropriate business rule.

5.1.8 Writing Alternate Courses of Action

When writing alternate courses of action I follow several best practices:

1. **Briefly describe the condition.** An alternate course includes a description of the condition that must be met to invoke the alternate course.

2. **Indicate that the alternate course exists within the basic course of action.** For example, in step 3 you see that there is a reference to alternate course A. Step 5 shows a slightly different style; in this case it also indicates the condition. This is a little wordier but makes it more obvious what is going on. Pick a style and apply it consistently.

3. **You need an identification scheme.** My preferred approach is to identify the first alternate course as *A*, the second as *B*, and so on. Also, notice the numbering scheme for the steps of the alternate course.

4. **Set a consistent step numbering strategy.** In this case each step starts with the letter of the alternate course, followed by the number of the step in the basic course of the use case it replaces. For example, the first step of the first alternate course (*A*) replaces step 3 in the basic course of action.

Student	System
1. The student wants to enroll in a seminar.	
2. The student inputs his name and student number into the system via *UI23 Security Log-in Screen*.	3. The system verifies the student is eligible to enroll in seminars at the university, according to business rule *BR129 Determine Eligibility to Enroll*.
	4. The system displays *UI32 Seminar Selection Screen*, which indicates the list of available seminars.
5. The student indicates the seminar in which she wants to enroll.	
	6. The system validates the student is eligible to enroll in the seminar, according to the business rule *BR130 Determine Student Eligibility to Enroll in a Seminar*.
	7. The system validates the seminar fits into the existing schedule of the student, according to the business rule *BR43 Validate Student Seminar Schedule*.
	8. The system calculates the fees for the seminar based on the fee published in the course catalog, applicable student fees, and applicable taxes. Apply business rules *BR 180 Calculate Student Fees* and *BR45 Calculate Taxes for Seminar*.
	9. The system displays the fees via *UI33 Display Seminar Fees Screen*.
	10. The system asks the student whether he still wants to enroll in the seminar.
11. The student indicates he wants to enroll in the seminar.	12. The system enrolls the student in the seminar.
	13. The system informs the student the enrollment was successful via *UI88 Seminar Enrollment Summary Screen*.

Figure 5.12. Basic course of action for *Enroll in Seminar* written in action–response style.

14. The system bills the student for the seminar, according to business rule *BR100 Bill Student for Seminar.*
15. The system asks the student if he wants a printed statement of the enrollment.
16. The student indicates he wants a printed statement.
17. The system prints the enrollment statement *UI89 Enrollment Summary Report.*
18. The use case ends when the student takes the printed statement.

FIGURE 5.12 (*continued*)

5. **End the alternate course.** The last step in each alternate course should indicate either that the use case ends, using the same terminology you would for the last step of the basic course of action, or that the use case continues at another step. Alternate courses *A* and *B* both resulted in the use case ending—the error condition was too grave a problem to continue—whereas for alternate course *C* it was possible to continue.

6. **Each step should do one thing.** My experience is that alternate courses are easier to write when your use case statements do one thing and one thing only. Notice how alternate course A in Fig. 5.11 was easy to write: the step in the basic course of action that it branched from did one thing and one thing only, making it straightforward to define the error condition. Alternate courses B and C are another matter. Step 4 describes two actions: first that the system presents a list of available seminars to the student and the student picks from this list. It affects alternate course B because this is the step that B returns to: do you really need to display the list again? I doubt it. It affects C because this is the step C branches from, the fact that the student does not see a seminar in which she is interested. The impact is not that large in this case, but it could have been. The point is it simplifies things if a use case step does one thing and one thing only. Furthermore, imagine trying to add alternate courses to the prose-style use case of Fig. 13. I doubt you could do it effectively.

7. **Focus on business issues.** The conditions described in the alternate courses focus on business issues, such as the student not having the right

> **TIP**
>
> **The Goal Is Mutual Understanding, Not Documentation**
>
> The fundamental goal of the requirements gathering process is to understand what it is that your project stakeholders want. Whether you create a detailed document describing those requirements, or perhaps just a collection of hand-drawn sketches and notes, is a completely different issue. Having well-documented requirements is completely useless if the developers do not understand what needs to be built. Even worse is developers who think they "know the requirements" without this interaction with project stakeholders.

prerequisites, not technical ones. Yes, database errors, network errors, and operating system errors still occur, but those are technical design issues, not behavioral requirements issues. For now, assume these types of things are handled by the system, although if you have not already done so, then you should consider identifying reliability issues such as this as technical requirements.

5.1.9 Other Use Case Styles

The use case of Fig. 5.11 is written in narrative style—where the basic and alternate courses of action are written one step at a time. A second style, called the action–response style, presents use case steps in columns, one column for each actor and a second column for the system. Figure 5.11 presents the basic course of action for Fig. 5.11 rewritten using this style. For the sake of brevity, I did not include rewritten versions of the alternate courses. There are two columns, one for the *Student* actor and one for the system, because only one actor is involved in this use case. The advantage of action–response style is it is easier to see how actors interact with the system and how the system responds. The disadvantages are that it is a little harder to understand the flow of logic of the use case and that it is hard to maintain use cases in this format. This is particularly true for alternate courses and their references to other courses of action or when there are several actors involved. The style you choose is a matter of preference. What is important is that your team and, ideally, your organization selects one style and sticks to it—remember AM's *apply modeling standards* practice.

Figure 5.13 presents a different, and simpler approach to documenting use case: instead of writing numbered steps, you simply write prose. I sometimes

Name: Enroll in Seminar

Description:
A student wants to enroll in a seminar so he submits his name and student number to the registrar; therefore, he may be validated to become an eligible student at the university. Once the registrar verifies him, the student indicates the seminar he wants to enroll in from the list of those available. The registrar validates the student is eligible to enroll in the seminar and that the seminar fits into the student's existing schedule. The registrar calculates the fees for the seminar—based on the fee published in the course catalog, applicable student fees, and applicable taxes—and informs the student. The registrar verifies with the student that he still wants to enroll in the seminar, and then enrolls the student in the seminar. The registrar adds the appropriate fees to the student's bill and provides the student with a confirmation that he is enrolled.

FIGURE 5.13. *Enroll in Seminar* written as simple prose.

take this approach at first to understand what each use case is about, but I believe in tightening up the writing, along the lines of Fig. 5.11, to ensure that I have truly captured the logic of the use case.

5.1.10 Comparing Essential and System Use Cases

At this point I think that there is significant value in discussing the differences between essential and system use cases. Chances are pretty good that you have seen some form of use cases before and that if so those examples were likely system use cases and they were likely very different from what you see in Fig. 5.7.

Let us consider two versions of the *Enroll in Seminar* use case—Fig. 5.7, the essential use case, and Fig. 5.14, the system use case (also called a traditional or concrete use case). There are several things to notice:

1. **The system use case is much more detailed.** The essential use case focuses on the bare minimum information to explore the system usage, whereas the system use case uses much more verbiage.

2. **The system use case includes implementation details.** For example, it indicates that a system does much of the work, indicating a decision has been made to automate many of the mundane aspects of enrollment. A decision to do this manually via a human registrar could also have been made; thus the use case would be worded differently. The writer of system use cases is analyzing and describing requirements imposed by the problem, intermingled with implicit decisions about what the user interface is going to be like, whereas the writer of an essential use case is not.

3. **The system use case makes references to screen and reports.** Note the references to *UI23 Security Log-in Screen* and *UI89 Enrollment Summary Report*. Once again this reflects implementation details: someone has decided the system will be implemented as screens, as opposed to HTML pages perhaps, and printed reports. However, the essential use case could just as easily have referred to user-interface (UI) elements; the essential version of screens and reports, and, truthfully, this is a practice I recommend. Essential UI prototyping is described in Chapter 6.

4. **Both versions of the use case reference business rule definitions.** For example, both use cases refer to *BR129 Determine Eligibility to Enroll*. Business rules reflect essential characteristics of your domain that your system must implement. I will describe business rules, as well as other types of requirements, in their own separate definitions whenever I am building complex

---

TIP

Your Requirements Only Need to Be Good Enough

You do not need complete models in order to move forward to the next stage. For example, I would consider the system use case of Fig. 5.14 to be more than good enough to start designing from it if not coding from it. Yet I clearly do not have complete information. For example, it references business rules but I do not have the details of how to implement those rules. An hour or so into coding I may discover that I need more information. At that point I could ask the project stakeholder(s) who are active working with the project or I could simply stub the code out for now; in other words write an operation that returns a fake answer, and then go back and implement it properly when I do have the details (after talking with one or more stakeholders). Similarly, I could take the same approach with the UIs referenced but not yet defined. This is what evolutionary development is all about: you iterate between various development tasks as needed instead of following a strict procedural approach.

Name: **Enroll in Seminar**

Description:
Enroll an existing student in a seminar for which she is eligible.

Preconditions:
The Student is registered at the University.

Postconditions:
The Student will be enrolled in the course she wants if she is eligible and room is available.

Basic Course of Action:

1. A student wants to enroll in a seminar.
2. The student inputs her name and student number into the system via *U123 Security Log-in Screen*.
3. The system verifies the student is eligible to enroll in seminars at the university according to business rule *BR129 Determine Eligibility to Enroll*.
4. The system displays *U132 Seminar Selection Screen*, which indicates the list of available seminars.
5. The student indicates the seminar in which she wants to enroll.
6. The system validates the student is eligible to enroll in the seminar according to the business rule *BR130 Determine Student Eligibility to Enroll in a Seminar*.
7. The system validates the seminar fits into the existing schedule of the student according to the business rule *BR143 Validate Student Seminar Schedule*.
8. The system calculates the fees for the seminar based on the fee published in the course catalog, applicable student fees, and applicable taxes. Apply business rules *BR180 Calculate Student Fees* and *BR45 Calculate Taxes for Seminar*.
9. The system displays the fees via *U133 Display Seminar Fees Screen*.
10. The system asks the student whether she still wants to enroll in the seminar.
11. The student indicates she wants to enroll in the seminar.
12. The system enrolls the student in the seminar.
13. The system informs the student the enrollment was successful via *U188 Seminar Enrollment Summary Screen*.

FIGURE 5.14. *Enroll in Seminar* as a traditional system use case.

14. The system bills the student for the seminar, according to business rule *BR100 Bill Student for Seminar*.
15. The system asks the student whether she wants a printed statement of the enrollment.
16. The student indicates she wants a printed statement.
17. The system prints the enrollment statement *U189 Enrollment Summary Report*.
18. The use case ends when the student takes the printed statement.

FIGURE 5.14 (*continued*)

systems. For very simple systems without very many complex business rules I will often keep it simple and document the rule within the use case. Different situations call for different approaches, hence the importance of AM's *local adaptation* principle.

5. **The system use case has more steps than the essential use case version.** This, in fact, reflects my style of writing use cases; I believe each use case step should do one thing and one thing only.

Why essential use cases? Traditional/system use cases typically contain too many built-in assumptions, often hidden or implicit, about the underlying technology implementation and the UI yet to be designed. This is a good feature during your analysis and design efforts, but not so good for your requirement efforts. An essential use case, on the other hand, is based on the purpose or intentions of a user, rather than on the concrete steps or mechanisms by which the purpose or intention might be carried out.

5.1.11 Reuse in Use Case Models: <<extend>>, <<include>>, and Inheritance

One of your goals during analysis is to identify potential opportunities for reuse, a goal you can work toward as you are developing your use case model. Potential reuse can be modeled through four generalization relationships supported by UML use case models: extend relationships between use cases, include relationships between use cases, inheritance between use cases, and inheritance between actors.

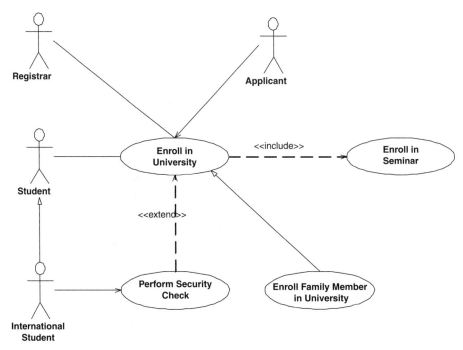

FIGURE 5.15. The opportunities for reuse in use case models.

An extend association, formerly called an extends relationship in UML v1.2 and earlier, is a generalization relationship where an extending use case continues the behavior of a base use case. The extending use case accomplishes this by conceptually inserting additional action sequences into the base use case sequence. This allows an extending use case to continue the activity sequence of a base use case when the appropriate extension point is reached in the base use case and the extension condition is fulfilled. When the extending use case activity sequence is completed, the base use case continues. In Fig. 5.15, you see the use case *Perform Security Check* extends the use case *Enroll in University*, the notation for doing so being simply a normal use case association with the stereotype of <<extend>>. Stereotypes are a mechanism for defining common and consistent extensions to the UML notation. We say that *Enroll in University* is the base use case and *Perform Security Check* is the extending use case. An extending use case is, effectively, an alternate course of the base use case. In fact, a good rule of thumb is you should introduce an extending use case whenever the logic for an alternate course of action is at a complexity level similar to that of your basic course of action. I also like to introduce an extending use case whenever I need an alternate course for an alternate course; in this case, the extending use case would encapsulate both alternate courses. Many use case modelers avoid the use of extend associations as this technique has a tendency to make use case diagrams difficult to understand. My preference is to use extend associations sparingly.

Just as you indicate the point at which the logic of an alternate course replaces the logic of a portion of the basic course of action for a use case, you need to be able to do the same thing for an extending use case. This is accomplished using an extension point, which is simply a marker in the logic of a base use case indicating where extension is allowed. Figure 5.16 depicts the basic course of action for the *Enroll in University* use case of Fig. 5.15, which includes an example of how an extension point would be indicated within a use case (see step 7). This extension point is applicable from steps 7 through 17. The implication is that at any time, the security check may occur but you do not know exactly when it will occur. Notice how the identifier and the name of the use case are indicated. If several use cases extended this one from the same point, then each one would need to be listed. A condition statement, such as *Condition: Enrollee is an international student* could have been indicated immediately following the name of the extending use case, but, in this example, it was obvious what was happening.

A second way to indicate potential reuse within use case models is to include associations. An include association, formerly known as a uses relationship in UML v1.2 and earlier, is a generalization relationship denoting the inclusion of the behavior described by another use case. The best way to think of an include association is that it is the invocation of a use case by another one. In Fig. 5.15, you see the use case *Enroll in University* includes *Enroll in Seminar*, the notation for doing so being simply a normal use case association with the stereotype of <<include>>. Step 11 in Fig. 5.16 presents an example of how you would indicate where the use case is included in the logic of the including use case. Similar to calling a function or invoking an operation within source code, isn't it? Object-oriented programming is covered in Chapter 13.

You use associations whenever one use case needs the behavior of another. Introducing a new use case that encapsulates similar logic that occurs in several use cases is quite common. For example, you may discover several use cases need the behavior to search for and then update information about students, indicating the potential need for an *Update Student Information* use case included by the other use cases.

Use cases can inherit from other use cases, offering a third opportunity to indicate potential reuse. Figure 5.15 depicts an example of this, showing that

Name: Enroll in University

Identifier: UC 19.

Description:
Enroll someone in the university.

Preconditions:
The Registrar is logged into the system.
The Applicant has already undergone initial checks to verify that they are eligible to enroll.

Postconditions:
The Applicant will be enrolled in the university as a student if they are eligible.

Basic Course of Action:

1. An applicant wants to enroll in the university.
2. The applicant hands a filled out copy of form *U113 University Application Form* to the registrar. [Alternate Course A: Forms Not Filled Out]
3. The registrar visually inspects the forms.
4. The registrar determines that the forms have been filled out properly. [Alternate Course B: Forms Improperly Filled Out]
5. The registrar clicks on the *Create Student* icon.
6. The system displays *U189 Create Student Screen*.
7. The registrar inputs the name, address, and phone number of the applicant. [Extension Point: *UC34 Perform Security Check*. Applicable to Step 17]
8. The system determines that the applicant does not already exist within the system according to *BR37 Potential Match Criteria for New Students*. [Alternate Course F: Students Appears to Exist within the System].
9. The system determines that the applicant is on the eligible applicants list. [Alternate Course G: Person Is Not Eligible to Enroll]
10. The system adds the applicant to its records. The applicant is now considered to be a student.
11. The registrar helps the student to enroll in seminars via the use case *UC 17 Enroll in Seminar*.
12. The system calculates the required initial payment in accordance to *BR16 Calculate Enrollment Fees*.
13. The system displays *U115 Fee Summary Screen*.

FIGURE **5.16.** The *Enroll in University* use case.

14. The registrar asks the student to pay the initial payment in accordance to *BR19 Fee Payment Options.*
15. The student pays the initial fee. [Alternate Course D: The Student Cannot Pay at This Time]
16. The system prints a receipt.
17. The registrar hands the student the receipt.
18. The use case ends.

Alternate Course A: . . . .

FIGURE 5.16 (continued)

Enroll Family Member in University inherits from the *Enroll in University* use case. Inheritance between use cases is not as common as the use of either extend or include associations, but it is still possible. The inheriting use case would completely replace one or more of the courses of action of the inherited use case. In this case, the basic course of action is completely rewritten to reflect that new business rules are applied when the family member of a professor is enrolling at the university. Family members are allowed to enroll in the school, regardless of the marks they earned in high school; they do not have to pay any enrollment fees, and they are given top priority for enrollment in the university.

Inheritance between use cases should be applied whenever a single condition, in this case, the student is a family member of a professor, would result in the definition of several alternate courses. Without the option to define an inheriting use case, you need to introduce an alternate course to rework the check of the student's high-school marks, the charging of enrollment fees, and for prioritization of who is allowed to enroll in the given semester.

The inheriting use case is much simpler than the use case from which it inherits. It should have a name, description, and identifier, and it should indicate from which use case it inherits. This includes any section that is replaced, particularly the preconditions and postconditions as well as any courses of action. If something is not replaced, then leave that section blank, assuming it is inherited from the parent use case (you might want to put text, such as "see parent use case," in the section).

The fourth opportunity for indicating potential reuse within use case models occurs between actors: an actor on a use case diagram can inherit from another actor. An example of this is shown in Fig. 5.15; the *International Student* actor inherits from *Student.* An international student is a student, the

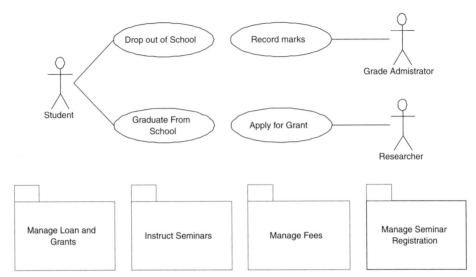

FIGURE 5.17 Reorganizing the use case diagram with packages.

only difference being is he or she is subject to different rules and policies (the international student pays more in tuition and must undergo a security check during the registration process). The standard UML notation for inheritance, the open-headed arrow, is used and the advice presented about the appropriate use of inheritance still applies: it should make sense to say the inheriting actor is or is like the inherited actor.

5.1.12 Packages

Figure 5.17 depicts how you could reorganize Fig. 5.4 using packages. A UML package is a mechanism for representing a collection of model elements—in this case, the elements of a use case diagram. Packages can be used on any type of UML diagram, although their use is most common on use case diagrams and class diagrams (Ambler 2003c). By introducing packages, the use case diagram becomes simpler and easier to understand, each package, in turn, would be documented by another use case diagram. For example, Fig. 5.18 depicts the resulting use case diagram for the *Manage Seminar Registration* package. Notice how the *Student* and *Registrar* actors both appear on this diagram: they are involved with the use cases that appear on the diagram and, therefore, should also appear on it. In Fig. 5.18 I could have included a system boundary box to represent the boundary of the package.

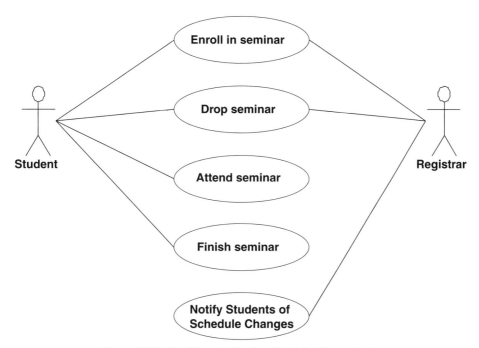

FIGURE **5.18.** *The Manage Seminar Registration package.*

If Fig. 5.18 only contained packages as well as any dependencies between them then it would actually be considered a UML package diagram. Package diagrams are covered in detail in Chapter 10.

5.1.13 Use Case Modeling Tips

Here is a collection of tips and techniques that I have found useful over the years to improve the quality of my system use case models:

1. **Associations between actors and use cases indicate the need for interfaces.** When the actor is a person, then to support the association, you need to develop UI components, such as screens and reports. When the actor is an external system, then you need to develop a system interface, perhaps a data file transfer or a real-time online link to the external system. For example, in the *Enroll in Seminar* use case of Fig. 5.11, the *Student* actor interacts with the system via several major UI components, particularly *UI23 Security Log-in Screen, UI32 Seminar*

*Selection Screen, UI33 Display Seminar Fees Screen, UI88 Seminar Enroll-
ment Summary Screen*, and *UI89 Enrollment Summary Report.*

2. **Write use cases under the assumption that you can exit at any time.** For
   example, in the middle of the *Enroll in Seminar* use case, the student may
   decide to give up and try again later or the system may crash because the
   load on it is too great. The description of the use case does not include
   these as alternate courses because it would greatly increase the complexity
   of the use case without adding much value. Instead, it is assumed if one
   of these events occurs, that the use case simply ends and the right thing
   will happen. However, your subject matter experts (SMEs) may want to
   define nontechnical requirements that describe how situations like this
   should be handled.

3. **Do not overuse the reuse techniques.** Include associations and, to a lesser
   degree, extend associations, lead to functional decomposition within your
   use case model. Use cases are not meant to describe functions within your
   source code; they are meant to describe series of actions that offer value to
   actors. A good rule of thumb is if you are able to describe a use case with a
   single sentence, then you have likely decomposed it too much, something
   that occurs when you apply include associations too often. Another rule
   of thumb is if you have more than two levels of include associations, for
   example, if use case *A* includes use case *B*, which includes use case *C*,
   then two levels of include exist, and then you are in danger of functional
   decomposition. The same is true of extend associations and inheritance
   between use cases.

4. **Write use cases from the point of view of the actor in the active voice.**
   Use cases should be written in the active voice: "The student indicates
   the seminar," instead of in the passive voice, "The seminar is indicated by
   the student." Furthermore, use cases should be written from the point of
   view of the actor. After all, the purpose of use cases is to understand how
   your users will work with your system.

5. **Write scenario text, not functional requirements.** A use case describes
   a series of actions that provide value to an actor; it does not describe
   a collection of features. For example, the use case of Fig. 5.11 describes how a student interacts with the system to enroll in a seminar. It does not describe what the UI looks like or how it works.
   You have other models to describe this important information, such
   as your UI model and your supplementary specifications. Follow AM's

practice of *apply the right artifact* and use each technique for its strengths.

6. **A use case is neither a class specification nor a data specification.** This sort of information should be captured by your conceptual domain model, described in Chapter 8. You are likely to refer to classes described in your conceptual model; for example, the *Enroll in Seminar* use case includes concepts, such as seminars and students, both of which would be described by your conceptual model. Once again, use each model appropriately.

7. **Create a use case template.** As you can see in Fig. 5.11, use cases include a fair amount of information, information that can easily be documented in a common format. You should consider either developing your own template based on what you have learned in this book or adopting an existing one you have either purchased with an object modeling tool or downloaded from the Internet.

8. **Organize your use case diagrams consistently.** Common practice is to draw inheritance and extend associations vertically, with the inheriting/extending use case drawn below the parent/base use case. Similarly, include associations are typically drawn horizontally. Note that these are simple rules of thumb, rules that, when followed consistently, result in diagrams that are easier to read.

9. **Remember the system responses to the actions of actors.** Your use cases should describe both how your actors interact with your system and how your system responds to those interactions. With the *Enroll in Seminar* use case, had the system not responded when the student indicated they wanted to enroll in a seminar, I suspect the student would soon become discouraged and walk away. The system was not doing anything to help the student fulfill her goals.

10. **Alternate courses of action are important.** Start with the happy path, the basic course of action, but do not forget the alternate courses as well. Alternates courses will be introduced to describe potential usage errors, as well as business logic errors and exceptions. This important information is needed to drive the design of your system, so do not forget to model it in your use cases.

11. **Do not get hung up on <<include>> and <<extend>> associations.** I am not quite sure what happened, but I have always thought the

proper use of include and extend associations, as well as uses and extends associations in older versions of the UML, were never described well. As a result, use case modeling teams had a tendency to argue about the proper application of these associations, wasting an incredible amount of time on an interesting, but minor, portion of the overall modeling technique. Use them to provide clarity to the use case model; do not go looking for chances to apply them just because you can. If the model is not clearer using <<include>> or <<extend>>, rethink using them.

12. **Use cases drive user documentation**. The purpose of user documentation is to describe how to work with your system. Each use case describes a series of actions taken by actors using your system. In short, use cases contain the information from which you can start writing your user documentation. For example, the "how to enroll in a seminar" section of your system's user documentation could be written using the *Enroll in Seminar* use case as its base.

13. **Use cases drive presentations**. Part of software development is communicating your work efforts with project stakeholders, resulting in the occasional need to give presentations. Because use cases are written from the point of view of your users, they contain valuable insight into the type of things your users are likely to want to hear about in your presentations. In other words, use cases often contain the logic from which to develop presentation scripts.

In my opinion use case modeling has received far more attention within the industry than it actually deserves. Yes, it is a useful technique but, no, it is not the be-all-and-end-all of requirements and analysis modeling. Essential use case modeling is one technique of several you can use to gather requirements, and system use case modeling is one of several analysis techniques. Do not let the marketing hype of CASE tool vendors and object-oriented consultants deceive you into thinking everything should be "use case driven." Use case modeling is merely one of many important techniques you should have in your modeling toolkit.

5.1.14 Remaining Agile

It is very easy for use case modeling to become unagile so I thought I should expand on my early advice. To prevent this from happening you need to focus on creating artifacts that are just barely good enough; they do not need to be perfect. I have seen too many projects go astray because people thought that the requirements had to be worded perfectly; in other words they are suffering from analysis paralysis. You are not writing the Magna Carta! For example, in Fig. 5.16 there are several imperfections: the alternate courses are not labeled in order (D appears after F and G) and the letters C and E are not used (they were at some point in the past but then were dropped). The use case is not perfect, yet the world has not ended. Yes, I could invest time to fix these issues but what would the value be. Nothing. Always remember AM's *maximize stakeholder investment* principle and only do things that add value. Repeat after me: "My use cases need to be just good enough. My use cases need to be just good enough. My use cases need to be just good enough." Why does this work? Because in an agile environment you will quickly move to writing code based on those requirements, you will discover that you do not fully understand what is required, you will work closely with your stakeholder to do so, and you will build something that meets their actual needs. It is software development, not documentation development.

Always be prepared to iterate. The idea of logging into the system each time you want to enroll in a seminar is clearly a bad idea. The *Enroll in Seminar* use case of Fig. 5.11 should be rewritten so that it assumes the person is already logged into the system just as *Enroll in University* of Fig. 5.16 does. We might also want to introduce a *Log-on to System* use case to support the required functionality.

Another important issue is not doing more than you need to. For example, I will only create essential use cases when fundamental architecture decisions have yet to be made. Once technology decisions have been made, which is often at the very start of a project, there is not a lot of value in using technology-independent techniques such as essential use cases and essential UIs. Instead, I will jump straight to system use cases and concrete UI models (Chapter 6).

You should also strive to keep your use case diagrams simple. For example, the small diagram of Fig. 5.15 is much easier to understand than the complex diagram of Fig. 5.8. In addition, as I indicated in Chapter 4, I prefer to draw use case diagrams on whiteboards: it is faster and just as effective, as AM's *use the simplest tools* practice recommends.

5.2 USER STORIES

User stories (Beck 2000) are one of the primary development artifacts for XP project teams. A user story is a very high-level definition of a requirement, containing just enough information so that the developers can produce a

---

- Students can purchase monthly parking passes online.
- Parking passes can be paid via credit cards.
- Parking passes can be paid via PayPal.
- Professors can input student marks.
- Students can obtain their current seminar schedule.
- Students can order official transcripts.
- Students can only enroll in seminars for which they have prerequisites.
- Transcripts will be available online via a standard browser.

FIGURE 5.19. Example user stories.

reasonable estimate of the effort to implement it. A good way to think about a user story is that it is a reminder to have a conversation with your customer (in an XP project stakeholders are called customers). As you can see in Fig. 5.19 user stories are small, much smaller than use cases. In XP a user story must be able to be implemented by two people in a single iteration/cycle; therefore if you are working in one-week iterations each user story must describe less than one week's worth of work.

Each of the statements in Fig. 5.19 represents a single user story. User stories are often written on index cards as you see in Fig. 5.20. Index cards are very easy to work with and are therefore an inclusive modeling technique. You can easily maintain a stack of prioritized requirements by moving the cards around in the stack as appropriate. You can see that the user story card includes an indication of the priority; I often use a scale of 1 to 10 with 1 being the highest priority. Other prioritization approaches are possible—priorities of high/medium/low are often used instead of numbers and some people will

---

TIP

Use Simple, Inclusive Tools and Techniques

It is possible, and in fact desirable, for stakeholders to be actively involved in modeling. However, stakeholders typically are not trained in modeling techniques nor complex modeling tools such as TogetherCC (http://www.borland.com) or ERWin (http://www.ca.com). Although one option would be to invest several months training your stakeholders in modeling tools and techniques a much easier approach is to use simple tools, such as whiteboards and paper, and simple modeling techniques (such as those described in this chapter). Simple tools and techniques are easy to teach and are therefore inclusive because anyone can work with them. Do not scare people with technology if it is not needed!

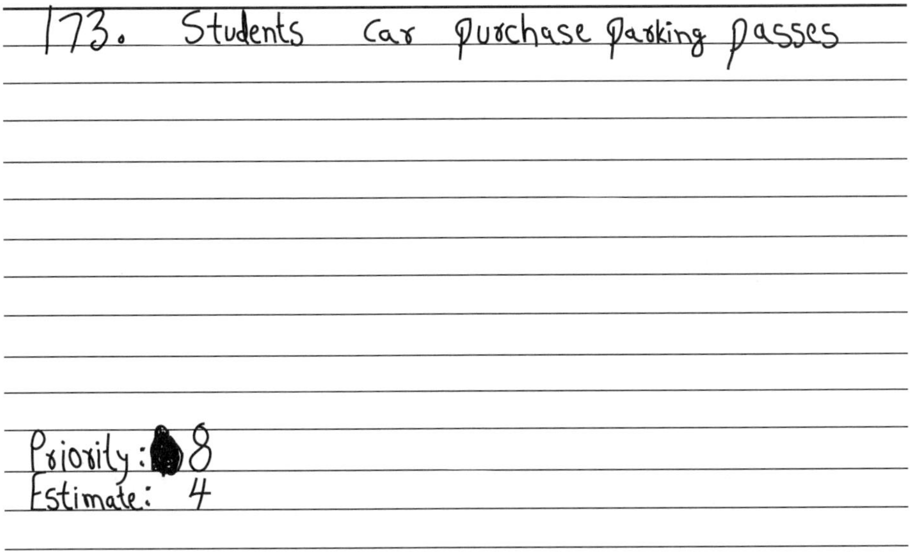

173. Students Car Purchase Parking passes

Priority: 8
Estimate: 4

FIGURE 5.20. A user story card.

even assign each card its own unique priority order number (e.g., 344, 345, etc.). Pick a strategy that works well for your team.

You also see that the priority changed at some point in the past—this is a normal thing—motivating the team to move the card to another point in the stack. The implication is that your prioritization strategy needs to support this sort of activity. My advice is to keep it simple.

The card also includes a unique identifier for the user story, in this case 173, and an estimate for the effort to implement the user story. One way to estimate is to assign user story points to each card, a relative indication of how long it will take a pair of programmers to implement the story. The team then knows that it currently takes them on average 2.5 hours per point; therefore the card in Fig. 5.20 will take around 10 hours to implement.

An important concept is that your project stakeholders write the user stories, not the developers. User stories are simple enough that people can learn to write them in a few minutes, so it makes sense that the domain experts (the stakeholders) write them.

You often create a stack of user stories during cycle 0 to identify the scope of your system. During development cycles you will identify new user stories, split existing user stories when you realize that they are too large to be implemented in single cycle, reprioritize existing stories, or remove stories that are no longer considered to be in scope. The point is that your user stories evolve over time just like other types of requirements models evolve. A significant advantage of user stories is that because they are often described using a very simple technology, index cards, and because they are small, they are very easy to work with and to evolve.

User stories can be used to describe a wide variety of requirements types. For example, in Fig. 5.19 the *Students can purchase parking passes online* user story is a usage requirement similar to a use case (Section 5.1), whereas the *Transcripts will be available online via a standard browser* is closer to a technical requirement (Chapter 7). The point is that although the name "user story" is similar to "use case," whereby user stories are simply a small version of a use case, they are in fact a different type of development artifact.

Because user stories contain so little information you will need to flesh them out a bit when you first work with them. During the estimation effort it is quite common to list programming tasks required to implement the user story. When you start to work on implementing the user story you may decide to create some rough sketches of what you are going to build, perhaps a sketch of a screen or a UML activity diagram (Chapter 9) representing the relevant business logic. User stories are merely the starting point.

5.2.1 What About System User Stories?

If there is such a thing as system use cases, why are there not system user stories as well? Because the techniques are different. Essential use cases and user stories are both requirements artifacts, although user stories are at a much higher level. Essential use cases, if you create them, are typically followed by system use cases because you want to start bringing architecture and design considerations into your work (yes, purists cringe at this concept but that is the way it works). User stories, on the other hand, are best followed by other artifacts such as screen sketches (if it is a UI-oriented story), a list of programming tasks, process models (Chatper 9), class models, data models, or even source code. In short, follow AM's practice of *apply the right artifact*.

5.3 FEATURES

A feature is a small, client-valued function expressed in the form <action>the<result> <by|for|to| . . . ><object>. As the name implies, features are an important aspect of feature-driven development (FDD) (Palmer and Felsing 2002). Figure 5.21 shows several features for the university

- Add a student to a seminar waiting list.
- Calculate fee for a parking pass.
- Calculate the average mark on a transcript.
- Display the name and address of a student on a transcript.
- Drop a student from a seminar.
- Enroll a student in a seminar.
- List the prerequisites for a seminar.
- List the seminars of a student on a transcript.
- Track number of parking passes.

FIGURE **5.21. Example features.**

system. Features are very small and typically can be implemented within a few hours.

The features in Fig. 5.21 are basically a formalized version, wording-wise at least, of traditional features. Another formalized approach is to write features as shall statements. For example, "Calculate the average mark on a transcript" would be worded "The system shall calculate the average mark on a transcript." Although the wording changes slightly in the end, features and shall statements are effectively the same thing in my experience.

Although one of the primary advantages of features is that their small size makes them easy to estimate and to implement, their size also poses a problem

TIP

Invest Time Learning Multiple Modeling Techniques

I spent a significant amount of time describing use cases, less time on user stories, and even less on features. That is because use cases are more complex than user stories, which in turn are slightly more complex than features. As a result it is harder to learn use cases as compared to user stories and features. The implication is that the simpler techniques may be better options than use cases because your project stakeholders can learn to work with them faster. Although working with user stories and features may not be an option for you if you are following a process that requires use cases, such as the RUP, it is still important to know about them because you will not always be on a RUP project. This is one of the reasons AM's *multiple models* principle is so important—the more modeling techniques you know about, the greater the chance that you will pick the right one for the situation that you are in. If you only know about the official UML models then you are doing well, but you are clearly not as effective as someone who understands more than just UML techniques.

Transcript

- Calculate the average mark on a transcript.
- List the seminars of a student on a transcript.
- Display the name and address of a student on a transcript.

Enrollment

- List the prerequisites for a seminar.
- Enroll a student in a seminar.
- Drop a student from a seminar.
- Add a student to a seminar waiting list.

Parking Passes

- Calculate fee for a parking pass.
- Track number of parking passes.

FIGURE 5.22. Feature sets.

in that one feature by itself rarely provides significant value to stakeholders. The solution is to organize features into groups called "feature sets." Figure 5.22 depicts how the features of Fig. 5.21 would be organized into three feature sets—*Transcript*, *Enrollment*, and *Parking Passes*. As you can see each feature set contains two or more related features.

From a requirements point of view features are to FDD as use cases are to the RUP and user stories are to XP—they are a primary source of requirements and the primary input into your planning efforts. However, from a size point of view feature sets are much closer conceptually to use cases. Features are estimated and prioritized in a manner similar to that of user stories. Because features are so simple to create it is common to use very simple tools—such as index cards or a spreadsheet—to capture them.

5.4 WHAT YOU HAVE LEARNED

Successful software systems are based on requirements, and because modern software systems are complex you need a wide variety of techniques to address this complexity. In this chapter you were introduced to several usage modeling techniques—essential use cases, UML use case diagrams, user stories, and features. These techniques can be used to explore how people will work with your system, a critical form of requirement.

5.5 REVIEW QUESTIONS

1. Develop a use case diagram for the bank case study described in Chapter 1.
2. Identify the three most important use cases in your diagram from Question 1 and develop essential use cases for each.
3. Justify why the three use cases that you chose in Question 2 are the most important ones.
4. Using index cards, write ten user stories for the bank case study. Play the role of a specific stakeholder and prioritize each user story. Estimate the amount of effort, in hours, that it would take you and a colleague to implement the user story (assume that the system is partially built already). On the back of the card justify, in point/bullet form, your prioritization and estimation decision.
5. Write twenty features for the bank case study.
6. Discuss the term "use case–driven," as in use case–driven testing and use case–driven development. When does this term make sense? When does it not? Can you suggest a better, more generic term? Why is it better?
7. Compare and contrast the narrative style for writing use cases with the action–response style. What are the advantages and disadvantages of each? When would or would you not use each approach?
8. Search the Web for documentation templates for use cases, actors, and UI specifications. For use case templates, compare and contrast the content they capture with what has been suggested in this book.
9. Search the Web for papers and information about usage modeling. Compare and contrast the various techniques. Formulate why differences exist among the various approaches and discuss the advantages and disadvantages of having different approaches available to you.

CHAPTER 6

User-Interface Development

To your users, the user interface is the system.

If you build an ineffective user-interface (UI) to your system then it really does not matter how good the rest of your system is: your users are going to hate what you have built for them. Effective developers understand, and then apply, at least the fundamentals of UI development. The implication is that you will need techniques (summarized in Table 6.1) to help you to explore the UI with your stakeholders, both to analyze their needs and then to design a UI that meets those needs.

This chapter discusses

- Essential UI prototyping;
- Traditional UI prototyping;
- UI flow diagrams;
- Usability;
- UI design strategies; and
- Agile stakeholder documentation.

TABLE 6.1. User-Interface Development Artifacts	
Artifact	Description
Essential UI prototype	A technology-independent prototype created using paper that can be used to identify UI requirements.
Screen/report sketch	A hand-drawn sketch depicting the layout of a major UI element such as a screen, HTML page, or report; typically used to explore the layout of the UI element.
Traditional UI prototype	A "working" user interface that appears to be the system, or at least a part of the system, to the users; often created in order to design a user interface in detail.
UI flow diagram	A diagram that depicts major UI elements and how users transition between them; used to explore the high-level usability of a system or to overview/ document the user interface of a system.

6.1 ESSENTIAL USER-INTERFACE PROTOTYPING

The UI is the portion of software with which a user directly interacts. An essential UI prototype (Constantine and Lockwood 1999) is a low-fidelity model, or prototype, of the UI for your system. It represents the general ideas behind the UI, but not the exact details. Essential UI prototypes represent UI requirements in a technology-independent manner, just as essential use case models do for behavioral requirements. An essential UI prototype is effectively the initial state—the beginning point—of the UI prototype for your system. It models UI requirements, requirements evolved through analysis and design to result in the final user interface for your system.

Two basic differences exist between essential UI prototyping and traditional UI prototyping. First, with essential UI modeling the goal is to focus on your users and their usage of the system, not system features. This is one of the reasons you want to perform essential use case modeling and essential UI prototyping in tandem: they each focus on usage. Second, your prototyping

---

TIP

Active Stakeholder Participation Is Crucial

Project stakeholders must be available to provide requirements, to prioritize them, and to make decisions in a timely manner. It is critical that your project stakeholders understand this concept and are committed to it from the beginning of any project.

---

tools are simple, including whiteboards, flip chart paper, and sticky notes. The minute you introduce electronic technology to your prototyping efforts you have most likely made a design decision about the implementation technology. If you use an HTML development tool to build a UI prototype, then you may immediately narrow your design space to the functionality supported within browsers. If you choose a Java development environment, then you may narrow your design space to Java, and if you choose a Windows-based prototyping tool, you may narrow your design space to whatever is supported on the Windows platform. Right now, you should be focused on requirements, not design; therefore, you do not currently want to use technology-based prototyping tools. Understand the problem first, and then solve it.

So how do you use sticky notes and flip chart paper to create an essential UI prototype? Let us start by defining several terms. A major UI element represents a large-grained item, potentially a screen, HTML page, or report. A minor UI element represents a small-grained item, widgets such as user input fields, menu items, lists, or static text fields such as labels. When a team is creating an essential UI prototype, it iterates between the following tasks:

1. **Explore system usage**. Your team will explore system usage via several means. First, you will likely work together on a whiteboard to discuss ideas, work on initial drawing together, and generally take advantage of the dynamic nature of whiteboards to come to an understanding quickly of the portion of the system you are discussing. For example, with the university system, you may gather around a whiteboard to make an initial drawing of what a university transcript would contain or what a seminar enrollment submission would contain. Second, as you have seen, essential use case modeling (Chapter 5) is an effective technique for understanding the behavioral requirements for your system. You will see in Chapter 8 there are several effective techniques for understanding the domain concepts your system must support.

2. **Model major UI elements.** Major UI elements, such as potential screens and reports, can be modeled using flip chart paper. I say potential because whether something is a screen or printed report is a design decision—a university transcript could be implemented as an HTML page your users view in a browser, as a paper report printed and mailed to students, or as an application screen. Each piece of flip chart paper is given a name, such as *Student Transcript* or *Seminar Enrollment Request*, and has the appropriate minor UI elements added to it as needed. Pieces of flip-chart paper have several advantages: they can be taped to a wall; they are good for working in groups because they make it easier for everyone to see and interact; they are large enough so you can put many smaller items such as sticky notes on them; you can draw on them; and they can be stored away between modeling sessions.

3. **Model minor UI elements.** Minor UI elements, such as input fields, lists, and containers (minor UI elements that aggregate other minor UI elements) are modeled using sticky notes. Constantine and Lockwood (1999) suggest using different color notes for different types of components, for example, bright colors (yellow or red) for active UI elements such as input fields versus subdued colors (white or tan) for passive interface elements such as containers. Figure 6.1 depicts an essential UI prototype to enroll students in seminars. The *Student name* sticky note is a container that includes four active elements: *First name*, *Surname*, *Middle*, and *Title*. The other sticky note represents a list of the seminars a student has taken or is currently enrolled in. Notice how each sticky note has a name that describes its purpose, but not how it is implemented. You can look at the sticky note and immediately know how it is used. Different sizes of sticky notes are used, indicating the relative size of each UI element. Also notice how the relative order of the UI elements are indicated by the order of the sticky notes: a student's title comes before his first name, then comes his middle name, and then his surname. This ordering may change during design but for now it is close enough.

   Whenever you realize you may need a minor UI element, you simply take a sticky note, label it appropriately, and place it in the general area on a major UI element where your stakeholder believe it belongs. Sometimes you identify a minor UI element that may not have a major UI element on which to place it. Don't worry. This is an iterative process, so attempt to identify an appropriate major UI element and continue. The very fact that sticky notes do not look like a real graphical UI (GUI) widget is a constant

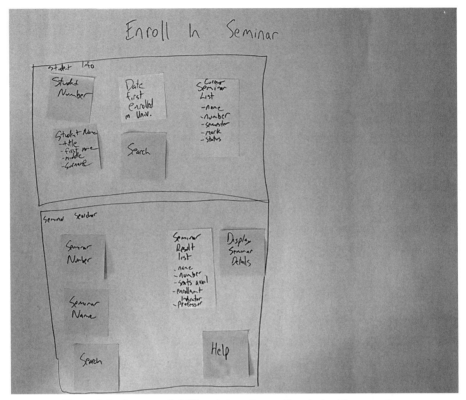

FIGURE **6.1.** An essential UI prototype to enroll a student in a seminar.

visual reminder to your team that you are building an abstract model of
the user interface and not the real thing. Each sticky note is, effectively, a
placeholder that says you need something there, but you do not yet know
yet the best way to implement it, so for now, you want to leave it open.

4. **Explore the usability of your UI**. Highly usable systems are learnable,
   they enable user productivity, their use is easy to remember, and they are
   supportable. Ensuring system usability is discussed in Section 6.4.

Let us examine Fig. 6.1 in greater detail. This prototype was created using
a standard piece of flip chart paper; you should use one piece of flip chart
paper per major UI element. Alternatively you might simply use a whiteboard
instead of the flip chart paper, although this is not as physically portable.
The name, in this case *Enroll in Seminar*, is typically written across the top.
Notice how there is two containers, which I drew on the paper to help bound

different sections of the UI. The pink sticky notes, such as *Student Number* and *Student Name*, represent input fields, whereas the yellow ones are display only. *Student Name* is interesting because it is a bit of a cheat, listing four separate data elements on the one sticky note. I will often do this when I know some things always come in a group and when I think I will need the room, which, as you can see in Fig. 6.1, I do. The blue sticky notes, such as *Search* and *Help*, represent action items. Action items are often implemented as push buttons, function keys, or "hot key" combinations, such as CTRL-SHIFT-S. All of the lists support selection of the information within them; for lists that do not support selection, you should indicate this information.

Although Fig. 6.1 represents something that will very likely be implemented as either a screen or an HTML page you can still use this technique to model UI elements that could be implemented as reports. For example, Fig. 6.2 shows how you would model a student transcript, something that could potentially be implemented as printed output.

I like to ask questions about how your essential UI prototypes would be used. For example, what should happen if a student really wants to enroll in a seminar that is currently full? Should she be given the opportunity to add herself to a waiting list? If so, how does that affect the UI? You likely need to support the capability to indicate a waiting list of X number of people already exists, as well as a way to request being added to, or removed from, the waiting list. Should obtaining detailed information about the professor teaching a seminar be possible? Should obtaining detailed information about the seminars in the prerequisite list be possible? In Fig. 6.1 you see it is possible to search for a seminar by inputting its number or name. Should searching by the department that offers the seminar be possible? Or by day of the week on which it is offered (when I was a student I had a 1.5-hour commute, so I tried to enroll in seminars that all were held on the same days)? Or by the name of the instructor teaching it? These are all interesting questions, the answers for which could potentially result in new requirements.

TIP

You Will Still Need to Explain the Techniques

Even when you use simple techniques you will still need the time to explain them to your stakeholders. Because people learn best by doing it is often a good idea to lead stakeholders through the creation of several examples.

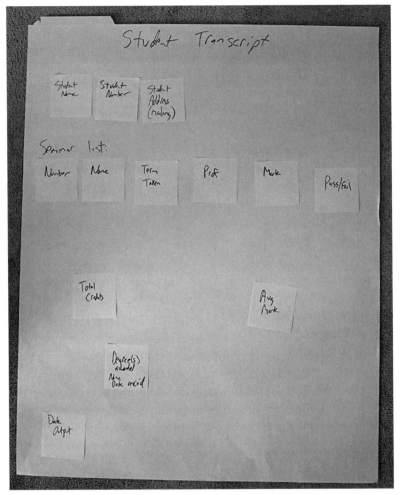

FIGURE 6.2. An essential UI prototype for a student transcript.

However, always remember that your project stakeholders are the official source of requirements, not developers. If you identify some new functionality that you think is required you need to convince your stakeholder that it is a good idea, have them prioritize it, and add the new requirement to the stack. When you are following agile modeling's practice of *active stakeholder participation* this is very easy to accomplish because your stakeholder(s) would have been part of the modeling exercise to begin with.

We have been jumping through hoops not indicating implementation decisions for the major UI elements. The reality is that you know that the seminar enrollment prototype of Fig. 6.1 is going to be implemented as either a screen

---

TIP

Create Several Models in Parallel

I perform user-interface modeling in parallel with usage models such as use cases, user stories, or features. I will iterate back and forth between the various models and evolve them together. This approach allows me to use each one for its strengths as well as to avoid analysis paralysis—when I get stuck describing a use case I will switch to modeling a major UI element that supports that use case, or better yet I will decide to start coding what I currently understand.

---

or an HTML page, so why not admit it? Furthermore, you know the student transcript prototype modeled in Fig. 6.2 will be some sort of report because all the information is display only. Granted, it could be implemented as a printed report, as an electronic file, as a browser page, as a screen, or several of these. When a major UI element contains one or more minor UI elements that permit editing, then you know it is going to be a screen or a page. When it contains no editable elements, then it will be a report. If you are going to a lot of "unnatural" effort to make your major UI elements independent of implementation technology, then you may want to loosen up a bit and distinguish between reports and screens/pages. In fact, once the architectural decision of how we are going to deploy the system has been made (see Chapter 10), I have a tendency to draw screen sketches on a whiteboard, which enables me to get a more accurate rendering of what the screen/report may look like. However, as always my advice is always to choose the most appropriate tools and techniques for your situation.

6.2 TRADITIONAL USER-INTERFACE PROTOTYPING

UI prototyping is an iterative analysis technique in which users are actively involved in the mocking-up of the UI for a system. UI prototypes have several purposes:

- As an analysis artifact that enables you to explore the problem space with your stakeholders;
- As a design artifact that enables you to explore the solution space of your system;
- As a vehicle for you to communicate the possible UI design(s) of your system; and

---

TIP

Good Things to Understand about Prototyping

Constantine and Lockwood (1999) provide valuable insight into the process of UI prototyping. First, you cannot make everything simple. Sometimes your software will be difficult to use because the problem it addresses is inherently difficult. Your goal is to make your UI as easy as possible to use, not simplistic. Second, they differentiate between the concepts of WYSIWYG, "What You See Is What You Get," and WYSIWYN, "What You See Is What You Need." Their point is a good UI fulfills the needs of the people who work with it. It is not loaded with a lot of interesting, but unnecessary, features. Third, consistency is important in your UI. Inconsistent UIs lead to less usable software, more programming, and greater support and training costs. Fourth, small details can make or break your UI. Have you ever used some software, and then discarded it for the product of a competitor because you did not like the way it prints, saves files, or some other feature you simply found too annoying to use? I have. Although the rest of the software may have been great, that vendor lost my business because a portion of its product's user interface was deficient.

- As a potential foundation from which to continue developing the system (if you intend to throw the prototype away and start over from scratch then you do not need to invest the time writing quality code for your prototype).

As you see in the activity diagram depicted in Fig. 6.3, there are four high-level steps in the UI prototyping process. The first step is to analyze the UI needs of your users. UI modeling moves from requirements definition into analysis at the point you decide to evolve all or part of your essential user-interface prototype into a traditional UI prototype. This implies you convert your hand drawings, flip chart paper, and sticky notes into something a little more substantial. You begin this process by making platform decisions, which in effect is an architectural decision (Chapter 10). For example, do you intend to deploy your system so it runs in an Internet browser, as an application with a Windows-based GUI, as a cross-platform Java application, or as a mainframe-based set of "green screens"? Different platforms lead to different prototyping tools: for a browser-based application, you need to use an HTML-development tool, whereas a Java-based application would require a Java development tool and a different approach to the user-interface design.

While you are determining the needs of your stakeholders you may decide to transform your essential UI prototypes, if you created them to begin with,

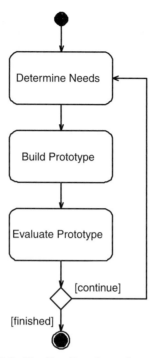

FIGURE **6.3. The iterative steps of prototyping.**

with sketches. Figure 6.4 depicts a sketch of two potential screens or HTML pages based on the essential UI prototype of Fig. 6.1. Transform really is not the right word here seeing as I am using a completely different modeling technology now (a whiteboard instead of paper) so in effect I am replacing the essential UI prototype with the sketches.

I chose to split the original prototype into two screens for cohesion issues—I prefer screens that fulfill a single purpose, in this case capturing basic student information and enrolling a student in seminars, respectively. This is arguably a design issue (there is a fine line between analysis and design, which you will cross all the time). The sketches provide a finer level of detail than the paper prototypes do; for example it is much easier to get a feel for how the screen will be implemented when you look at Fig. 6.4 than when you look at Fig. 6.1. However, the sketch is not as flexible as the paper prototype: it is hard to shift widgets from one part of the diagram to another, whereas with the paper it is very easy.

As you iterate through UI prototyping you will often discover information better captured by other artifacts. That is okay; you can follow the AM practice

---

TIP

Agile Software Development Is an Evolutionary Process

When you are analysis modeling on an agile project you will typically focus on a very small subset of the requirements at a time. For example, on an XP project you and your programming pair may work with a project stakeholder to analyze a single user story, one of hundreds, and then move on to design and implement it. This analysis effort often takes several minutes, depending on the nature of the user story, as does the design effort. Then you will spend several hours or days implementing the requirement only to start again with a new user story. Other agile approaches, such as feature-driven development (FDD) (Palmer and Felsing 2002), may invest a bit more time in analysis and design but they still work in a similar, evolutionary, manner.

---

iterate to another artifact and capture that information in the proper place. It also points to the importance of the AM practice *create several models in parallel*—you often need to work on several things at once to get the job done. Agile software development is an evolutionary process, so this is normal.

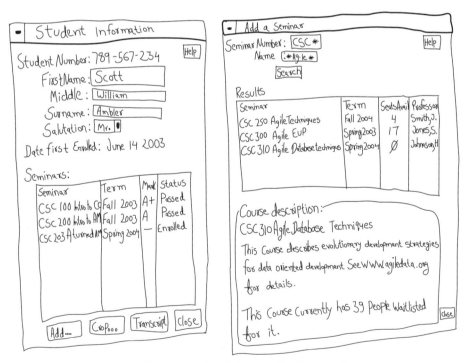

Figure 6.4. Screen sketch for enrolling in a seminar.

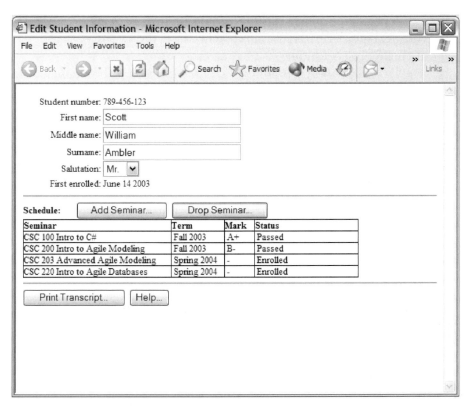

FIGURE **6.5. An HTML page for enrolling in a seminar.**

Once you understand the UI needs of your stakeholders, the next step is to actually build a prototype. Using a prototyping tool or high-level language, you develop the screens, pages, and reports needed by your users. With the UI platform selected, you can begin converting individual aspects of your essential UI prototype into your traditional UI prototype. You may want to create sketches such as you see in Fig. 6.4 or go straight to a concrete implementation, such as the HTML page depicted in Fig. 6.5. The sketches are more inclusive, and your stakeholders can be actively involved in creating them, although the actual HTML page is much closer to working code (your primary goal).

It is critical to understand that you do not need to create a prototype for the entire system. It is very common to prototype a small portion of the UI, perhaps a single screen or HTML page, before moving onto implementing it. Remember that agile developers work in an evolutionary manner—they do not need to define everything up front before moving on. Sometimes you will need to prototype a large portion of your system, perhaps as part of an envisioning exercise or perhaps even to help define the system scope so that you can obtain project funding.

After a version of the UI prototype is built, it needs to be evaluated by your stakeholders to verify that it meets their needs. Sometimes this is as easy as asking someone to spend a few minutes to look at what you have built and other times it is as complicated as scheduling a meeting so that you can demonstrate the software to a group of people. I prefer the first approach. When evaluating a UI prototype I have always found that the following questions provide me with significant feedback:

- What is good about the UI prototype?
- What is bad about the UI prototype?
- What is missing from the UI prototype?

After evaluating the prototype, you may find you need to scrap parts of it, modify parts, and even add brand-new parts. You want to stop the UI prototyping process when you find the evaluation process is no longer generating any new ideas or it is generating a small number of not-so-important ideas. Otherwise, return to exploring your stockholder's UI needs.

I have found the following tips and techniques have worked well for me in the past while UI prototyping:

1. **Work with the real users.** The best people to get involved in prototyping are those who will actually use the application when it is done. These are the people who have the most to gain from a successful implementation; these are the people who know their own needs best.

2. **Get your stakeholders to work with the prototype.** Just as if you want to take a car for a test drive before you buy it, your users should be able to take an application for a test drive before it is developed. Furthermore, by working with the prototype hands-on, they can quickly determine whether the system will meet their needs. A good approach is to ask them to work through some use case scenarios using the prototype as if it were the real system.

3. **Understand the underlying business.** You need to understand the underlying business before you can develop a prototype that will support it. In other words, you need to base your UI prototype on your requirements. The more you know about the business, the more likely it is you can build a prototype that supports it.

4. **You should only prototype features that you can actually build.** Christmas wish lists are for kids. If you cannot possibly deliver the functionality, do not prototype it.

5. **Get an interface expert to help you design it.** UI experts understand how to develop easy-to-use interfaces, whereas you probably do not. A general rule of thumb is if you have never taken a course in human factors, you probably should not be leading a UI prototyping effort.

6. **Explain what a prototype is.** The biggest complaint developers have about UI prototyping is their users say "That's great. Install it this afternoon." This happens because users do not realize more work is left to do on the system. The reason this happens is simple: From your user's point of view, a fully functional application is a bunch of screens and reports tied together by a menu. Unfortunately, this is exactly what a prototype looks like. To avoid this problem, point out that your prototype is like a Styrofoam model that architects build to describe the design of a house. Nobody would expect to live in a Styrofoam model, so why would anyone expect to use a system prototype to get his job done?

7. **Avoid implementation decisions as long as possible.** Be careful about how you name these user-interface items. Strive to keep the names generic, so you do not imply too much about the implementation technology. For example, the name *UI23 Security Log-in Screen* implies I intend to use GUI technology to implement this major UI item. Had I named it *UI23 Security Log-in* I would not have implied an implementation technology.

6.3 USER-INTERFACE FLOW DIAGRAMMING

UI prototypes are an excellent means of exploring your user interface, but unfortunately it is easy to quickly become bogged down in the details of the UI and not see the bigger picture. Consequently, you often miss high-level relationships and interactions within your system's UI. User-interface flow diagrams—also called storyboards, interface flow diagrams (Ambler 1998a), Windows navigation diagrams (Page-Jones 2000), and context-navigation maps (Constantine and Lockwood 1999)—enable you to model the high-level relationships between major user-interface elements.

In Figure 6.6 you see the start at a UI flow diagram for the university system. The boxes represent major user interface elements, modeled as you would instances/objects, and the arrows represent the possible flow between them, modeled as you would transitions in activity diagrams. For example,

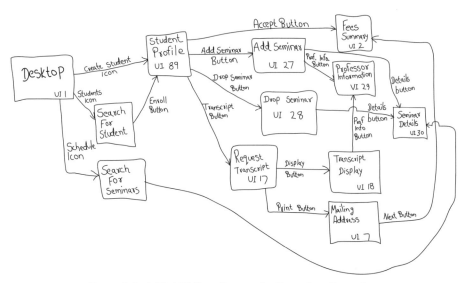

FIGURE **6.6. Initial UI flow diagram for the university system.**

when you are on the *Desktop* screen, you can use the *Students Icon* to take you to the *Search for Students* screen. Once you are there, you can either go back to the desktop (going back is always assumed) or go to the *Student Profile* screen.

UI flow diagrams are typically used for one of two purposes. First, they are used to model the interactions that users have with your software, as defined in a single use case. For example, a system use case will not only refer to several screens it also provides insight into how those screens are used. Based on this information, you can develop a UI flow diagram that reflects the behavioral view of the single use case. Second, as you see in Fig. 6.6, they enable you to gain a high-level overview of the UI for your application. This overview is effectively the combination of all the behavioral views derived from your use cases, the result being called the architectural view of your UI (Constantine and Lockwood 1999). I prefer to take the high-level overview approach, also referred to as the architectural approach, because it enables me to understand the complete UI for a system.

Because UI flow diagrams offer a high-level view of the interface of a system, you can quickly gain an understanding of how the system is expected to work. It puts you in a position where you can validate the overall flow of your application's user interface. For example, does the flow make sense? I am not so sure. Why can't I get from *Seminar Details* to *ProfessorInformation*? When you are viewing the information for a seminar, isn't it possible you might want to view the information for the instructor of that seminar? Furthermore, UI flow diagrams can be used to determine whether the user interface will be usable. If there are many boxes and many connections, it may be a signal to you that your system is too large for people to learn and understand.

Unfortunately, the UML does not yet support this sort of diagram. In the past (Ambler 2001) I have used a modified version of a UML collaboration/communication diagram, whereas others have suggested modified UML activity diagrams or even UML state machine diagrams for this. Our solutions all look something like what you see in Fig. 6.6, albeit using slightly different notations. Because the UML is not yet complete, we find ourselves in exactly the situation that the UML is meant to avoid—people using different notations to model the software that they are building. My hope is that the Object Management Group (OMG) will eventually define a profile for UI flow modeling.

6.4 Usability

An important issue to consider when developing an essential UI prototype, or any UI prototype for that matter, is usability. Constantine and Lockwood (1999) suggest five factors affect the usability of your software:

1. **Access.** Your system should be usable, without help or instruction, by a user who has knowledge and experience in the application domain, but no prior experience with the system.

2. **Efficacy.** Your system should not interfere with or impede use by a skilled user who has substantial experience with the system.

TIP

Requirements Change over Time

People often do not know what they want nor do they know how to communicate it well. Furthermore, people change their minds—it is quite common to hear stakeholders say, "now that I think about this some more . . ." or "this really isn't what I meant." Worse yet, the external environment changes: perhaps your competitors announce a new strategy or the government releases new legislation. Effective developers accept the fact that change happens and better yet they embrace change (Beck 2000).

3. **Progression.** Your system should facilitate continuous advancement in knowledge, skill, and facility, and accommodate progressive change in use as the user gains experience with the system.

4. **Support.** Your system should support the real work users are trying to accomplish by making it easier, simpler, faster, or more fun by making new things possible.

5. **Context.** Your system should be suited to the real conditions and actual environment of the operational context in which it will be used and deployed.

Why is usability important? First, by focusing primarily on use and usability instead of on features or functionality, on your users and their usage more than on user interfaces, your system can be turned into a better tool for the job that is smaller, simpler, and ultimately less expensive. Second, the best systems give pleasure and satisfaction, they make people feel good about using them, and in short, they are usable. Third, the harder a system is to use, the harder and more expensive it is to learn how to use and to support. Unusable features that are difficult to master lead to requests for changes, increasing future maintenance costs. Fourth, as users have grown accustomed to using computer applications, they have also grown less patient with them and, in particular, less patient with poorly designed software. The bar has been raised.

6.5 USER-INTERFACE DESIGN STRATEGIES

As you develop the user interface of your system you should be aware of basic UI design issues. My experience is that your best strategies are to applying common UI design principles and techniques in parallel to applying your organizations chosen UI design standards. UI design is a complex task, one that requires a wide range of skills to be successful. Although my advice to most project teams is to hire a UI design expert onto your team, the reality is few people are available with the appropriate skillset. Most decisions regarding the design of your system's UI, or affecting its usability, are made by ordinary developers. Therefore it is important that all developers have an understanding of the basics of UI design.

Let us start with the fundamentals of UI design. Constantine and Lockwood (1999) describe a collection of principles for improving the quality of your UI design. These principles are

text is worded poorly, then your interface will be perceived poorly by your users. Using full words and sentences, as opposed to abbreviations and codes, makes your text easier to understand. Your messages should be worded positively, imply that the user is in control, and provide insight into how to use the application properly. For example, which message do you find more appealing: "You have input the wrong information" or "An account number should be eight digits in length"? Furthermore, your messages should be worded consistently and displayed in a consistent place on the screen. Although the messages "The person's first name must be input" and "An account number should be input" are separately worded well, together they are inconsistent. In light of the first message, a better wording of the second message would be "The account number must be input" to make the two messages consistent.

8. **Understand the UI widgets**. You should use the right widget for the right task, helping to increase the consistency in your application and probably making it easier to build the application in the first place. The only way you can learn how to use widgets properly is to read and understand the user-interface standards and guidelines your organization has adopted.

9. **Look at other applications with a grain of salt**. Unless you know another application has been verified to follow the user-interface standards and guidelines of your organization, do not assume the application is doing things right. Although looking at the work of others to get ideas is always a good idea, until you know how to distinguish between good and bad user-interface design, you must be careful. Too many developers make the mistake of imitating the user interface of poorly designed software.

10. **Use color appropriately**. Color should be used sparingly in your applications and, if you do use it, you must also use a secondary indicator. The problem is that some of your users may be color blind and if you are using color to highlight something on a screen, then you need to do something else to make it stand out if you want these people to notice it. You also want to use colors in your application consistently, so you have a common look and feel throughout your application.

11. **Follow the contrast rule**. If you are going to use color in your application, you need to ensure that your screens are still readable. The best way to do this is to follow the contrast rule: Use dark text on light backgrounds and light text on dark backgrounds. Reading blue text on a white background

is easy, but reading blue text on a red background is difficult. The problem is not enough contrast exists between blue and red to make it easy to read, whereas there is a lot of contrast between blue and white.

12. **Align fields effectively.** When a screen has more than one editing field, you want to organize the fields in a way that is both visually appealing and efficient. I have always found the best way to do so is to left-justify edit fields—in other words, make the left-hand side of each edit field line up in a straight line, one above the other. The corresponding labels should be right-justified and placed immediately beside the field. This is a clean and efficient way to organize the fields on a screen.

13. **Expect your users to make mistakes.** How many times have you accidentally deleted some text in one of your files or in the file itself? Were you able to recover from these mistakes or were you forced to redo hours, or even days, of work? The reality is that to err is human, so you should design your user interface to recover from mistakes made by your users.

14. **Justify data appropriately.** For columns of data, common practice is to right-justify integers, decimal align floating-point numbers, and left-justify strings.

15. **Your design should be intuitable.** In other words, if your users do not know how to use your software, they should be able to determine how to use it by making educated guesses (Raskin 1994). Even when the guesses are wrong, your system should provide reasonable results from which your users can readily understand and ideally learn.

16. **Do not create busy user interfaces.** Crowded screens are difficult to understand and, hence, are difficult to use. Experimental results (Mayhew 1992) show that the overall density of the screen should not exceed 40 percent, whereas local density within groupings should not exceed 62 percent.

17. **Group things effectively.** Items logically connected should be grouped together on the screen to communicate they are connected, whereas items that have nothing to do with each other should be separated. You can use white space between collections of items to group them and/or you can put boxes around them to accomplish the same thing.

For more information about object-oriented user interface (OOUI) design, I suggest reading *Building Object Applications That Work* (Ambler 1998a).

6.6 AGILE STAKEHOLDER DOCUMENTATION

User documentation is part of the user interface for an application and well-written user documentation is no excuse for a poorly designed user interface (Mayhew 1992). My experience confirms these beliefs—because modern systems are complex, your users often require significant documentation that describes how to use them effectively. Because different types of users have different needs, you also discover you need to develop several kinds of user documentation. Don't worry: it is not as hard as it sounds, particularly if you have developed the models this book recommends.

Weiss (1991) points out the need for different kinds of manuals to support the needs of different types of users. The lesson to be learned is one manual does not fit all. He suggests a tutorial manual for novice users, a user manual for intermediate users, and a reference manual for expert users. Tourniaire and Farrell (1997) also recommend you develop a support user's guide describing the support services provided to your user community, a document typically less than a page in length.

When appropriate, your user documentation should include a description of the skills needed to use your system. For example, your users may require training in your business domain or in basic computer skills, such as using a mouse. This information is needed to develop training plans for users and by support engineers when they are attempting to determine the source of a problem. Quite often, support engineers will receive support calls where the solution is to send the user for additional training.

What were you trying to accomplish the last time you looked at a user manual? You were likely trying to determine how to accomplish a task, a task that probably would be described via a use case or activity diagram in your analysis model. My experience is the easiest way to write your user documentation is to start with the models that describe how your users will work with your system: your use case model and your activity diagrams. Use cases describe how users will interact with your system and, as you saw in Chapter 5, UML activity diagrams are often used to describe high-level business logic. This is exactly the type of information your user documentation should reflect.

Start your user manual with a description of the system itself, probably several paragraphs, information you likely have in your supplementary specification. Then add a section describing any high-level business processes, processes where you should have documented the logic for using a UML activity diagram. For large systems, you may find you have a section for each UML package within your use case model or even a separate user manual.

Then, for each use case, add an appropriate subsection describing it; the use case text will drive the body of that section. You will likely want to combine steps into paragraphs to make your documentation more readable. Wherever you reference a UI element, you may decide to include a relevant picture of that portion of your user interface (my suggestion is to wait until you have baselined your user-interface design before investing the time to generate the pictures). You may also decide to replace references to business rules with their descriptions to help increase your user's understanding of how the system actually works. Although many in the industry call this a use case—driven approach to writing user documentation, it really is a model-driven approach because your use cases simply are not sufficient for this purpose.

Tutorials are developed in a manner similar to that of user manuals, although a few differences exist. First, tutorials focus on the most critical uses of the system, whereas a user manual should focus on the entire system. Second, tutorials should have a more explicit focus on learning a product, so they will include more detailed use instructions than a user manual might. The assumption is anyone using a tutorial likely knows little about the system and, therefore, needs more help, whereas someone using a user manual is probably familiar with the system itself, but needs help with a specific aspect of it.

Your reference manual, because it has a slightly different purpose, is generally driven by your user-interface model, instead of your use cases and activity diagrams. I generally include an overview of the system, sections for each major portion of your system, and subsections describing the major user-interface elements. The subsections should describe the purpose of the relevant screen/report/page and how to work with it.

You will often hear advice within the software industry to write your documentation before you write you code. Although this is a reasonably good

---

TIP

Hire a Technical Writer

Writing is hard and writing good user documentation is even harder. It takes a lot of effort and significant skill to do well—the type of skill technical writers have. If possible, hire a technical writer to work with you to produce your user documentation. This will improve the quality of your documentation and, hence, the quality of your overall user interface. Hiring a technical writer will also free you to focus on other development activities, such as modeling, coding, and testing.

practice, why do people give this advice? I believe the motivation is that writing user documentation first forces you to think about how your system will be used before you start to build it. My advice is different: invest the time to understand your system by developing requirements for it, analyzing it, and designing it, and then allow this understanding to drive the development of your source code and your user documentation. I have worked on several systems where we developed the user documentation in parallel with the source code, not before it, and it worked out well.

6.7 WHAT YOU HAVE LEARNED

In this chapter you learned several techniques to explore the user interface of a system, including essential user-interface prototyping to explore UI requirements, traditional UI prototyping for the analysis of those requirements and for the design of the UI, and UI flow diagramming for exploring usability issues. You also learned the fundamental concepts behind usability as well as a collection of techniques for creating usable screens and reports.

6.8 REVIEW QUESTIONS

1. Develop essential user-interface prototypes to support one or more of your essential use cases developed in Chapter 5. Update your essential use cases to reflect your improved understanding of the system based on your essential user-interface prototyping efforts.
2. Choose a user-interface platform, such as HTML or Microsoft Windows, and transform your essential user-interface prototypes into traditional user-interface prototypes.
3. Discuss the advantages and disadvantages of essential UI prototyping with traditional UI prototyping. When would you use each technique?
4. Develop UI flow diagrams for system use cases that you developed for the bank case study. Create one diagram for each use case, then create an overall diagram for all of them.
5. Choose an application or development tool that you regularly use. Identify five potential user-interface design flaws with it. Justify why you think that they are flaws and propose.
6. Search the Web for papers and information about user-interface modeling. Compare and contrast the various techniques. Formulate why differences

exist between the various approaches and discuss the advantages and disadvantages of having different approaches available to you.

7. For the platform you chose in Question 2, search the Web for user-interface design guidelines applicable to it. How comprehensive are those guidelines? Identify one potential issue that the guidelines do not address, or you do not agree with, and contact the original author with your suggestion.

CHAPTER 7

Supplementary Requirements

The true goal of requirements engineering is not to create documentation; it is to convey ideas from project stakeholders to developers.

Modern-day businesses are complex, as are the systems that support them. To make matters worse, there are various aspects to the complexities. For example there are business complexities that you need to understand, technical complexities, even constraints imposed on you by outside authorities. The implication is that you need techniques with which to explore these complexities, techniques that produce something that I will call "supplementary requirements" in this book. Table 7.1 summarizes the supplementary requirements artifacts described in this chapter.

This chapter discusses

- Business rules;
- Technical requirements;
- Constraints;
- Object constraint language (OCL);
- Glossaries; and
- Supplementary specifications.

TABLE 7.1. Supplementary Requirements Artifacts	
Artifact	Description
Business rules	A business rule defines or constrains one aspect of your business that is intended to assert business structure or influence the behavior of your business. Business rules often supplement usage or user interface requirements.
Constraints	A constraint is a restriction on the degree of freedom you have in providing a solution. Constraints will supplement other development artifacts, in particular architecture and design-oriented models.
Glossary	A glossary is a collection of definitions that supplements a wide range of development artifacts by defining a common business and technical vocabulary.
Technical requirements	A technical requirement pertains to the technical aspects that your system must fulfill, such as performance-related, reliability, and availability issues. Technical requirements are often the main driver of your technical architecture (Chapter 10).

7.1 BUSINESS RULES

A business rule defines or constrains one aspect of your business that is intended to assert business structure or influence the behavior of your business. Business rules often focus on access control issues; for example, professors are allowed to input and modify the marks of the students taking the seminars they instruct, but not the marks of students in other seminars. Business rules may also pertain to business calculations, for example, how to convert a percentage mark (for example, 91 percent) that a student receives in a seminar into a letter grade (for example, A-). Some business rules focus on the policies of your organization; perhaps the university policy is to expel for one year anyone who fails more than two courses in the same semester.

Figure 7.1 summarizes several examples of business rules. Notice how each business rule has a unique identifier. My convention is to use the format of BR#, but you are free to set your own numbering approach. The unique

> ### TIP
> ### You Need Multiple Models
>
> The requirements for a system are typically complex, dealing with a wide variety of issues. Because every model has its strengths and weaknesses no one single model is sufficient for your needs; therefore you will need several types of models to get the job done.

identifier enables you to refer easily to business rules in other development artifacts, such as class models and use cases. You saw an example of this in the use cases of Chapter 5.

In some situations you will discover that business rules can be described very simply, perhaps with a single sentence. In other situations this is not the case. Figure 7.2 presents one way to fully document BR123. There are several sections in this figure:

- **Name.** The name should give you a good idea about the topic of the business rule.

- **Description.** The description defines the rule exactly. Although I used text to describe this rule it is quite common to see diagrams such as flow charts or UML activity diagrams (Chapter 6) used to describe an algorithm. Other options include business rule languages such as object constraint language (OCL) (http://www.omg.org), the ILOG rules language (http://www.ilog.com), or business rules markup language (BRML) (http://xml.coverpages.org/brml.html). As agile modeling (Chapter 4) suggests, *apply the right artifact* for your situation.

- **Example (optional).** An example of the rule is presented to help clarify it.

- BR123 Tenured professors may administer student grades.
- BR124 Teaching assistants who have been granted authority by a tenured professor may administer student grades.
- BR177 Table to convert between numeric grades and letter grades.
- BR245 All master's degree programs must include the development of a thesis.

Figure 7.1. **Example business rules (summarized).**

Name:	Tenured professors may administer student grades
Identifier:	BR123
Description:	Only tenured professors are granted the ability to initially input, modify, and delete grades students receive in the seminars that they and they only instruct. They may do so only during the period a seminar is active.
Example:	Dr. Bruce, instructor of "Biology 301 Advanced Uses of Gamma Radiation," may administer the marks of all students enrolled in that seminar, but not those enrolled in "Biology 302 Effects of Radiation on Arachnids," which is taught by Dr. Peters.
Source:	University Policies and ProceduresDoc ID: U1701Publication date: August 14, 2000
Related rules:	BR12 Qualifying for TenureBR65 Active Period for SeminarsBR200 Modifying Final Student Grades
Revision History:	Defined March 2, 2001, by D. Prince. Updated October 10, 2001, by G. Stacy to reference-related rule BR200.

FIGURE 7.2. A fully documented business rule.

- **Source (optional).** The source of the rule is indicated so it may be verified (it is quite common that the source of a rule is a person, often one of your project stakeholders, or a team of people).

- **Related rules (optional).** A list of related business rules, if any, is provided to support traceability between rules.

- **Revision history (optional).** An indication of the date a change was made, the person who made the change, and a description of the change.

Figure 7.2 is clearly a lot wordier than most project teams need. A more agile approach would be to simply write the name of the business rule, the business rule number, and the description on an index card and leave it at that. Or you might want to get a little fancier and type the business rule into a Wiki page (http://www.wiki.org) or a word processor. Remember to keep your models as simple as possible.

Business rules are identified in the normal course of requirements gathering and analysis. While you are usage modeling, perhaps with use cases or user

---

TIP

You Only Need a Subset of the Models

When you fix something at home you will only use a few of the tools, such as a screwdriver and a wrench, in your tool box. The next time you fix something you will use different tools. Even though you have multiple tools available, you will not use them all at any given time. It is the same thing with software development; although you have several techniques in your "intellectual toolbox" you will only use a subset on any given project.

---

stories, you will often identify business rules. A rule of thumb is if something defines a calculation or operating principle of your organization then it is likely a good candidate to be documented as a business rule. You want to separate business rules out from your other requirements artifacts because they may be referred to within those artifacts several times. For example, BR129 was referenced by the *Enroll Student in Seminar* use case and likely would be referenced by your class models (Chapter 6) and perhaps even your source code. However, if you have only a handful of business rules or use cases, you may choice to document them right in the use cases. A rule of thumb: start out including them in the use cases until it becomes obvious, or painful, to do so. This may be because the sheer number of business rules is dominating the use case or because the same business rule is referenced in two or more use cases.

A good business rule is cohesive: in other words, it describes one, and only one, concept. By ensuring that business rules are cohesive, you make them easier to define and increase the likelihood they will be reused (every time one of your artifacts refers to a business rule, even other business rules, it is effectively being reused). Unfortunately, because business rules should focus on one issue, you often must identify a plethora of rules.

Ross (2003) describes several basic principles of what he calls "the business rule approach." He believes that rules should

- Be written and made explicit;
- Be expressed in plain language;
- Exist independent of procedures and workflows (e.g., multiple models);
- Build on facts, and facts should build on concepts as represented by terms (see Section 7.5, Glossaries);
- Guide or influence behavior in desired ways;
- Be motivated by identifiable and important business factors;

TIP

Use the Terminology of Your Stakeholders

Do not force artificial, technical jargon onto your project stakeholders. They are the ones doing the modeling and they are the ones the system is being built for; therefore, you should use their terminology to model the system. As Constantine and Lockwood (1999) say, avoid geek-speak.

- Be accessible to authorized parties (e.g., collective ownership);
- Be single sourced;
- Be specified directly by those people who have relevant knowledge (e.g., active stakeholder participation); and
- Be managed.

Many business rules can actually be thought of as constraints (see Section 7.3), and in fact constraints can apply to either technical or business issues. In the UML business rules are often described on diagrams using OCL (Warner and Kleppe 1999), which can add to people's confusion regarding the differences between the two concepts. Don't worry about it. The important thing is to identify and understand the requirement, not categorize it.

7.2 TECHNICAL REQUIREMENTS

A technical requirement pertains to the technical aspects that your system must fulfill, such as performance-related issues, reliability issues, and availability issues. These types of requirements are often called service-level requirements or nonfunctional requirements (I do not like that term as it makes them sound like requirements that will not work). Examples of technical requirements are presented in Fig. 7.3. As you can see, technical requirements are summarized in a manner similar to that of business rules: they have a name and a unique identifier (my convention is to use the format TR#, where TR stands for technical requirement). You document technical requirements in the same manner as business rules, including a description, an example, a source, references to related technical requirements, and a revision history.

I am a firm believer that you should minimize the number of purely technical requirements. Technology changes quickly and often requirements based on technology change just as quickly. An example of a pure technical requirement is that an application be written in Java or must run on the XYZ

- TR34 The system shall be available 99.99 percent of the time for any 24-hour period.
- TR78 A seminar search will occur within less than three seconds 95 percent of the time.
- TR79 A seminar search will occur within no more than ten seconds 99 percent of the time.

FIGURE **7.3. Potential technical requirements for the university system.**

computer. Whenever you have a requirement based purely on technology, try to determine the real underlying business needs being expressed. To do this, keep asking why your application must meet a requirement. For example, when asked why your application must be written in Java, the reply was it must run on the Internet. When asked why it must run on the Internet, the reply was your organization wants to take orders for its products and services on the Internet. The real requirement is to sell things to consumers at their convenience; one technical solution to this need (and a good one) is to write that component in Java that can be accessed via the Internet. A big difference exists between having to write the entire application in Java and having to support the sales of some products and services to consumers over the Internet.

Many technical requirements can actually be thought of as constraints (see Section 7.3) and in fact constraints can apply to either technical or business issues.

7.3 CONSTRAINTS

A constraint is a restriction on the degree of freedom you have in providing a solution (Leffingwell and Widrig 2000). Constraints are effectively global requirements, such as limited development resources or a decision by senior

TIP

Requirements Must Be Prioritized

Your project stakeholders must prioritize the requirements, enabling you to constantly be working on the most important requirements and thus provide the most value for their IT investment.

- C24 The system will work on our existing technical infrastructure—no new technologies will be introduced.
- C56 The system will only use the data contained in the existing corporate database.
- C73 The system shall be available 99.99 percent of the time for any 24-hour period.
- C76 All master's degree programs must include the development of a thesis.

FIGURE 7.4. Potential constraints for the university system.

management that restricts the way you develop a system. Constraints can be economic, political, technical, or environmental and pertain to your project resources, schedule, target environment, or to the system itself. Figure 7.4 presents several potential constraints for the university system. Like business rules and technical requirements, constraints are documented in a similar manner.

An interesting thing about Fig. 7.4 is that it contains two constraints, C73 and C76, which were previously identified as a technical requirement and a business rule, respectively. Constraints can be a little confusing because of their overlap with business rules and technical requirements. Don't worry about it. The important thing is that you have identified the requirement. If you happen to miscategorize it as a constraint instead of a business rule that is perfectly okay; the world is not going to end as a result (unless of course you are working on a nuclear missile guidance system). I would not identify the same requirement as both a business rule and a constraint—that would be busy work—but I would not waste any time arguing over whether something is a constraint or another type of requirement.

As with business rules, you identify constraints as you are developing other artifacts, such as your use case model and user-interface model.

7.4 OBJECT CONSTRAINT LANGUAGE (OCL)

One way to describe business rules, technical requirements, or constraints is via the object constraint language. The OCL is a formal language similar to structured English to express side-effect-free constraints within UML models (Warner and Kleppe 1999). OCL can appear on any UML diagram or in the supporting documentation describing a diagram, such as business rule definitions. OCL can be used for a wide variety of purposes, including specifying the invariants of classes, preconditions and postconditions on operations, and constraints on operations. The reality is that a graphical model, such as a UML class diagram, is not sufficient for a precise and unambiguous specification. You must describe additional constraints about the objects in the model, constraints defined in your supplementary specification.

I rarely use OCL when I am modeling. First, few people know how to read OCL, let alone write it, so you are restricting the audience of your models when you use it. Second, it is complex. OCL statements are depicted on UML diagrams in the format "{constraint description}," where the constraint description may be in any format, including predicate calculus. I personally find that free-form text, along the lines of Fig. 7.2, is far more effective. Third, if I want to describe rules in such a way that I can generate working software from them I will use a real programming language such as Java or C# to do it.

The OCL was an interesting concept but it has not been adopted by the industry. Because it shows no signs of being adopted any time soon, in my opinion it is not worth the effort to learn.

7.5 GLOSSARIES

A glossary is a collection of definitions of terms, an example of which is presented at the back of this book. Every company has its own specialized jargon, and you need to understand it if you want to communicate effectively with the experts with which you working.

You may want to include both technical and business terms in your glossary. Although you may understand what terms such as XP, C#, J2EE, and application server all mean your stakeholders likely do not. Similarly your stakeholders may understand what business terms such as convocation, grant, and transcript mean, but some developers may not. A glossary that includes

---

TIP

Reuse Existing Resources

Your organization may already have an existing glossary in place; if so then reuse appropriate terms from it. Often your industry will already have a specialized dictionary describing common terms that you may want to adopt as well.

both the relevant technical and business terminology goes a long way to improving the communications between developers and users—if you do not understand each other's language you cannot communicate effectively.

The best advice that I can give about creating a glossary is to be realistic. You are not *Webster's*—you do not have to get the definitions perfect, they just need to be good enough. Furthermore, dictionaries have multiple definitions for most words so do not be afraid to do the same. Ideally you want a single definition; realistically it often is not worth the effort to argue it out if it is even possible to come to agreement.

An important issue with glossaries, with all artifacts for that matter, is to make them available to people. This is one of the reasons AM includes the *display models publicly* practice. You might want to consider documenting your glossary as a single HTML page that everyone can access and hopefully edit (remember the practice of *collective ownership*). Another option, particularly if editing a major concern, is to use a Wiki (http://www.wiki.org).

7.6 SUPPLEMENTARY SPECIFICATIONS

A supplementary specification is a RUP document that contains requirements not contained directly in your use cases. This often includes business rules, technical requirements, and constraints. The best way to think of a supplementary specification is that it is a container into which you place other requirements. In my opinion supplementary specifications are not models in their own right but instead are the documentation of models.

7.7 WHAT YOU HAVE LEARNED

Successful software systems are based on requirements, and because modern software systems are complex you need a wide variety of techniques to address this complexity. In this chapter you were introduced to several requirements modeling techniques—business rules, constraints, and technical requirements. You also saw how these techniques could be applied in an agile manner, by working closely with your stakeholders (some techniques can be applied by the stakeholders themselves), and by taking an iterative and incremental approach to development.

In addition to understanding the technical aspects of requirements gathering, the philosophical aspects are also critical. You learned that your project stakeholders are the best source of requirements because they are the experts. You also learned that requirements have nothing to do with the development paradigm you are following—any of these techniques could be used with object technology, component technology, structured technology, or any other technologies.

7.8 REVIEW QUESTIONS

1. Identify the three most important business rules referenced by your use cases in Question 2 of Chapter 5 and describe them appropriately.
2. What were the benefits of developing the three models of Questions 1 through 3 of Chapter 5 in parallel? Discuss, from the point of view of the quality of the requirements, their consistency and their reliability.
3. Discuss the term "supplementary specification." Is it a good name? Discuss the subconscious implications of the name.
4. How are essential use cases, essential user-interface prototypes, and business rules interrelated? Discuss from the point of view of the changes you made to the three models from Questions 1 through 3 of Chapter 5. What are the strengths and weaknesses of each technique? Do you need all of them?
5. Compare and contrast small development groups of three or four people versus larger development groups of ten to twenty people. Take into consideration management issues, communication issues, logistical issues, decision-making ability, group dynamics, skills, and knowledge. What do you believe is the ideal size for a development team? Why?
6. With several other people, go through a brainstorming session to identify nonfunctional requirements and constraints for the university system. Identify potential sources for these requirements, such as roles within the organization (the Dean, an instructor, a registrar, and so on) and documents.
7. Identify the categories of tools, such as requirements management systems and computer-aided software engineering (CASE) tools, which you could potentially use during requirements gathering. For each category, present three examples of them in the marketplace: one should be an open-source software (OSS) tool and one should be a commercial package. Identify how each category is used and the potential skills required of the people using them.

CHAPTER 8

Conceptual Domain Modeling

You need to understand the fundamental concepts within your problem domain.

Your requirements artifacts, although effective for understanding what your users want to have built, is not as effective at understanding what will be built. You need techniques to help you to flesh out the details of what needs to be built. Conceptual domain modeling, also called conceptual modeling or domain modeling, is the task of discovering the entity types that represent the things and concepts, and their relationships, pertinent to your problem space. Another way to look at it is that conceptual models are used to depict your detailed understanding of the problem space for your system. For example, the conceptual model for a university might include entity types such as student, instructor, tenured professor, seminar, transcript, and registrar. As you can imagine, nouns and noun phrases within your requirements models are good candidates for concepts that should be included in your conceptual model. Many of the entities that appear in your conceptual model will also appear in your glossary (Chapter 7). Conceptual modeling is often referred to as domain modeling—some people will actually distinguish between the two types of modeling although I do not.

Why am I using the term entity type instead of class? Because you have several very good options available to you when you are conceptual modeling.

TIP

Essential Reading

The book *Domain Driven Design: Tackling Complexity in the Heart of Software* by Eric Evans (2004) describes a design pattern language that "starts" with conceptual domain modeling.

Two, class responsibility collaborator (CRC) models and UML class diagrams are object-oriented modeling artifacts. Although you can make a very good argument (Hay 2003) that object-oriented artifacts bring technology issues into your analysis efforts, the reality is that most modern systems use object technology and therefore in my mind the point is moot. Two other options, object-role model (ORM) diagrams and logical data models (LDMs), are not object-oriented models. ORM diagrams, as you will see, are arguably technology independent, whereas LDMs lean towards data-oriented technologies. Table 8.1 summarizes the various models used for conceptual domain modeling.

Let us explore the various types of models that you might want to use for conceptual domain modeling:

- Robustness diagrams;
- Object role model (ORM) diagrams;
- Class responsibility collaborator (CRC) models;
- UML class diagrams;
- Logical data models (LDMs);
- Analysis patterns; and
- UML object diagrams.

8.1 ROBUSTNESS DIAGRAMS

In *Use Case Driven Object Modeling with UML* Doug Rosenberg and Kendall Scott (1999) describe a technique called robustness analysis, something the rational unified process (RUP) refers to as use case analysis (IBM 2003). The basic idea is that you can analyze the steps of a use case to validate the business logic within it and to ensure that the terminology is consistent with other use cases that you have previously analyzed. In other words, you can use them to ensure that your use cases are sufficiently robust to represent the usage requirements for the system you are building. Another use is to identify

TABLE 8.1. Conceptual Domain Modeling Artifacts	
Model	Description
Class diagram	A unified modeling language (UML) diagram that shows the classes within your problem domain (or a portion thereof) and the associations between them.
CRC model	A collection of CRC cards that model all or part of a system. A CRC card is a standard index card that has been divided into three sections, one indicating the name of the class the card represents, one listing the responsibilities of the class, and the third listing the names of the other classes that this one collaborates with to fulfill its responsibilities.
Logical data models (LDMs)	A model depicting domain entities and the relationships between those entities.
Object diagram	A UML diagram that depicts objects and their relationships at a point in time, typically a special case of either a class diagram or a communication diagram.
Object role model (ORM) diagram	A diagram that depicts objects (entity types), the relationships (fact types) between them, the roles that the objects play in those relationships, constraints within the problem domain, and, optionally, examples (called fact-type tables).
Robustness diagram	A simplified UML communication/collaboration diagram (Chapter 11) that uses graphical symbols to represent interface/boundary, process/control, and entity classes. Robustness diagrams are very useful for identifying domain concepts captured within usage requirements (Chapter 5).

potential objects or object responsibilities to support the logic called out in the use case, effectively acting as a bridge to other diagrams such as UML sequence diagrams (Chapter 11) and UML class diagrams (Section 8.4).

A robustness diagram is a simplified UML communication/collaboration diagram (Chapter 11) that use the graphical symbols depicted in Fig. 8.1. Robustness diagrams depict several types of concepts:

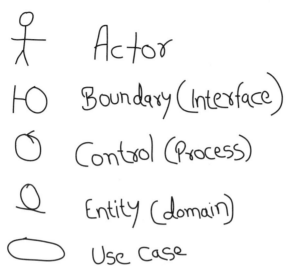

FIGURE 8.1. Visual stereotypes used on robustness diagrams.

- **Actors.** This is the same concept as actors on a UML use case diagram.

- **Boundary elements.** These represent software elements such as screens, reports, HTML pages, or system interfaces that actors interact with. Also called interface elements.

- **Control elements.** These serve as the glue between boundary elements and entity elements, implementing the logic required to manage the various elements and their interactions; they are also known as process elements or simply as controllers. It is important to understand that you may decide to implement controllers within your design as something other than objects—many controllers are simple enough to be implemented as a method of an entity or boundary class, for example.

- **Entity elements.** These are entity types typically found in your conceptual model. Examples include *Student* and *Seminar*.

- **Use cases (optional).** Because use cases can invoke other use cases, you need to be able to depict this on your robustness diagrams.

Figure 8.2 shows a whiteboard sketch of a robustness diagram representing the logic contained in the *Enroll in University* use case of Fig. 8.3. To create the sketch I merely followed the logic of the use case and applied the following heuristics:

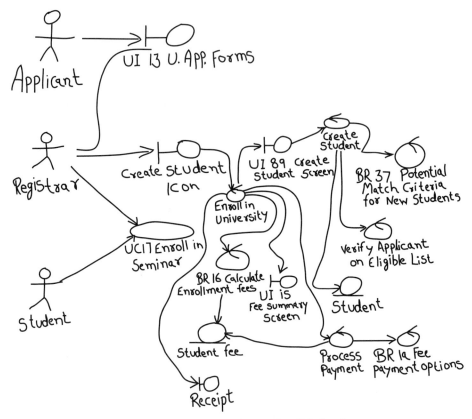

FIGURE 8.2. A robustness diagram for the *Enroll in Seminar* use case.

- Add a boundary element for each major user-interface element such as a screen or a report. Although some very detailed use cases will describe how actors work with buttons and edit fields I prefer to stay at a higher level and not show these details. I did, however, choose to show the *Create Student Icon* on the diagram although in hindsight this boundary class would be better labeled *Desktop*. I chose not to update the diagram because I follow the agile modeling (AM) practice *update only when it hurts* and it is not important enough to fix this minor issue. These classes are likely to appear on your interface flow diagrams (Chapter 6) if you choose to create them.

- Add a controller to manage the overall process of the scenario being modeled. In Fig. 8.2 this is the *Enroll in University* element. As you can see, it provides the glue that keeps the diagram together. In your design

Name: Enroll in University

Identifier: UC 19.

Description:
Enroll someone in the university.

Preconditions:
The Registrar is logged into the system.
The Applicant has already undergone initial checks to verify that they are eligible to enroll.

Postconditions:
The Applicant will be enrolled in the university as a student if they are eligible.

Basic Course of Action:

1. An applicant wants to enroll in the university.
2. The applicant hands a filled out copy of form *U113 University Application Form* to the registrar. [Alternate Course A: Forms Not Filled Out]
3. The registrar visually inspects the forms.
4. The registrar determines that the forms have been filled out properly. [Alternate Course B: Forms Improperly Filled Out]
5. The registrar clicks on the *Create Student* icon.
6. The system displays *U189 Create Student Screen.*
7. The registrar inputs the name, address, and phone number of the applicant. [Extension Point: *UC34 Perform Security Check.* Applicable to Step 17]
8. The system determines that the applicant does not already exist within the system according to *BR37 Potential Match Criteria for New Students.* [Alternate Course F: Students Appears to Exist within the System].
9. The system determines that the applicant is on the eligible applicants list. [Alternate Course G: Person Is Not Eligible to Enroll]
10. The system adds the applicant to its records. The applicant is now considered to be a student.
11. The registrar helps the student to enroll in seminars via the use case *UC 17 Enroll in Seminar.*
12. The system calculates the required initial payment in accordance to *BR16 Calculate Enrollment Fees.*
13. The system displays *U115 Fee Summary Screen.*

FIGURE 8.3. The *Enroll in University* use case.

14. The registrar asks the student to pay the initial payment in accordance to *BR19 Fee Payment Options*.
15. The student pays the initial fee. [Alternate Course D: The Student Cannot Pay at This Time]
16. The system prints a receipt.
17. The registrar hands the student the receipt.
18. The use case ends.

Alternate Course A: . . . .

FIGURE 8.3 (*continued*)

this element could very likely be implemented as a class, one or more operations, or some sort of workflow engine.

- **Add a controller for each business rule.** This helps to make the business rules explicit on your diagram. Some people will not model the business rules at all, keeping their diagrams simple, but as a result, they miss very important information in their diagrams. Try both ways and then choose the approach that works best for you.

- **Add a controller for activities that involve several other elements.** An example of this is the *Create Student* element, which interacts with a business rule as well as the *Student* entity.

- **Add an entity for each business concept.** The *Student* and *Student Fee* classes are examples of this. These elements are likely to appear on your conceptual model if you chose to create one.

- **Add a use case whenever one is included in the scenario.** I chose to depict the invocation of the *Enroll in Seminar* use case using standard UML notation for use cases. Another option is to depict the use case as a controller, although in my experience this is not as clear to project stakeholders. Remember the AM principle *content is more important than representation* and do whatever is best for your situation.

By drawing this robustness diagram we quickly gain a sense for the work that we need to do to implement this use case because it helps to visualize the potential elements we will have to build. The boundary elements will help to bridge your use cases to your user-interface development (Chapter 6) and your legacy system analysis (Chapter 14) efforts. Some of those classes are entity elements, things that should definitely appear on a conceptual model. The controllers are much closer to design concepts, so robustness diagrams help to bridge to your design.

How do you keep robustness diagrams agile? My experience is that the following AM practices are very relevant:

- **Active stakeholder participation.** Robustness diagrams can be a very good technique, in some situations, to perform analysis with your stakeholders. As you can see in Fig. 8.2 robustness diagrams are very straightforward and easy to draw, making them an inclusive modeling technique.

- **Discard temporary models.** Robustness diagrams are typically drawn on a whiteboard in order to analyze the logic of a use case. Once the use case has been improved the robustness diagram will be kept around long enough to act as a bridge to the next development step, see below, then erased.

- **Apply the right artifacts.** Some modelers, including myself, will stop creating robustness diagrams when their stakeholders get used to making the logical jump from use cases to other development artifacts such as sequence diagrams. In other words, robustness diagrams are used to help train stakeholders to think abstractly and then abandoned as a technique once this goal is reached. Other modelers will continue to use robustness diagrams because the models still add significant value to their overall efforts.

What is next after robustness diagrams? Robustness diagrams often act as a bridge from use cases to other models such as UML sequence diagrams (Chapter 11), which represent the detailed design logic required to support the use case. It is also common to focus on the user interface for your system, perhaps via prototyping or better yet just getting right into the "real" coding, because robustness diagrams explicitly include boundary/interface elements. Furthermore, because robustness diagrams depict major business entities it is quite common to use them as an input to your conceptual/domain modeling efforts.

8.2 OBJECT ROLE MODEL (ORM) DIAGRAMS

ORM diagrams, thoroughly described in *Information Modeling and Relational Databases* (Halpin 2001) at http://www.orm.net, are in my opinion an incredibly effective way to explore domain concepts with your stakeholders. An ORM diagram depicts objects (entity types), the relationships (fact types)

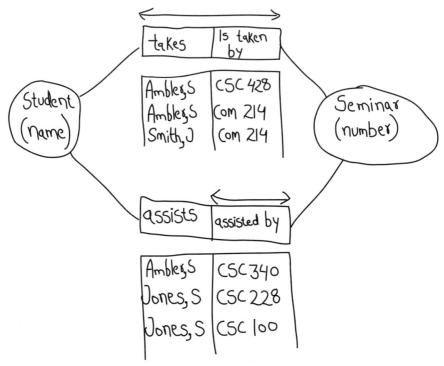

FIGURE 8.4. Simple ORM diagram.

between them, the roles that the objects play in those relationships, constraints within the problem domain, and, optionally, examples (called fact-type tables).

Figure 8.4 depicts a simple example of an ORM diagram. The ovals represent entity types (Halpin uses the term object although ORM diagrams can be used to model systems that do not use object technology at all) and the rectangles roles that the objects play in relationships. Notice how the roles are described in both directions: in the top relationship the *Student* is in the *takes* role and *Seminar* is in the *is taken by* role. The double arrowhead above the roles indicates uniqueness constraints. Because the arrowhead is above both the *takes*/*is taken by* roles it indicates that the combination of student/seminar must be unique in this relationship—a student can take many seminars and a seminar is taken by many students, but a student can take a given seminar once and once only. Consider the other relationship. In this case the double arrowhead is only above the *assisted by* role, indicating that a seminar may only appear once in the fact-type table (in other words, this is a one-to-many relationship). As you can see in the fact table, each seminar appears once,

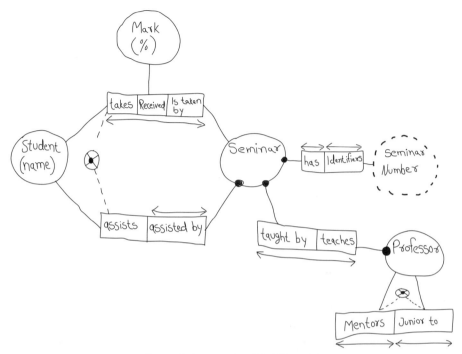

FIGURE 8.5. Complex ORM diagram.

yet Sally Jones appears twice—there is no uniqueness constraint over the *assists* role so this is allowed. Had there been individual arrowheads over each role this would model a one-to-one relationship because each object could only appear at most once in each role. Where there are no arrowheads at all above the roles that indicate an unrestricted many-to-many relationship (e.g., a student could take the same seminar several times).

In Fig. 8.4 each object has an attribute listed in the oval—name for *Student* and number for *Seminar*—indicating the example information listed in the fact-type tables immediately below the roles. This style of ORM diagram is often referred to as a knowledge base diagram although for the sake of simplicity I do not bother to differentiate between various styles of ORM diagrams. Knowledge bases are used to provide examples of the relationships that the entity types experience when they are fulfilling the given roles, enabling you to easily and explicitly explore the relationship with your stakeholders. I will often draw a knowledge base when the relationship is not clear, particularly when we are trying to explore the multiplicity of the relationship.

Figure 8.5 presents a more complex example. It does not include fact-type tables and as a result explores a wider range of concepts—you can only fit so much on a whiteboard, and AM recommends that you *model in small increments* regardless. The relationships between *Student* and *Seminar* have been fleshed out a bit. The top relationship has evolved from a binary relationship to a ternary relationship, which involves three entity types. It is possible to model *n*-ary relationships on ORM diagrams simply by adding more roles to the relationship although I rarely find the need to do so. You see that there is an exclusive or (XOR) relationship, depicted by the dotted circle with the X through it, between the *takes* role and the *assists* role, indicating that either a student can take a seminar or they can assist it but not both. A dotted circle without the X would indicate a simple OR relationship. ORM defines a wide variety of constraint symbols that you can apply, although I find OR and XOR the ones that I most commonly use.

You see that there is a large black dot on the line between *Professor* and the *teaches* role, indicating that it is mandatory for a professor to teach a seminar. The dot can appear at either end of the line, although I prefer to place it on the object end (sometimes an object will be involved in many mandatory relationships that can clutter your object symbols so it is good to have the option to move the dot to the other end of the line).

The dashed oval represents an attribute of an object, showing a more detailed way to represent the concept that seminars have seminar numbers than the short form that we used in Fig. 8.4. I prefer to follow the *depict models simply* practice and use the short form but I wanted to provide an example of the long form for you.

Another interesting concept is the recursive/self relationship that *Professor* is involved in. One professor may mentor other professors and a professor may be junior to several professors that mentor her.

How do you remain agile when working with ORM diagrams? I prefer to use ORM diagrams with my stakeholders, modeling around a whiteboard with them in order to explore the problem domain. Although the notation is rather complex I have found that stakeholders quickly pick up the basics, particularly when fact tables are used frequently at the beginning. Once we understand the details of an issue that we are exploring with an ORM diagram I typically capture the information in a higher-level artifact, such as a UML class diagram (Section 8.4), and erase the ORM diagram once I am through with it. Sometimes I will skip the class diagram completely and move straight to code, depending on the situation.

If your project stakeholders do not like the ORM notation then you may find UML object diagrams (Section 8.7) to be a good option, as are CRC models.

FIGURE 8.6. The layout of a CRC card.

8.3 CLASS RESPONSIBILITY COLLABORATOR (CRC) CARDS

A class responsibility collaborator model (Beck and Cunningham 1989; Wilkinson 1995; Ambler 1998a) is a collection of standard index cards that have been divided into three sections, as depicted in Fig. 8.6. A class represents a collection of similar objects, a responsibility is something that a class knows or does, and a collaborator is another class that a class interacts with to fulfill its responsibilities.

Although CRC cards were originally introduced as a technique for teaching object-oriented concepts, they have also been successfully used as a full-fledged modeling technique. My experience is that CRC models are an incredibly effective tool for conceptual modeling as well as for detailed design. CRC cards feature prominently in extreme programming (XP) (Beck 2000) as a design technique. My focus here is on applying CRC cards for conceptual modeling with your stakeholders.

A class represents a collection of similar objects. An object is a person, place, thing, event, or concept relevant to the system at hand. For example, in a university system, classes would represent students, tenured professors, and seminars. The name of the class appears across the top of a CRC card and is typically a singular noun or singular noun phrase, such as *Student, Professor,* or *Seminar.* You use singular names because each class represents a generalized version of a singular object. Although there may be the student John O'Brien, you would model the class *Student.* The information about a student describes a single person, not a group of people. Therefore, it makes sense to use the name *Student* and not *Students.* Class names should also be simple. For example, which name is better: *Student* or *Person who takes seminars?*

Student	
Student number Name Address Phone number Enroll in a seminar Drop a seminar Request transcripts	Seminar

FIGURE **8.7. An example CRC card.**

A responsibility is anything that a class knows or does. For example, students have names, addresses, and phone numbers. A student knows these things. Students also enroll in seminars, drop seminars, and request transcripts. A student does these things. The things a class knows and does constitute its responsibilities. Important: A class is able to change the values of the things it knows, but it is unable to change the values of what other classes know.

Sometimes a class has a responsibility to fulfill, but not have enough information to do it. For example, as you see in Fig. 8.7, students enroll in seminars. To do this, a student needs to know whether a spot is available in the seminar and, if so, he then needs to be added to the seminar. However, students only have information about themselves (their names and so forth), and not about seminars. What the student needs to do is collaborate/interact with the card labeled *Seminar* to sign up for a seminar. Therefore, *Seminar* is included in the list of collaborators of *Student*.

Collaboration takes one of two forms: A request for information or a request to do something. For example, the card *Student* requests an indication from the card *Seminar* whether a space is available, a request for information. *Student* then requests to be added to the *Seminar*, a request to do something. Another way to perform this logic, however, would have been to have *Student* simply request *Seminar* to enroll himself into itself. Then have *Seminar* do the work of determining whether a seat is available. If the seat is available, then enroll the student; if not, then inform the student that he was not enrolled.

So how do you create CRC models? Iteratively perform the following steps:

1. **Find classes.** I will employ several strategies to find potential classes. First, I look for some sort of customer class, such as *Student* in a university system and *Passenger* in an airline reservation system. I "follow the money" by identifying how it is earned and what it is spent on to identify core business classes for the system surrounding products and services. I will look for the

three—five main classes right away, for example, *Student, Professor, Course, Seminar,* and *Room* for a university information system. The business terms in your glossary are potential classes in your system. Events, such as graduation and commencement at the university, are potential classes because there will be significant responsibilities required to support these activities (for example, *Graduation* would know how to schedule people, would maintain a list of students graduating, and would know its date and location). I will sometimes include reports, such as *Transcript,* in my CRC models. Because there is an existing user-interface prototype for it I do not need to describe its responsibilities in great detail. Instead I will simply add a comment on the card such as "*₊*See the protoype**" as you see in Fig. 8.8 and leave it at that—there is no need to capture the same information in several places.

2. **Find responsibilities.** You should ask yourself what a class does. For example, transcripts must be able to calculate their average marks and rooms must be able to indicate when they are available (so that seminars can be scheduled into them). Another way to identify responsibilities is to ask yourself what information you need to record about a class. For the class *Student* you need to keep track of their names, addresses, student numbers, and phone numbers. When a class needs to collaborate with another class, this means the second class now has the responsibility to fulfill that collaboration. In other words, as you find responsibilities, you need to define collaborations, and as you define collaborations, you will often find new responsibilities.

3. **Define collaborators.** An important concept to understand is that collaboration must occur when a class needs information it does not have. Similarly, collaboration occurs when a class needs to modify information it does not have because any given class class can update only the information it knows. This implies that if it needs to have information updated in another class, then it must ask that class to update it.

4. **Move the cards around.** CRC modeling is typically performed by a group of people around a large desk. As the CRC cards are created, they are placed on the desk, so everyone can see them. Two cards that collaborate with one another should be placed close together on the table, whereas two cards that do not collaborate should be placed far apart. Furthermore, the more two cards collaborate, the closer they should be on the desk. By having cards that collaborate with one another close together, it is easier to understand the relationships between classes. The main advantage is

when you look at the cards from above (which is exactly the viewpoint you have standing around the table), you can get an overall view of the system, seeing how each class interacts with the others. Furthermore, you can concentrate on any given section of the system and know you will have all the cards involved with that section right there in front of you. Another advantage is that when someone wants to move a card, it will often engender a discussion along the lines of "you cannot move that card there because XYZ over here collaborates with it." Conversations like this help you to grow the model. You are likely to find new responsibilities and to help everyone understand the nuances of the model. Finally, when you convert your CRC model into a class model (Section 8.4) the cards on the table are in reasonably good positions for transcribing them onto the class model.

Figure 8.8 depicts a small CRC model for the university information system. These cards were identified by working closely with a project stakeholder who understood this part of the domain. Because CRC cards are a simple technique you will quickly discover that your stakeholders will learn how to work with them, particularly for high-level conceptual modeling.

Here are a few tips I have learned over the years when CRC modeling:

1. **List a collaborator once on a card.** Although the *Seminar* class in Fig. 8.8 likely collaborates several times with *Student* it only has this collaborator listed once. Another approach you can take is to list all the collaborators for each responsibility adjacent to the responsibility, although this seems like a lot of needless busy work to me.

2. **List a collaborator only if there is collaboration.** Sometimes the set of collaborations between two classes is two-way (bidirectional), and sometimes only one way (unidirectional). For example, the collaboration between *Transcript* and *Seminar* is unidirectional. *Transcript* requests information from *Seminar*; however, *Seminar* asks nothing of *Transcript*. Therefore, I listed *Seminar* as a collaborator of *Transcript*, but not the other way around. The general rule is Class A is listed as a collaborator of Class B if and only if *A* does something for *B*.

3. **Sometimes the collaborator does most of the work.** For example, consider enrolling a student in a seminar. *Student* collaborates with *Seminar* to see whether any seats are left and, if so, then asks to be added to the seminar list. *Seminar* is doing all the work. *Seminar* must determine how many seats are left, as well as update the list of students in the given

Professor	
Name Address Phone number Email address Salary Provide information Seminars instructing	Seminar

Transcript	
See the prototype Determine average mark	Student Seminar Professor Enrollment

Seminar	
Name Seminar number Fees Waiting list Enrolled students Instructor Add student Drop student	Student Professor

Enrollment	
Mark(s) received Average to date Final grade Student Seminar	Seminar

Student Schedule	
See the prototype	Seminar Professor Student Enrollment Room

Student	
Name Address Phone number Email address Student number Average mark received Validate identifying info Provide list of seminars taken	Enrollment

Room	
Building Room number Type (Lab, class, º) Number of Seats Get building name Provide available time slots	Building

Building	

Building Name
Rooms
Provide name
Provide list of available
  rooms for a given time
  period
	Room

FIGURE **8.8.** **Some of the CRC cards for a university information system.**

seminar. On the other hand, *Student* merely manages (directs) the entire process.

4. **Expect to be moving the cards around a lot at the beginning.** Because people have a tendency to identify the most obvious responsibilities first, and because these responsibilities tend to lead to the main collaborations, you will find that you can determine the "right" position for your cards fairly quickly.

5. **Put "busy" cards towards the center of the table.** The busiest cards are often the core of the system, so it makes sense to have the core at the

center. One good rule of thumb is to put the customer at or near the center of the table.

6. **Create cards immediately.** When you think you have identified a class, create a new card for it immediately. Think of it like this: the time you spend trying to determine whether you have identified a class costs far more than the card itself.

7. **Actually move the cards around.** There is a tendency for people to fill the cards out, and then put them down on the table wherever there is room. Do not underestimate the value of moving the cards around.

8. **People will identify associations between classes as they move them around.** Typically, one person will pick up a card and say she wants to put it beside another because they collaborate. Somebody else will then say the card should go somewhere else because it is related to another card. You should listen closely to this conversation and record any associations or important business rules that come out of it.

9. **The context determines whether something is a class or a responsibility.** Why isn't *Student name* a class with responsibilities such as *First name*, *Surname*, and *Middle initials*? Well, depending on your domain, *Person Name* might be a valid class. For a university system, it likely is not. A good rule of thumb is that a possessive noun, such as the noun student in *Student name*, is a likely indicator that *Student* is a class, but *Student name* is a responsibility of that class.

10. **Choose a consistent style for "data" responsibilities.** An interesting stylistic issue is how to depict data-oriented responsibilities. The *Student* card includes responsibilies such as *Name* and *Phone number*, whereas the real responsibilies are *Know name* and *Know phone number.* Although some people will insist on using the *Know name* form, I prefer the short form, *Name*, because it is simpler to use. Although both techniques are valid, I prefer to follow the AM practice *depict models simply.* The important thing is you choose one style and stick to it to ensure consistency within your model—follow the AM practice *apply modeling standards* in doing so.

I will create a CRC model whenever I want to actively involve my project stakeholders in the modeling process. Yes, they are involved with other forms of conceptual domain modeling but CRC modeling often becomes more hands-on because we are using physical cards. My experience is that the cards often work better than the diagrams because they are easy to understand and work with.

8.4 ANALYSIS CLASS DIAGRAMS

UML class diagrams (Object Management Group 2003) are the mainstay of object-oriented modeling. Class models show the classes of the system, their interrelationships (including inheritance, aggregation, and association), and the operations and attributes of the classes. Class diagrams are used for a wide variety of purposes, including both conceptual/domain modeling and detailed structural design modeling (Chapter 12). Although I prefer to create domain models on whiteboards (simple tools are more inclusive) most of the diagrams that I will show in this section are drawn using a software-based drawing tool so you may see the exact notation.

Figure 8.9 depicts a start at a simple UML class diagram for the conceptual model for the university. Classes are depicted as boxes with three sections: the top one indicates the name of the class, the middle one lists the attributes of the class, and the third one lists the methods. By including both an attribute and a method box in the class I am arguably making design decisions in my model, something I should not be doing if my goal is conceptual modeling. Another approach would be to have two sections, one for the name and one for the responsibilities. This would be closer to the CRC model of Fig. 8.8 although if I wanted to take this sort of approach I would use CRC cards instead of a UML class diagram. I could also use class boxes that show just the name of the class, enabling me to focus on just the classes and their relationships. However, if that was my goal I would be more likely to create an ORM diagram (Section 8.2) instead. In short, I prefer to follow AM's *apply the right artifact(s)* practice and use each modeling technique for what it is best suited for.

The *Enrollment* class uses new notation that you did not see in Chapter 2. *Enrollment* is an associative class, also called a link class, which is used to model associations that have methods and attributes (*Enrollment* is the same as the *Mark* object in the ORM diagram of Fig. 8.5). Associative classes are typically modeled during analysis and then refactored into what I show in Fig. 8.10 during design. To date, at least to my knowledge, no mainstream programming language that supports the notion of associations that have responsibilities exists. Because you cannot directly build your software in this manner, I have a tendency to stay away from using association classes and

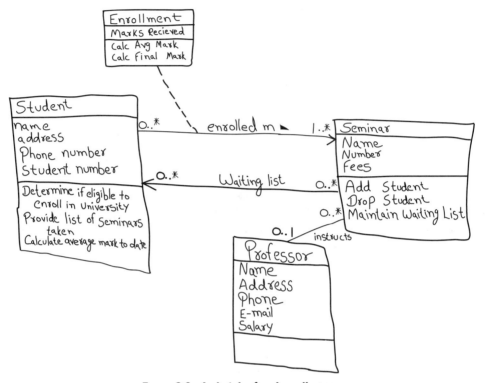

FIGURE 8.9. A sketch of a class diagram.

instead resolve them during my analysis efforts. This is not a purist way to model, but it is pragmatic because the other members on the team, including project stakeholders, do not need to learn the notation and concepts behind associative classes. The disadvantage is that analysis classes arguably do a better job of portraying the domain. As always, choose an approach that works for you and stick with it.

Figure 8.10 depicts a reworked version of Fig. 8.9; the associative class has been resolved. The *on waiting list* association between *Seminar* and *Student* models the similarly named responsibility on the *Seminar* CRC card of Figure 8.8. I could have added an attribute in the *Seminar* class called *Waiting List* but, instead, chose to model it as an association because that is what it actually represents: that seminar objects maintain a waiting list of zero or more student objects. Attributes and associations are called properties in UML 2.0. I also showed associations are implemented as a combination of attributes and operations—I prefer to keep my models simple and assume that the attributes and operations exist to implement the associations. Furthermore that

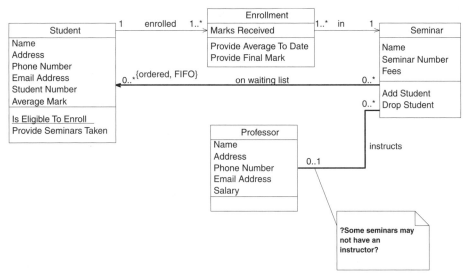

FIGURE **8.10. A formalized UML class diagram.**

would be a detailed design issue anyway, something that is not appropriate on a conceptual model.

The *on waiting list* association is unidirectional because there is not yet a need for collaboration in both directions. Follow the AM practice of *create simple content* and do not over model—you do not need a bidirectional association right now so do not model it. The *enrolled in* association between the *Student* and *Enrollment* classes is also unidirectional for similar reasons. For this association it appears student objects know what enrollment records they are involved with, recording the seminars they have taken in the past, as well as the seminars in which they are currently involved. This association would be traversed to calculate their student object's average mark and to provide information about seminars taken. There is also an *enrolled in* association

---

TIP

Models Evolve over Time

You may start with an essential use case but quickly decide to evolve it into several system use cases. Or you may decide to develop a collection of ORM diagrams on a whiteboard as input into your design-level UML class diagram, which in turn will evolve into Java source code. It is quite common to discard the interim artifacts and only keep the final products—remember AM's *travel light* principle.

between *Enrollment* and *Seminar* to support the capability for student objects to produce a list of seminars taken. The *instructs* association between the *Professor* class and the *Seminar* class is bidirectional because professor objects know what seminars they instruct and seminar objects know who instruct them.

When conceptual modeling, my style is to name attributes and methods using the formats *Attribute Name* and *Method Name*, respectively. Following a consistent and sensible naming convention helps to make your diagrams readable, an important benefit of AM's *apply modeling standards* practice. Also, notice in Fig. 8.10 how I have not modeled the visibility of the attributes and methods to any great extent. Visibility is an important issue during design but, for now, it can be ignored. Also, notice I have not defined the full method signatures for the classes. This is another task I typically leave to design.

I was able to determine with certainty, based on this information, the multiplicities for all but one association and for that one I marked it with a note so I know to discuss it further with my stakeholders. Notice my use of question marks in the note. My style is to mark unknown information on my diagrams this way to remind myself that I need to look into it.

In Fig. 8.10, I also modeled a UML constraint (Chapter 7), in this case {*ordered FIFO*} on the association between *Seminar* and *Student*. The basic idea is that students are put on the waiting list on a first-in, first-out (FIFO) basis. In other words, the students are put on the waiting list in the order they applied for the seminar. UML constraints are used to model complex and/or important information accurately in your UML diagrams. UML constraints are modeled using the format "{constraint description}" format, where the constraint description may be in any format, including predicate calculus. My preference is to use UML notes with English comments, instead of formal constraints, because they are easier to read.

Class models contain a wealth of information; they can be used for both the analysis and design of systems. To create and evolve a class model, you need to model these items:

- Classes;
- Responsibilities;
- Associations;
- Dependencies;
- Inheritance relationships;
- Composition associations; and
- Association classes.

8.4.1 Modeling Classes and Responsibilities

An object is any person, place, thing, concept, event, screen, or report applicable to your system. Objects both know things (they have attributes) and they do things (they have methods). A class is a representation of an object and, in many ways, it is simply a template from which objects are created. Classes form the main building blocks of an object-oriented application. Although thousands of students attend the university, you would only model one class, called *Student*, which would represent each individual student in the entire collection.

Classes are typically modeled as rectangles with three sections: the top section for the name of the class, the middle section for the attributes of the class, and the bottom section for the methods of the class. The initial classes of your model can be identified in the same manner as they are when you are CRC modeling (Section 8.3), as will the initial responsibilities (its attributes and methods). Attributes are the information stored by an object (or at least information temporarily maintained about an object), while methods are the things an object or class do. For example, students have student numbers, names, addresses, and phone numbers. Those are all examples of the attributes of a student. Students also enroll in courses, drop courses, and request transcripts. Those are all examples of the things a student does, which get implemented (coded) as methods. You can think of methods as the object-oriented equivalent of functions and procedures.

An important consideration is the appropriate level of detail. Consider the *Student* class modeled in Fig. 8.10, which has an attribute called *Address*. When you stop and think about it, addresses are complicated things. They have complex data, containing street and city information, for example, and they potentially have behavior. An arguably better way to model this is depicted in Fig. 8.11. Notice how the *Address* class has been modeled to include an attribute for each piece of data it comprises and two methods have been added: one to verify it is a valid address and one to output it as a label (perhaps for an envelope). By introducing the *Address* class, the *Student* class has become more cohesive. It no longer contains logic (such as validation) pertinent to addresses. The *Address* class could now be reused in other places, such as the *Professor* class, reducing your overall development costs. Furthermore, if the need arises to support students with several addresses—during the school term, a student may live in a different location than his permanent mailing address, such as a dorm—information the system may need to track. Having a separate class to implement addresses should make the addition of this behavior easier to implement.

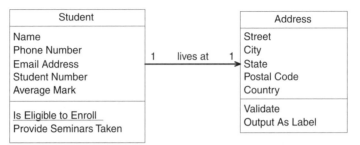

Figure 8.11. The *Student* and *Address* classes.

An interesting feature of the *Student* class is its *Is Eligible to Enroll* responsibility. The underline indicates that this is a class-level responsibility, not an instance-level responsibility (for example, *Provide Seminars Taken*). A good indication that a responsibility belongs at the class level is one that makes sense that it belongs to the class but that does not apply to an individual object of that class. In this case this operation implements BR129 *Determine Eligibility to Enroll* called out in the *Enroll in Seminar* use case of Fig. 8.12.

The *Seminar* class of Fig. 8.10 is refactored into the classes depicted in Fig. 8.13. Refactoring such as this is called class normalization (Ambler 2003b), a process in which you refactor the behavior of classes to increase their cohesion and/or to reduce the coupling between classes. A seminar is an offering of a course; for example, there could be five seminar offerings of the course "CSC 148 Introduction to Computer Science." The attributes *name* and *fees* where moved to the *Course* class and *courseNumber* were introduced. The *getFullName()* method concatenates the course number "CSC 148" and the course name "Introduction to Computer Science" to give the full name of the course. This is called a getter method, an operation that returns a data value pertinent to an object. Although getter methods, and the corresponding setter methods, need to be developed for a class they are typically assumed to exist and are therefore not modeled (particularly on conceptual class diagrams) to not clutter your models.

Figure 8.14 depicts *Course* from Fig. 8.13 as it would appear with its getter and setter methods modeled. Setters and getters are described in detail in Chapter 13. Getters and setters are details not appropriate for conceptual models and in my experience are not even appropriate for detailed design diagrams—instead I would set a coding guideline that all properties will have getter and setter methods and leave it at that. Some people do choose to model getters and setters but I consider them visual noise that clutter your diagrams without adding value.

Name: **Enroll in Seminar**

Description:
Enroll an existing student in a seminar for which she is eligible.

Preconditions:
The Student is registered at the University.

Postconditions:
The Student will be enrolled in the course she wants if she is eligible and room is available.

Basic Course of Action:

1. A student wants to enroll in a seminar.
2. The student inputs her name and student number into the system via "U123 Security Long-in Screen."
3. The system verifies the student is eligible to enroll in seminars at the university according to business rule "BR129 Determine Eligibility to Enroll."
4. The system displays "U132 Seminar Selection Screen," which indicates the list of available seminars.
5. The student indicates the seminar in which she wants to enroll.
6. The system validates the student is eligible to enroll in the seminar according to the business rule "BR130 Determine Student Eligibility to Enroll in a Seminar."
7. The system validates the seminar fits into the existing schedule of the student according to the business rule "BR143 Validate Student Seminar Schedule."
8. The system calculates the fees for the seminar based on the fee published in the course catalog, applicable student fees, and applicable taxes. Apply business rules "BR 180 Calculate Student Fees" and "BR45 Calculate Taxes for Seminar."
9. The system displays the fees via "U133 Display Seminar Fees Screen."
10. The system asks the student whether she still wants to enroll in the seminar.
11. The student indicates she wants to enroll in the seminar.
12. The system enrolls the student in the seminar.
13. The system informs the student the enrollment was successful via "U188 Seminar Enrollment Summary Screen."

FIGURE **8.12.** *Enroll in Seminar* **as a traditional system use case.**

14. The system bills the student for the seminar, according to business rule "BR100 Bill Student for Seminar."
15. The system asks the student whether she wants a printed statement of the enrollment.
16. The student indicates she wants a printed statement.
17. The system prints the enrollment statement "U189 Enrollment Summary Report."
18. The use case ends when the student takes the printed statement.

FIGURE 8.12 (*continued*)

FIGURE 8.13 Normalizing the *Seminar* class.

Course
Name
Course Number
Fees
getFullName()
getCourseNumber()
setCourseNumber(number)
getFees()
setFees(amount)
getName()
setName(name)

FIGURE 8.14 *Seminar* with its getter and setter methods modeled.

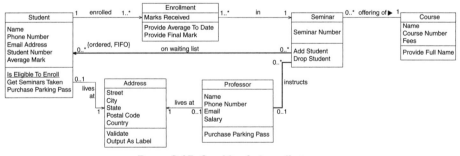

FIGURE 8.15 Combined class diagram.

FIGURE 8.16. Notation overview for modeling associations on UML class diagrams.

Figure 8.15 presents the class diagram that results when Fig. 8.10, Fig. 8.11, and Fig. 8.13 are combined. Notice how *Professor* now references the *Address* class, taking advantage of the work we did to improve the *Student* class.

8.4.2 Modeling Associations

Objects are often associated with, or related to, other objects. For example, as you see in Fig. 8.15, several associations exist: students are *on waiting list* for seminars, professors *instruct* seminars, seminars are an *offering of* courses, a professor *lives at* an address, and so on. Associations are modeled as lines connecting the two classes whose instances (objects) are involved in the relationship.

When you model associations in UML class diagrams, you show them as a thin line connecting two classes, as you see in Fig. 8.16. Associations can become quite complex; consequently, you can depict some things about them on your diagrams. The label, which is optional, although highly recommended, is typically one or two words describing the association. For example, professors instruct seminars.

However, it is not enough simply to know professors instruct seminars. How many seminars do professors instruct? None, one, or several? Furthermore, associations are often two-way streets: not only do professors instruct seminars, but also seminars are instructed by professors. This leads to questions like how many professors can instruct any given seminar and is it possible to have a seminar with no one instructing it? The implication is you also need to identify the multiplicity of an association. The multiplicity of the association is labeled on either end of the line, one multiplicity indicator for each direction (Table 8.2 summarizes the potential multiplicity indicators you can use).

For each class involved in an association, there is always a multiplicity for it. When the multiplicity is one and one only (for example, one and one only person may be president of the United States at any given time), then it is common practice not to indicate the multiplicity and, instead, to assume it

TABLE 8.2. UML Multiplicity Indicators

Indicator	Meaning
$0..1$	Zero or one
1	One only
$0..*$	Zero or more
$1..*$	One or more
n	Only n (where $n > 1$)
$0..n$	Zero to n (where $n > 1$)
$1..n$	One to n (where $n > 1$)

is one. I believe this is a mistake. If the multiplicity is one then indicate it as such. When something is left off a diagram, I cannot tell whether that is what is meant or whether the modeler simply has not gotten around to working on that aspect of the model yet. I always assume the modeler has not done the work yet.

Another option for associations is to indicate the direction in which the label should be read. This is depicted using a filled triangle, called a direction indicator, an example of which is shown on the *offering of* association between the *Seminar* and *Course* classes of Fig. 8.15. This symbol indicates the association should be read "a seminar is an offering of a course," instead of "a course is an offering of a seminar." Direction indicators should be used whenever it is not clear which way a label should be read. My advice, however, is if your label is not clear, then you should consider rewording it.

At each end of the association, the role, the context an object takes within the association, may also be indicated. My style is to model the role only when the information adds value; for example, knowing the role of the *Student* class is *enrolled student* in the *enrolled in* association does not add anything to the model. I follow the AM practice *depict models simply* and indicate roles when it is not clear from the association label what the roles are, if there is a recursive association, or if there are several associations between two classes. In Fig. 8.17, I have evolved our class diagram to include two associations between *Professor* and *Seminar*. Not only do professors instruct seminars, they also assist in them. When several associations are between two classes, something relatively common, you often find you need to indicate the roles to understand the associations fully. In this case, I indicated the roles professors take, but

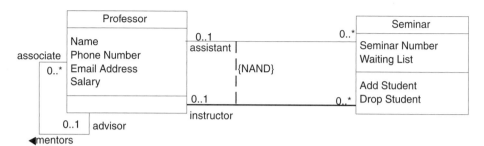

FIGURE **8.17. Modeling roles in associations.**

not seminars, because the role of the seminar objects was not very interesting. Both roles are modeled for the *mentors* recursive association that the *Professor* class has because it is interesting to know that the mentoring professor is called an advisor and the mentored professor is called an associate.

Figure 8.17 is also interesting because it uses a UML contraint to indicate a professor may instruct a given seminar, may assist a seminar, may not be involved in the seminar, but would not be both an assistant and an instructor for the same seminar. The contraint description *NAND* represents the logical concept of "not and."

8.4.3 Introducing Reuse between Classes via Inheritance

Similarities often exist between different classes. Very often two or more classes will share the same attributes and/or the same methods. Because you do not want to have to write the same code repeatedly, you want a mechanism that takes advantage of these similarities. Inheritance is that mechanism. Inheritance models "is a" and "is like" relationships, enabling you to reuse existing data and code easily. When *A* inherits from *B*, we say *A* is the subclass of *B* and *B* is the superclass of *A*. Furthermore, we say we have "pure inheritance" when *A* inherits all the attributes and methods of *B*. The UML modeling notation for inheritance is a line with a closed arrowhead pointing from the subclass to the superclass.

In Fig. 8.15, many similarities occur between the *Student* and *Professor* classes. Not only do they have similar attributes, but they also have similar methods. To take advantage of these similarities, I created a new class called *Person* and had both *Student* and *Professor* inherit from it, as you see in Fig. 8.18. This structure would be called the *Person* inheritance hierarchy

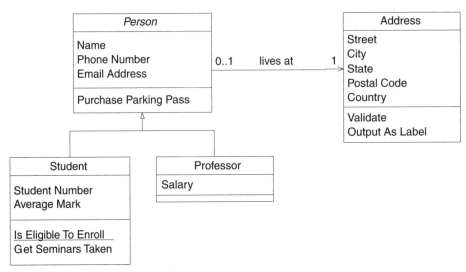

FIGURE 8.18. The *Person* inheritance hierarchy.

because *Person* is its root class. The *Person* class is abstract: objects are not created directly from it, and it captures the similarities between the students and professors. Abstract classes are modeled with their names in italics, as opposed to concrete classes, classes from which objects are instantiated, whose names are in normal text. Both classes had a name, e-mail address, and phone number, so these attributes were moved into *Person*. The *Purchase Parking Pass* method was also common between the two classes, so that was also moved into the parent class. By introducing this inheritance relationship to the model, I reduced the amount of work to be performed. Instead of implementing these responsibilities twice, they are implemented once, in the *Person* class, and reused by *Student* and *Professor*.

In the class diagram of Fig. 8.15, I was lucky because I used similar names for the attributes in both classes. However, you will often find situations where one class has an attribute called name, whereas another one has *First Name*, *Middle Initial*, and *Last Name*. You then need to decide whether these are, in fact, the same thing and if they are, be prepared to refactor your existing model, and perhaps even code to reflect whichever approach to storing a person's name you accept. A similar issue can also occur with methods and associations.

An interesting aspect of Fig. 8.18 is the association between *Person* and *Address*. First, this association was pushed up to *Person* because both

Professor and *Student* had a *lives at* association with *Address*. I could do this because associations are implemented by the combination of attributes and methods. Because attributes and methods can be inherited, any association they implemented can also be inherited by implication. It made sense to apply inheritance here because the associations represented the same concept: a person lives at an address (I was also lucky because the direction of the associations, as well as their multiplicities, were identical).

Another interesting aspect of Fig. 8.18 is, although both *Professor* and *Student* had associations with *Seminar*, that I did not chose to push this association up into *Person*. The issue is that the semantics of the two associations are different. First, one association is unidirectional whereas the other is bidirectional, a good indication that they are significantly different. Second, the multiplicities are different, another good indication the associations are different. Third, and most important, the two associations are completely different from one another. One represents the fact that professors instruct seminars, whereas the other one represents that students are on waiting lists to enroll in a seminar.

8.4.4 Modeling Composition and Associations

Sometimes an object is made up of other objects. For example, an airplane is made up of a fuselage, wings, engines, landing gear, flaps, and so on. Figure 8.19 presents an example using composition, modeling the fact that a building is composed of one or more rooms, and then, in turn, that a room may be composed of several subrooms (you can have recursive composition). UML 2 no longer supports the concept of aggregation, a weaker form of composition, which was depicted in UML 1.x using a hollow diamond.

When deciding whether to use composition over association, Craig Larman (2002) says it best: If in doubt, leave it out. Unfortunately many modelers will agonize over when to use composition when the reality is little difference exists among association and composition at the coding level, something you see in Chapter 13. The only difference when it comes to design is that composition gives you hints about object creation/deletion, i.e., a composed object is typically created when the composer is created and deleted when the composer is deleted; this is not usually true of simple association. Other than that, given today's modern programming language, there is very little difference when implementing an association and a composition.

Figure 8.19. Buildings and rooms.

8.4.5 Modeling Vocabularies

In *Agile Database Techniques* (Ambler 2003b) I discussed the importance of vocabularies when it comes to modeling XML data structures. A vocabulary defines the semantics of entity types and their responsibilities, the taxonomical relationships between entity types, and the ontological relationships between entity types. Semantics is simply a fancy word for meaning—when we are defining the semantics of something we are defining its meaning. Taxonomies are classifications of entity types into hierarchies, an example of which is presented for university persons in Fig. 8.20. Ontology goes beyond taxonomy. Where taxonomy addresses classification hierarchies ontology will represent and communicate knowledge about a topic as well as about a set of relationships and properties that hold for the entities included within that topic.

The semantics of your conceptual model are best captured in a glossary (Chapter 7). Figure 8.20 depicts taxonomies for persons within the university.

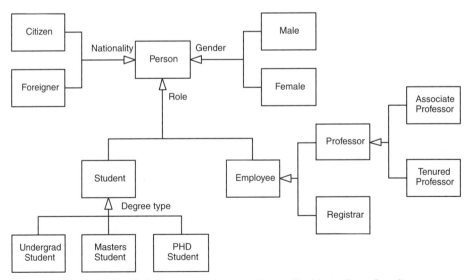

Figure 8.20. Modeling people taxonomies applicable to the university.

There are several interesting aspects of this diagram:

- It takes a "single section" approach to classes, instead of the three-section approach that we have seen in previous diagrams, because we are exploring relationships between entity types but not their responsibilities.
- It uses UML 2.0's generalization set concept, just an inheritance arrowhead with a label representing the name of the set. In UML 1.x this label was called a discriminator. There are three generalization sets for *Person*: *Nationality*, *Role*, and *Gender*.
- These generalization sets overlap—a person can be classified via each of these roles (e.g., someone can be a male foreign student). This is called multiple classification.
- You can indicate "sub-generalization" sets, for example, *Student* within the *Role* generalization set.
- Some generalization sets are mutually exclusive from others, not shown in the example, where an entity type may only be in one set. This is referred to as single classification and would be modeled using an XOR constraint between the two (or more) discriminators.

Fowler (2004) points out that generalization sets are by default disjointed. For example, in the *Role* generalization set you are a student or an employee but not both. He also discusses the concept of dynamic versus static classification—with dynamic classification an object can change its subtype within the generalization structure; with static classification it may not. He argues that dynamic classification is a useful concept for conceptual modeling; for example, it is reasonable to expect a student to become an employee. Fowler also points out that it can be difficult to implement and therefore you see most UML class diagrams sticking with single static classification (e.g., the inheritance hierarchy of Fig. 8.18).

8.5 LOGICAL DATA MODELS (LDMs)

Data modeling is the act of exploring data-oriented structures. Like other modeling artifacts, data models are used for a variety of purposes, from conceptual models to physical design models (Chapter 12). Logical data models are used to explore domain concepts and their relationships. This could be done for the scope of a single project or for your entire enterprise. From the

> ### TIP
> #### Essential Reading
>
> The book *Requirements Analysis: From Business Views to Architecture* by David Hay (2003) is the best source of information regarding how to use LDMs for conceptual modeling.

point of view of an object-oriented developer, data modeling is conceptually similar to class modeling. With data modeling, you identify data entities and assign data attributes to them, whereas with class modeling you identify classes and assign responsibilities to them. There are associations between entities, similar to the associations between classes—relationships, inheritance, and composition are all applicable concepts in data modeling.

Figure 8.21 depicts a partial LDM for the university, corresponding to the conceptual class model of Fig. 8.15. There are several common data modeling notations available to you, although for the sake of consistency with the rest of this book this diagram conforms to the data modeling profile described at http://www.agiledata.org/essays/umlDataModelingProfile.html. At the time of this writing the UML still does not yet officially include a data model, which is truly unfortunate considering how common physical data modeling is. The notation used is a subset of class diagramming notation; methods are not an issue on LDMs for example. You will also notice that in the bottom right-hand corner a stereotype has been added to the diagram, indicating that it is an LDM instead of a class diagram.

Much of the advice for creating conceptual class diagrams is applicable to creating LDMs so I am not going to go into a lot of detail in this section. To create a LDM, iteratively perform the following steps:

- **Identify entity types.** An entity type represents a collection of people, places, things, events, or concepts. Figure 8.21 depicts *Student*, *Professor*, and *Address* entity types (amongst others). If you were class modeling you would expect to discover classes with the exact same names. Ideally, an entity type should be "normal," the data modeling world's version of cohesive. A normal entity type depicts one concept, just like a cohesive class models one concept. For example, the entity types *Student* and *Address* are cohesive; *StudentAndAddress* is not because it clearly depicts two separate concepts.

- **Identify relationships.** In the real world entities have relationships with other entities, just as classes have relationships with other classes. The

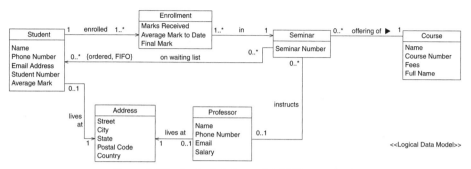

FIGURE 8.21. Logical data model (UML notation).

advice presented in Section 8.4.2 applies to LDMs as well as to class diagrams.

- **Identify attributes.** Each entity type will have one or more data attributes, such as *Name* and *Phone Number* in the *Student* entity. Attributes should also be cohesive from the point of view of your domain, which is often a judgment call. For example, should it be *Name* as a single attribute or *First Name, Middle Initial*, and *Last Name* as attributes of *Student*? The answer depends on your requirements.

- **Apply naming conventions.** Your organization should have standards and guidelines applicable to data modeling, something you should be able to obtain from your enterprise administrators (if they do not exist you should lobby to have some put in place). Follow AM's *apply modeling standards* practice.

Project teams will typically create LDMs as a primary analysis artifact when their implementation environment is predominantly procedural in nature, for example, when they are using structured COBOL as an implementation language. LDMs are also a good choice when a project is data-oriented in nature; perhaps a data warehouse or reporting system is being developed. However, in my experience LDMs are often a poor choice when a project team is using object-oriented or component-based technologies (because they would rather work with object and component models) or simply when the project is not data-oriented in nature (e.g., you are building embedded software). I find LDMs inferior to class models because they only show the data aspects of your domain. For example, when you compare the LDM in Fig. 8.21 with the class diagram of Figure 8.15 you see that there has been information loss. The LDM does not communicate the fact that professors and students purchase parking passes, nor does it show that addresses can validate themselves.

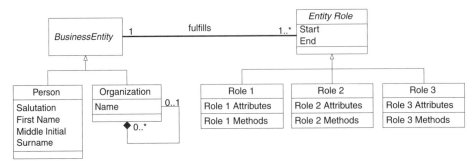

FIGURE 8.22. The *Business Entity* analysis pattern.

8.6 APPLYING ANALYSIS PATTERNS EFFECTIVELY

Analysis patterns (Hay 1996; Fowler 1997; Ambler 1998a) describe solutions to common problems found in the analysis/business domain of a system. Analysis patterns are typically more specific than design patterns (Chapter 12) because they describe a solution for a portion of a business domain. This does not mean an analysis pattern is applicable only to a single line of business, although it could be. In this section I overview two analysis patterns I have used in various business domains, patterns I believe you will find useful when you are conceptual modeling.

The real value of analysis patterns is the thinking behind them. A pattern might not be the total solution to your problem, but it might provide enough insight to help save you several hours or days during development. Consider analysis patterns as a good start at solutions.

For example, every organization must deal either with other organizations or with people, usually both. As a result, you need to keep track of them. The solution for the *Business Entity* analysis pattern (Ambler 1998a), similar to the *Party* pattern (Hay 1996; Fowler 1997), is presented in Figure 8.22. This pattern is a specialization of Peter Coad's *Roles Played* pattern (Coad 1992) for modeling the different types of organizations and people with whom your company interacts. In the case of the university, this pattern could be applied to model concepts such as professor, student, and registrar.

The basic idea of this pattern is to separate the concept of a business entity, such as a person or company, from the roles they fulfill. For example, Tony may be an employee and a customer. Furthermore, one day he may also sell your company services, also making him a supplier. The person does not change, but the role(s) he has with your organization does, so you need to find a way to model this, which is what this pattern does. Each business entity

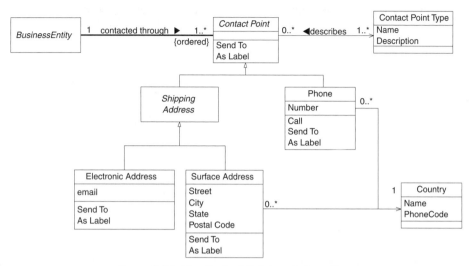

FIGURE 8.23. The *Contact Point* analysis pattern.

has one or more roles with your organization and each role has a range during which it was applicable (the *start* and *end* attributes). Each role implements the behavior specific to it, such as placing an order with a supplier or the hiring and promotion of an employee.

Another example is the *Contact Point* analysis pattern (Ambler 1998a), the solution for which is depicted in Fig. 8.23. It describes an approach for keeping track of the various means by which you interact with business entities. Your organization most likely sends information and bills to, as well as ships products to, the surface addresses of your customers. Perhaps it e-mails information to customers and employees, or faxes information to them. It also probably needs to keep track of the contact phone number for anyone with whom it interacts. The *Contact Point* pattern models an approach to supporting this functionality. It could be applied directly to the class model of Fig. 8.18 to rework the approach to basic contact information currently modeled via the *Person* and *Address* classes.

The basic idea behind this pattern is that surface addresses, e-mail addresses, and phone numbers are really the same sort of thing—a means by which you can contact other business entities. Subclasses of *Contact Point* need to be able to do at least two things: they need to know how things/information can be sent to them and they need to know how to output their "label information." You can send faxes to phone numbers, e-mail to electronic addresses, and letters and packages to surface addresses. You also need to be able to

TABLE 8.3. Advantages and Disadvantages of Analysis Patterns

Advantages	Disadvantages
Increase developer productivity by enabling them to reuse the thinking of others.	You need to learn a large number of patterns.
Increase the consistency between applications.	Hard-core developers are not interested in analysis patterns because they are not code.
Potentially better than reusable code because they can be applied in a wide range of environments, as they are not environment-specific.	Can be unnaturally "forced" to fit into your models when they do not truly belong.

print contact point information on labels, letterhead, and reports. To do so, contact points collaborate with instances of *Contact Point Type* for descriptor information. For example, you want to output "Fax: (416) 555–1212," not just "(416) 555–1212." Furthermore, the *Phone* class should have the capability to be dialed automatically. The different varieties of contact point types would include things like voice phone line, fax phone line, work address, home address, billing address, and personal e-mail ID.

It is interesting to note that I applied the *Item-Item Description* pattern (Coad 1992; Ambler 1998a) when modeling the *Contact Point* and *Contact Point Type* classes. This points out an important principle of object-oriented patterns—they can be used in combination to solve larger problems.

Table 8.3 lists the primary advantages and disadvantages of analysis patterns. I maintain a Web page, http://www.ambysoft.com/processPatterns Page.html, which provides links and references to printed literature pertaining to patterns and the software process. From this page, I link to the major patterns sites online, including sites specializing in analysis patterns.

8.7 UML Object Diagram

UML object diagrams, sometimes referred to as instance diagrams, are useful for exploring "real-world" examples of objects and the relationships between

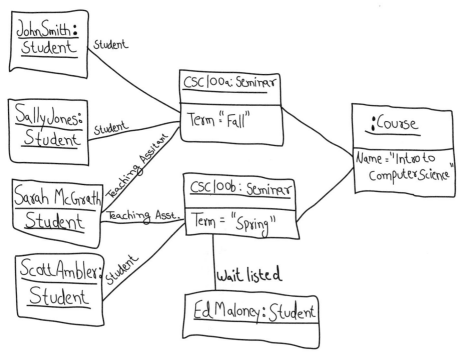

FIGURE 8.24. UML object diagram.

them. Although UML class diagrams are very good at describing this information some people find them too abstract—a UML object diagram can be a good option for explaining complex relationships between classes.

For example, the object diagram of Fig. 8.24 explores the concepts that a student can attend a seminar, be wait listed for a seminar, or can be a teaching assistant within a seminar. The diagram explores an example where *John Smith* and *Sally Jones* are both students in *CSC 100a*, whereas *Sarah McGrath* is the teaching assistant for it. *Sarah* is also the teaching assistant in *CSC 100b*, *Scott Ambler* is an enrolled student, and *Ed Maloney* is wait-listed. The diagram also shows that the two seminars are both sections of the *Introduction to Computer Science* course. This diagram makes the three relationships among students and seminars, as well as the relationship between seminars and courses, much more explicit.

The notation used on UML object diagrams is very simple—they show objects and the connections among them. When you depict an object you need to include enough information so that it is a recognizable instance. As a result I will use one of two formats: a single box-named instance such as

Sarah McGrath: Student or a double box instance listing one or more identifying attribute values in the format *attribute = value* such as *name = "Intro to Computer Science"*. Connections between objects are shown as lines with roles, such as *Teaching Assistant*, optionally indicated. If you need to, you can list several values, such as the year in addition to the term that a seminar is held in, in order to specify which object instance you are referring to.

As you can see UML object diagrams are effectively notational subsets of UML communication diagrams, although object diagrams are used to explore structure whereas communication diagrams explore behavior. It is common for object diagrams to evolve into communication diagrams simply by adding messages to the diagram.

I will typically draw object diagrams on whiteboards in order to explore the relationships between objects. Once we have explored said relationships we will use whatever we have learned to update our class models or source code as appropriate then erase the diagram. Remember, the value is often in the act of modeling and not in the model itself. I have seen object diagrams retained as part of the description of a complex business rule but this is pretty rare in my experience.

8.8 KEEPING CONCEPTUAL DOMAIN MODELING AGILE

In this section, I want to share a collection of tips and techniques that I have found useful over the years to improve the quality of my conceptual modeling efforts:

1. **You do not need a complete model.** Remember, agile software developers work in an evolutionary manner, not a "big design up front" manner. You can and should create very small conceptual models then move forward into design and implementation in order to prove that your models actually reflect the needs of your stakeholders.

2. **Use the right model for the job.** I prefer to use simple ORM diagrams, object diagrams, and/or CRC cards with my project stakeholders as I find them to be very inclusive modeling techniques. ORM diagrams are very good at exploring nuances, whereas CRC cards are better at higher-level concepts. I will use UML class diagrams to capture a structural view of the domain, often capturing the insights gained from ORM diagrams.

this detracted from your model in any way? If so, how? Do you need to verify this change with your stakeholders? Why or why not?

7. Create one or more ORM diagrams to explore the relationships between the different types of customers of a bank and the various types of accounts. Also, model the features of those accounts.

8. Compare and contrast the information content of your CRC model and your conceptual class model for the bank case study. What are the strengths and weaknesses of each model? Why? Would you keep either of these models as permanent documentation? Why or why not?

9. Search the Web for papers and information about conceptual domain modeling. Compare and contrast the various techniques. Formulate why differences exist between the various approaches and discuss the advantages and disadvantages of having different approaches available to you.

CHAPTER 9

Business Process Modeling

Process modeling has been a mainstay of software development for decades and will continue to as long as we need to build business systems.

Process models allow us to describe the often-complicated flow of logic within a system. Process models typically depict sources of information outside the scope of your system, which are called actors in use case models (Chapter 5), and the way that they interact with the system. Process models also show, albeit at a high level sometimes, how information is processed by the system to support these interactions, depicting process/activities and the information flowing between them. Process models can be used to analyze an existing system, to analyze an existing business process, to design a new business process, or to design a new system.

This chapter describes three types of models that I typically use for process modeling—data flow diagrams (DFDs), flowcharts, and UML activity diagrams—summarized in Table 9.1. The RUP (Kruchten 2000) suggests creating business use case models, which are very similar to essential use case models, for process modeling. However, my experience is that use cases do not work very well for this purpose—use cases are very effective for exploring the usage of a system but not so good at exploring business processes because

TABLE 9.1. Artifacts for Process Modeling	
Model	Description
Activity diagram	A unified modeling language (UML) diagram used to model high-level business processes, including data flow, or to model the logic of complex logic within a system.
Data flow diagram (DFD)	A diagram that shows the movement of data within a system between processes, entities, and data stores.
Flowchart	A diagram depicting the logic flow of a single process or method.

they do not depict information flow at all. My expectation is that we will eventually see the RUP move away from use cases for business process modeling in favor of some, if not all three, techniques, which I describe below.

9.1 DATA FLOW DIAGRAMS (DFDs)

In the late 1970s, *data-flow diagrams* were introduced and popularized for structured analysis and design (Gane and Sarson 1979). DFDs show the flow of data from external entities into the system, show how the data move from one process to another, and data's logical storage. In Fig. 9.1 we see an example of a DFD using the Gane and Sarson notation. There are only four symbols:

1. Squares representing *external entities*, which are sources or destinations of data.
2. Rounded rectangles representing *processes*, which take data as input, do something to it, and output it.
3. Arrows representing the *data flows*, which can be either electronic data or physical items.
4. Open-ended rectangles representing *data stores*, including electronic stores such as databases or XML files and physical stores such as filing cabinets or stacks of paper.

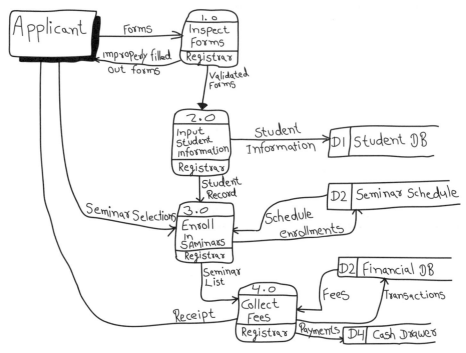

FIGURE 9.1. Data flow diagram for enrolling in the university.

To create the diagram I simply worked through a usage scenario, in this case the use case logic described in Fig. 9.2. On actual projects, it is far more common just to stand at a whiteboard with one or more project stakeholders and simply sketch as we talk through a problem. In this case, I started with the applicant, the external entity in the top left corner, and simply followed the flow of data throughout the system. I introduced the *Inspect Forms* process to encapsulate the initial validation steps. I assigned this process identifier 1.0, indicating that it is the first process on the top-level diagram. A common technique with DFDs is to create detailed diagrams for each process to depict more granular levels of processing. Were I to do that for this process I would number the subprocesses 1.1, 1.2, and so on. Subprocesses of 1.1 would be numbered 1.1.1, 1.1.2, and so on. I would not bother to expand this process to more detailed DFD, as it is clear what is happening in it and therefore the new diagram would not add any value. I also indicated who/what does the work in the bottom section of the process bubble, in this case the registrar. This information is optional although very useful in my experience. You can see how the improperly filled out forms are returned to the applicant if required.

Name: Enroll in University

Identifier: UC 19

Description:
Enroll someone in the university.

Preconditions:
The Registrar is logged into the system.
The Applicant has already undergone initial checks to verify that they are eligible to enroll.

Postconditions:
The Applicant will be enrolled in the university as a student if they are eligible.

Basic Course of Action:

1. An applicant wants to enroll in the university.
2. The applicant hands a filled out copy of form *U113 University Application Form* to the registrar. [Alternate Course A: Forms Not Filled Out]
3. The registrar visually inspects the forms.
4. The registrar determines that the forms have been filled out properly. [Alternate Course B: Forms Improperly Filled Out]
5. The registrar clicks on the *Create Student* icon.
6. The system displays *U189 Create Student Screen*.
7. The registrar inputs the name, address, and phone number of the applicant. [Extension Point: *UC34 Perform Security Check*. Applicable to Step 17]
8. The system determines that the applicant does not already exist within the system according to *BR37 Potential Match Criteria for New Students*. [Alternate Course F: Students Appears to Exist within the System].
9. The system determines that the applicant is on the eligible applicants list. [Alternate Course G: Person Is Not Eligible to Enroll]
10. The system adds the applicant to its records. The applicant is now considered to be a student.
11. The registrar helps the student to enroll in seminars via the use case *UC 17 Enroll in Seminar*.
12. The system calculates the required initial payment in accordance to *BR16 Calculate Enrollment Fees*.
13. The system displays *U115 Fee Summary Screen*.

FIGURE **9.2.** The *Enroll in University* use case.

---

14. The registrar asks the student to pay the initial payment in accordance to *BR19 Fee Payment Options*.
15. The student pays the initial fee. [Alternate Course D: The Student Cannot Pay at This Time]
16. The system prints a receipt.
17. The registrar hands the student the receipt.
18. The use case ends.

Alternate Course A: ....

FIGURE 9.2 (*continued*)

I then continued to follow the logic of the use case, concentrating on how the data are processed by each step. The second process encapsulates the logic for creating a student record, including the act of checking to see whether the person is eligible to enroll as well as whether they are already in the database. Notice how each data flow on the diagram has been labeled. Also, notice that the names of the data change to reflect how they have been processed.

Now that I look closer at the diagram, the arrow between the *Input Student Information* process and the *Student DB* data store should be two-way because this process searches the database for existing student records. Unfortunately, I have erased this diagram from my whiteboard so it is not easy to address this minor problem. Yes, I could use a drawing program to update the arrowhead but it is more important to make the point that agile models do not need to be perfect; they just need to be good enough. AM recommends that you follow the practice *update models only when it hurts* and in this case this issue does

---

TIP

Common DFD Modeling Rules

- All processes must have at least one data flow in and one data flow out.
- All processes should modify the incoming data, producing new forms of outgoing data.
- Each data store must be involved with at least one data flow.
- Each external entity must be involved with at least one data flow.
- A data flow must be attached to at least one process.

not hurt enough to invest the two or three minutes it would take to fix the diagram.

The *Collect Fees* process is interesting because it interacts with an electronic data store, *Financial DB*, as well as a physical one, *Cash Drawer*. DFDs can be used to model processes that are purely physical, purely electronic, or more commonly a mix of both. Electronic data stores can be modeled via data models, particularly if they represent a relational database. Physical data stores are typically self-explanatory.

Traditionally the DFD modeling process was to create five sets of diagrams with accompanying documentation (descriptions for each process, data flow, data store, and external entity):

1. **Context DFD**. This was a single process bubble connected via data flows to major external entities. The purpose of this diagram was to describe the context in which the system existed.

2. **Current physical DFDs**. These diagrams, typically created in a hierarchy to capture the varying levels of details, modeled the current processes as they are implemented today.

3. **Current logical DFDs**. These diagrams depict the business process from a technology independent point of view. The goal was to step back and ask yourself what was really happening (very similar to essential modeling as described in Chapter 5).

4. **Proposed logical DFDs**. These diagrams depict the new design for your business processes in a technology-independent manner.

5. **Proposed physical DFDs**. These diagrams depict one or more potential detailed designs for the system, taking technology and architectural decisions into account.

As you can imagine this is a lot of work, the epitome of big design up front (BDUF). Very few project teams actually did this in practice, although it was quite common to do a context DFD, a current physical DFD, and a proposed physical DFD for the chosen implementation approach. Still far too much modeling, in my opinion.

Although this idea helped to improve the analysis-and-design process, it unfortunately had its problems. First, drawing and documenting DFDs proved a long and drawn out process. Second, a simple change in business rules would often result in significant changes to the DFDs. Third, there was little if any

---

TIP

Feedback Is Your Friend

Never forget that you are a mere mortal just like everyone else on your team. Expect to receive feedback about your work—I suggest you actively seek it—and be prepared to consider it and act accordingly. Not only will your system be the better for it, but you will likely learn something in the process.

---

correlation between the model and the code, the result being that the code would quickly get out of synch with the model.

Many people will deride DFDs for these reasons, telling you that you do not need them to model a system. Yes, it is clearly possible to apply DFDs in dysfunctional ways, but you can also do so in an agile manner as well. Keep your diagrams small, as I did above. Use simple tools, such as whiteboards, to create them with your stakeholders. Travel light and erase them when you are through with them. Create them if they are going to add value, not simply because your process tells you to do so. The bottom line is that some of the modeling methodologies may have been flawed but the need to represent the data flow within a system is still required.

9.2 FLOWCHARTS

Flowcharts are a modeling technique introduced in the 1940/50s and popularized for structured development in the 1970s (Gane and Sarson 1979) as well as for business modeling. Figure 9.3 depicts a flowchart for the *Enroll in University* use case. There are three symbols depicted on this flowchart: Squares that represent activities or tasks, diamonds that represent decision points, and arrows that represent flow of control. Flowcharts support other types of symbols, such as off-page connectors (for when your diagrams get too big) and input/output symbols to represent printed reports and data storage options. I typically do not use off-page connectors as I prefer small flowcharts although I will occasionally model reports (a four-sided shape with a curvy bottom edge) and databases (as a cylinder).

Notice the differences between the flowchart and the DFD of Fig. 9.1. Unlike DFDs, which are used to describe data flow within a system, flowcharts are typically used to describe the detailed logic of a business process or business rule. In the past, it was quite common to use flowcharts to model the logic of large software modules, such as a 30,000-line COBOL program. However,

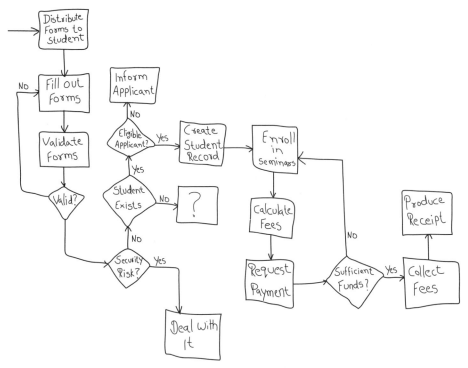

FIGURE **9.3. Flowchart for enrolling in the university.**

because object methods are much smaller (a 30-line method would be considered quite large) flowcharts have dropped out of favor with programmers in recent years. That is okay, as they are still useful for process modeling. It is important to note that although the flowchart is much more detailed than the DFD I could just as easily gone to the same level of detail in both diagrams.

To create this diagram I simply worked through the business logic a step at a time. I started at the top left corner of the board; you can see the arrow coming from nowhere into the side of the *Distribute Forms to Student* step. It is interesting to note that the use case does not specifically call this out as the first step, but it does seem to be implied and this step is required if the registrar determines that the forms are not valid.

Each time a decision is made I introduced a diamond. In this example all the decision points were yes/no questions but that is not always the case. I could just as easily ask a question such as "What is the day of the week?" and had seven arrows leaving the diamond, one for each day. Each arrowhead leaving a decision should be labeled with the appropriate condition but as you can see

I forgot to label the *yes* arrow coming out of the *Valid* diamond—remember, agile models just need to be barely good enough.

It is interesting that by drawing this flowchart I seem to have picked up some logic errors in my use case. First, the box with a question mark in it indicates that I still need to think through an alternate course in the use case—no big deal. The real logic problem is that I check to see whether the person exists in the database before I check to see whether they are on the list of expected applicants. This does not feel right to me so this is something I should discuss with my stakeholders, pointing out the value of AM's *active stakeholder participation* practice. If the stakeholder is working with me on this model we can resolve this issue right away; if not, then I must either wait for them to be available to discuss the issue or simply make something up on the spot and risk having to fix it later on.

The best way to stay agile when working with flowcharts is to keep things simple. Sketch them on whiteboards with your stakeholders to discuss important business logic, take a digital photo if you want to save it, or simply erase it once you are through. The value often is not in the models that you create but instead it is in the act of modeling because it helps you to think things through. For example, the flowchart of Fig. 9.3 has helped my team to identify a potential problem with our use case, but once we have fixed that problem, the flowchart is not going to be of much value any more.

I do not use flowcharts much any more because I prefer to use UML activity diagrams instead, and in fact activity diagrams are arguably sophisticated flowcharts (there is more to them than this though). Regardless, it is important to be aware of flowcharts because you will still see them used by experienced IT professionals from time to time.

9.3 UML Activity Diagrams

UML 2.x activity diagrams (Object Management Group 2003) are typically used for business process modeling, for modeling the logic captured by a single use case or usage scenario, or for modeling the detailed logic of a business rule (Chapter 7). Although UML activity diagrams could potentially model the internal logic of a complex operation it would be far better to simply rewrite the operation so that it is simple enough that you do not require an activity diagram. In many ways UML activity diagrams are the object-oriented equivalent of flowcharts and DFDs from structured development.

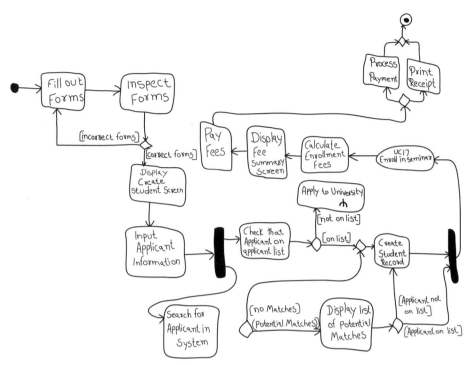

Figure 9.4. A UML activity diagram for enrolling in university for the first time.

Let us start by describing the basic notation that I have used in Fig. 9.4 and Fig. 9.5:

- **Initial node.** The filled circle is the starting point of the diagram. An initial node is not required although it does make it significantly easier to read the diagram.

- **Activity final node.** The filled circle with a border is the ending point. An activity diagram can have zero or more activity final nodes.

- **Activity.** The rounded rectangles represent activities that occur. An activity may be physical, such as *Inspect Forms*, or electronic, such as *Display Create Student Screen.*

- **Flow/edge.** The arrows on the diagram. Although there is a subtle difference between flows and edges, I have never seen a practical purpose for the difference although I have no doubt one exists. I will use the term flow.

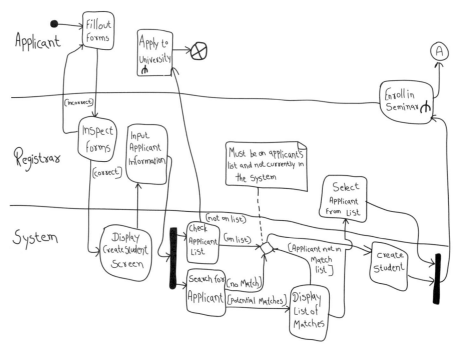

FIGURE 9.5. A UML activity diagram partitioned by actor.

- **Fork.** A black bar with one flow going into it and several leaving it. This denotes the beginning of parallel activity.

- **Join.** A black bar with several flows entering it and one leaving it. This denotes the end of parallel processing.

- **Condition.** Text such as [*Incorrect Form*] on a flow, defining a guard that must evaluate to true in order to traverse the node.

- **Decision.** A diamond with one flow entering and several leaving. The flows leaving include conditions although some modelers will not indicate the conditions if it is obvious.

- **Merge.** A diamond with several flows entering and one leaving. The implication is that all incoming flows must reach this point until processing continues, unless otherwise noted as in Fig. 9.5 (discussed below).

- **Partition.** Figure 9.5 is organized into three partitions, also called swim lanes, indicating who/what is performing the activities (the *Applicant, Registrar,* or *System*).

- **Subactivity indicator.** The rake in the bottom corner of an activity, such as in the *Apply to University* activity, indicates that the activity is described by a more finely detailed activity diagram. In Figure 9.5 the *Enroll in Seminar* activity includes this symbol.

- **Flow final.** The circle with the X through it. This indicates that the process stops at this point.

- **Note.** Figure 9.5 includes a standard UML note to indicate that the merge does not require all three flows to arrive before processing can continue. An alternative way to model this would have been with an OR constraint between the *no match* and *applicant not on match* list flows. I prefer notes because stakeholders find them easier to understand.

- **Use case.** In Fig. 9.4 I indicated that the *Enroll in Seminar* use case is invoked as one of the activities. This is a visual cheat I use to indicate an included use case is being invoked. To tell you the truth I am not sure whether this is officially allowed by the UML, but clearly, it should be. Another way to depict this is shown in Fig. 9.5 via the use of a normal activity although I do not think this is as obvious as using a use case.

The activity diagram of Fig. 9.4 depicts one way to model the logic of the *Enroll in University* use case of Fig. 9.2, a very common use of activity diagrams because they enable you to depict both the basic course of action and the alternate courses. Activity diagrams that cross several use cases or that address just a small portion of a use case can also be drawn. You can also use activity diagrams without use cases being involved at all; for example, a pair of eXtreme Programming (XP) developers (Beck 2000) could draw activity diagrams with their customer (the XP term for stakeholder) to analyze a user story or a larger business process that a user story supports.

TIP

Analysis Is So Important You Should Do It Every Day

Analysis is not a phase when you are working in an evolutionary manner. Analysis involves working with your stakeholders, as well as with your fellow developers, to understand the problem domain whenever you need to. Analysis could be something as simple as asking a stakeholder "What did you mean by this?" or as complex as drawing several diagrams to explore an aspect of what you are building. It is an informal process requiring open and honest communication.

Figure 9.4 is notable for several things:

1. It depicts the notation that you are likely to use 90 percent of the time (I will discuss the more esoteric notation later).
2. The use of diamonds for decisions and merges is visually wordy but unfortunately all too common. In Fig. 9.5 I address this issue by placing conditions on flows leaving activities instead of introducing additional diamonds to represent decision points.
3. It uses a fork to indicate parallel processing; in this case, we have decided that we can perform some of the checks on the applicant in parallel, something that was not easy to indicate using flowcharts.
4. It shows how activity diagrams can get large very quickly. Even though it models the logic of a single use case, I was forced to have it wind around the whiteboard because I ran out of space. Ideally, the diagram should be wider, with the logic going from left to right across the board. Better yet, it would be nice to have more whiteboard space.
5. It includes a common mistake. At the very end, I applied a decision just before the *Process Payment* and *Print Receipt* processes to indicate that they can be done in parallel. I should have used a fork, not a decision, for that. I should also use a balancing join, instead of a merge, although either one would be allowed. The join or merge is required because both processes need to finish before the overall process ends; without doing this a race condition effectively exists where the first process to finish would end things.

Figure 9.5 depicts the *Enroll in University* use case but takes an approach different than that of Fig. 9.4. As noted above it avoids the use of decision points. It also uses the concept of partitions, also called swim lanes, to indicate who/what is performing the activity. In this diagram I simply labeled the partitions with the text *Applicant, Registrar*, and *System* although it is also common to put actor symbols (stick figures) to make it very clear that an actor is performing some activities. Partitions are useful because they provide more information, but they also elongate the diagram—I ran out of room and was forced to finish the diagram on another whiteboard (not shown), using a connector (the circle with the letter A in it), to help show how the physical separate portions fit together. A common use of connectors is to avoid a line going from one side of a diagram to another. Instead, you show a flow entering a connector and a second flow leaving a similarly labeled connector, e.g., both connectors have the letter B in them, going into the target activity.

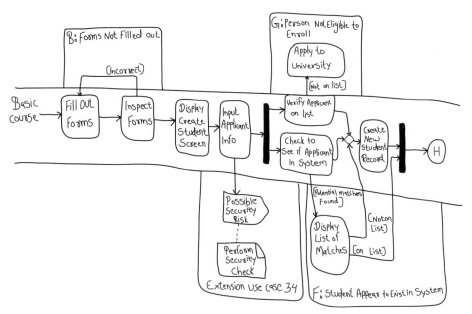

FIGURE 9.6. A UML activity diagram partitioned by courses of action.

Figure 9.5 also depicts how to apply a flow final, the circle with the X through it, as well as a note to indicate a constraint on a merge, as noted above.

The style of partitions in Fig. 9.5 is often referred to as "swim lanes" because the partitions look like the lanes in a swimming pool. Figure 9.6 takes a different approach; I guess you could call the partitions "swim areas." As you can see, swim areas take up less room than swim lanes. It is also interesting to note that the partitioning strategies between the two diagrams are different—Fig. 9.6 is partitioned by actor, whereas Fig. 9.10 is partitioned by courses of action within a use case. As always, my advice is to use the strategy best suited for your situation.

Figure 9.6 uses a notation that we have not seen before: the five-sided *Possible Security Risk* signal. This symbol indicates that an event has occurred, that we have determined that there is a possible security risk, and therefore that the *Perform Security Check* use case may need to be triggered.

Figure 9.7 depicts a UML activity diagram for the *Distribute Schedules* use case and this time I have used a drawing tool so you can see a clean example of the notation. The activity starts when the *Schedule Printed* signal is received. This signal would be sent from one or more other activity diagrams, and it is April 1 (or later). The hourglass symbol represents time, and because all of the

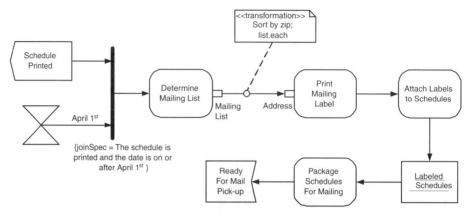

FIGURE 9.7. A UML activity diagram for the *Distribute Schedules* use case.

flows going into a join must occur before processing can continue, the way that you would read this is that the schedules must be printed and it must be at least April 1. In fact, I have chosen to indicate this with a join specification, a constraint associated to a join in the format {joinSpec = . . . }. In this case, the join specification is completely redundant so there is not any value in indicating it other than the fact that I wanted to show you an example. The only time that I indicate join specifications is when there is a constraint that is not obvious from the incoming flows. For example, if the schedules needed to be distributed before April 21 then I would likely indicate this with a join specification.

The square on the side of the *Determine Mailing List* activity in Fig. 9.7 is called a pin, and the one on the side of the *Print Mailing Label* activity is a parameter. The circle on the flow indicates a transformation; in this case, the people on the mailing list are sorted by zip code (the post office charges less

---

TIP

Focus on the Problem, Not the Techniques

Your goal is to develop software that supports the efforts of your user community. Rosenberg and Scott (1999) advise you to ruthlessly focus on answering the fundamentally important questions about the system you are building and refuse to get caught up in the superfluous modeling issues. I have been on several projects where the most pressing issue to the modelers was the correct usage of extend and include associations on use case diagrams, or which notation to use to develop their data models. Interesting issues, but not important ones when your goal is develop a system that works.

for bulk mailings sorted in this manner) and then each individual is listed so that a mailing label can then be printed for each individual.

The *Labeled Schedule* box is an example of an object being passed between activities. I rarely show objects in this manner as I feel this notation is a little bit goofy. You can usually read between the lines and determine what is flowing between activities; for example, it is clear that labels are being passed from the *Print Mailing Label* activity to the *Attach Labels to Schedules* activity.

9.4 WHAT YOU HAVE LEARNED

Process models enable you to explore in detail how your business works, often at a physical level. You have three basic models to choose from—data flow diagrams, flowcharts, and UML activity diagrams—for process modeling. Although UML activity diagrams offer the potential to replace flowcharts they still are not as good as DFDs when it comes to exploring data flow within a system. As always, use the right artifact for your situation.

9.5 REVIEW QUESTIONS

1. Develop a UML activity model describing the business logic of the *Enroll in Seminar* system use case described in Chapter 5. Be sure to include the alternate courses. Are any alternate courses missing in the use case? If so, model them in your activity diagram. Is there any opportunity for performing some activities in parallel?
2. Create a data flow diagram for the *Enroll in Seminar* use case.
3. Create a flowchart for the *Enroll in Seminar* use case.
4. Compare and contrast your three diagrams. Which was the most useful? Why?
5. Search the Web for papers and information about process modeling. Compare and contrast the various techniques. Formulate why differences exist between the various approaches and discuss the advantages and disadvantages of having different approaches available to you.

CHAPTER 10

Agile Architecture

*If you always think what you have thought you will always get
what you have got.*

Architecture provides the foundation from which systems are built, and models are one way to define the vision on which your architecture is based. The scope of architecture can be that of a single application, of a family of applications, for an entire organization, or for an international infrastructure such as the Internet. The focus of this chapter is on architectural modeling for a single system, although much of the advice is pertinent to larger efforts. Regardless of the scope, my experience is that you can take an agile approach to the modeling, development, and evolution of architectures. Table 10.1 overviews the artifacts described in this chapter for architectural modeling.

For our purposes the architecture for a system is simply its high-level design. Good architectures are based on requirements—developers taking on the role of architect will often analyze the pertinent requirements as part of the architectural modeling process. One way to look at architecture is that it, along with analysis, is the bridge between requirements and design. Architects will also consider high-level design decisions such as "What will we build this system from?", "How will the parts of this system fit together?", and "How can we ensure this system will work under less-than-perfect (or real-world) conditions?"

	TABLE 10.1. Architecture Models	
Model	**Description**	
Change case	A potential requirement that your system may need to support in the future; a primary source of architecture requirement.	
Component diagram	A unified modeling language (UML) diagram that depicts the components (as well as their interrelationships, their interactions, and their public interfaces) that compose an application, system, or enterprise. Used to model the physical software architecture of a component-based system.	
Deployment diagram	A UML diagram showing the execution architecture of systems, including nodes, either hardware or software execution environments, and the middleware connecting them. Used to model the physical hardware and software architecture of a system.	
Free-form diagram	A diagram that does not follow a defined notation, exactly as the name implies;very useful for exploring a wide range of issues.	
Network diagram	A diagram commonly used to depict hardware nodes as well as the connections between them; arguably a high-level form of a UML deployment diagram with extensive use of visual stereotypes.	
Package diagram	A UML diagram that shows how model elements are organized into packages as well as the dependencies between packages. Often used to organize other models or to depict the physical structure of source code libraries.	

This chapter is organized into several sections:

- Architecture techniques and concepts;
- Looking to the future with change cases;
- UML package diagrams;
- UML component diagrams;
- Free-form diagrams;
- UML deployment diagrams;
- Network diagrams; and
- Layering your architecture.

> ## TIP
> ## There Is Nothing Special about Architecture
>
> Agile modeling (AM)'s (Chapter 4) value of humility states that everyone has
> equal value on a project; therefore anyone in the role of architect and their efforts
> are just as important but no more so than the efforts of everyone else. Yes, good
> architects have a specialized skillset appropriate to the task at hand and should
> have the experience to apply those skills effectively. The exact same thing can
> be said, however, of good developers, of good coaches, of good senior managers,
> and so on. Humility is an important success factor for your architecture efforts
> because it is what you need to avoid the development of ivory tower architecture
> and to avoid the animosity of your teammates. The role of architect is valid for
> most projects; it just should not be a role fulfilled by someone atop a pedestal.
> Check all egos at the door.

10.1 ARCHITECTURE TECHNIQUES AND CONCEPTS

It takes years of experience to become an effective architect. Having said this,
there are several fundamental techniques and concepts that good architects
seem to follow:

- Put architectural decisions off as long as possible;
- Accept that some architectural decisions are already made;
- Prove it with code;
- Set an architectural change strategy;
- Consider reuse;
- Roll up your sleeves;
- Be prepared to make trade-offs;
- Consider adopting the Zachman framework; and
- Apply architectural patterns gently.

10.1.1 Put Architectural Decisions Off As Long As Possible

In general, the more information available to you the greater your ability
to make effective decisions. You gain more and more information, either a
greater understanding of the requirements or greater experience with the
technologies that you are working with, as a software development project
progresses. Therefore, the longer you are able to put an architectural decision

---

TIP

Think Through Big Issues Early

Following an agile model–driven design (AMDD) approach you will invest a short period of time during "cycle 0" to identify the initial candidate architecture for your system. Your goal is to identify a potential vision for how you will approach building your system, a vision that will evolve in later cycles as you learn more about the requirements and the technologies that you are working with.

---

off the greater flexibility your team will have to provide the right solution to your stakeholders.

There are limits, of course. You can put off decisions so long that you become stuck in analysis paralysis. Be cognizant of this.

10.1.2 Accept That Some Architectural Decisions Are Already Made

Many architectural decisions, in particular technical platform decisions, will already have been made for you. These decisions are often captured as technical constraints (Chapter 7) that your system must fulfill. For example, your organization has very likely settled on a standard relational database, and although your team may prefer one vendor's product to another, the fact still remains that your organization has a standard in place. Accept this and move forward. There may also be standard hardware configurations, operating systems, and middleware platform standards in place. Yes, these standards should evolve over time and it should be possible for your team to not follow standards given just cause. However, I have seen too many teams waste their time and energy fighting for their preferred approach when an existing corporate standard met their actual needs. Pick your battles wisely.

10.1.3 Prove It with Code

Agile architects ensure that their technical ideas actually work by writing a small version of it to validate the idea. This is called a spike solution in extreme programming (XP) (Jeffries, Anderson, and Hendrickson 2001) and a technical prototype or skeleton in the unified process (Kruchten 2000; Nalbone, Vizdos, and Ambler 2003). The idea is that you write just enough code to verify that what you think will work actually does. This helps to reduce technical risk because you are making technology decisions based on known facts instead of good guesses. This is different, and in my experience far more effective, than the traditional approach of creating comprehensive architectural models and submitting them for review.

10.1.4 Set an Architectural Change Strategy

Change happens. Any successful software product needs to change and evolve over its lifetime; that is, changes are motivated by new and/or modified requirements. Extensibility, the responsiveness of software to change, has been touted as one of the great benefits of object orientation, of component-based development, and of virtually any development environment with which you have ever worked. The reality is that software is extensible because its design supports the required changes, not because you implemented objects, not because you implemented components, and certainly not because you used the latest version of tool XYZ.

There are two lines of thought when it comes to architectural change strategies:

1. **Architect for change.** One line of thought says that you need to think through all of the potential situations that you can and then architect your system to support those potential situations (or at least the most likely ones). This results in you overbuilding your software, requiring you to invest in features that you *may* need at some point in the future instead of features that you know you need today. This approach reduces your ability to meet your stakeholder's immediate needs and increases your immediate development costs because you are building and maintaining more than you need to. This approach assumes that you can in fact identify all potential changes, a dubious concept at best, and then actually produce an architecture that addresses them effectively.

2. **Trust that you can meet tomorrow's needs tomorrow.** This is the approach promoted by XP (Beck 2000). The basic idea is to solve today's needs today and wait until tomorrow to address tomorrow's needs. Beck also suggests that you keep your design as simple as possible, that you produce a high-quality design, and that you ruthlessly focus on keeping your design this way. With a simple, high-quality design in place it is very likely that you

> **TIP**
>
> **Keep It Simple**
>
> A critical concept is that your architecture models and documents just need to be good enough; they do not need to be perfect. My experience is that a hand-drawn sketch today can often be far more valuable than a fully documented and validated document several months from now. By keeping your architecture artifacts simple you increase the chances that your audience will use and understand them. Overly detailed documents might look impressive sitting on a shelf, but a simple model that project teams actually use is far more impressive.

can in fact address potential changes as they occur. The primary risk of this approach is that a radically different requirement could force a major change in the design of your system, a potentially expensive endeavor. The primary benefits are that you do not waste resources overbuilding your system and as a result deliver software to your stakeholders faster and less expensively.

10.1.5 Consider Reuse

Reuse and architecture go hand-in-hand. Common reuse-oriented questions that you should consider when developing your architecture include:

- Will you build something from scratch?
- Will you adopt open source software (OSS) solutions?
- Will you start an OSS project to share resources with your peers?
- Will you reuse an existing resource as is?
- Will you modify an existing resource to meet your unique needs?
- Will you take advantage of a common business architecture framework?
- Will you develop common business architecture and then reuse it?
- Will you reuse, or develop for reuse, common technical infrastructure functionality such as that described in Table 10.2?

> **TIP**
>
> **Essential Reading**
>
> Visit http://www.flashline.com for a very good collection of articles written about reuse.

TABLE 10.2. Common Infrastructure Functionality

Service	Description
Data sharing	This service encapsulates the management of common data formats, such as XML and EDI files.
File management	This service encapsulates and manages access to files.
Interprocess communication (IPC)	This service implements middleware functionality, including support for messaging between nodes, queuing of services, and other applicable system communication services.
Persistence	This service encapsulates and manages access to permanent storage devices, such as relational databases, object databases, and object-relational databases.
Printing	This service implements the physical output of your system onto paper or to an electronic "print" format such as PDF files.
Security	This service implements security access control functionality, such as determining who is entitled to work with certain objects or portions thereof, as well as encryption/decryption and authentication.
System management	This service implements system management features, such as audit logging, real-time monitoring (perhaps via SNMP), error management, and event management.
Transaction management	This service manages transactions, single units of work that either completely succeed or completely fail, across potentially disparate nodes within your system.

10.1.6 Roll Up Your Sleeves

Although modeling and documentation is an important part of the job of an architect, that should not be their primary focus. Instead, supporting the architecture within and coaching developers both in the architecture and in architecture skills should be. The best way to do this is to get actively involved in development, to become "embedded within a project team" and work with developers to help them understand the architecture and to try it out in practice. This approach yields several benefits:

- You quickly discover whether your ideas work, and if so then how well they work.
- You improve the chance that project teams understand the architecture because you are working with them face-to-face.
- You gain experience in the tools and technologies that the project team works with, as well as the business domain itself, improving your own understanding of what it is that you are architecting.
- You obtain concrete feedback that you can act on to improve the architecture, enabling you to evolve it over time to meet the actual needs of your organization.
- You gain the respect of your primary customers, the developers, because they see that you are participating and not simply pontificating.
- You actively help build software-based systems, the primary goal of IT professionals.
- You can mentor the developers on the project teams in modeling and architecture, improving their skillsets—and learning more yourself.
- You provide clear benefit to application teams because you are helping them to fulfill their immediate goals, forsaking the "do all this extra work because it is good for the company" attitude for a more attractive "let me help you achieve your goals, and by doing so together we will do something good for the company" attitude.

10.1.7 Be Prepared to Make Trade-offs

No architecture is perfect. Requirements often contradict each other, priorities change, and sometimes you may find that you simply do not have the resources to do everything that you would like. The point is that you cannot always get what you want and that you need to be prepared to make trade-offs as you architect a system.

10.1.8 Consider Adopting the Zachman Framework

The Zachman framework (ZF) (ZIFA 2002; Hay 2003) summarizes a collection of perspectives pertinent to enterprise architecture, a modified version of which is depicted in Fig. 10.1. The rows represent the views of different

	Structure (What)	Activities (How)	Locations (Where)	People (Who)	Time (When)	Motivation (Why)
Objectives/ Scope (Planner's View)	Most significant business concepts	Mission	International view of where organization operates	Human resource philosophies and strategies	Annual planning	Enterprise vision
Enterprise Model (Business Owner's View)	Business language used	Strategies and high-level business processes	Offices and relationships between them	Positions and relationships between positions	Business events	Goals, objectives, business policies
Model of Fundamental Concepts (Architect's View)	Specific entities and relationships between them	Business functions and tactics	Roles played in each location and relationships between roles	Actual and potential interactions between people	System events	Detailed business rules
Technology Model (Designer's View)	System representation of entites and relationships	Program functions/ operations	Hardware, network, middleware	User interface design	System triggers	Business rule design
Detailed Representation (Builder's View)	Implementation strategy for entities and relationships	Implementation design of functions/ operations	Protocols, hardware components, deployed software items	Implementation of user interface	Implementation of system triggers	Implementation of business rules
Functioning System	Classes, components, tables, ...	Deployed functions/ operations	Deployed hardware, middleware, and software	Deployed user interface (including documentation)	Deployed systems	Deployed software

Computation Independent Models

Platform Independent Models (PIMs)

Platform Specific Models (PSMs)

FIGURE 10.1. The modified Zachman framework.

types of stakeholders and the columns represent different aspects or views of your architecture. There are three important concepts to understand about the ZF:

1. Within a column the models are evolved or translated to reflect the views of the stakeholders for each row.
2. The models within a single row should be consistent with one another, although because agile models are just barely good enough, the models only need to be sufficiently consistent when taking an agile approach.
3. The ZF does not define an architectural process for architecture; instead it defines the various perspectives that architecture should encompass.

The modifications that I have made are straightforward. First, I adopted David Hay's (2003) interpretation of the framework because I believe that he has evolved it in a good direction. Second, I renamed the first column from *Data* to *Structure* to remove methodological bias. The original name reflects a data-oriented approach to development, although object-driven and component-driven are also viable approaches. Third, unlike other methodologists I have not filled in the boxes with suggested artifacts but instead have indicated the perspective that each cell represents. For example, in the *Structure* column David Hay suggests that you create a language divergent data model in row 2, a convergent entity/relationship model in row 3, and a database design in row 4. Moriarty (2001) suggests a business class diagram, a class diagram, and a schema data model, respectively, in the same rows. Based on previous writings (Ambler 1998a; Ambler and Constantine 2000b) I would have suggested a component model, a class diagram, and another class diagram for these rows. All three approaches are valid, but all three represent the experiences and prejudices of the individual methodologists. Far better advice would be to understand the perspective represented by each box, understand the strengths and weaknesses of each type of modeling artifact (e.g., adopt the AM principle *know your models*), and then follow

---

TIP

Focus on People, Not Technology or Techniques

Agile architects will work with their customers, including developers, in the most effective manner possible. Sometimes this will be face-to-face drawing sketches with them at a whiteboard, sometimes they will work with project teams via video conferencing, sometimes they will answer questions via e-mail, and sometimes they will publish models and documents.

the practice *apply the right artifact(s)* to meet your actual needs. Finally, I have mapped the rows to the terms used by the Object Management Group (OMG)'s model-driven architecture (MDA), indicating which rows should be supported via platform-independent models (PIMs) versus platform-specific models (PSMs).

The primary strength of the ZF is that it explicitly shows that there are many views that need to be addressed by enterprise architecture. An immediate benefit of Fig. 10.1 is that it reminds you of the issues that you need to consider in your architecture, whether or not you decide to adopt the ZF. Another implication is that one model does not fit all, as AM's *multiple models* principle implores. Furthermore a single level of detail is not sufficient either because the audience for each row changes. A related strength is that the ZF explicitly communicates that there are several architectural stakeholders.

Unfortunately there are several potential problems with the ZF. First, the 36 cells of the ZF can motivate a documentation-heavy approach. Agile architects prefer to travel light and focus on developing software, not extraneous documentation. Second, the ZF can lead to a methodology-biased approach as we have seen with the vast majority of writings regarding the ZF. Agile architects, instead, choose the right artifacts for their situation. Third, the ZF can lead to a process-heavy approach to development, perhaps one that requires significant levels of traceability or many model reviews. Agile architecture follows the AM principle *maximize stakeholder investment* and only perform activities that add value. Fourth, the ZF is not well accepted within the development community although this is slowly changing. Fifth, the ZF promotes a top-down approach to development although this does not have to be the case. Agile architects will start in whatever cell is most appropriate for their situation and then iterate from there.

TIP

Work Iteratively and Incrementally

Agile architects work in an iterative and incremental manner, preferring an evolutionary approach where the architecture evolves over time as opposed to a "big design up front" (BDUF) approach where they would attempt to get the architecture "right" before coding. Yes, there will always be some "up front" modeling even with an agile approach, as you saw in Chapter 4's discussion of cycle 0, but doing just enough architectural modeling up front is a world of difference than a BDUF approach. Agile architects will follow the principles and practices of AM in order to be effective members on agile software development teams.

TIP
Essential Reading

There are several very good books describing common architectural patterns. The three that I recommend are

- *A Systems of Patterns: Pattern-Oriented Software Architecture* (Buschmann et al. 1996)
- *Patterns of Enterprise Application Architecture* (Fowler et al. 2003)
- *Core J2EE Patterns: Best Practices and Design Strategies, 2nd edition* (Alur, Crupi, and Malks 2003)

10.1.9 Apply Architectural Patterns Gently

The reuse of existing patterns is one of the most effective forms of reuse, in my experience, and a significant productivity enhancement that all developers should take advantage of. An architectural pattern describes a proven solution to a common architectural problem, and good architects will learn a wide range of architectural patterns over time in order to increase their effectiveness.

However, patterns are not perfect. Because there is the danger of overbuilding your system by applying patterns too early agile software developers prefer to follow the AM practice of *apply patterns gently* and ease into a pattern when there is clear evidence that it is applicable. You likely would not invest the time to layer a "hello world" application although you would a typical business application. Layering is likely the most common architectural pattern, and is described in detail in Section 10.8.

10.2 LOOKING TO THE FUTURE WITH CHANGE CASES

Change cases (Bennett 1997) are used to describe new potential requirements for a system or modifications to existing requirements. Change cases are modeled in a simple manner. You describe the potential change to your existing requirements, indicate the likeliness of that change occurring, and indicate the potential impact of that change. Figure 10.2 presents three change cases, two potential changes motivated by technical innovation—in this case the need to support several platforms and the transition to a new database vendor—and a third by a change in your business environment. Notice how both change

Change case: Need to support both Linux and Microsoft platforms.
Likelihood: Very likely to happen for application and database servers within six months; medium probability that Linux will be adopted by the school for desktop machines.
Impact: Unknown. Currently application servers for other applications run Microsoft-based operating systems and will likely continue to do so. New servers will likely have Linux installed. Desktop impact is hard to quantify as the Linux market is evolving rapidly. Should be re-evaluated six months from now.

Change case: Need to support new database vendor.
Likelihood: Medium. The school is currently renegotiating the contract with our existing vendor.
Impact: Potentially large if SQL is hard-coded into the application.

Change case: The University will open a new campus.
Likelihood: Certain. It has been announced that a new campus will be opened in two years across town.
Impact: Large. Students will be able to register in classes at either campus. Some instructors will teach at both campuses. Some departments, such as Computer Science and Philosophy, are slated to move their entire programs to the new campus. The likelihood is great that most students will want to schedule courses at only one of the two campuses, so we will need to make this easy to support.

FIGURE 10.2. Examples of change cases for the university.

cases are short and to the point, making them easy-to-understand. The name of a change case should describe the potential change itself.

Change cases can be identified throughout the course of your overall development efforts, although I have a tendency to create them when I am focusing

TIP

Base Your Architecture on Requirements

Architects who do not base their work on requirements are effectively "hacking in the large"; they are making things up instead of addressing the actual needs of their stakeholders. Technical requirements (Chapter 7) will drive much of your architecture.

on architectural modeling. Change cases are often the result of brainstorming with your project stakeholders. Good questions to consider include:

- How can the business change?
- What is the long-term vision for our organization?
- What technology can change?
- What legislation can change?
- What is your competition doing?
- What systems will we need to interact with?
- Who else might use the system and how?

My experience is that you can use change cases in a very agile manner. First, they enable you to consider long-term issues and potential changes that your system may need to support. This puts you in a position to make better architectural decisions, such as choosing one platform over another, and thus increases the chances that you are taking the best approach. This in turn reduces your desire to overbuild your system because you are not as worried about the architectural choices you have made. Second, change cases provide an easy way for you to justify architectural decisions that you have made because you can show that you have considered a wide range of issues. This can help to reduce the politics that your team must endure, allowing you to spend more time actually building software instead of attending meetings. Third, if you identify a very high-likelihood change case you can simply write it up as a normal requirement(s) with your stakeholders. They can prioritize the requirement(s) as usual and your team can then implement it as appropriate. Your architecture should be based on real requirements—from real stakeholders on the project—otherwise, you risk gold-plating your system with "really cool" features that your stakeholders do not actually need. If your architecture sports features not needed by your known requirements, or by your high-likelihood change cases, then you have overbuilt it and should scale it back.

In many ways, the change cases for a system are simply a risk assessment for changing requirements.

10.3 UML PACKAGE DIAGRAMS

Packages are UML constructs that enable you to organize model elements into groups, making your UML diagrams simpler and easier to understand.

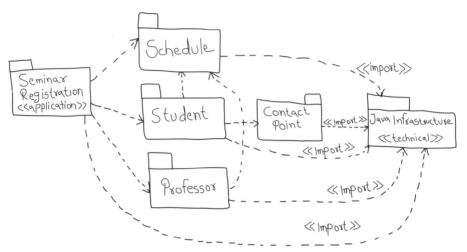

FIGURE 10.3. Package diagram that organizes classes.

Packages are depicted as file folders and can be used on any of the UML diagrams, although they are most common on use case diagrams and class diagrams because these models have a tendency to grow.

A UML package diagram is a style of diagram that only shows packages and the dependencies between them. Although a package diagram can be used to organize any type of classifier, I typically create package diagrams to organize either classes, data entities, or use cases. All three styles are effectively business architecture diagrams in my mind.

10.3.1 Class Package Diagrams

When it comes to "class package diagrams" I apply several rules of thumb. First, classes in the same inheritance hierarchy typically belong in the same package. Second, classes related to one another via composition often belong in the same package. Third, classes that collaborate with each other—information reflected by your sequence diagrams (Chapter 11) and communication diagrams (Chapter 11)—often belong in the same package.

Figure 10.3 depicts the start at a package diagram for the university. It shows several packages and the dependencies between them. Notice how the *Contact Point* package has the "flap" drawn on the right-hand side instead of the left—remember the AM principle that *content is more important than representation.*

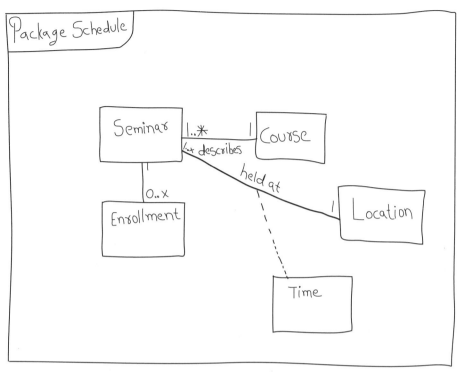

FIGURE 10.4. The contents of the *Schedule* package.

I have applied several UML stereotypes on Fig. 10.3. The *application* stereotype is applied to the *Seminar Registration* package, indicating that this package contains user-interface (UI) classes and application-specific business classes for registering students in seminars. Similarly the *technical* stereotype is applied to the *Java Infrastructure* package, indicating that it contains technical classes, perhaps a user-interface framework such as *Apache Struts* (http://jakarta.apache.org/struts) or a persistence framework such as *Prevayler* (http://www.prevayler.org). Both the *application* and *technical* stereotypes are my own convention, albeit very common ones. The import stereotype, a UML standard, is applied to several dependencies, indicating that the *Java Infrastructure* package is imported into the other packages on this diagram.

Each package in Fig. 10.3 would lead to a more detailed diagram, perhaps another package diagram for a very complicated system or more likely to a UML class diagram. Figure 10.4 depicts a UML frame, which is used to depict the contents of the *Schedule Package*, in this case, a high-level conceptual class diagram (Chapter 8). Frames can be used to show the detailed contents of any type of UML model, such as packages, components, classes, or operations. The heading is depicted with a name tag, the rectangle with the cutoff bottom-right corner, in the format *[<kind>]Name[<parameters>]*. Had the frame represented a component the heading would have read *Component Schedule* and had it been for an operation it may have read something like *Operation EnrollStudent(Student)*.

10.3.2 Data Package Diagrams

Because you can use the UML to model data it makes sense that you can also have "data model package diagrams." In this case packages are used to organize data entities into large-scale business domains. If you were to remove the *Seminar Registration* and *Java Infrastructure* packages from Fig. 10.3 you would have such a diagram, the only difference being that the packages would lead to UML data models (Chapter 12) instead of UML class models.

10.3.3 Use Case Package Diagrams

Figure 10.5 depicts a UML use case diagram that has had its use cases organized into packages (the actors are still indicated on the diagram, although they could have been moved into packages as well). Is this really a use case diagram now or is it really a UML package diagram? The important thing is that the diagram somehow adds value to your efforts—how you categorize the diagram is of little real consequence.

When I am creating a use case package diagram I will follow two rules of thumb. First, included and extending use cases belong in the same package as the base/parent use case. This heuristic works well because these use cases typically were introduced by "pulling out" their logic from the base/parent use case to start. Second, I then analyze the use cases with which my main actors are involved. What I typically find is that each actor will interact with the system to fulfill a few main goals; for example, students interact with the university to enroll in it, to manage their schedules, to pay fees, and to manage their loans and grants. Because these four sets of goals are each reasonably cohesive it suggests the need for four separate packages.

Figure 10.5 is interesting because it shows my typical reason to use packages—to organize a large diagram into several smaller ones. A good rule of thumb is that a diagram should have 7 ± 2 bubbles on it, a bubble being

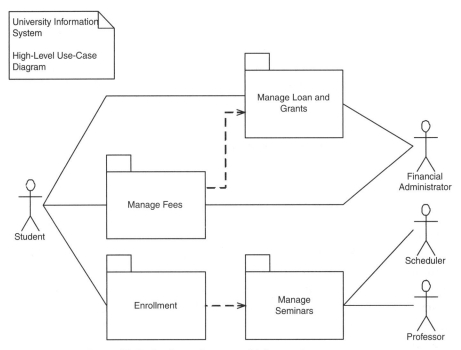

FIGURE 10.5. Package diagram, which organizes use cases.

a use case or class. When a diagram has more bubbles than this it starts to become unwieldy and therefore difficult to understand.

Packages should be cohesive. Anything you put into the package should make sense when considered with the rest of the contents of the package. To determine whether a package is cohesive, a good test is you should be able to give your package a short, descriptive name. If you cannot, then you may have put several unrelated things into the package.

I rarely create UML package diagrams in their own right, although I do apply packages on diagrams (particularly when I am using a CASE tool). I

TIP

Communication Is the Key

It does not matter how elegant or efficient an architecture is if it is not communicated and understood. Architecture should be public at all times and must be understood by all parties to be effective. In addition, communication must be two-way. Avoid architectural pontificating; respect and incorporate (or at least address) the architectural concerns of developers and others.

have heard of Java development teams using package diagrams to depict the high-level organization of their code base; Java natively supports packages of classes, although I do not see how it adds anything beyond the code-browsing capabilities of Java development environments. The fact is that I find physical diagrams such as UML component diagrams much more useful.

10.4 UML Component Diagrams

Component-based development (CBD) and object-oriented development go hand-in-hand, and it is generally recognized that object technology is the preferred foundation from which to build components. I typically use UML component diagrams as an architecture-level artifact, either to model the business software architecture, the technical software architecture, or more often than not both of these architectural aspects. Physical architecture issues, in particular hardware issues, are better addressed via UML deployment diagrams (Section 10.6) or network diagrams (Section 10.7). In fact I will often iterate back and forth between these diagrams as they are highly related to one another.

Component diagrams are particularly useful with larger teams. Your initial architectural modeling efforts during cycle 0 should focus on identifying the initial architectural landscape for your system. UML component diagrams are great for doing this as they enable you to model the high-level software components, and more importantly the interfaces to those components. Once the interfaces are defined, and agreed to by your team, it makes it much easier to organize the development effort between subteams. You will discover the need to evolve the interfaces to reflect new requirements or changes to your design as your project progresses, changes that need to be negotiated among the subteams and then implemented appropriately.

Figure 10.6 presents an example component model, using the UML 2 notation, for the university system. Figure 10.7 depicts the same diagram using UML 1.x notation. As you can see, there are several notational differences. UML 2 components are modeled as simple rectangles, whereas in UML 1.x they were depicted as rectangles with two smaller rectangles jutting out from the left-hand side. As you can see UML 2 uses this symbol as a visual stereotype within the rectangle to indicate that the rectangle represents a component although the textual stereotype of *component* is also acceptable (as you see with the *Schedule* component in Fig. 10.6). Both diagrams model dependencies, either between components or between components and interfaces. You can also see that both diagrams use the lollipop symbol to indicate an implemented

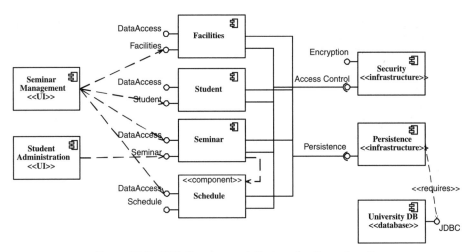

FIGURE **10.6. UML 2 component diagram for the university.**

interface although the UML 2 version introduces the socket symbol to indicate a required interface. As far as I am concerned the socket symbol is effectively a visual stereotype applied to a dependency; the equivalent textual stereotype is shown on the dependency between the *Persistence* component and the *JDBC* interface.

Diagrams such as Fig. 10.6 are often referred to as "wiring diagrams" because they show how the various software components are "wired together" to build your overall application. The lines between components are called

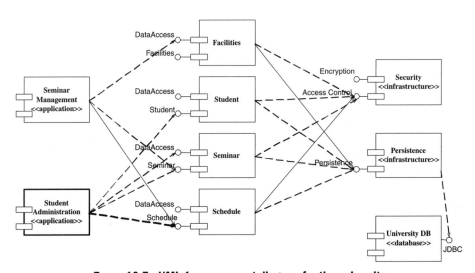

FIGURE **10.7. UML 1.x component diagram for the university.**

> **TIP**
> **Manage the Seams**
>
> Booch, Rumbaugh, and Jacobson (1999) suggest you "manage the seams in your system" by defining the major interfaces for your components. What they mean is you want to define the interfaces to components early in design, so you are free to work on the internals of each component without having to worry about how you will affect other components.

connectors, the implication being that some sort of messaging will occur across them.

I usually draw component diagrams on whiteboards although for both of the examples I have used a drawing tool to depict the notation accurately. You can use component diagrams for both logical and physical modeling although I prefer to use them for physical modeling of the software architecture of a system. Figure 10.6 shows the large-scale domain components for the system we are building, including two user-interface components that map to two different applications that we are building as part of the overall system. This diagram includes both business and technical architecture aspects—the components with the *infrastructure* and *database* stereotypes are clearly technical in nature—and that is perfectly fine. The important thing is that we are considering both business and technical aspects in our architecture, not just technical issues, and for whatever reason we have chosen to create a single diagram that includes both views.

I have modeled a *Persistence* component in Fig. 10.6 for two reasons. First, one of the change cases in Fig. 10.2 discussed the chance that we will soon need to support another database vendor. Because a persistence framework helps to decouple an object schema from a data schema it will make this potential change much easier to support. Second, a persistence framework should increase the productivity of the developers as it simplifies the effort of persisting objects. There is a cost for purchasing/downloading the framework, installing it, operating and maintaining it, and learning to work with it. These sorts of costs are typically much less than the benefits of doing so. Persistence issues are discussed in detail in Chapter 14.

10.4.1 Interfaces and Ports

Components may both provide and require interfaces. An interface is the definition of a collection of one or more methods, and zero or more attributes,

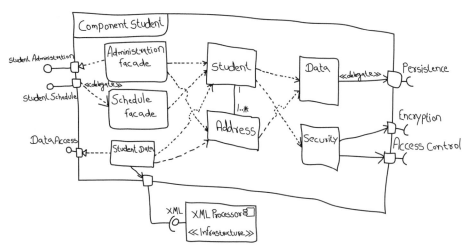

FIGURE **10.9. Designing the *Student* component.**

it indicates the flow of communication and as a result seems to be easier to understand.

3. The *Data* and *Security* classes use the same names as the corresponding ports in Fig. 10.8.
4. Classes such as *AdministrationFacade, ScheduleFacade, StudentData, Data,* and *Security* implement the façade design pattern (Gamma et al. 1995). The basic idea is that they implement the public operations required by the interfaces, operations that typically just delegate messages to the appropriate classes. Together the *AdministrationFacade, ScheduleFacade,* and *StudentData* classes implement the public interface of the *Student* component. *StudentData, Data,* and *Security* wrap access to external components so that the internal classes are not directly coupled to other physical components.
5. Expect to adapt incoming/outgoing interactions back and forth between data- and object-oriented messages. An incoming message may be implemented as a Web service, which takes XML as a parameter and returns XML as the result. The internal objects within the component, on the other hand, need messages sent to them with either objects or data as parameters and return values. The implication is that you need to marshal the data and objects back and forth between each other, something addressed by the *Adapter* design pattern (Gamma et al. 1995).
6. Another way to implement the public interface would have been to implement a single façade class called *StudentComponent,* which implements the required public interfaces and delegates appropriately.

7. When designing the *StudentData* class the team realized that it needed to work with our existing *XMLProcessor* component; therefore we added the connection to this component.

Figure 10.9 makes it obvious that building components is costly. Creating the *Student* component as shown in Fig. 10.9 does not make much sense—I have added five new classes to support two domain classes, a clear case of overbuilding. This approach would make sense if there were twenty classes, and would make a lot of sense for fifty domain classes, because the additional five classes reduce the coupling within your system while at the same time implement a large-scale, reusable domain component. The point is that you should only take a component-based approach when the benefit of doing so outweighs the additional cost. Good heuristics would be that you should have a large number of business classes in your system, at least 100, which can be organized into several cohesive components. Furthermore, there should be a good chance that your components could be potentially reusable by other applications (perhaps within the same suite/family).

10.4.3 Creating Component Models

There are two fundamental strategies for developing a component model, either top down or bottom up. Given the choice I prefer the top-down approach because it provides a good mechanism for identifying the "software landscape" early in the project, which is particularly important for teams composed of several subteams because you want to work towards the same vision. Unfortunately a top-down approach suffers from the tendency to promote overarchitecting, and hence overbuilding, of your system. For example, Fig. 10.6 calls out *Security* and *Persistence* components but you might not yet need anything even remotely that complicated. It would be a serious mistake to focus on building these two components instead of implementing actual business functionality that your stakeholders actually need.

A second way to develop component models is from the bottom up. I will do this when we have an existing collection of classes that have been developed and we decide to componentize our design. Componentizing is often done to rescue reusable functionality out of an existing application or to split an application up so it can be easily dispersed between subteams. When I am componentizing an existing object design I will often iterate through the following steps:

1. **Keep components cohesive.** A component should implement a single, related set of functionality. This may be the user-interface logic for a single
   user application, business classes composing a large-scale domain concept, or technical classes representing a common infrastructure concept.

2. **Assign user-interface classes to application components.** User-interface
   classes, those that implement screens, pages, or reports, as well as those
   that implement "glue logic" such as identifying which screen/page/... to
   display should be placed in components with the *application* stereotype.
   In Java these types of classes would include Java Server Pages (JSPs),
   servlets, and screen classes implemented via user interface class libraries
   such as Swing.

3. **Assign technical classes to infrastructure components.** Technical classes,
   such as those that implement system-level services such as security, persistence, or middleware should be assigned to components that have the
   infrastructure stereotype.

4. **Define class contracts.** A class contract is any method that directly responds to a message sent from other objects. For example, the contracts
   of the *Seminar* class likely include operations such as *enrollStudent()* and
   dropStudent(). For the purpose of identifying components, you can ignore
   all the operations that are not class contracts because they do not con-
   tribute to communication between objects distributed in different components.

5. **Assign hierarchies to the same component.** I can safely say that 99.9
   percent of the time I find that it makes sense to assign all of the classes
   of a hierarchy, either an inheritance hierarchy or a composition hierarchy,
   to the same component.

6. **Identify domain components.** A domain component is a set of classes that
   collaborate among themselves to support a cohesive set of contracts. The
   basic idea is that classes, and even other domain components, are able to
   send messages to domain components either to request information or
   to request an action be performed. On the outside, domain components
   appear simple; actually they appear like any other type of object, but,
   on the inside, they are often quite complex because they encapsulate
   the behavior of several classes. A key goal is you want to organize your
   design into several components in such a way as to reduce the amount
   of information flowing between them. Any information passed between

components, in the form of either messages or the objects returned as the result of a message send, represents potential traffic on your network (if the components are deployed to different nodes). Because you want to minimize network traffic to reduce the response time of your application, you want to design your domain components in such a way that most of the information flow occurs within the components and not between them.

7. **Identify the "collaboration type" of business classes.** To determine which domain component a business class belongs to, you need to analyze the collaborations it is involved with to determine its distribution type. A server class is one that receives messages, but does not send them. A client class is one that sends messages, but does not receive them. A client/server class is one that both sends and receives messages. Once you have identified the distribution type of each class, you are in a position to start identifying potential domain components.

8. **Server classes belong in their own component.** Pure server classes belong in a domain component and often form their own domain components because they are the "last stop" for message flow within an application.

9. **Merge a component into its only client.** If you have a domain component that is a server to only one other domain component, you may decide to combine the two components.

10. **Pure client classes do not belong in domain components.** Client classes do not belong in a domain component because they only generate messages, they do not receive them, whereas the purpose of a domain component is to respond to messages. Therefore, client classes have nothing to add to the functionality offered by a domain component and very likely belong in an application component instead.

11. **Highly coupled classes belong in the same component.** When two classes collaborate frequently, this is an indication they should be in the same domain component to reduce the network traffic between the two classes. This is especially true when that interaction involves large objects, either passed as parameters or received as return values. By including them in the same domain component you reduce the potential network traffic between them. The basic idea is that highly coupled classes belong together.

12. **Minimize the size of the message flow between components.** Client/ server classes belong in a domain component, but there may be a choice as to which domain component they belong to. This is where you need

TABLE 10.3. Design Principles for Components	
Principle	Description
Acyclic dependencies	Allow no cycles in the dependencies graph between components. For example disallow A → B → C → A because it includes a cycle.
Common closure	The classes of a component should be closed together against the same kinds of changes. A change that affects a class within a component should not affect classes outside that component. In other words your components should be cohesive in that sweeping changes across several components are not required.
Common reuse	The classes in a component are reused together. If you reuse one class in a component you reuse them all. This is another principle addressing cohesion.
Dependency inversion	Abstractions should not depend on details; instead details should depend on abstractions.
Open-closed	Software elements should be open for extension but closed for modification.
Release-reuse equivalency	The granule of reuse is the granule of release. In other words you should not reuse only part of a released software element.
Stable abstractions	A component should be as abstract as it is stable. A component should be sufficiently abstract so that it can be extended without affecting its stability.
Stable dependencies	Depend on the direction of stability—If component A depends on component B, then B should be more stable (e.g., less likely to change) than A.

to consider issues such as the information flow going into and out of the class. Communication within a component will often be simple message sends between objects in memory; communication between components may require an expensive marshaling effort in which a message and its parameters are converted to data, transmitted, and then converted back into a message again.

13. **Define component contracts.** Each component will offer services to its clients, each such service being a component contract.

Table 10.3 summarizes several design principles presented in *Agile Software Development* (Martin, Newkirk, and Koss 2003) for components and packages.

I summarize them here because I find them of great value when it comes to component modeling.

10.4.4 Remaining Agile

My most successful use of component models was with a team where we drew a diagram similar to Fig. 10.6, albeit a much larger one with over twenty components, on a whiteboard. This whiteboard was situated in the teamwork area where everyone could see the board. We developed the diagram early in the project and updated it as required throughout the project. We kept it on the board because it provided a high-level map of the architecture of our software, a map that we used from time to time as we worked and more importantly engendered many interesting conversations regarding the overall system design.

There are several advantages to components that promote agility. First, components are reusable building blocks from which you can build software, increasing your productivity as a developer. Second, components can improve your testing productivity because they can be treated as elements, which you can black-box unit and integration test. Testing was discussed in detail in Chapter 3.

10.5 FREE-FORM DIAGRAMS

One of the most useful, and most common, types of model is a free-form diagram. Yet they rarely seem to be recognized as an "official" diagram type, perhaps because it is difficult to set free-form modeling standards or convince you that you need an expensive tool to create them—whiteboards work just fine, thank you. Figure 10.10 depicts a free-form diagram of the technical architecture for the university system. I regularly see whiteboard drawing like this at clients as well as depicted in architecture books (although these diagrams are usually drawn with a tool such as Microsoft Visio to make them look pretty).

This diagram shows the architectural layering (Section 10.8), software components such as the business rule and security engines, middleware such as Web services and the message bus, and hardware nodes such as the mainframe and application servers. A mishmash of information that would likely require

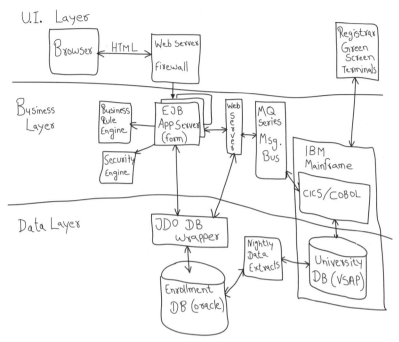

FIGURE 10.10. A free-form diagram for the technical architecture of the system.

several UML diagrams to capture; yet this single sketch seems to communicate the architectural landscape for your system nicely.

It is interesting to note that some of your most important architectural decisions, such as the use of XML to transport data between hardware nodes, will often be made by a group of people drawing a free-form diagram on a whiteboard. I think the idea of free-form diagrams is self-explanatory so I am not going to go into any more detail. The important point is to realize that they are a valid architectural modeling option that is available to you.

TIP

You Must Make Architecture Attractive to Your Customers

Agile architects realize that they need to make their efforts attractive to developers and business stakeholders. If your customers perceive that you have value to add, that your architecture efforts will aid them in their jobs, then they are much more likely to work with you. If, on the other hand, they think that you are wasting their time they will not work with you. They will find ways to avoid you, to cancel or postpone meetings with you, and to find ways to work around you.

10.6 UML Deployment Diagrams

A UML 2 deployment diagram depicts a static view of the run-time configuration of processing nodes and the components that run on those nodes. In other words, deployment diagrams show the hardware for your system, the software installed on that hardware, and the middleware used to connect the disparate machines to one another. You want to create a deployment diagram for applications deployed to several machines, for example, a point-of-sales application running on a thin-client network computer that interacts with several internal servers behind your corporate firewall or a customer service system deployed using a Web services architecture such as Microsoft's.NET. Deployment diagrams can also be created to explore the architecture of embedded systems, showing how the hardware and software components work together. In short, you may want to consider creating a deployment diagram for all but the most trivial of systems.

Figure 10.11 presents an example of a fully rendered UML 2 deployment diagram for the student administration application. The three-dimensional boxes represent nodes, either software or hardware. Physical nodes should be labeled with the stereotype *device*, to indicate that it is a physical device such as a computer or switch. As you can see I did not indicate that *WebServer* is a device—it will at least be some sort of software artifact and very well may be one or more physical devices as well but my team has not made that decision yet. Remember that models evolve over time. Connections between nodes are represented with simple lines, and are assigned stereotypes such as *RMI* (remote method invocation) and *message bus* to indicate the type of connection.

This version of the diagram was drawn three months into the project, having evolved over time as we gained a better understanding of the environment. During the second month our enterprise architecture group decided to standardize on Solaris-based application servers. We had originally thought that Linux-based servers would be chosen, as you can see from our change cases of Fig. 10.2—you do not always guess right. We did, however, guess right about the database decision: senior management decided that our project would by the pilot test project for Oracle (previously we were strictly an IBM DB2 shop). The adoption of Oracle is not guaranteed; if we run into significant challenges or discover that the operating cost is higher than expected we may need to migrate back to DB2. The architectural choice of using a persistence framework is looking more prescient every day. Furthermore, based on the potential need to support a Linux desktop as well as a Microsoft one we have

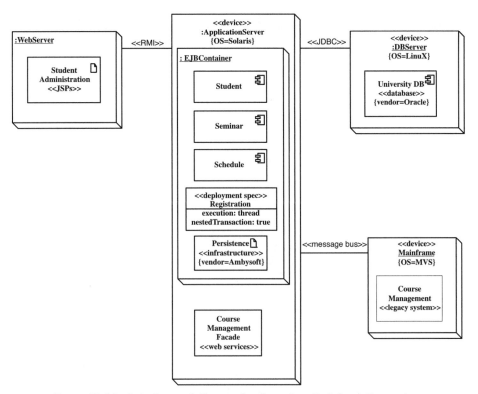

FIGURE 10.11. A deployment diagram for the university information system.

made the decision to build a browser-based system using JSPs to render the user interface.

When you stop and think about it, the stereotypes that I have applied to the connections are not correct. In reality the software on the Web server is communicating via the RMI protocol over the connection to the software on the application server. The physical connection between the physical hardware nodes is at a lower level, perhaps an Ethernet connection, so in reality I really should have modeled a connection between the hardware nodes with *Ethernet* as a stereotype and a second connection between software elements with the *RMI* stereotype. I would also need to model a dependency relationship between the software connection and the hardware connection, perhaps with the stereotype of *over*. Although this would be more accurate it would be a lot of work that I likely would not get much benefit from. Remember that agile models do not need to be perfect; they need to be just good enough.

TIP

Look at the Whole Picture

Agile architects believe in the AM principle *multiple models* and thus strive to look at the whole picture. They do not just focus on data models, or object/component models, or business models, or whatever type of model might tickle their fancy. Instead they strive to model from several points of view so that their understanding and description of the architecture is more robust. Why several views? First, architecture has several audiences—the business community, application developers, DBAs, network professionals, and so on—each of whom has different priorities. Second, each type of model has its strengths and weaknesses and because architecture is such a complex issue no single view is sufficient.

Nodes can contain other nodes or software artifacts. The *ApplicationServer* node contains *EJBContainer* (a software node), which in turn contains three software components, a deployment specification, and a software artifact. The software components use the same notation as component diagrams (I could have annotated them with their interfaces although that would not have added any value in my opinion). Deployment specifications are basically configuration files, such as an Enterprise Java Beans (EJB) deployment descriptor, which define how a node should operate. They are depicted as two-sectioned rectangles with the stereotype *deployment spec*; the top box indicates the name and the bottom box lists the deployment properties (if any) for the node. In my opinion the deployment properties is superfluous as this is the type of information contained in the actual deployment specification file at run time. Software artifacts are shown with the visual stereotype of a page with a folded corner or with the textual stereotype *artifact* (or both sometimes, which I also believe is superfluous). In this case the software artifact is a fictional persistence framework purchased from AmbySoft (the vendor is indicated with a UML property string).

I never draw deployment diagrams following the style show in Fig. 10.11, except when I am writing about deployment modeling, because in my opinion this notation is visually wasteful. A better example is shown in Fig. 10.12. Software elements are now simply listed by their physical filenames, information that developers are very likely to be interested in, and thus a more compact diagram is possible. I have also used a drum as a visual stereotype for the *University DB* database, making it easier to distinguish on the diagram. Another difference is that the concise version shows less details; not as many tagged values are shown as this information can be captured in either supporting documentation, configuration files, or source code. Deployment diagrams

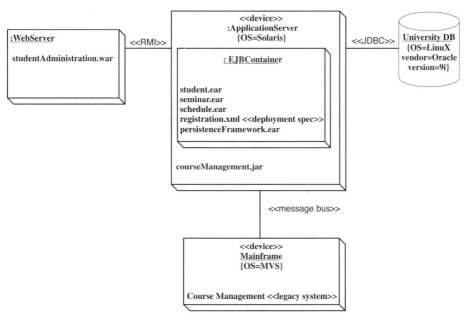

FIGURE **10.12. A concise deployment diagram.**

tend to become very large very quickly because they reflect the physical complexities of your system; therefore a concise notation becomes critical to your success.

How agile are deployment diagrams? As always, it depends on your goals. Very often less-detailed network diagrams (Section 10.7), which are arguably deployment diagrams with extensive use of visual stereotypes, are a better option. This is particularly true when you are modeling an environment consisting of many interconnected machines. Sometimes a high-level free-form diagram (Section 10.5) is a better option because the notation is much more flexible. The information contained in Fig. 10.12 can just as readily be captured in either a network diagram or a free-form diagram in combination with

TIP

Keep the Politics to a Minimum

As Mitch Kapor advises, architecture is politics. Architecture sets the foundation for your system, and effective politicians understand that this is one of the most effective spots to affect your efforts. Working together as a team, following practices such as open and honest communication, and proving things with code help to reduce the negative aspects of architectural politics.

installation scripts. When you think about it installation scripts are effectively "deployment source code."

To determine whether you need to create a deployment model, ask yourself this: if you knew nothing about the system and someone asked you to install it and/or maintain and support it, would you want a description of how the parts of the system fit together? When I ask this question of the project teams I work with, we almost always decide to develop some form of deployment model. More important, practice has shown that deployment modeling is well worth it. Deployment models force you to think about important deployment issues long before you must deliver the actual system.

When determining how to model the deployment architecture for a system, regardless of the artifacts chosen, I will typically do the following:

1. **Identify the scope of the model.** Does the diagram address how to deploy a version of a single application or does it depict the deployment of all systems within your organization?

2. **Consider fundamental technical issues.** What existing systems will yours need to interact/integrate with? How robust does your system need to be (will there be redundant hardware to failover to)? What/who will need to connect to and/or interact with your system and how will they do it (via the Internet, exchanging data files, and so forth)? What middleware, including the operating system and communications approaches/protocols, will your system use? What hardware and/or software will your users directly interact with (PCs, network computers, browsers, and so forth)? How do you intend to monitor the system once it has been deployed? How secure does the system need to be (do you need a firewall, do you need to physically secure hardware, and so forth)?

3. **Identify the distribution architecture.** Do you intend to take a fat-client approach where the business logic is contained in a desktop application or a thin-client approach where business logic is deployed to an application server? Will your application have two tiers, three tiers, or more? Your distribution architecture strategy will often be predetermined for your application, particularly if you are deploying your system to an existing technical environment.

4. **Identify the nodes and their connections.** Your distribution strategy will define the general type of nodes you will have, but not the exact details. You need to make platform decisions, such as the hardware and operating

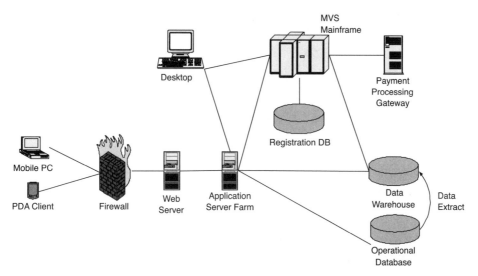

FIGURE 10.13. A network diagram for the university.

systems to be deployed, including how the various nodes will be connected (perhaps via RMI and a message bus as in Fig. 10.12).

5. **Distribute software to nodes.** Both versions of the deployment diagrams indicate the software deployed on each node, critical information for anyone involved in development, installation, or operation of the system.

10.7 NETWORK DIAGRAMS

Network diagrams, an example of which is depicted in Fig. 10.13, are commonly used to depict hardware nodes as well as the connections between them. Network diagrams are arguably a high-level form of UML deployment diagram with extensive use of visual stereotypes.

Network diagrams are often drawn using software-based drawing tools; Fig. 10.13 was drawn using Microsoft Visio, although there is nothing stopping you from using simpler tools such as whiteboards. Hand-drawn network diagrams are often used as the starting point for either a "clean" network diagram created with a drawing tool or a more detailed UML deployment diagram.

The scope of a network diagram can be a single application, a family of applications, or even your entire enterprise. An enterprise network diagram is

---

TIP

Your Architecture Must Support Many Releases

Good architects consider the issue of deploying future releases over existing ones. It is relatively easy to build a system that can be installed once. It is much more difficult to architect it to be updated on a regular basis, not to mention to have a previous version reinstalled.

---

often used as the starting point, when available, for either an application-level network diagram or UML deployment diagram. A combination of a network diagram and installation script is often used as an alternative to a detailed UML deployment diagram.

10.8 LAYERING YOUR ARCHITECTURE

Very likely the most critical architectural practice, in my opinion, is that of layering. While technically an architectural pattern (Section 10.1.9) and not an architectural technique, it is important enough, and comes up so often, that it justifies a discussion by itself.

Layering is the concept of organizing your software design into layers/collections of functionality that fulfill a common purpose, such as implementing your user interface or the business logic of your system. A class-type architecture provides a strategy for layering the classes of your software to distribute the functionality of your software among classes. Furthermore, class-type architectures provide guidance as to what other types of classes a given type of class will interact with, and how that interaction will occur. This increases the extensibility, maintainability, and portability of the systems you create.

What are the qualities that make up good layers? First, it seems reasonable that you should be able to make modifications to any given layer without affecting any other layers. This will help to make our system easy to extend and to maintain. Second, layers should be modularized. You should be able either to rewrite or to replace a layer and, as long as the interface remains the same, the rest of the system should not be affected. This will help increase the portability of your software. For example, if you create a separate layer for your user interface (a common approach), you can provide a Visual Basic UI for the first version of your application and later develop an HTML interface without changing any other part of the system.

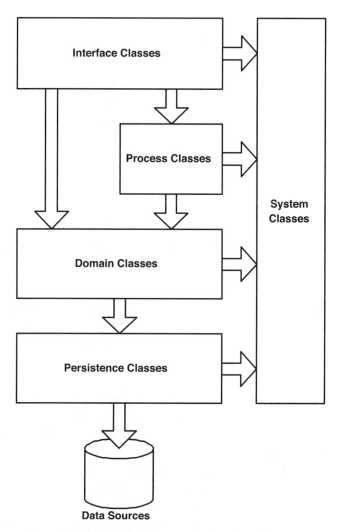

FIGURE **10.14. Layering your system based on class types.**

Figure 10.14 depicts five-layer class-type architecture for the design of object-oriented software. These are the layers:

1. **Interface classes.** These classes wrap access to the logic of your system. There are two categories of interface class—UI classes that provide people access to your system and system interface (SI) classes that provide access to external systems to your system. JSPs and graphical user interface (GUI) screens implemented via the Swing class library are commonly used to

implement UI classes within Java. Web services and CORBA wrapper classes are good options for implementing SI classes.

2. **Domain classes.** These classes implement the concepts pertinent to your business domain such as *Student* or *Seminar*, focusing on the data aspects of the business objects, plus behaviors specific to individual objects. EJB entity classes are a common approach to implementing domain classes within Java.

3. **Process classes.** Also called controller classes, these classes implement business logic that involves collaborating with several domain classes or even other process classes.

4. **Persistence classes.** These classes encapsulate the capability to store, retrieve, and delete objects permanently without revealing details of the underlying storage technology. Persistence is covered in greater detail in Chapter 14.

5. **System classes.** These classes provide operating-system-specific functionality for your applications, isolating your software from the operating system (OS) by wrapping OS-specific features, increasing the portability of your application.

Collaboration between classes is allowed within a layer; for example, UI classes can send messages to other UI classes and business/domain classes can send messages to other business/domain classes. Collaboration can also occur between classes in layers connected by arrows. As you see in Fig. 10.14, interface classes may send messages to domain classes but not to persistence classes. Domain classes may send messages to persistence classes, but not to interface classes. By restricting the flow of messages to only one direction, you dramatically increase the portability of your system by reducing the coupling between classes. For example, the domain classes do not rely on the user interface of the system, implying that you can change the interface without affecting the underlying business logic.

All types of classes may interact with system classes. This is because your system layer implements fundamental software features such as inter-process communication (IPC), a service classes use to collaborate with classes on other computers, and audit logging, which classes use to record critical actions taken by the software. For example, if your user-interface classes are running on a personal computer (PC) and your domain classes are running on an EJB application server on another machine, then your interface classes will send messages to the domain classes via the IPC service in the system layer. This service is often implemented via the use of middleware.

It is important to understand that this is not the only way to layer an application, but instead that it is a very common one. The important thing is that you identify the layers pertinent to your environment and then act accordingly.

10.9 WHAT YOU HAVE LEARNED

Every system has an underlying architecture; whether you choose to invest time modeling that architecture is your decision. My advice is to do so. This chapter began with a discussion of techniques and concepts for effective and agile architecture efforts. It also overviewed common architecture-oriented models, including UML package diagrams, UML component diagrams, UML deployment diagrams, change cases, network diagrams, and free-form diagrams. Every developer should understand at least the fundamentals of architecture and ideally all developers should be skilled at this important aspect of software development. This chapter introduced you to these skills.

10.10 REVIEW QUESTIONS

1. Organize the classes of your conceptual model into a UML package diagram. Describe each package with a single paragraph or several point-form sentences.
2. Why did you choose the form (paragraph vs. point-form) of documentation in Question 1? When would you choose the other? What value does the documentation add?
3. Create a business component diagram; do not worry about technical components for now, for the bank case study. Write some documentation describing each component.
4. Create a deployment diagram for the bank case study. As you create the model identify the architectural decisions that you are making, for example, the choice of an operating system.
5. Create a free-form diagram overviewing the architecture for the bank case study. Identify any new architectural decisions, if any, that you have made beyond those already identified for the deployment diagram in the previous question.

6. Compare and contrast your business component diagram, your deployment diagram, and your free-form diagram. What are the strengths and weakness of each? How do they relate to one another? Do you need all three? In which situations would you create each one? Why?

7. In the role of business stakeholder, identify and document five different change cases for the bank case study.

8. In the role of developer, identify and justify the potential impact of each change case from Question 5. Write this in terminology that your business stakeholders would understand (assume that they are not developers but are familiar with computing technology).

9. Is it important to be able to describe technical issues to non-technical people? Why or why not?

10. Of the requirements and analysis artifacts that you learned about in Chapters 4 and 6, identify the three most important ones for input into the creation of a network diagram. Rank them in priority order and describe how each one provides input into the creation of a network diagram.

11. Repeat Question 10 for component diagrams.

12. Search the Web for papers and information about architectural modeling. Compare and contrast the various techniques. Formulate why differences exist among the various approaches and discuss the advantages and disadvantages of having different approaches available to you.

CHAPTER 11

Dynamic Object Modeling

No matter what happens, someone will find a way to take it too seriously.

Dynamic object modeling focuses on identifying the behavior and collaborations between objects within your system. It is a critical aspect of object-oriented (OO) design, as is structural object design (Chapter 12). Table 11.1 summarizes six dynamic modeling techniques described in this chapter, all of them defined by the unified modeling language (UML) (Object Management Group 2003).

The purpose of design is to determine how you are going to build your system, information needed to drive the actual implementation of your system (object-oriented programming is covered in Chapter 13). First, just like other aspects of development, design is also an iterative process. Second, analysis and design are highly interrelated as are design and programming.

This chapter addresses the following topics:

- UML sequence diagrams;
- UML communication diagrams;
- UML state machine diagrams;
- UML timing diagrams;
- UML interaction overview diagrams; and
- UML composite structure diagrams.

TABLE 11.1. Dynamic Modeling Techniques	
Model	Description
Communication diagram	A UML diagram that shows instances of classes, their interrelationships, and the message flow between them. Communication diagrams typically focus on the structural organization of objects that send and receive messages and are used to get a "bird's-eye view" of those collaborating objects.
Composite structure diagram	A UML diagram that depicts the internal structure of a classifier (such as a class, component, or use case), including the interaction points of the classifier to other parts of the system. Typically used to explore the detailed implement required to support a critical transaction or collaboration.
Interaction overview diagram	A UML diagram (Chapter 9) that overviews the control flow within a system or business process. Each node/activity within the diagram can represent another interaction diagram. Used to connect a collection of detailed diagrams together.
Sequence diagram	A UML diagram that models the sequential logic, in effect the time ordering of messages between classifiers. This diagram is the mainstay of dynamic modeling; it is often used as a bridge between usage requirements (Chapter 5) and detailed structural designs (Chapter 12) or to model the detailed design of an operation or service.
State machine diagram	A UML diagram that describes the states an object or interaction may be in, as well as the transitions between states. Typically used to explore the design of a complex class or component.
Timing diagram	A UML diagram that depicts the change in state or condition of a classifier instance or role over time. Typically used to show the change in state of an object over time in response to external events.

11.1 UML Sequence Diagrams

UML sequence diagrams model the flow of logic within your system in a visual manner, enabling you both to document and validate your logic, and are commonly used for both analysis and design purposes. In fact they are often described as the bridging technique between analysis artifacts such as system use cases and robustness diagrams and design-oriented artifacts such as UML class diagrams. Sequence diagrams are the most popular UML artifact for dynamic modeling. Sequence diagrams, along with class diagrams and physical data models (Chapter 12), are in my opinion the most important design-level models for modern business application development.

Sequence diagrams are typically used to model the following:

- **Usage scenarios.** A usage scenario is a description of a potential way your system is used. The logic of a usage scenario may be part of a use case, perhaps an alternate course. It may also be one entire pass through a use case, such as the logic described by the basic course of action or a portion of the basic course of action, plus one or more alternate scenarios. The logic of a usage scenario may also be a pass through the logic contained in several use cases. For example, a student enrolls in the university, and then immediately enrolls in three seminars.

- **The logic of methods.** Sequence diagrams can be used to explore the logic of a complex operation, function, or procedure. One way to think of sequence diagrams, particularly highly detailed diagrams, is as visual object code.

- **The logic of services.** A service is effectively a high-level method, often one that can be invoked by a wide variety of clients. This includes Web services as well as business transactions implemented by a variety of technologies such as CICS/COBOL or CORBA-compliant object request brokers (ORBs).

Let us start with three simple examples. Figure 11.1 depicts a UML sequence diagram for the *Enroll in University* use case of Fig. 11.2, taking a system-level approach where the interactions among the actors and the system are shown. Figure 11.3 depicts a sequence diagram for the detailed logic of a service to determine whether an applicant is already a student at the university. Figure 11.4 shows the logic for how to enroll in a seminar. I will often develop a system-level sequence diagram with my stakeholders to help to both visualize and validate the logic of a usage scenario. It also helps me to identify significant methods/services, such as checking to see whether the applicant already exists as a student, which my system must support.

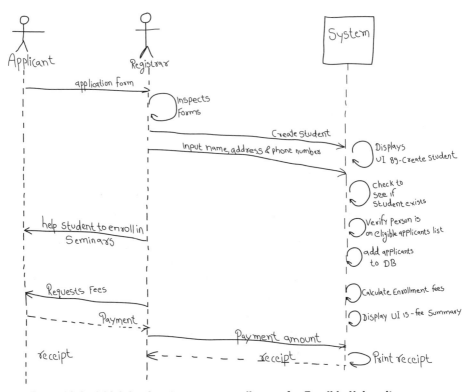

FIGURE 11.1. A high-level system sequence diagram for *Enroll in University* use case.

Name: Enroll in University

Identifier: UC 19

Description:
Enroll someone in the university.

Preconditions:
The Registrar is logged into the system.
The Applicant has already undergone initial checks to verify that they are eligible to enroll.

FIGURE 11.2. The *Enroll in University* use case.

Postconditions:

The Applicant will be enrolled in the university as a student if they are eligible.

Basic Course of Action:

1. An applicant wants to enroll in the university.
2. The applicant hands a filled out copy of form *U113 University Application Form* to the registrar. [Alternate Course A: Forms Not Filled Out]
3. The registrar visually inspects the forms.
4. The registrar determines that the forms have been filled out properly. [Alternate Course B: Forms Improperly Filled Out]
5. The registrar clicks on the *Create Student* icon.
6. The system displays *U189 Create Student Screen*.
7. The registrar inputs the name, address, and phone number of the applicant. [Extension Point: *UC34 Perform Security Check*. Applicable to Step 17]
8. The system determines that the applicant does not already exist within the system according to *BR37 Potential Match Criteria for New Students*. [Alternate Course F: Students Appears to Exist within the System].
9. The system determines that the applicant is on the eligible applicants list. [Alternate Course G: Person Is Not Eligible to Enroll]
10. The system adds the applicant to its records. The applicant is now considered to be a student.
11. The registrar helps the student to enroll in seminars via the use case *UC 17 Enroll in Seminar*.
12. The system calculates the required initial payment in accordance to *BR16 Calculate Enrollment Fees*.
13. The system displays *U115 Fee Summary Screen*.
14. The registrar asks the student to pay the initial payment in accordance to *BR19 Fee Payment Options*.
15. The student pays the initial fee. [Alternate Course D: The Student Cannot Pay at This Time]
16. The system prints a receipt.
17. The registrar hands the student the receipt.
18. The use case ends.

Alternate Course A: . . . .

FIGURE 11.2 (continued)

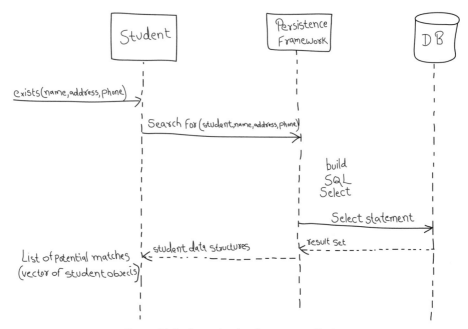

FIGURE 11.3. A service-level sequence diagram.

The reason they are called sequence diagrams should be obvious: the sequential nature of the logic is shown via the ordering of the messages (the horizontal arrows). The first message starts in the top left corner, the next message appears just below that one, and so on.

The boxes across the top of the diagram represent classifiers or their instances, typically use cases, objects, classes, or actors. Because you can send messages to both objects and classes, objects respond to messages through the

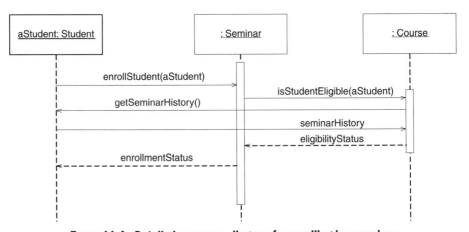

FIGURE 11.4. Detailed sequence diagram for enrolling in a seminar.

invocation of an operation and classes do so through the invocation of static operations; it makes sense to include both in sequence diagrams. Because actors initiate and take an active part in usage scenarios, they can also be included in sequence diagrams. Objects have labels in the standard UML format *name: ClassName*, where "name" is optional (objects that have not been given a name on the diagram are called anonymous objects). Classes have labels in the format *ClassName*, and actors have names in the format *Actor Name*. Notice how object labels are underlined, classes and actors are not. For example, in Fig. 11.4, you see the *Student* object has the name *aStudent*—this is called a named object—whereas the instance of *Seminar* is an anonymous object. The instance of *Student* was given a name because it is used in several places as a parameter in messages, whereas the instance of the *Seminar* did not need to be referenced anywhere else in the diagram and thus could be anonymous. In Fig. 11.3 the *Student* class sends messages to the *PersistenceFramework* class (which could have been given the stereotype <<infrastructure>> but was not to keep the diagram simple). Any message sent to a class is implemented as a static method; more on this later.

The dashed lines hanging from the boxes are called object lifelines, representing the life span of the object during the scenario being modeled. The long, thin boxes on the lifelines are activation boxes, also called method-invocation boxes, which indicate processing is being performed by the target object/class to fulfill a message. I will only draw activation boxes when I am using a tool that natively supports them, such as a sophisticated CASE tool, and when I want to explore performance issues. Activation boxes are too awkward to draw on whiteboards or with simple drawing tools that do not easily support them.

The *X* at the bottom of an activation box, an example of which is presented in Fig. 11.5, is a UML convention to indicate an object has been removed from memory or that it has been "let go." In languages such as C++ where you need to manage memory yourself you need to invoke an object's destructor, typically

---

TIP

Design Is So Important You Should Do It Every Day

It is critical to think through how you are going to build something, to actually design it, before you build it. Your design efforts may take the form of a sketch on a whiteboard, a detailed model created with a sophisticated modeling tool, or a simple test that you write before you write business code. Agile developers realize that design is so important that they do it every day, that design is not just a phase that you do early in the project before getting to the "real work" of writing the source code.

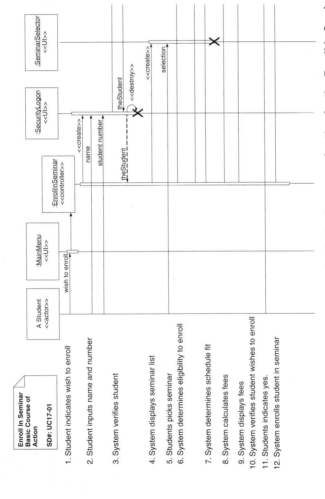

Enroll In Seminar
Basic Course of
Action

SD#: UC17-01

1. Student indicates wish to enroll

2. Student inputs name and number

3. System verifies student

4. System displays seminar list

5. Students picks seminar

6. System determines eligibility to enroll

7. System determines schedule fit

8. System calculates fees

9. System displays fees

10. System verifies student wishes to enroll

11. Students indicates yes.

12. System enrolls student in seminar

FIGURE 11.5. A UML sequence diagram for the basic course of action for the *Enroll in Seminar* use case.

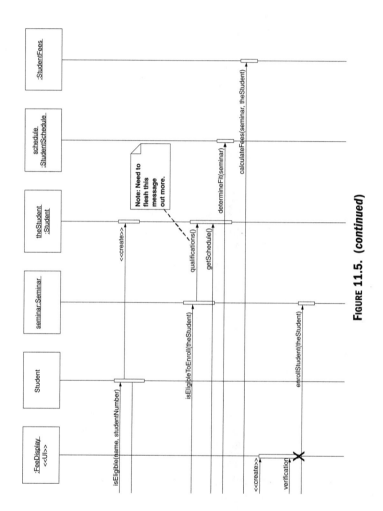

FIGURE 11.5. (*continued*)

modeled as a message with the stereotype of <<destroy>>. In languages such as Java or C# where memory is managed for you and objects that are let go are automatically removed from memory, something often referred to as garbage collection. I generally do not bother with modeling object destruction at all and will instead trust that the programmers, often myself, will implement low-level details such as this appropriately.

Figure 11.5 presents a complex UML sequence diagram for the basic course of action for the *Enroll in Seminar* use case. This is an alternative way for modeling the logic of a usage scenario; instead of doing it at the system-level such as Fig. 11.1 you simply dive straight into modeling the detailed logic at the object-level. I will take this approach when I am working with developers who are experienced sequence diagrammers and I have a large working space (either a huge whiteboard or a CASE tool installed on a workstation with a very large screen and good graphic card). Most of the time I will draw system-level diagrams first and then create small diagrams along the lines of what is shown in Fig. 11.3 and Fig. 11.4.

Messages are indicated on UML sequence diagrams as labeled arrows. When the source and target of a message is an object or class the label is the signature of the method invoked in response to the message. However, if either the source or target is a human actor, then the message is labeled with brief text describing the information being communicated. For example, in Fig. 11.5 the *EnrollInSeminar* object sends the message *isEligibleToEnroll(theStudent)* to the instance of *Seminar*. Notice how I include both the method's name and the name of the parameters, if any, passed into it. The *Student* actor provides information to the *SecurityLogon* object via the messages labeled *name* and *student number* (these really are not messages; they are actually user interactions).

Return values are optionally indicated using a dashed arrow with a label indicating the return value. For example, the return value *theStudent* is indicated coming back from the *Student* class as the result of invoking a message, whereas no return value is indicated as the result of sending the message *isEligibleToEnroll(theStudent)* to *Seminar*. My style is not to indicate the return values when it is obvious what is being returned, so I do not clutter my sequence diagrams (as you can see, sequence diagrams get complicated fairly quickly). Figure 11.6 shows an alternate way for indicating return values using the format *message: returnValue* for messages, as you would with *isEligibleToEnroll(theStudent): false*.

In Fig. 11.5 the steps of the use case are summarized down the left-hand side of the diagram. Notice how I used an informal wording for the use case

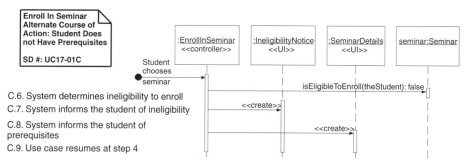

FIGURE **11.6. Modeling an alternate course of action.**

steps—formal wording is often too wordy to fit nicely on a diagram. What is critical is that the step numbers correspond to those in the use case and the general idea of the step is apparent to the reader of the diagram. With this approach the reader can easily see which messages correspond to which use case steps, offering a very straightforward and simple traceability between models.

Notice the use of stereotypes throughout the diagrams. For the boxes, I applied the stereotypes <<actor>>, <<controller>>, and <<UI>>, indicating they represent an actor, a controller class, or a user-interface (UI) class, respectively. I have also used visual stereotypes on some diagrams—a stick figure for actors; the robustness diagram visual stereotypes for controller, interface, and entity objects in Fig. 11.7; and a drum for the database. Stereotypes are also used on messages. Common practice on UML diagrams is to indicate creation and destruction messages with the stereotypes of <<create>> and <<destroy>>, respectively. For example, you see the *SecurityLogon* object is created in this manner (actually, this message would likely be sent to the class that would then result in a return value of the created object, so I cheated a bit). This object later destroys itself in a similar manner, presumably when the window is closed.

I used a UML note in Fig. 11.5; notes are basically free-form text that can be placed on any UML diagram, to provide a header for the diagram, indicating its title and identifier (as you may have noticed, I give unique identifiers to

TIP

Design Models Need to Be Just Barely Good Enough

You do not need to model every single detail in your models, and the models do not need to be perfect.

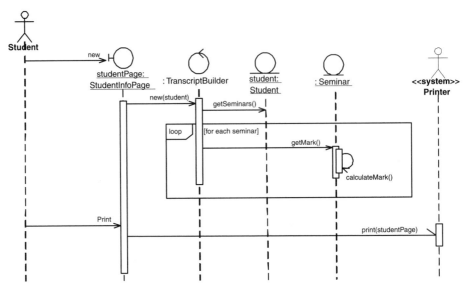

FIGURE 11.7. Modeling how transcripts are output.

all artifacts that I intend to keep). Notes are depicted as a piece of paper with the top-right corner folded over. I also used a note to indicate future work that needs to be done, during either analysis or design, in this diagram—the *qualifications*() message likely represents a series of messages sent to the student object. Common UML practice is to anchor a note to another model element with a dashed line when appropriate; in this case the note is attached to the message.

Although Fig. 11.5 models the logic of the basic course of action for the *Enroll in Seminar* use case, how would you go about modeling alternate courses? The easiest way to do so is to create a single sequence diagram for each alternate course, as you see depicted in Fig. 11.6. This diagram models only the logic of the alternate course, as you can tell by the numbering of the steps on the left-hand side of the diagram, and the header note for the diagram indicates it is an alternate course of action. Also notice how the ID of this diagram includes that this is alternate course *C*, yet another modeling rule of thumb I have found useful over the years.

Let us consider other sequence diagramming notation. Figure 11.6 includes an initial message, *Student chooses seminar*, which is indicated by the filled in circle. This could easily have been indicated via a method invocation, perhaps *enrollIn(seminar)*. Figure 11.7 shows another way to indicate object creation—sending the *new* message to a class. We have actually seen three ways to achieve

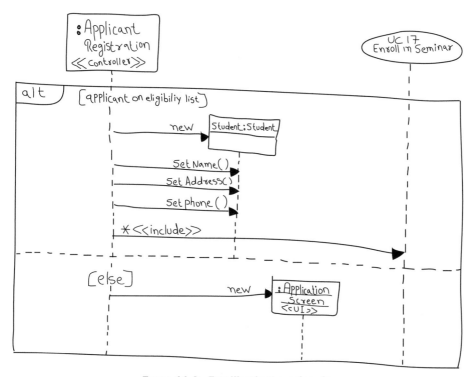

FIGURE 11.8. Enrolling in the university.

this, the other two being to send a message with the <<create>> stereotype and/or to send a message into the side of the classifier symbol (for example, in Fig. 11.5 the message going into the side of *EnrollInSeminar* or in Fig. 11.7 the message going into the side of *StudentInfoPage*). My advice is to choose one style and stick to it.

Figure 11.7 and Fig. 11.8 each depict a way to indicate looping logic. One way is to show a frame with the label loop and a constraint indicating what is being looped through, such as *for each seminar* in Fig. 11.7. Another approach is to simply precede a message that will be invoked several times with an asterisk, as you see in Fig. 11.8 with the inclusion of the *Enroll in Seminar* use case.

Figure 11.7 includes an asynchronous message, the message to the system printer that has the partial arrowhead. An asynchronous message is one where the sender does not wait for the result of the message; instead it processes the result when and if it ever comes back. Up until this point all other messages have been synchronous, messages where the sender waits for the result before continuing on. It is common to send asynchronous messages to hardware devices or autonomous software services such as message buses.

The method of modeling the inclusion of use cases used in Fig. 11.8 is something that I first proposed in *The Elements of UML Style* (Ambler 2003b) although I have no doubt that others use this approach as well. I basically show the use case as a bubble across the top of the diagram, just like any other classifier, and show a message sent to it with the <<include>> stereotype. This is consistent with both use case diagramming and sequence diagramming practices.

Figure 11.8 is also interesting because it shows how to model conditional logic. In this case a frame with the label *alt* is used along with a guard, in this case *applicant on eligibility list*. The frame is separated into regions separated by dashed lines. In this case there are two regions, one for each alternative, although you can have as many regions as you require (to support the visual equivalent of a case statement). Each region requires a guard.

11.1.1 Visual Coding Via Sequence Diagrams

Earlier I stated that sequence diagrams are effectively a form of visual coding, or perhaps another way to think of it is that sequence diagrams can be used for very detailed design. When I developed the sequence diagram of Fig. 11.5 I made several decisions that could potentially affect my other models. For example, as I modeled Step 10, I made the design decision that the fee display screen also handled the verification by the student that the fees were acceptable.

Also, as I was modeling Steps 2 and 3, I came to the realization that students should probably have passwords to get into the system. When you are

---

TIP

Design for Your Implementation Environment Judiciously

Take advantage of features of your implementation environment, but be smart about it. Trade-offs are normal, but understand the implications and manage the risks involved. Every time you take advantage of a unique performance enhancement in a product (such as a database, operating system, or middleware tool) you are likely coupling your system to that product and, thus, reducing its portability. To minimize the impact of your implementation environment on your systems, you can layer your software (Chapter 10) and wrap specific features to make them appear general to their users. Wrapping is discussed in detail in *Building Object Applications That Work* (Ambler 1998a).

following the AM practices of *active stakeholder participation* and *model with others* it is easy to find out whether ideas such as this make sense because all you need to do is ask. In this case I discovered I was wrong: the combination of name and student number is unique enough for our purposes and the university did not want the added complexity of password management. This is an interesting decision that would potentially be recorded as a business rule because it is an operating policy of the university, indicating the need to follow the practice *iterate to another artifact* and jot down the rule if we are interested in keeping a permanent record of it.

11.1.2 How to Draw Sequence Diagrams

I have been trying to explain to people how to draw sequence diagrams for years, and what I have discovered is that the people who get it are either very good at thinking in a logical manner and/or they are good at writing software code. Sequence diagramming really is visual coding, even when you are modeling a usage scenario via a system-level sequence diagram.

When I am creating a sequence diagram I will start by identifying the scope of what I am trying to model, and because I prefer to follow the AM practice *model in small increments* I will typically tackle small usage scenarios at the system level or a single method/service at the detailed object level. A diagram such as Fig. 11.5 is too complex to be useful in my experience.

I will then work through the logic with at least one more person, laying out classifiers across the top as I need them. I automatically add the object lifelines but, as I indicated earlier, will typically not invest time adding activation boxes. The heart of the diagram is in the messages, which I add to the diagram one at a time as I work through the logic. I rarely indicate return values; instead I will give messages intelligent names, which often make it clear what is being returned.

It is interesting to note that as you sequence diagram you will identify new responsibilities for classes and objects, and, sometimes, even new classes. The implication is that you may want to update your class model appropriately; agile modelers will follow the practice *create several models in parallel*, something that CASE tools will do automatically. Remember that each message sent to a class invokes a static method/operation on that class; each message sent to an object invokes an operation on that object.

Regarding style issues for sequence diagramming, I prefer to draw messages going from left to right and return values from right to left, although that does not always work with complex objects/classes. I justify the label on messages and return values, so they are closest to the arrowhead. I also prefer to layer the sequence diagrams: from left to right. I indicate the actors, then the controller class(es), and then the user interface class(es), and, finally, the business class(es). During design, you probably need to add system and persistence classes, which I usually put on the right-most side of sequence diagrams. Laying your sequence diagrams in this manner often makes them easier to read and also makes it easier to find layering logic problems, such as user-interface classes directly accessing persistence classes.

11.1.3 Keeping It Agile

The most important thing that you can do is to keep your diagrams simple, both content wise and tool wise. I will sketch sequence diagrams on white-boards to think something through, either to verify the logic in a use case or to design a method or service. I rarely keep sequence diagrams as I find their true value is in their creation.

A common mistake is to try to create a complete set of sequence diagrams for your system. I have seen project teams waste months creating several sequence diagrams for each of their use cases, one for the basic course of action and one for each alternate course. My advice is to only create a sequence diagram when you have complex logic that you want to think through—if the logic is straightforward the sequence diagram will not add any value; you had might as well go straight to code.

11.2 UML Communication Diagrams

A fundamental concept of the UML is that you use different diagrams for different purposes. Class diagrams are used to model the static nature of your system, sequence diagrams are used to model sequential logic, and state machine diagrams are used to model the behavior of complex classes. But what happens when you need to show the behavior of several objects collaborating together to fulfill a common purpose? This is what UML communication diagrams, formerly known as collaboration diagrams in UML 1.x, can be used for because they provide a bird's-eye view of a collection of collaborating objects.

Communication diagrams show the message flow between objects in an OO application and also imply the basic associations (relationships) between classes. Figure 11.9 presents a simplified collaboration diagram for displaying

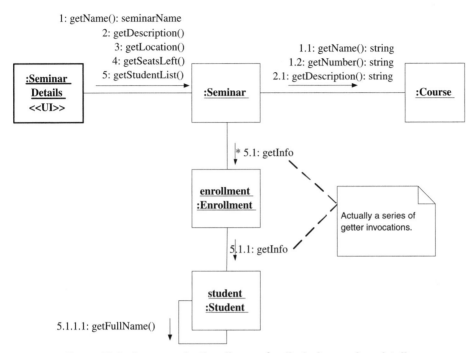

Figure 11.9. A communication diagram for displaying seminar details.

a seminar details screen or page. The rectangles represent the various objects involved that make up the application. The lines between the classes represent the relationships (associations, composition, dependencies, or inheritance) between them. The same notation for classes and objects used on UML sequence diagrams are used on UML communication diagrams, another example of the consistency of the UML. The details of your associations, such as their multiplicities, are not modeled because this information is contained on your UML class diagrams: remember that each UML diagram has its own specific purpose and no single diagram is sufficient on its own. Messages are depicted as a labeled arrow that indicates the direction of the message, using a notation similar to that used on sequence diagrams.

Figure 11.10 summarizes the basic notation for modeling messages on communication diagrams. Optionally, you may indicate the sequence number in which the message is sent, indicate an optional return value, or indicate the method name and the parameters (if any) passed to it. Sequence numbers should be in the format A.B.C.D to indicate the order in which the messages where sent. In Fig. 11.9 message 1 is sent to the *Seminar* object, which in turn sends messages 1.1 and then 1.2 to the *Course* object. Message 5 is sent to the *Seminar* object, which sends message 5.1 to *enrollment*, which in turn sends

```
[sequenceNumber:] methodName(parameters) [: returnValue]
```

FIGURE **11.10. The basic notation for invoking a message on a communication diagram.**

message 5.1.1 to *student*, and it finally sends message 5.1.1.1 to itself. Notice how a recursive connection, or a self connection, is required so that *student* can do this.

Although Fig. 11.9 applies sequence numbers to the messages, my experience is if you feel the need to use sequence numbers on communication diagrams this is a good indication you should be using sequence diagrams instead. The main difference between communication diagrams and sequence diagrams is that sequence diagrams are good at showing sequential logic but not that good at giving you a "big picture view" whereas communication diagrams are the exact opposite.

In Fig. 11.9, you see the *Seminar Details* user-interface object collaborates with the seminar object to obtain the information needed to display its information. It first invokes the getter method to obtain the name of the seminar. To fulfill this responsibility, the seminar object then collaborates with the course object that describes it to obtain the name of the course. In this example I showed return values for some messages but not others to provide examples of how to do it. I will either indicate the type of the return value, for example, *string*, or the result, such as *seminarName*. Normally I would not show return values on this diagram because the messages are named well—my heuristic is to only model return values when it is not clear what the message returns. Better yet I try to find a new name for the message (remember that messages map to operations implemented by your classes).

Another trick I often use is to consolidate trivial messages such as getter invocations. In Fig. 11.9 I modeled the series of getter method invocations

---

TIP

You Typically Only Need a Few Models

Any given project team will only require a subset of the models described in this book. Think of it like this: in your toolbox at home you have a wide array of screwdrivers, wrenches, pliers, and so on. For any given repair job you will use only a few of the tools. Different jobs, different tools. You never need all of your tools at once, but over time you will use them in a variety of manners.

to obtain the information needed to display the list of students enrolled in a seminar as the single message *getInfo*. I also added a note to the diagram to make it clear what I was doing, but I typically do not do that. Why is this important? Because agile developers will only do things that add value, and defining an exact list of getter invocations would not have added value.

You draw communication diagrams in the same way as you draw sequence diagrams, the only real difference being that you lay out the notation in a different manner. To tell you the truth I rarely find the need to create communication diagrams although I have found them useful in situations where we did not have use cases as the primary requirements artifact. Sequence diagrams and use cases seem to go hand in hand because of how easy it is to model the sequential logic of a use case using a sequence diagram. Communication diagrams seem to be preferred by people with a "structure bent," people that focus on UML class diagrams or class responsibility collaborator (CRC) cards, because of the similarity of communication diagrams with those types of artifacts. As always, follow the AM practice *apply the right artifact(s)* and use the most appropriate technique for your situation.

11.3 UML State Machine Diagrams

Objects have both behavior and state or, in other words, they do things and they know things. Some objects do and know more things, or at least more complicated things, than other objects. Some objects are incredibly complicated, so complex that developers can have difficulty understanding them. To understand complex classes better, particularly those that act in different manners depending on their state, you should develop one or more UML state machine diagrams, formerly called state chart diagrams in UML 1.x, describing how their instances work.

UML state machine diagrams depict the various states that an object may be in and the transitions between those states. In fact, in other modeling languages, it is common for this type of a diagram to be called a state-transition diagram or even simply a state diagram. A state represents a stage in the behavior pattern of an object, and like UML activity diagrams it is possible to have initial states and final states. An initial state, also called a creation state, is the one that an object is in when it is first created, whereas a final state is one in which no transitions lead out of. A transition is a progression from one state to another and will be triggered by an event that is either internal or external to the object.

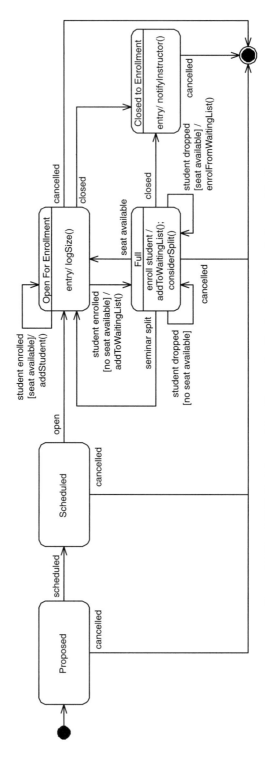

FIGURE 11.11. A UML 2 state machine diagram for the *Seminar* class during registration.

```
event [guard][/method list]
```

FIGURE **11.12. The format for transitions labels.**

Figure 11.11 presents an example state machine diagram for the *Seminar* class during registration. The rounded rectangles represent states: you see that instances of *Seminar* can be in the *Proposed, Scheduled, Open For Enrollment, Full*, and *Closed to Enrollment* states. An object starts in an initial state, represented by the closed circle, and can end up in a final state, represented by the bordered circle. This is the exact same notation used by UML activity diagrams, a perfect example of the consistency of the UML.

The arrows in Fig. 11.11 represent transitions, progressions from one state to another. For example, when a seminar is in the *Scheduled* state, it can be either opened for enrollment or cancelled. Figure 11.12 depicts the notation for the labels on transitions. It is mandatory to indicate the event that causes the transition, such as *open* or *cancelled*. Guard, conditions that must be true for the transition to be triggered, are optionally indicated. The [*no seat available*] guard is shown on the *student enrolled* transition from the *Open For Enrollment* to the *Closed To Enrollment* state. Guards can be described in any manner, including both free-form text or formal language—when I am whiteboarding I will use free-form text to ensure that it is readable by everyone, but with a sophisticated CASE tool I would consider using either a programming language such as Java or a modeling language such as object constraint language (OCL) if the tool has the ability to actually process that information into something useful (such as executable code). The invocation of methods, such as *addToWaitingList()*, can optionally be indicated on transitions. The order in the listing implying the order in which they are invoked.

States are represented by the values of the attributes of an object. For example, a seminar is in the *Open For Enrollment* state when it has been flagged as open and seats are available to be filled. It is possible to indicate the invocation of methods within a state; for example, upon entry into the *Closed To Enrollment* state the method *notifyInstructor()* is invoked. The notation used within is the same as that used on transitions, the only difference being that the method list is mandatory and the event is optional. For example in the *Full* state the operations *addToWaitingList()* and *considerSplit()* are invoked whenever a student is enrolled. Had there been no event indicated those methods would be invoked continuously (in a loop) whenever the object is

---

TIP

Agile Designs Are Emergent, They Are Not Defined Up Front

Although you will do some modeling during "cycle 0" (just enough to get your team going), you do not need to get a fully documented set of models in place before you may begin coding. Your overall system design will emerge over time, evolving to fulfill new requirements and take advantage of new technologies as appropriate.

---

in that state. I indicate the methods to run during the state when I want to indicate a method is to be run continuously: perhaps a method that polls other objects for information or a method that implements the logic of an important business process. Methods to be invoked when the object enters the state are indicated by the keyword *entry*, as you see with both the *Open For Enrollment* and *Closed To Enrollment* states in Fig. 11.11. Methods to be invoked as the object exits the state are indicated by the keyword *exit*. The capability to indicate method invocations when you enter and exit a state is useful because it enables you to avoid documenting the same method several times on each of the transitions that enter or exit the state, respectively.

Transitions are the result of the invocation of a method that causes an important change in state. Understanding that not all method invocations will result in transitions is important. For example, the invocation of a getter method likely would not cause a transition because it is not changing the state of the object (unless lazy initialization is being applied). Furthermore, Fig. 11.11 indicates an attempt to enroll a student in a full seminar may not result in the object changing state, unless it is determined that the seminar should be split, even though the state of the object changes (another student is added to the waiting list). You can see that transitions are a reflection of your business rules. For example, you see that you can attempt to enroll a student in a course only when it is open for enrollment or full, and that a seminar may be split (presumably into two seminars) when the waiting list is long enough to justify the split. You can have recursive transitions, also called self transitions, that start and end in the same state. An example of which is the *student dropped* transition when the seminar is full.

For the sake of convention, we say an object is always in one and only one state, implying transitions are instantaneous. Although we know this is not completely true (every method is going to take some time to run), this makes life a lot easier for us to assume transitions take no time to complete.

Because the lifecycle of a seminar is so complex Fig. 11.11 only depicts part of it. Figure 11.13 depicts the entire lifecycle, with Fig. 11.11 shown as

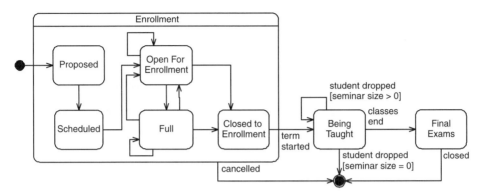

FIGURE **11.13. The complete *Seminar* lifecycle.**

a substate of the *Enrollment* state. I could have included all of the details in Fig. 11.13 but chose not to in order to keep the diagram simple—I prefer to follow the AM practices *depict models simply* and *model in small increments*. In fact, instead of creating a diagram such as Fig. 11.13 I typically prefer something more along the lines of the high-level view of Fig. 11.14 with detailed views such as Fig. 11.11. This approach keeps the diagrams small and easy to understand.

Figure 11.15 depicts a slightly different take on state machine diagrams; this time it is much closer to an analysis level diagram because it shows what is happening to the seminar while it is in this state from the point of view of the people involved. It is organized into two parallel swim lanes representing concurrent substates—one from the point of view of the professor teaching the seminar and the other showing the actions of the teaching assistant responsible for keeping the seminar material up to date. Concurrent substates are common with hardware but very uncommon in business classes, hence the goofy example. Normally I would depict this sort of information using

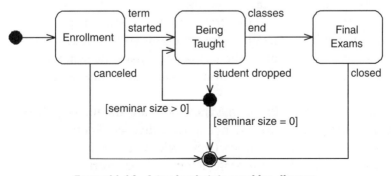

FIGURE **11.14. A top-level state machine diagram.**

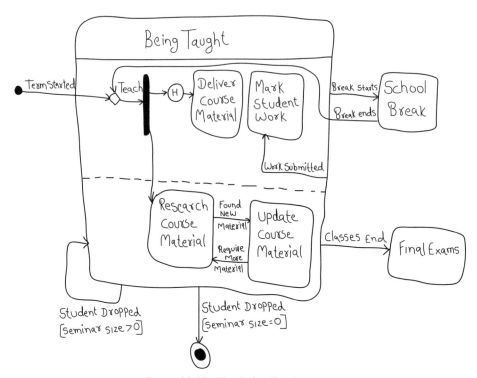

FIGURE 11.15. The *Being Taught* state.

either a UML activity diagram or a UML timing diagram (Section 11.4) but I needed an example to show extra notation.

Figure 11.15 shows several ways to depict transitions. The *Break Starts* transition exiting from the *Being Taught* states is applicable to all of the substates; you know this because it exits from the superstate instead of an individual substate. The *Work Submitted* transition is potentially triggered by several sources; you know this because it is attached to the outside edge of the superstate, whereas the source of the *Break ends* transition is explicitly defined as the *School Break* state. The initial transition into this state is the *Term Started* transition, indicated through the use of an initial state symbol. I could also have modeled this state coming from an *Enrollment* state; either approach is fair.

The *Term Started* and *Break Ends* transitions are first merged, then they lead to a fork, which in turn leads to one or the other set of concurrent substates. A history pseudo-state is shown (the circle with the H), indicating that if *Seminar* was previously in this state, left it, and the returns that it will go back to the substate it was originally in. The arrow leaving the history pseudo-state

TIP

State Modeling Often Reveals Potential Error Conditions

Identifying potential error conditions while you are state machine modeling is common because you are constantly asking "should this transition be allowed when the object is in this state?" When the answer is yes, you need to add the transition to your diagram. When the answer is no, you may need to document this potential issue so your programmers develop the proper error checking code, so the transition is not allowed to occur.

indicates that the *Deliver Course Material* substate is the default the very first time that *Seminar* enters the *Begin Taught* superstate.

When drawing a state machine diagram the thing you want to do is to identify the creation state and whether any final states exist. After you have done this, ask yourself what other states or stages in the life of an object does it pass through? You can often find states by looking at the boundary values of your attributes. For example, when the number of students in a seminar reaches the maximum, it becomes full. *Full* is a valid state because different rules now apply: when a student tries to enroll, he is put on a waiting list and the seminar is a candidate to be split in two.

Once you have identified as many states as you can, start looking for transitions. For each state, ask yourself how the object can get out of it, if possible. This will give you a transition. Because all transitions lead from one state to another, ask yourself what new state the transition leads you to (do not forget about recursive transitions that lead to the same state). You should also look at the methods you identified in your class diagram. Some of them will correspond to a transition in your state diagram.

Although being able to inherit state diagrams would be nice, it is extremely unlikely this will happen. The definition of inheritance says that although the subclass is similar to the superclass, *it is still different*. The behavior of the subclass is usually different than that of the superclass. This means you need to reconsider the state diagram when you inherit from a class with one. The one good thing is many of the states and transitions are reusable. You will probably find either you add new states and transitions or you will redefine some.

State machine modeling is a dynamic modeling technique, one that focuses on identifying the behavior within your system—in this case, behavior specific to the instances of a single class. My style is to draw one or more state machine diagrams when a class exhibits different behavior depending on its state. For example, the *Address* class is fairly simple, representing data you will display and manipulate in your system. *Seminar* objects, on the other hand, are fairly complex, and therefore it makes sense to create a state machine diagram for them.

In business applications it seems that a very small proportion of classes, perhaps 5 percent at most, are complex enough to warrant the creation of a state machine diagram. However, state machine diagrams are much more common in real-time systems (Douglass 1999).

11.4 UML TIMING DIAGRAMS

Timing diagrams are one of the new artifacts added to UML 2, although they have been one of the core diagrams within the hardware design and real-time communities for decades. They are used to explore the behaviors of one or more objects throughout a given time period. There are two basic flavors of timing diagram, the concise notation depicted in Fig. 11.16 and the robust notation depicted in Fig. 11.17. Timing diagrams are often used to design embedded software, such as control software for fuel injection system in an automobile, although they occasionally have their uses for business software too.

Figure 11.16 depicts the lifecycle of a single seminar, showing its timeline quite clearly. The *:Seminar* label indicates that the lifeline being explored is that of an instance of *Seminar*. The critical states that the seminar exhibits— *Proposed, Scheduled, Enrolling Students, Being Taught, Final Exams, Closed*—are listed across the diagram. The two lines surrounding the states are called a general value lifeline. In this case I am using them to show the value of the state of a seminar, but you could also explore the value of a single attribute of an object if you so choose. When the two lines cross one another it indicates a transition point between states. Along the bottom of the diagram timing constraints are shown, in this case indicating the period of time during which the seminar is in each state.

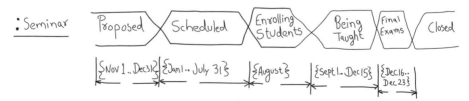

FIGURE 11.16. UML timing diagram (concise notation) for the lifecycle of a seminar.

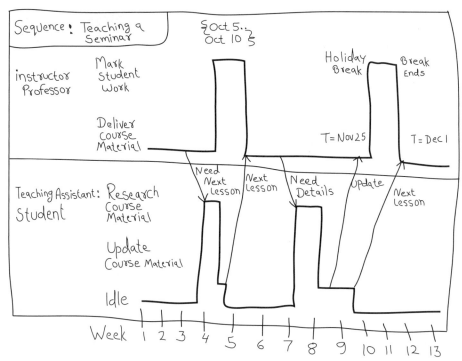

Figure 11.17. UML timing diagram (robust notation) for teaching a seminar.

It is interesting to note the differences between the timing diagram of Fig. 11.16 and the state machine diagram of Fig. 11.13. Several states from the state machine diagram are encompassed by the *Enrolling Students* state of the timing diagram. That is perfectly fine because I am using each diagram for its individual strengths—concise timing diagrams are good at exploring one or more objects throughout a period of time and state machine diagrams are good at exploring the detailed transitions between states as the result of events (either external or internal). Remember AM's *apply the right artifact(s)* practice and use the right model for the job.

Figure 11.17 depicts a timing diagram that explores the details of what happens while a seminar is being taught. In this jaded example the professor delivers the seminar and marks student work and the teaching assistant develops the course material just in time for it to be taught. A UML frame is being used to bound the two lifelines (that of the professor and the teaching assistant); we could very easily have modeled more lifelines simply by adding other sections to the frame. The box lines are called state timelines; in this case there are discrete transitions between states resulting in a box line,

---

TIP

Prove It with Code

Never assume your design works; instead, obtain concrete feedback by writing
code that reflects your design as soon as possible.

---

although had the transitions been continuous in nature (such as the change
in temperature) a curvy line would have been drawn. The states/conditions
applicable to the lifeline, such as *Mark Student Work* and *Idle*, are listed along
the left-hand side of the diagram. Events/stimuli, such as *Holiday Break* and
Break Ends, are optionally labeled at transition points to indicate the reason for the change. The arrows between timelines are messages between the
objects.

Several ways to indicate time are shown in Fig. 11.17. A timing constraint,
{*Oct 5..Oct 10*} is shown as are time observations (*T=Nov 25* and *T=Dec
1*). Timing constraints and time observations can be applied to a variety of
UML diagrams, including all forms of interaction diagrams such as sequence
diagrams and communication diagrams, although I find them most useful on
timing diagrams. Unique to timing diagrams are timing rulers, depicted as
tick mark values along the bottom of the diagram.

Both notations have their purposes, although the robust notation seems
the more useful of the two particularly for objects that move back and forth
between states. The more lifelines you try to model at once the harder it is to
draw the diagram so two lifelines is about as complex as I like to get. I draw
timing diagrams on whiteboards; I do not know of any mainstream modeling
tool oriented towards business application development that supports this
kind of diagram.

In my opinion very few business application developers will find that they
need UML timing diagrams, so I really cannot recommend that you invest the
time to learn them. For the few times that you need to explore timing issues
free-form diagrams will very likely suffice.

11.5 UML INTERACTION OVERVIEW DIAGRAMS

UML interaction overview diagrams are variants on UML activity diagrams,
which overview control flow. Figure 11.18 depicts an interaction overview diagram for enrolling in a seminar. The nodes within the diagram are frames instead of the normal activities that you would see on an activity diagram. There

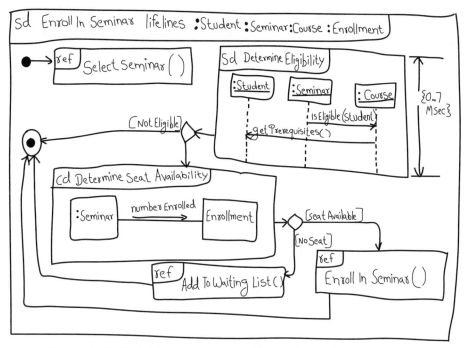

Figure 11.18. UML interaction overview diagram for enrolling in a seminar.

are two types of frame shown: interaction frames, which depict any type of UML interaction diagram (sequence diagram, communication diagram, timing diagram, interaction overview diagram), or interaction occurrence frames, which indicate an activity or operation to invoke. There are two interaction frames in the diagram, one that depicts a sequence diagram for determining whether a student is eligible to enroll in a seminar and a communication diagram to determine whether a seat is available in a seminar. These frames indicate the type of diagram (*sd* for sequence diagrams, *cd* for communication diagrams, *td* for timing diagrams, and *iod* for interaction overview diagrams) and optionally the name of the diagram. The interaction occurrence frames are of type *ref* and typically are anonymous as the name of the activity or operation to be invoked should make it clear what is happening (otherwise you need to rethink your naming strategy).

The other notation used on the diagram should be familiar to you. Decision points are shown as diamonds, exactly as on UML activity diagrams. There should be guards on all of the exiting flows although as you can see I will forgo labeling some guards when it is obvious what is meant. Remember that agile models do not need to be perfect, they just need to be good enough, but just barely! Duration constraints, such as {*0..7 msec*}, are shown using the

> **TIP**
>
> **Continue to Use the Terminology of Your Stakeholders**
>
> It was a good idea for your requirements/analysis modeling efforts and it is a good idea for your design modeling efforts as well.

same notation as on other types of interaction diagrams. The start and end points use the same notation as initial and end states on UML state machine diagrams and UML activity diagrams.

Although interaction overview diagrams are an interesting concept I doubt that they will be used much in practice. Interaction frames are virtually useless due to a lack of space—the diagrams that you can depict within the frames will be too small to be of value. My suspicion is that interaction overview diagrams will be abandoned within the marketplace in favor of UML activity diagrams because they do not work well on whiteboards and the CASE tool vendors can simply allow you to use other diagrams to describe the details of activities. Perhaps I am wrong about this. Time will tell.

11.6 UML COMPOSITE STRUCTURE DIAGRAMS

UML composite structure diagrams are used to explore run-time instances of interconnected instances collaborating over communications links. Figure 11.19 depicts a composite structure diagram for enrolling in a seminar. The dashed oval, *Enroll in Seminar*, models a collaboration. A collaboration enables you to model the relevant aspects of a cooperation between instances, indicating the objects and the roles that they take within the collaboration. The rectangles model instances of any type of classifier, including classes, objects, or interfaces. The properties used in the collaboration, such as the prerequisite seminars that a student has taken in the past, are optionally indicated with the classifier boxes.

An alternative form of this diagram is shown in Fig. 11.20, something I refer to as a collaboration-style composite structure diagram. I would really like to refer to this as a collaboration diagram, but my fear is that this name would be confusing for anyone familiar with UML 1.x's collaboration diagrams, which are now called communication diagrams. In this diagram the collaboration symbol contains a detailed composite structure diagram, showing how the composite structure diagrams can effectively be nested within one another.

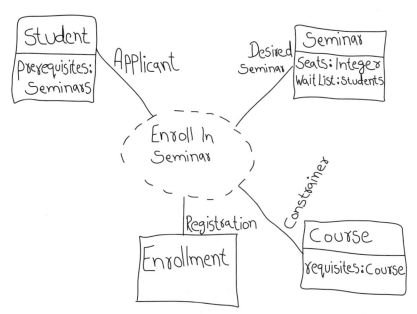

FIGURE 11.19. Composite structure diagram for enrolling in a seminar.

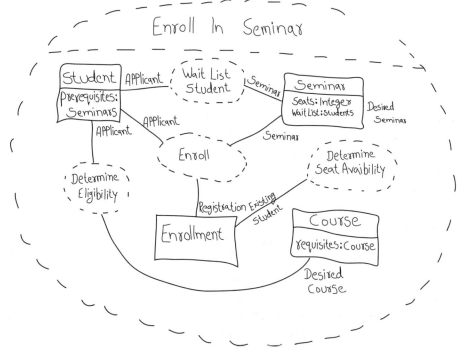

FIGURE 11.20. Collaboration-style composite structure diagram for enrolling in a seminar.

It is interesting to note that UML composite structure diagrams are very similar to object role model (ORM) diagrams (Chapter 8) in notation. Although the two diagrams explore similar issues, i.e., structure, they do so in different ways. ORM diagrams are very good for explored detailed relationships between entities whereas the focus of composite structure diagrams is on exploring collaborations between entities.

To be honest, I do not find composite structure diagrams to be of much use either. I would much rather use UML sequence diagrams for exploring a collaboration because the notation is much more robust and because far more developers understand the notation.

11.7 WHAT YOU HAVE LEARNED

Dynamic object modeling focuses on identifying the behavior and collaborations between objects within your system. It is a critical aspect of object-oriented design that leads into structural object design described in the next chapter. You learned that you have several dynamic object modeling options—UML sequence diagrams, UML communication diagrams, UML state machine diagrams, UML timing diagrams, UML interaction overview diagrams, and UML composite structure diagrams—as well as how to create them.

11.8 REVIEW QUESTIONS

1. Develop a state machine diagram for a bank account, based on the information in the bank case study in Chapter 1.
2. Using a UML sequence diagram, model the act of successfully transferring funds from a checking account to a savings account using an automated teller machine.
3. Model the usage scenario from Question 2 using a UML collaboration diagram.
4. Model the usage scenario from Question 2 using the detailed form of a UML timing diagram.
5. Model the usage scenario from Question 2 using a UML composite structure diagram.
6. Compare and contrast the diagrams of Questions 2 through 5. What are the advantages and disadvantages of each, and when would you use each? Why?

CHAPTER 12

Structural Design Modeling

Think before you code.

The purpose of structural design modeling is exactly what the name implies—to model the design of the structural aspects of your system. Structural design focuses on the identification of entities, classes or data structures, and the relationships among those entities. For modern systems there are two basic styles of structure that you need to be concerned about at the detailed design level. The first is the design of your object schema, something that is typically modeled with a class diagram. The second is the design of your database, something that is done with a physical data model (PDM).

This chapter addresses the following topics:

- UML class diagrams;
- Applying design patterns effectively; and
- Physical data modeling with the UML.

12.1 UML CLASS DIAGRAMS

The purpose of design is to model how the software will be built; as you would expect, the purpose of design class modeling is to model the static structure of how your software will be built. The techniques of analysis class modeling that you learned in Chapter 8 still apply. The only difference is your focus is on the solution domain instead of on the problem domain. In fact your analysis class model often evolves into your design class model—you simply introduce changes to your class model based on implementation technologies. Although modeling purists may insist that you keep your analysis and design models separate, the reality is that you will often work through requirements to analysis to design in a matter of minutes, sometimes even seconds. When moving from an analysis class modeling mindset to a design mindset perhaps you will do the following:

- Implement business rules using a business rules engine, which means your business/domain classes will invoke the rules, instead of directly implementing them in methods;
- Apply known design patterns, the topic of Section 12.2, to improve the design quality of your models;
- Decide to take a component-based approach as described in Chapter 10; and
- Decide to take advantage of features of your database, a topic covered in Chapter 14.

In this section, I describe a collection of topics important to your design class modeling efforts. These are the topics:

- Modeling methods and attributes during design;
- Association and dependency techniques;
- Inheritance techniques;
- Composition techniques;
- Modeling interfaces;
- Documenting design trade-offs; and
- Class modeling design tips.

12.1.1 Modeling Methods during Design

Methods, also called operations or member functions, are the object-oriented equivalent of functions and procedures. Until now, I have been modeling methods in a simple manner, indicating their names and the names of any

```
visibility name(param1:type1=default1, ...): returnType
  <<stereotype>>
```

<small>FIGURE</small> **12.1. The UML format for an operation signature.**

parameters passed to them. With the unified modeling language (UML), however, it is possible to model far more information about a method's signature than just this, as you can see in Fig. 12.1. During design, you should consider indicating these items:

1. **Visibility (optional).** This is the level of access that external objects have to a method, on your class diagrams. Method visibility is described in Section 12.1.1.1.

2. **Name.** Strategies for naming methods are described in Section 12.1.1.2.

3. **Parameters (optional).** The names of parameters, and optionally their types and default values (if any), should also be indicated for each method.

4. **Return value type (optional).** The type of the return value, if any, should be indicated.

5. **Stereotype(s) (optional).** Any applicable stereotypes (see Section 12.1.1.3) should be indicated. Although the UML suggests listing the stereotypes on the left-hand side I feel that stereotypes are the least important information regarding a method and therefore should be listed last, not first. This is a basic usability issue that the UML misses, in my opinion.

6. **Scope.** Whether a method is a static method that works on the class or an instance method that works on instances of the class should also be indicated. Static methods are underlined; instance methods are not.

Figure 12.2 depicts a simple analysis class diagram and Fig. 12.3 depicts the *Student* class from that diagram with its methods fully modeled. I added the accessor methods for the *averageMark* attribute so I had an example of an operation, *setAverageMark()*, with a visibility different from that of the other methods and the constructor *Student(studentNumber)*, so I had an example of a method with a stereotype. The *isEligible(...)* method is interesting for several reasons. First, you know it is a static method because it is underlined (instance methods are not underlined). Second, you know it is a publicly

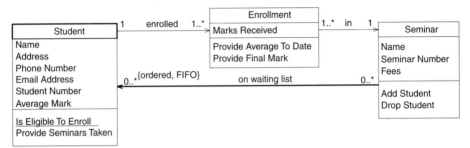

FIGURE **12.2. Students and seminars (analysis class diagram).**

accessible method because its visibility indicator is a + sign. Third, its name parameter is a simple string, whereas its *studentNumber* is an instance of the class *StudentNumber*—the type of a parameter may be either a primitive type or a class. Both Java and C++ have integers, floats, and string among its primitive types, but Smalltalk, a typeless language, by definition has no primitive types. Fourth, you see it returns a *Boolean* value, either true or false.

The other methods depicted in Fig. 12.3 are also worth noting. You see the *Student(studentNumber)* method is a constructor, a method that instantiates instances of *Student* (note the return value) and presumably sets the value of the *studentNumber* attribute within the object. Methods that do not take parameters have nothing listed in their parameter list, and operations that do not return anything have no return value indicated. Similarly, the *Student(studentNumber)* method has a stereotype indicated for it, but the other methods do not because no stereotypes are applicable to them. Finally, the accessor methods *getAverageMark()* and *setAverageMark(...)* deal with the

Student
name address phoneNumber emailAddress studentNumber averageMark
+ isEligible(name: string, studentNumber: StudentNumber): boolean + Student(studentNumber: StudentNumber): Student<<constructor>> + getSeminarsTaken(): Vector + purchaseParkingPass() + getAverageMark(): long - setAverageMark(newAverageMark: long)

FIGURE **12.3. The *Student* class with its methods fully modeled.**

same type, in this case long, implying that the *averageMark* attribute must also be of type long. Attributes are discussed in detail in Section 12.1.2.

12.1.1.1 Method Visibility

How a method is accessed by objects is defined by its visibility. In the UML, you have your choice of four levels of visibility, defined in Table 12.1: public, protected, private, and package (Object Management Group 2003). To reduce the coupling within your system, the general rule of thumb is to be as restrictive as possible when setting the visibility of a method. In other words, if a method does not have to be public, then make it protected. If it does not have to be protected, then make it private.

Table 12.2 indicates whether each class would be able to invoke the four methods implemented by *Superclass* in Fig. 12.4. For example, *protectedMethod()* is visible to *Subclass* but not *OtherClass*.

As an aside, notice how I have named the classes of Fig. 12.4—the word class is capitalized in *OtherClass*, but not in *Superclass* and *Subclass*. This is because superclass and subclass are actual words; therefore, it would not be appropriate to capitalize the *c* in class. Good class names are typically nouns,

TABLE 12.1. UML Method Visibilities

Visibility	Symbol	Description	Proper Usage
Public	+	A public method can be invoked by any other method in any other object or class.	When the method must be accessible by objects and classes outside of the class hierarchy in which the method is defined.
Protected	#	A protected method can be invoked by any method in the class in which it is defined or any subclasses of that class.	When the method provides behavior needed internally within the class hierarchy, but not externally.
Private	−	A private method can only be invoked by other methods in the class in which it is defined, but not in the subclasses.	When the method provides behavior specific to the class. Private methods are often the result of refactoring.
Package	~	A package method can only be invoked by other methods in objects belonging to the immediate namespace, e.g., the package the class is in.	When the method needs to be public to the other software elements within a package but private to everything else.

TABLE 12.2. Accessibility of Methods				
	Superclass	Subclass	OtherClass	ExternalClass
publicMethod()	Yes	Yes	Yes	Yes
protectedMethod()	Yes	Yes	No	No
privateMethod()	Yes	No	No	No
packageMethod()	Yes	Yes	Yes	No

two or three words at most, are fully spelled out, and are written in mixed case with the first letter of each word capitalized.

As a matter of style, I prefer to list static methods before instance methods in classes, as you can see in Fig. 12.3. Furthermore, for each type of method scope, I list public methods first, then protected methods, then private methods, and then package methods. Finally, for each visibility, I list the business methods before the accessor and scaffolding methods (such as those required to maintain associations). I also take a similar approach to listing attributes within a class.

12.1.1.2 Naming Methods

In most C-based languages, such as Java and C#, it is common to name methods with a full description, using mixed case with the first letter of any noninitial word capitalized in the format *methodName()*. Also common

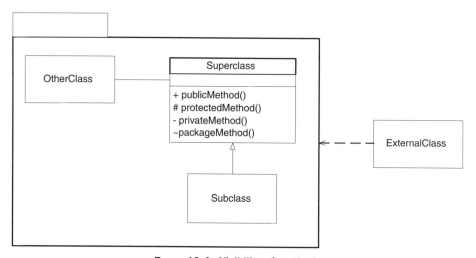

FIGURE 12.4. Visibility of methods.

TABLE 12.3. Example Names for Member Functions		
"Bad" Name	"Good" Name	Issue
openAcc()	openAccount()	An abbreviation was replaced with the full word to make the meaning clear.
mailingLabelPrint()	printMailingLabel()	The verb was moved to the beginning of the name to make it active.
purchaseparkingpass()	purchaseParkingPass()	Mixed case was applied to increase the readability of the name.
saveTheObject()	save()	The name was shortened because the term *TheObject* did not add any value.

practice is for the first word of a member function name to be a strong, active verb. Table 12.3 depicts examples of method names that were not ideal, presents an improved version of the name, and describes what changed and why.

These conventions result in methods whose purpose can often be determined just by looking at its name. Although this approach results in a little extra typing by developers—because it often results in longer method names—this is more than made up for by the increased understandability of your code.

12.1.1.3 Techniques for Methods

During design, what factors lead to high-quality methods? I find the following guidelines lead to superior methods:

1. **Develop consistent method signatures**. The greater the consistency within your designs, the easier they are to learn and to understand. First, method

names should be consistent with one another. Method names such as *get-FirstName()* and *fetchLastName()* are not consistent, whereas starting both method names with get would make them so. Second, parameter names should also be consistent with one another. For example, parameter names such as *theFirstName, firstName,* and *firstNm* are not consistent with one another, and neither are *firstName, aPhoneNumber,* and *theStudentNumber.* Pick one naming style for your parameters and stick to it. Third, the order of parameters should also be consistent. For example, the methods *doSomething(securityToken, startDate)* and *doSomethingElse(studentNumber, securityToken)* could be made more consistent by always passing *securityToken* as either the first or the last parameter.

2. **Define preconditions and postconditions for your methods.** A precondition describes something that must be true before a method may be invoked. A postcondition describes something that will be true once a method has completed (assuming the initial preconditions were met). Preconditions and postconditions are a vital aspect of the definition of a method, even if the answer is "none" for a given method, that other developers need to be able to determine whether they should invoke a method.

3. **Preconditions of an overridden method should be weaker.** Meyer (1997) points out that when a subclass overrides (redefines) an existing method, its preconditions must be the same or weaker than that of the method it is overriding. This is because the subclass must still conform to the preconditions of its superclass(es); therefore, the overriding method should at least be able to accept anything the original method can.

4. **Postconditions of an overridden method should be stronger.** Meyer (1997) also points out that when a subclass overrides (redefines) an existing method, its postconditions must be the same or stronger than that of the method it is overriding. This is because the subclass must still conform to the postconditions of its superclass(es); therefore, the overriding method should be as restrictive, or more so, than the original method.

5. **Model the appropriate stereotypes.** The UML allows for stereotypes to be applied to methods. I often apply stereotypes such as <<constructor>> and <<destructor>>, for constructors and destructors, respectively, to methods, but I stay away from <<getter>> and <<setter>> for accessor methods because I prefer to name them using a *getAttributeName()* and *setAttributeName()* format.

```
visibility name: type = initialValue <<stereotype>>
visibility name[*]: type <<stereotype>>
```

FIGURE 12.5. The UML formats for an attribute.

12.1.2 Modeling Attributes during Design

Attributes are the data aspects of objects. Until now I have just indicated their names, as you can see in Fig. 12.2. However, as Fig. 12.5 shows it is possible to model far more information about an attribute than just this. During design you should indicate these items:

- **Visibility (optional).** This is the level of access external objects have to an attribute, on your class diagrams. Visibility is described in Section 12.1.2.1.

- **Name.** Strategies for naming attributes are described in Section 12.1.2.2.

- **Type (optional).** The type of an attribute may be a primitive type, such as *string* or *int*, or a class such as *Address*.

- **Initial value (optional).** The initial value (if any) for an attribute should also be indicated.

- **Repeats (optional).** If the attribute repeats, it should be indicated with the "[*]" notation.

- **Scope.** Static attributes, those with class scope, are underlined. Instance attributes are not underlined.

Figure 12.6 depicts the *Student* and *StudentNumber* classes with their attributes fully modeled. In the static attribute, *nextStudentNumber*, you know it is static because it is underlined. In the *StudentNumber*, class is an incremental value. Each time an instance of *StudentNumber* is created, this static attribute is incremented by one, and then its value is assigned to the object (the instance). The instance attribute *averageMark* of the *Student* class is interesting because its type is long, one of Java's primitive types, which is consistent to the parameter passed to the corresponding setter, as well as the return value of the getter. Primitive types—such as *long, string,* and *int* in Fig. 12.6—are typically indicated in lowercase, whereas types that are classes are indicated

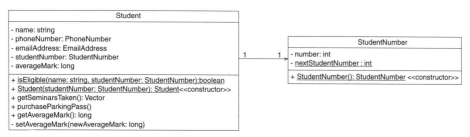

FIGURE 12.6. The *Student* and *StudentNumber* classes.

using the proper mixed case for the name of the class (such as *PhoneNumber* and *StudentNumber* in Fig. 12.6).

12.1.2.1 Attribute Visibility

Table 12.4 describes the four types of attribute visibility supported by the UML: public, protected, private, and package. As you can see, the rules and notation for attribute visibility are consistent with those for method visibility. My experience is that all fields should be declared private for purposes of information hiding and encapsulation. Some developers prefer to make attributes protected but I believe that is a mistake—when attributes are declared protected, there is the possibility of methods in subclasses will directly access them, effectively increasing the coupling within a class hierarchy. This makes your classes more difficult to maintain and to enhance; therefore, it should be avoided.

Attributes should never be accessed directly; instead, accessors should be used. The proper use of accessor methods is covered in Chapter 13.

TIP

Minimize the Public Interfaces of Software Elements

The public interface of a class is the collection of public methods and public attributes (if any) it either implements or inherits. Riel (1996) suggests you do not clutter the public interface of a class. In other words, you include only those methods and attributes that need to be public and no others. Minimizing the public interface of a class reduces the potential for coupling within your system—other classes may only access the public methods and attributes (its public interface) of a software element, so a smaller public interface implies less opportunity for coupling.

TABLE 12.4. UML Attribute Visibilities

Visibility	Symbol	Description	Proper Usage
Public	+	A public attribute can be accessed by any other method in any other object or class.	Don't.
Protected	#	A protected attribute can be accessed by any method in the class in which it is declared or by any method defined in subclasses of that class.	Don't.
Private	–	A private attribute can only be accessed by method in the class in which it is declared, but not in the subclasses.	All attributes should be private and accessed by getter and setter methods (accessors).
Package	~	A package attribute can only be accessed by methods in objects belonging to the immediate namespace, e.g., the package the class is in.	Don't.

Throughout this book I discuss a variety of modeling issues where there are several valid strategies you could take and, for each one, I suggested you choose one strategy and stick with it. For example, do you assume all accessor methods (methods that get and set the values of attributes) exist or do you show them on your diagrams? Do you assume the scaffolding code for managing associations exists or do you show it on your diagram? Not only should you choose each strategy, you should also document which strategy you have chosen so everyone on your team and, ideally within your organization, can follow the same set of modeling practices.

12.1.2.2 Naming Attributes

Like classes and methods, you should use full descriptions to name your attributes so it is obvious what the attribute represents, using the format *attributeName* for Java (other languages may take different approaches; my advice is to adopt and follow the industry standard). Attributes that are collections, such as arrays or vectors in Java, should be given names that are plural to indicate they represent multiple values. Furthermore, your attributes should be named in a consistent manner, at least within the definition of a single class, and ideally within all classes you develop. Also, if the name of the field begins with an acronym, such as *sqlDatabase*, then the acronym (in this case *sql*) should be completely in lowercase. Table 12.5 presents examples of how to improve attribute names.

12.1.2.3 Documenting Attributes

First and foremost an attribute's name should be clear enough so that other people understand how you are using it. However, you may discover that you need to optionally document:

1. **Applicable invariants.** The invariants of an attribute are the conditions that are always true about it. For example, an invariant about the attribute "day" might be that its value is between 1 and 31 (you could obviously get far more complex with this invariant by referring to the collection of business rules for calculating the number of days in each month). By documenting the restrictions on the value of an attribute you help to relate it to the applicable business rules, ensuring your class will be developed properly.

TABLE 12.5. Example Names for Attributes

"Bad" Name	"Good" Name	Issue
fName	firstName	Do not use abbreviations in attribute names.
firstname	firstName	Capitalizing the second word makes the attribute name easier to read.
personFirstName	firstName	This depends on the context of the attribute, but if this is an attribute of the *Person* class, then including *person* merely lengthens the name without providing any value.
nameLast	lastName	The name *nameLast* was not consistent with *firstName* (and it sounded strange anyway).
hTTPConnection	httpConnection	The abbreviation should be all in lowercase.
firstNameString	firstName	Indicating the type of the attribute, in this case *string*, couples the attribute name to its type. If the type changes, perhaps you decide to reimplement this attribute as an instance of the class *NameString*, then you would need to rename the attribute.
orderItemCollection	orderItems	The second version of the name is shorter and easier to understand.

2. **Examples.** For attributes that have complex business rules associated with them, you should provide several examples to make them easier to understand. An example is often like a picture: it is worth a thousand words.

3. **Visibility decisions.** If you have declared a field to be anything but private, then you should document why you have done so. You should have a good reason for not declaring a variable as private.

12.1.2.4 Techniques for Attributes

The most important technique for designing and using attributes effectively is not to access them directly in your code. My approach to attributes is to do the following:

- Assign private visibility to all attributes;
- Update attributes only in their setter methods;
- Directly access attributes only in their getter methods;
- Always invoke a setter method for an attribute to update its value, even within the class where it is defined;
- Always invoke a getter method for an attribute to obtain its value, even within the class where it is defined;
- Implement simple validation logic for an attribute in its setter method;
- Implement complex validation logic in separate methods; and
- Apply lazy initialization in getter methods for attributes that are rarely needed and have high overhead.

Simple validation logic for an attribute occurs when you only need to access the value of that single attribute. For example, simple validation logic for *firstName* would include rules such as the first name of a person must be defined and it is in mixed case, beginning with a capital letter. This sort of logic can easily be encapsulated in the setter method for *firstName*. Complex validation logic for an attribute, however, occurs when you need to access the value of the attribute in question, as well as the value of other attributes. For example, one part of validating the day attribute of a date would be to verify its value is between 1 and 30 when the month is April. In this case, you need to access the values of both day and month as part of your validation logic. Although this appears simple, it can lead to race conditions in your validation logic: if the validation logic for the month attribute also included verifying the value was consistent with day, you could find your code does not work correctly. With this validation logic in each setter, you would always have to set the value of month after you set the value of day (if the date is currently April 30 and you tried to set it to February 28, you would be unable to change the value of month because you would have an invalid date of February 30). A better approach is to implement the validation logic in a single method, perhaps *validate()*, that is invoked after the two attributes are set. An even better approach is not to allow the invocation of the individual setter methods by external objects at all but, instead, to have a bulk setter method that will set the value of all the attributes—in this case the year, month, and day—after validating that their values are consistent.

> **TIP**
>
> **Do Not Overdocument**
>
> You need to document your design, but you should not overdocument either. Remember that users pay you to build systems, not to document them. There is a fine line between underdocumenting and overdocumenting, and only through experience are you able to find it.

12.1.3 Inheritance Techniques

Similarities often exist between different classes. Quite often, two or more classes share the same attributes and/or the same methods. Because you do not want to have to write the same code repeatedly, you want a mechanism that takes advantage of these similarities. Inheritance is that mechanism. Inheritance models "is a" and "is like" relationships, enabling you to reuse existing data and code easily. Over the years, I have found the following techniques to be valuable for ensuring that I apply inheritance properly:

1. **The sentence rule works 95 percent of the time.** If it does not make sense to say "the subclass is a superclass" or at least "the subclass is a kind of superclass," then you are likely misapplying inheritance. An example of where this rule does not work is it makes sense to say that "a seminar is a course" when association but not inheritance makes sense between the corresponding classes. That is the problem with heuristics such as this; they do not work all the time.

2. **Beware of implementation inheritance.** Implementation inheritance, often called convenience inheritance, occurs when a class inherits from another class simply to reuse part or the entirety of its behavior, even though the sentence rule failed. Implementation inheritance is particularly common when developers want to take short cuts and have business classes inherit system or persistence behaviors, instead of accessing these services through collaboration.

3. **Any kind of class can inherit from any other kind.** Both abstract and concrete classes can inherit from either abstract or concrete classes. Remember that you inherit attributes and methods, not whether the class is concrete or abstract.

4. **You should be able to substitute an instance of a subclass for an instance of a superclass.** This advice is effectively a rewording of the Liskov

substitution principle (Liskov 1988), which is "If for each object o1 of type *S* there is an object o2 of type *T* such that for all programs *P* defined in terms of *T*, the behavior of *P* is unchanged with o1 is substituted for o2 then *S* is a subtype of *T*." For example, if you have written code that manipulates instances of the *Person* class, the code should also be able to work with instances of the *Professor* class as well if *Professor* inherits from *Person*. If you find you are writing code that checks the type of an object, in this case to see whether the object is an employee or an executive, then you likely have problems in your design.

5. **Beware of multiple inheritance.** Not only is multiple inheritance, the capability of a class to inherit directly from two or more classes, difficult to understand, it is also not an option for most development languages. For example, C++ and Eiffel support multiple inheritance, but Java and C# do not. C++ has an interesting concept called "mixin classes," where multiple inheritance is used to obtain behaviors implemented by another class. Uses of mixin classes are typically an indication of implementation inheritance, although, admittedly, their use is convenient at times. Riel (1996) suggests you should assume multiple inheritance within your model is a mistake and should be able to prove otherwise.

6. **Beware of inheritance only based on common data attributes.** If the only reason two classes inherit from each other is because they share common data attributes, it indicates one of two things: either you have missed some common behavior (this is likely if the sentence rule applies) or you should have applied association instead of inheritance.

7. **Superclasses should know nothing of their subclasses.** The basic idea is you should be free to create a class without having to change the code of any classes from which it inherits, either directly or indirectly (Riel 1996).

8. **Factor commonality as high as possible in your class hierarchy.** The higher in a class hierarchy a method is, the greater is its reuse. However, this does not mean you should place every single method in the root class. Instead, if Classes *B* and *C* both inherit from Class *A*, and they both need behavior *X*, then *X* should be implemented in *A*. If only Class *B* needs *X*, then *X* belongs in *B*.

9. **A subclass should inherit everything.** A subclass should inherit all the attributes and methods of its superclass and, therefore, all its relationships as well. When a subclass inherits everything from its superclass, we say we have "pure inheritance." The advantage of pure inheritance is you only have

---

TIP

Requirements, Then Analysis, Then Design, Then Code

Fundamentally, you need to determine what is wanted, then determine what you will build, then determine how you will build it, and then finally build it. Think first; act second.

---

to understand what a subclass inherits and not what it does not inherit. While this sounds trivial, in a deep class hierarchy, life is a lot easier if you only need to understand what each class adds and not what it takes away.

I am not saying you cannot override (redefine) attributes and methods. For example, the class *Dragon* inherits everything from the classes *Bird* and *Lizard*, including the method *Eat*. However, in the definition of *Dragon*, I needed to override *Eat* because dragons eat differently than either birds or lizards (dragons eat knights in shining armor). What I am saying is if you find your subclasses need to override methods, then perhaps you need to rethink your inheritance hierarchy.

12.1.4 Association and Dependency Techniques

In the real world, objects have associations to other objects. The associations between objects are important because they help us to define how they interact with each other. For example, students *take* courses and professors *teach* courses. Associations between objects enable collaboration—an object needs to know about another object to work with it. When a persistent association does not exist between two objects, but they need to collaborate with one another, you model a dependency relationship between the two classes. The following tips and techniques should help you when modeling associations and dependencies:

1. **Do not model the scaffolding for your associations.** Some developers will add the necessary attributes and methods needed to maintain associations, whereas others will assume they will handle it during programming. Both approaches are fine, although I prefer to not clutter my diagrams with scaffolding code.

2. **Multiplicity must be shown.** The multiplicities of an association should be modeled, one on each end of the association line. Table 12.6 lists the potential multiplicity indicators you can use on your UML class diagrams.

TABLE 12.6. UML Multiplicity Indicators	
Indicator	Meaning
0..1	Zero or one
1	One only
0..*	Zero or more
1..*	One or more
*	One or more
n	Only n (where $n > 1$)
0..n	Zero to n (where $n > 1$)
1..n	One to n (where $n > 1$)

3. **Question multiplicities involving minimums and maximums.** The problem with minimums and maximums is they change over time. For example, today you may have a business rule that states a student may enroll in no more than five seminars in any given term. Say you build your system to reflect this rule. Perhaps your design relies on a performance trick that works well for collections of five or less items and the rule changes, so students can take more than five seminars, then you may quickly find that to support this change you must rewrite a major portion of your system. My experience is it is interesting to know about any minimums and maximums. They often reflect important business rules at the time, but I do not take advantage of them when I design (unless I must for exceptionally good reasons) to avoid maintenance complications in the future.

4. **Associations and dependencies are inherited.** Because associations and dependencies are implemented as a combination of attributes and methods, and because attributes and methods are inherited, by implication, associations are also inherited.

5. **Collaboration goes hand-in-hand with relationships.** You need to have some sort of relationship—an association, dependency, aggregation association, or composition association—between two model elements to enable them to collaborate. Furthermore, if two model elements do not collaborate with one another, then no need exists for a relationship between them. The basic thinking is this: if the classes never take advantage of the relationship, why maintain it?

6. **Model a unidirectional association when collaboration is only one way.** Assume an assocation exists between Class *A* and Class *B*. If instances of

A send messages to instances of *B*, and instances of *B* send messages to instances of *A*, then you need a bidirectional assocation. If instances of *A* send messages to instances of *B*, but instances of *B* do not send messages to instances of *A*, then you need a unidirectional assocation from *A* to *B*. For example, student objects send messages to instances of *Enrollment* such as *getFinalMark()*, but no need occurs for messages going in the other direction (not yet at least), so a unidirectional assocation from *Student* to *Enrollment* is modeled in the analysis class diagram of Fig. 12.2.

7. **Model a dependency when one of the instances is transient.** When one of the classes is transient, it is not saved to permanent storage. It is an indication that you likely have a dependency. For example, user interface classes are transient, but their instances collaborate with persistent business objects, such as instances of the *Student* and *Seminar* classes.

8. **Model a dependency when an object interacts only with a class, but not the instance.** A perfect example of this is when an object interacts with a factory class (Gamma et al. 1995) whose responsibility is to create instances of other classes (similar conceptually to the idea that, in the real world, cars and trucks are built in factories). In software, an instance of *CarDealership* would collaborate with the *VehicleFactory* class to obtain instances of the *Car* and *Truck* classes, not an instance of *VehicleFactory*. The *CarDealership* class would have a dependency on *VehicleFactory* and assocations with *Car* and *Truck*.

9. **Do not model implied associations.** An implied association exists between students and seminars: students take seminars. Yet in Fig. 12.2 this association is not modeled between these two classes. A mistake? No, the association is implied by the *Enrollment* class: *Student* is associated to *Enrollment*, which, in turn, is associated to *Seminar*. These two associations, when taken together, implement the implied association that students take (enroll in) seminars. If you model this implied association, then somebody, your programmers, needs to implement it.

10. **The Liskov substitution principle applies to mirror hierarchies.** In Fig. 12.7 you see a UML class diagram representing portions of two class hierarchies and the associations between them. This is an example of what is known as mirror hierarchies, something that happens when two or more class hierarchies take on the same shape because they model highly related concepts. In this case, the type of equipment contained in a laboratory reflects the type of laboratory. Considering each class hierarchy in

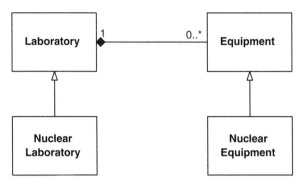

FIGURE **12.7. Classrooms and equipment class model.**

isolation, they appear to make sense because a nuclear laboratory is a laboratory and nuclear equipment is equipment. Taken together, however, they may not make as much sense. According to the Liskov substitution principle, you should be able to substitute instances of a subclass for its superclass, which indicates you should be able to use nuclear equipment wherever you can use equipment. According to Fig. 12.7, you can use equipment in a laboratory; therefore, you can use also nuclear equipment in a laboratory. That is not the intention of the model. Instead, nuclear equipment can only be used in a nuclear laboratory. Figure 12.8 presents a resolution of this issue. I made *Equipment* an abstract class and

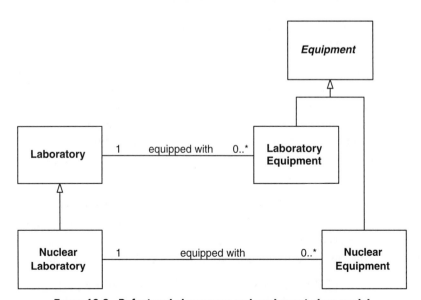

FIGURE **12.8. Refactored classrooms and equipment class model.**

introduced the class *LaboratoryEquipment*. I also introduced *equipped with* associations between the relevant classes; the fact that they are named the same and have the same multiplicities should let people know what is going on (adding a note would not hurt either). Most of the scaffolding attribute(s) and methods to implement these aggregation associations are likely to be implemented in *Equipment*, although *NuclearEquipment* is likely to include code that validates it is in a laboratory, which is able to contain it.

12.1.5 Composition Techniques

Sometimes an object is made up of other objects. For example, an airplane is made up of a fuselage, wings, engines, landing gear, flaps, and so on. A delivery shipment contains one or more packages. A team consists of two or more employees. These are all examples of the concept of composition, which represents "is part of" relationships. During design, several considerations are specific to composition:

1. **The advice for associations applies to composition.** Composition associations are merely specializations of the concept of association and, as a result, the heuristics for associations apply to them.

2. **The sentence rule should make sense for composition.** It should make sense to say that one object "is part of" or "composed of" another object.

3. **You should be interested in both the whole and the part.** For composition associations you should be interested in both the whole and the part separately. Another way to look at it is this: both the whole and the part should exhibit behavior that is of value to your system. For example, I could model the fact that my watch has hands on it, but if this fact is not pertinent to my system (perhaps I sell watches, but not watch parts), then no value exists in modeling this fact.

4. **You need to understand how the whole and the parts collaborate with each other.** If the whole and the parts do not collaborate, it is an indication that either a relationship does not exist between the two classes to begin with or you have not yet identified how they collaborate with each other.

5. **The majority of the interaction is from the whole to the part.** An engine is part of an airplane. To fly an airplane will collaborate with its engines,

> **TIP**
> **Document Complicated Things**
>
> If it is complicated, then document it thoroughly. Better yet, invest the time to design it so it is simple. Remember the agile modeling (AM) practice *create simple content*.

requesting they shut on or off, as well as increase or decrease their speed. It is unlikely that an engine will initiate much interaction with the airplane, except perhaps to inform it of a malfunction.

6. **Do not confuse inheritance with composition.** It is easy to get confused about when to use inheritance and when to use composition. Remember this: inheritance models "is a" or "is kind of" relationships, while composition models "is part of" relationships. By following the sentence rules (it should make sense to say a subclass *is a* superclass, etc.) you should be able to determine when to use each concept appropriately.

12.1.6 Introducing Interfaces into Your Model

An interface is the definition of a collection of one or more operation signatures and zero or more attributes, ideally one that defines a cohesive set of behaviors. Interfaces are implemented by classes and components. To implement an interface, a class or component must include methods that have the operation signatures defined by the interface. For example, Fig. 12.9 indicates that the class *Student* implements the *Serializable* interface and the *Searchable* interface. There are two ways to indicate something implements an interface: the lollipop notation used for the *Serializable* interface and the box notation used for the *Searchable* interface. The lollipop notation has the advantage that it is visually compact, whereas the box notation provides details about the

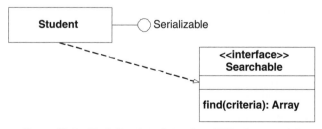

FIGURE 12.9. Modeling interfaces in a UML class model.

interface itself. The dashed arrow from *Student* to *Searchable* is a UML realizes relationship, indicating the *Student* class implements (realizes) the *Searchable* interface. The *Searchable* interface box is the same notation as a class, with the addition of the stereotype of <<interface>>. Any given class or component may implement zero or more interfaces, and one or more classes or components can implement any given interface.

Interfaces are named in the same manner as classes: they have fully described names in the format *InterfaceName*. In Java, it is common to have interface names such as *Serializable* that end in -able or -ible. In Microsoft environments, common practice is to prefix interface names with a capital *I*, resulting in names such as *IComponent*.

There are two sources of interfaces: existing interfaces you have purchased with your development environment or interfaces you have developed yourself. Java development environments come with predefined interfaces, such as *Serializable* in Fig. 12.9, as well as *Observer* and *EnterpriseBean*. You will choose to develop interfaces when you realize you need to implement something that needs to work with a wide range of objects in a similar manner. For example, consider how you would build a common facility for printing objects. This service would need to be able to work with instances of *Seminar*, *Student*, *Professor*, *Enrollment*, and so on. It would even need to work with classes you have not even identified yet. To solve this problem, you could have all these classes either directly or indirectly inherit from a common superclass, which assumes all classes in any given hierarchy would need to support printing. A better approach would be to have any class implement a common interface, perhaps named *Printable*, that defines the methods it must have to support printing. Your printing facility would then invoke these methods on each object as needed to print it.

By definition, the methods and attributes of interfaces are always public. Figure 12.10 depicts two interfaces, *Printable* and *Searchable*. Notice the application of the <<interface>> stereotype. Neither of the interfaces has attributes defined for them because this would not only go against the principle of information hiding—any attributes would be public—it would also constrain the classes that implement this interface. Attributes and methods are depicted the same way as you would for classes. When you are developing applications using object technology, it is likely you will need both of these interfaces and that you will need to refactor them to your environment. With respect to searching, Enterprise JavaBeans defines a common set of find methods, although they are not as sophisticated as the approach implied by the *Searchable* interface—the *RetrieveCriteria* class, described in a white paper

FIGURE **12.10. The *Printable* and *Searchable* interfaces.**

posted at http://www.ambysoft.com/persistenceLayer.html, supports a generic approach to finding objects that does not require the development of specific searching code.

Why interfaces? Interfaces are used to promote consistency within your models and source code, as well as to define new types for use within your system (class also define types). Coad and Mayfield (1997) argue that interfaces help to increase the flexibility, extensibility, and pluggability of your designs because your code is no longer hardwired for instances of specific classes. Instead, it is designed to work with objects that implement a common interface. This supports polymorphism within your design. Interfaces are also an alternative to multiple inheritance. Instead of using mixin classes to achieve common behavior, you simply develop common infrastructure components (see Chapter 10) that take as parameters objects that implement defined interfaces.

When would you decide to introduce a new interface? First, whenever you discover common behavior exhibited by several dissimilar classes, such as the need to support searching and printing capabilities throughout your business classes, you should attempt to generalize the common behaviors into the definition of an interface. Second, it is common to develop interfaces that support common design patterns, such as *Singleton* and *Façade*, as described in Section 12.2. This is actually a specific, albeit common, instance of the first case.

Important to note is that interfaces are not explicitly supported by all programming languages. For example, Java has built-in support for interfaces

---

TIP

Do Not Model the Methods of an Interface in Your Classes

My style is not to model the methods of an interface in the classes that implement them. The convention is that it is assumed the methods defined by the interface are implemented by that class (or at least by itself or by its subclasses if the class is abstract).

whereas C++ does not. If the language you are using does not support interfaces, you may instead develop a set of programming idioms for naming methods and attributes within your classes. Your language will not enforce the conformance of your class to a specific interface, but your coding guidelines can.

What factors make a good interface? First, interfaces should be cohesive; they should fulfill one well-defined purpose. Second, the methods and attributes should be well defined, exactly as you would for a class. For methods, this includes defining the preconditions and postconditions, if any, as well as the specific method signature (Douglass 1999). Third, the purpose of the interface should be defined as well as an indication of when it should and should not be implemented by a class.

12.1.7 Class Modeling Design Tips

This section summarizes a collection of class modeling design tips and techniques I have found useful over the years, such as:

- Follow the Law of Demeter;
- Minimize coupling;
- Maximize cohesion;
- Methods should do something;
- Separate commands from queries;
- Beware of connascent software elements; and
- Consider adding color to your diagrams.

12.1.7.1 *Follow the Law of Demeter*
The Law of Demeter (Lieberherr, Holland, and Riel 1988; Ambler 1998a) states that objects should send messages to themselves, a parameter of their methods, their own attributes, an element within a collection that is an attribute, or an object they create. Craig Larman (2002) encapsulates this concept with his *Don't Talk to Strangers* pattern.

12.1.7.2 *Minimize Coupling*
Coupling is a measure of how much two items, such as classes or methods, are interrelated. When one class depends on another class, we say they are coupled. When one class interacts with another class, but does not know

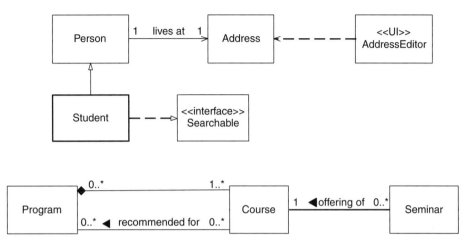

FIGURE **12.11. Sources of coupling in your object-oriented designs.**

any of the implementation details of the other class, we say they are loosely coupled. When one class relies on the implementation (that is, it directly accesses the data attributes of the other), we say they are tightly coupled.

A class is coupled to another class when it has knowledge of that other class. Coupling is important because when Class *A* is coupled to Class *B*, a change in *B* could necessitate a change in *A*. As a result, you want to reduce coupling wherever possible. In object-oriented designs, several sources of coupling exist:

1. **Coupling via associations.** Whenever an association exists between two classes, they are coupled. For example, in Fig. 12.11, the class *Person* is coupled to *Address* via the *lives at* association: a person object knows at what address it lives. Similarly, *Seminar* is coupled to *Course* via the *offering of* association. Furthermore, because this association is bi-directional, *Course* is also coupled to *Seminar*. It is important to understand that a class is coupled to another class only when it has knowledge of that other class. Therefore Class *A* can be coupled to Class *B* without *B* being coupled to Class *A*.

2. **Coupling via composition.** Because composition is simply a specialized type of association it also indicates coupling. In Fig. 12.11, the classes *Program* and *Course* are coupled to one another this way.

3. **Coupling via dependency.** Dependencies also indicate coupling between classes in the same manner as association does.

4. **Coupling via collaboration.** In a way, coupling via collaboration is related to coupling via association, aggregation, composition, or dependency (remember that without some sort of relationship you cannot have collaboration). The main point here is that collaborations increase coupling—not only does an object know of the existence of other objects, it also collaborates with them. For example, *Program* increases its coupling to *Course* via each collaboration it has with it. Riel (1996) suggests you should minimize the number of collaborations between two classes if possible.

5. **Coupling via realization.** The class *Student* is coupled to the definition of the *Searchable* interface via a realized relationship. If the definition of the interface changes, the *Student* class needs to be updated to reflect this change.

6. **Direct coupling via inheritance.** Subclasses are highly coupled to the implementations of their superclasses (a subclass knows and does everything its superclass does). For example, in Fig. 12.11, the *Student* class is coupled to the *Person* class in this manner. One way to reduce this kind of coupling is not to allow subclasses to modify the values of attributes defined in their superclasses. This implies you need to invoke accessors instead of directly accessing the values of attributes. While this is a little extra work, it makes your system more maintainable in the long run.

7. **Indirect coupling via inheritance.** Because a class inherits all the relationships and collaborations of its superclass(es), it also inherits any coupling with which the superclasses are involved. In this case, the *Student* class is indirectly coupled to *Address* via inheriting from *Person*.

12.1.7.3 *Maximize Cohesion*

Cohesion is a measure of how much an item, such as a class or method, makes sense. A good measure of the cohesiveness of something is how long describing it takes using only one sentence: the longer it takes, the less cohesive it likely is. You want to design methods and classes that are highly cohesive. In other words, it should be completely clear what a method or class is all about. A good rule of thumb is if you cannot describe a class or method with one sentence in less than 15 seconds, then it probably is not cohesive. Classes should represent only one kind of object, and methods should do one thing and one thing well.

12.1.7.4 Methods Should Do Something

Although this sounds obvious, in practice this advice is often ignored. Each method of a class should either access or modify the attributes of the class. A method should do something, and not just pass the buck to other methods.

12.1.7.5 Separate Commands from Queries

This is the command-query separation principle (Meyer 1997), which states functions should not produce abstract side effects. The basic idea is this: asking a question (a query), perhaps by invoking a getter or by asking for a calculated value, should not change the state target object. For example, it does not make sense that anything should change about a seminar just because you ask it how many students are currently enrolled in it. Commands can cause changes in the object. For example, a request to a seminar to enroll a student into itself would obviously change the state of the seminar. The student would be enrolled in it if she is eligible to take the seminar and there is room for her.

12.1.7.6 Beware of Connascent Software Elements

Connascence (Page-Jones 2000) is a measure of how well you have applied encapsulation within your system—have you minimized coupling and maximized cohesion? Two software elements are connascent either because of bad design (therefore, fix it) or, by their nature, they fulfill a common goal. For example, mirror hierarchies are connascent: their structures reflect that they fulfill a common goal.

12.1.7.7 Consider Adding Color to Your Diagrams

Coad, Lefebrvre, and DeLuca (1999) provide excellent advice in their book *Java Modeling in Color with UML* for improving the understandability of your diagrams by applying color to them. Your models are part of your communication interface with other developers and, just like user interfaces, can be improved by the effective application of color; so can your UML diagrams. In addition to applying UML stereotypes to your classes, you can also apply color; perhaps controller classes are rendered in blue, business entity classes in green, and system classes in yellow. Other uses for color include indicating the implementation language of a class (for example, blue for Java and red for C++), the development priority of a use case (for example, red for Phase 1, orange for Phase 2, and yellow for future phases), or the target platform (for example, blue for an application server, green for a client machine, and

> **TIP**
>
> **Essential Reading**
>
> The best pattern resource available to you is the Portland Pattern Repository at http://c2.com.

pink for a database server) for a software element. Deployment modeling is discussed in further detail in Chapter 10.

12.2 Applying Design Patterns Effectively

Design patterns describe a solution to common problems found in the design of systems. I will not discuss every existing design pattern in this section—there are too many to list in one book and people are discovering new patterns every day anyway. However, I will describe two useful design patterns that you should be able to apply immediately to the applications you are developing. These patterns are *Singleton* and *Façade* (Gamma et al. 1995).

12.2.1 The *Singleton* Design Pattern

Discovering classes in your application that should only have one instance is common. Perhaps there should only be one instance of a certain editing screen open at any given time, perhaps you have configuration information you want to store in one place only, or perhaps you have one or more constant values you need to maintain somewhere. In all these examples, you need to have a single instance of the class in question: a single instance of the dialog box, a single instance of the configuration information, and a single instance of the constants.

Singleton is a design pattern that shows how to ensure that only one single instance of a class exists at any one time. In Figure 12.12 you see the definition

> **TIP**
>
> **Iterate, Iterate, Iterate**
>
> With an iterative approach to development you work a bit on requirements, do a bit of analysis, do a bit of design, some coding, some testing, and iterate between these activities as needed. You will also iterate back and forth between working on various artifacts, working on the right artifact at the right time.

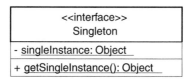

FIGURE **12.12. The solution to the** *Singleton* **design pattern.**

for an interface describing the Singleton design pattern. Note that a static attribute keeps track of the single instance, and a class method creates the instance if it does not already exist. The interface for this pattern is one of the few times I have actually seen a valid use for including an attribute in the definition of an interface. However, this is an invalid use of an attribute within an interface because I have assigned it private visibility instead of public (remember that interfaces define a public interface to be implemented by a class). Although *Singleton* is a simple pattern, I suspect it is one you will use over and over again when developing object-oriented software.

12.2.2 The *Façade* Design Pattern

The purpose of the *Façade* design pattern is to provide a unified interface to a subsystem or component, making it easier to use. The solution for the *Façade* pattern is presented in Fig. 12.13. The gist of the pattern is that objects external to the subsystem or component send messages to the façade class, which, in turn, routes them to the appropriate "internal" classes and objects.

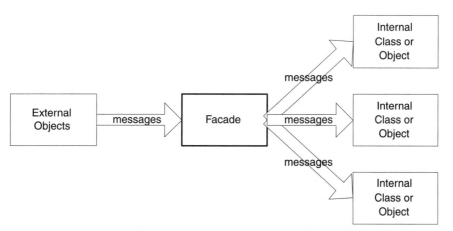

FIGURE **12.13. The solution to the** *Façade* **design pattern.**

The *Façade* pattern provides several advantages. First, it provides a simple and standard way to implement components using object technology. The façade class implements the public interface of the component and the internal classes implement the behaviors provided by the component. Component modeling is covered in detail in Chapter 10. Second, it provides a mechanism to reduce the coupling within your system because the external classes now interact only with the façade class, not all of the classes internal to your component or subsystem. Third, the external classes are not prevented from collaborating with the internal classes if need be, providing flexibility, albeit at the cost of increased coupling. Finally, because the communication to the internal classes of a component or subsystem are focused through a common point, the façade class, it provides a single point where you can potentially add important system features, such as security access control and load balancing.

12.2.3 Tips for Applying Patterns Effectively

The following tips can help you to apply patterns successfully in your work:

1. **Read widely.** Although patterns became popular in the early to mid-1990s within the object community, they have quickly gained prominence and significant work has been accomplished in a few short years. The end result is hundreds, if not thousands, of design patterns have been published. The Wiki at http://c2.com is a good place to start.

2. **Understand the patterns.** Simply reading about patterns is not enough; you also need to understand them. Most patterns describe both when and when not to apply them, important information you need to understand to use them successfully.

3. **Patterns are not the solution to everything.** Many patterns are out there at your disposal, but not every design problem can be solved via the application of one or more patterns. The secret is to have a good grasp of what patterns exist and to look them up when you think you have a situation where they can be applied.

4. **Remember several types of patterns exist.** As you have seen throughout this book, analysis patterns, design patterns, and process patterns exist, to name a few.

12.3 PHYSICAL DATA MODELING WITH THE UML

Data modeling is the act of exploring data-oriented structures. Like other modeling artifacts data models can be used for a variety of purposes, from high-level conceptual models (Chapter 8) to PDMs. Physical data modeling is conceptually similar to design class modeling, the goal being to design the internal schema of a database, depicting the data tables, the data columns of those tables, and the relationships between the tables.

Figure 12.14 presents a partial PDM for the university—you know that it is not complete by the fact that the *Seminar* table includes foreign keys to tables not shown, and quite frankly it is obvious that many domain concepts such as course and professor are clearly not modeled. All but one of the boxes represent tables, the one exception being *UniversityDB*, which lists the stored procedures implemented within the database. Because the diagram is given the stereotype *Physical Data Model* you know that the class boxes represent tables; without the diagram stereotype I would have needed to use the stereotype *Table* on each table. Relationships between tables are modeled using standard UML notation; although not shown in the example it would be reasonable to model composition and inheritance relationships between tables. Relationships are implemented via the use of keys (more on this below).

When you are physical data modeling, the following tasks are performed in an iterative manner:

1. **Identify tables.** Tables are the database equivalent of classes; data are stored in physical tables. As you can see in Fig. 12.14 the university has a *Student* table to store student data, a *Course* table to store course data, and so on. Figure 12.14 uses a UML-based notation that is described in detail at http://www.agiledata.org/essays/umlDataModelingProfile.html. This is a publicly defined profile that anyone can provide input into.

   If you have a class model in place a good start is to do a one-to-one mapping of your classes to data tables, an approach that works well in

---

TIP

Models Need to Be Just Barely Good Enough

Keep your models as simple and light-weight as possible. Focus on understanding, not documentation. Use the simplest, most inclusive tools available to you. Recognize that your models do not need to be perfect.

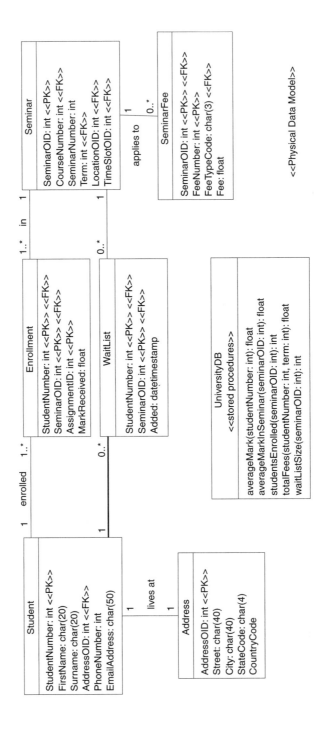

Figure 12.14. A PDM for part of the university database.

TABLE 12.7. Data Normalization Rules	
Level	Rule
First normal form (1NF)	An entity type is in 1NF when it contains no repeating groups of data.
Second normal form (2NF)	An entity type is in 2NF when it is in 1NF and when all of its nonkey attributes are fully dependent on its primary key.
Third normal form (3NF)	An entity type is in 3NF when it is in 2NF and when all of its attributes are directly dependent on the primary key.

"greenfield" environments where you have the luxury of designing your database schema from scratch. Because this rarely happens in practice you need to be prepared to be constrained by one or more legacy database schemas. which you will then need to map your classes to. In these situations it is unlikely that you will need to do much data modeling; you will simply need to learn to live with the existing data sources, but you will need to be able to read and understand existing models. In some cases you may need to perform legacy data analysis (Chapter 14) and model the existing schema before you can start working with it.

2. **Normalize tables.** Data normalization is a process in which data attributes within a data model are organized to increase the cohesion of tables and to reduce the coupling between tables. The fundamental goal is to ensure that data are stored in one and only one place. This is an important consideration for application developers because it is incredibly difficult to store objects in a relational database if a data attribute is stored in several places. The first three rules of data normalization are summarized in Table 12.7. There are many more normalization rules (Date 2001) but these are the three critical ones. The tables in Fig. 12.14 are in third normal form (3NF).

3. **Identify columns.** A column is the database equivalent of an attribute, and each table will have one or more columns. For example, in Fig. 12.14 the *Student* table has attributes such as *FirstName* and *StudentNumber*. Unlike attributes in classes, which can be either primitive types or other objects,

a column may only be a primitive type such as a *char* (a string), an *int* (integer), or a *float*.

4. **Identify stored procedures**. A stored procedure is conceptually similar to a global method implemented by the database. In Fig. 12.14 you see that stored procedures such as *averageMark()* and *studentsEnrolled()* are modeled as operations of the class *UniversityDB*. These stored procedures implement code that work with data stored in the database; in this case they calculate the average mark of a student and count the number of students enrolled in a given seminar respectively. Although some of these stored procedures clearly act on data contained in a single table they are not modeled as part of the table (along the lines of methods being part of classes). Instead, because stored procedures are a part of the overall database and not a single table, they are modeled as part of a class with the name of the database.

5. **Apply naming conventions**. Your organization should have standards and guidelines applicable to data modeling, and if not you should lobby to have some put in place. As always, you should follow AM's practice of *apply modeling standards* (Chapter 4).

6. **Identify relationships**. There are relationships between tables just like there are relationships between classes. The advice presented in Sections 12.1.4 and 12.1.5 are applicable to PDMs as well as to UML class models.

7. **Apply data model patterns**. Some data modelers will apply common data model patterns; David Hay's (1996) book *Data Model Patterns* is the best reference on the subject. Data model patterns are conceptually closest to analysis patterns (Chapter 8) because they describe solutions to common domain issues. Hay's book is a very good reference for anyone involved in analysis-level modeling, even when you are taking an object approach instead of a data approach because his patterns model business structures from a wide variety of business domains.

8. **Assign keys**. A key is one or more data attributes that uniquely identify a row in a table. A key that is two or more attributes is called a composite key. A primary key is the preferred key for an entity type, whereas an alternate key (also known as a secondary key) is an alternative way to access rows within a table. In a physical database a key would be formed of one or more table columns whose value(s) uniquely identifies a row within a relational table. In Fig. 12.14 primary keys are indicated using the <<PK>> stereotype and foreign keys via <<FK>>.

There are two strategies for assigning keys to tables: natural keys and surrogate keys. A key formed of attributes that already exist in the real world is called a natural key. For example, U.S. citizens are issued a Social Security Number (SSN) that is unique to them. A key formed completely of artificial values is called a surrogate key. Because student numbers are unique the column *StudentNumber* can be used as a natural key of the *Student* table in Fig. 12.14. There is no natural key for addresses, except perhaps the combination of all data attributes, so I introduced a new column called *AddressOID* for the key. The primary advantage of natural keys is that they exist already; you do not need to introduce a new "unnatural" value to your data schema. However, the primary disadvantage of natural keys is that because they have business meaning it is possible that they may need to change if your business requirements change. For example, if your users decide to make *StudentNumber* alphanumeric instead of numeric then in addition to updating the schema for the *Student* table (which is unavoidable) you would have to change every single table where *StudentNumber* is used as a foreign key. If the *Student* table instead used a surrogate key then the change would have been localized to just the *Student* table itself (*StudentNumber* in this case would just be a non0key column of the table). If you needed to make a similar change to your surrogate key strategy, perhaps adding a couple of extra digits to your key values because you have run out of values, then you would have the exact same problem. This points out the need to set a workable surrogate key strategy; strategies for calculating surrogate keys are presented in Table 12.8.

Although similar notation is used, it is interesting to note the differences between the PDM of Fig. 12.14 and the UML class diagrams presented in Section 12.1:

TIP

Designers Should Also Code

Whenever a model is handed over to someone else to code there is significant danger that the programmer will not understand the model, or at least will miss some of its nuances, and may even ignore the model completely in favor of their own approach. Furthermore, even when hand-offs are successful you will discover that you need far more details in your models than if you had simply coded it yourself. In short, separating design from programming is a risky and expensive proposition. It is far more effective to have generalizing specialists on your team that can both design and code.

TABLE 12.8. Surrogate Key Strategies

Strategy	Description
Key values assigned by the database	Most of the databases implement a surrogate key strategy called incremental keys. The basic idea is that they maintain a counter within the database server, writing the current value to a hidden system table to maintain consistency, which they use to assign a value to newly created table rows. Every time a row is created, the counter is incremented and that value is assigned as the key value for that row. Implementation strategies vary—sometimes the values assigned are unique across all tables, whereas sometimes values are unique only within a single table.
MAX() + 1	Use an integer column as the key with a starting value of 1. When a new row is added, set the value to the maximum value in this column plus one using the SQL MAX() function. This approach is simple but suffers from performance problems with large tables and only guarantees a unique key value within the table.
Universally unique identifiers (UUIDs)	UUIDs are 128-bit values created from a hash of the ID of your Ethernet card, or an equivalent software representation and the current datetime of your computer system. The UUID algorithm is defined by the Open Software Foundation (http://www.opengroup.org) and produces a unique value across all organizations using this strategy.
Globally unique identifiers (GUIDs)	GUIDs are a Microsoft standard that extends UUIDs, using a software ID when an Ethernet card is not available. When the software ID is used, the value is only guaranteed to be unique to the machine that created it so it is not actually globally unique as the name implies.
High–low strategy	A persistent object identifier (POID), often referred to simply as an object identified (OID), is in two logical parts: A unique *high* value that you obtain from a defined source and an N-digit *low* value that your application assigns itself. Each time that

Strategy	Description
	a *high* value is obtained the *low* value will be set to zero. For example, if the application that you are running requests a value for *high* it will be assigned the value 1234. Assuming that N, the number of digits for *low*, is four then all persistent object identifiers that the application assigns to objects will be a combination of 12340000, 12340001, 12340002, and so on until 12349999. At this point a new value for high is obtained, *low* is reset to zero, and you continue again. If another application requests a value for *high* immediately after you it will given the value of 1235, and the OIDs that will be assigned to objects that it creates will be 12350000, 12350001, and so on. As long as *high* is unique then all POID values will be unique. Several Java implementations of *high–low* generators can be found at http://www.theserverside.com.

1. **Keys.** Where it is common practice to not model scaffolding properties on class models it is common to model keys (the data equivalent of scaffolding).

2. **Visibility.** Visibility is not modeled for columns because they are all public. However, because most databases support access control rights you may want to model them using UML constraints, UML notes, or as business rules. Similarly stored procedures are also public so they are not modeled either.

3. **No many-to-many associations.** Relational databases are unable to natively support many-to-many associations, unlike objects, and as a result you need to resolve them via the addition of an associative table. The closest thing to an associative table in Fig. 12.14 is *WaitList*, which was introduced to resolve the *on waiting list* many-to-many association depicted in the class diagram of Fig. 12.2. A pure associative table comprises the primary key columns of the two tables that it maintains the relationship between, in this case *StudentNumber* from *Student* and *SeminarOID* from *Seminar*. Notice how in *WaitList* these columns have both a *PK* and an *FK* stereotype

because they make up the primary key of *WaitList* while at the same time are foreign keys to the other two tables. *WaitList* is not truly an associative table because it contains nonkey columns, in this case the *Added* column, which is used to ensure that the first people on the waiting list are those given the opportunity to enroll if a seat becomes available. Had *WaitList* been a pure associative table I would have applied the *associative table* stereotype to it.

I will often use a CASE tool to create physical data models. The two features I require of a data modeling tool are the ability to generate data definition language (DDL) code required to create the database schema and the ability to reverse-engineer a data model from an existing database schema. Virtually all data modeling tools still on the market today support these features. Chapter 14 discusses a wide range of database-oriented development activities.

12.4 What You Have Learned

In this chapter you learned that structural design modeling is an important part of software development. You saw how to model the detailed structural design of your object schema using UML class diagrams and how to model the detailed structural design of a relational database using PDMs. You were also introduced to design patterns, proven solutions to common design problems. Every developer should be skilled at detailed structural design and this chapter presented the basics of exactly that.

12.5 Review Questions

1. Identify ten common design patterns, taking them from at least three different sources, and summarize each pattern in one or two paragraphs. For each pattern indicate how it could or could not be applied to your analysis class model for the bank case study. For the patterns that could not be applied, indicate why you felt they were inappropriate.
2. Modify your analysis class diagram for the bank case study to reflect the application of the design patterns chosen in Question 1.
3. What are the advantages and disadvantages of applying the design patterns that you have chosen in Questions 1 and 2?
4. Section 12.1.1.3 suggests the precondition(s) of an overriding method must be the same or weaker than those of the method it is replacing and its

postcondition(s) must be the same or stronger. Justify why this is true (or why it is not true). Provide at least two examples.

5. Section 12.1.2.4 discusses the use of accessor methods (getters and setters), using a *Date* class as an example. Model a date class, including definitions of the attributes (*year*, *month*, and *day*), as well as the relevant methods. In addition to being able to represent dates accurately, it should also be able to calculate the difference in days between two dates and to add or subtract a given number of days from an existing date. Discuss your visibility decisions for each attribute and method in your design.

6. Create two versions of a physical data model to model the fact that a professor may teach many seminars and that a seminar is taught by one or more professor, one using foreign keys in each data entity and one using an associative table to resolve the association. Compare and contrast the advantages of the two approaches, suggesting when you would want to apply each one.

7. In a physical data model, what would be the advantages (if any) and disadvantages (if any) of using an associative table to resolve a many-to-one association?

8. Consider the additional requirements presented in Section 12.5.1. First, update your requirements models to reflect these changes. Then update your analysis models appropriately (hopefully, you baselined your original models), maintaining traceability back to your requirements models. Then update your design models to reflect these changes.

9. When you updated your models to reflect the new requirements presented in Section 12.5.1, what general changes did you need to make? How easy was it to accomplish? What was difficult? Why? What could you have done to ease this change? Present your findings as if it was a report to your organization's senior management.

12.5.1 The Bank Case Study Six Months Later

Your banking system has been in place for six months and it is running fine. During this time, the bank has been preparing to expand into other countries. Not only will the bank do business in the USA, it will also start doing business in Canada, Mexico, Great Britain, and France. The bank wants to be able to do business in each of those countries in their own currencies. For example, Mexican accounts will be handled in pesos, Canadian accounts in Canadian dollars, French accounts in francs, and so on. Because many of their customers do business internationally, it is certain that some customers will have accounts in several countries. ABC's corporate strategy is to be second-to-none in the banking industry. This means it must provide the best service to their customers. As a result, its accounts must be robust. That means if somebody wants to transfer money between an American account and a Mexican account, the bank can do it. If someone wants to deposit $20 in American dollars into a British account, it can do it and at both a teller and an automated teller machine (ATM).

CHAPTER 13

Object-Oriented Programming

Ouch! My paradigm shifted.

The purpose of object-oriented programming is to build your actual system, to develop the code that fulfills your system's design. Your design artifacts, such as unified modeling language (UML) class and state machine diagrams, drive the development of your source code. Design and programming are highly interrelated and iterative and you will often move back and forth between them. Your programming efforts will quickly reveal weaknesses in your design that need to be addressed, and your design efforts will reveal potential strategies to code the system effectively.

Developers will typically focus on two types of source code: object-oriented code, such as Java or C#, and database-oriented code, such as data definition language (DDL), data manipulation language (DML), stored procedures, and triggers. Section 13.4 describes how to implement common object-oriented concepts in Java and Chapter 14 describes database coding. The end goal of your programming efforts is to produce a component, subsystem, or even a full-fledged application that can undergo testing in the large (described in Chapter 3).

This chapter discusses these topics:

- Philosophies for effective programming;
- Programming tips and techniques for writing high-quality code;
- Test-driven development (TDD);
- From object design to Java code; and
- What you have learned.

13.1 Philosophies for Effective Programming

Over the years I have found that the following philosophies have helped improve my effectiveness as a programmer:

1. **Always write high-quality, clean code.** Quality work is one of the practices of extreme programming (XP) (Beck 2000), and my experiences confirm the importance of writing high-quality code at all times. High-quality code is easier to write, easier to understand, and easier to enhance. Sloppy code will only slow you down.

2. **Refactor ruthlessly.** Refactoring (Fowler 1999) is a technique where you make small changes to your code to improve its design without adding new functionality. Refactorings include changes such as renaming a method, splitting a method in two, moving a method up a class hierarchy, and introducing an assertion. Agile software developers write clean code from the very beginning and ruthlessly refactor it to maintain its quality.

3. **Think before you code.** Rushing to code results in systems that are fragile, difficult to maintain or to extend, and difficult to understand, which can be perilous. Agile software developers will first think through the design of their code before writing the code. They do this at a high level by following an agile modeling–driven development (AMDD) approach (Chapter 4) and at the detailed level via a test-driven development (TDD) approach (Section 13.3).

4. **Develop in small steps.** I have always found that developing in small steps—writing a few lines of code, testing it, and then writing a few more lines—is often far more effective than writing a whole bunch of code all at once, and then trying to fix it. It is much easier to test and fix ten lines of code than one hundred lines. In fact, I can safely say you could program,

test, and fix 100 lines of code in 10 ten-line increments in less than half the time than you could write a single 100-line block of code that did the same work. The reason for this is simple. Whenever you are testing your code and you find a bug, you almost always discover it is in the new code you just wrote, assuming the rest of the code was pretty solid to start. You can hunt down a bug faster in a small section of code than in a big one. By developing in small incremental steps, you reduce the average time it takes to find a bug, which, in turn, reduces your overall development time.

5. **Write understandable code.** Whenever the original programmer can only understand code, this is a sign the person is a bad coder, not the coding genius he most likely thinks he is. Most programmers typically work on teams, not alone, and people who were not its original developer(s) typically maintain most code. By writing clean, understandable code, you make it easier for others to work with it, increasing the chance they can maintain and enhance the code effectively. In short program for people.

6. **Adopt and follow coding standards and guidelines.** Your team, and ideally your organization, must come to a consensus as to the standards and guidelines it will follow during development. Programming standards and guidelines are critical to ensuring the work produced by your developers is of the quality your organization requires. Developers should follow the standards and guidelines when working on your application. These standards and guidelines should be in place by the time programming begins, so your team starts with a solid foundation. I maintain a page linking to a variety of coding standards and guidelines at http://www.ambysoft.com/javaCodingStandards.html (although it was originally a Java page, I now link to standards for many languages).

7. **Add documentation to improve code readability.** I am a firm believer that comments should add to the clarity of your code. Nagler (1995) points out that the reason you document your code is to make it more understandable to you, your co-workers, and to any other developer who comes after you. The implication is your documentation should add value. The goal is not to write a lot of documentation; it is to write just enough documentation to explain your work.

8. **Write the documentation before you write the code.** In addition to modeling and writing test code before business code, another way to think

before you code is to write the code documentation first. This gives you an opportunity to think about how the code will work before you write it and it ensures the documentation gets written. Alternatively, you should at least document your code as you write it. Because documentation makes your code easier to understand, you are able to take advantage of this fact while you are developing it. The downside of this approach is that you might write more documentation than you actually need.

9. **Follow the 30-second rule.** I have always believed another programmer should be able to look at a method, a class, or an interface definition and be able to fully understand what it does, why it does it, and how it does it in less than 30 seconds (Ambler 1998a). If he or she cannot, then your code is too difficult to maintain and should be improved. A class can be made understandable in less than 30 seconds by informative header documentation. A method can be made understandable in less than 30 seconds by effective heading documentation, adherence to common naming and programming conventions, and effective internal documentation.

10. **Smaller methods are usually better.** Everything else being equal, a small method is much easier to understand than a large method because there is less material to learn. Methods difficult to understand are difficult to maintain and enhance, increasing your maintenance costs. Furthermore, large methods indicate that your code is actually function oriented, as opposed to object oriented (Lorenz and Kidd 1994). Objects get things done by collaborating with each other and not by doing everything themselves. This results in short methods, not long ones. Although you will occasionally run into long methods, they are few and far between. If your methods are long, this is an indication that a problem exists.

11. **Optimize your code only as a last resort.** Optimizing your code is one of the last things programmers should be thinking about, not one of the first. My experience is you want to leave optimization to the end because you want to optimize only the code that needs it. Make it right then make it fast. Often a small percentage of your code results in the vast majority of the processing time and this is the code you should be optimizing. A classic mistake is to try to optimize all your code, even code that already runs fast enough. Personally, I prefer to optimize the code that needs it,

```
public boolean validate()
{
if (this.getStartDate() != null &&
    this.getTenuredAnniversary() != null) {
long start = this.getStartDate().getTime();
long tenureDate = this.getTenuredAnniversary().getTime();
return tenureDate >= start;
} else
return false;
}
```

FIGURE **13.1. Unparagraphed source code.**

and then move on to more interesting things than trying to squeeze out every single CPU cycle.

13.2 Programming Tips and Techniques for Writing High-Quality Code

Philosophies are not enough; you also need some fundamental techniques, which lead to high-quality code. Although Java examples are presented, these tips are applicable to a wide range of programming languages.

1. **Paragraph/indent your code.** One way to improve the readability of a method is to paragraph it; in other words, indent your code within the scope of a code block. Any code within braces, the { and } characters, forms a block. The basic idea is the code within a block should be uniformly indented one unit (a unit is typically between two and four spaces). Figure 13.1 presents a version of a method that does not apply any sort of paragraphing, whereas Fig. 13.2 presents a paragraphed version of the same code. Notice how following the flow of logic in the paragraphed version is easier because the indentation is visually grouping code that is at the same logical scope. Most IDEs (and some editors) provide the capability to do this for you automatically; take advantage of this.

2. **Paragraph and punctuate multiline statements.** A related issue to paragraphing your code occurs when a single statement requires several lines of code, an example of which appears in Fig. 13.3. Notice how I indent

```
public boolean validate()
{
  if (this.getStartDate() != null &&
      this.getTenuredAnniversary() != null) {
    long start = this.getStartDate().getTime();
    long tenureDate = this.getTenuredAnniversary().
      getTime();
    return tenureDate >= start;
  } else
    return false;
}
```

FIGURE **13.2. Paragraphed source code.**

the second and third lines two units, visibly indicating that they are still part of the preceding line. Also notice how the final comma in the second line immediately follows the parameter and is not shown on the following line (word processors also work this way).

3. **Use whitespace in your code.** A few blank lines or spaces, called whitespace, added to your Java code can help to make it much more readable by breaking the code up into small, easy-to-digest sections. I like to use a single blank line to separate logical groups of code, such as control structures, and two blank lines to separate method definitions. Without whitespace the code is difficult to read and to understand. Notice how the readability of the code improves from Fig. 13.4 to Fig. 13.5 by the simple addition of a blank line between setting the counter and the lines of code to calculate the grand total. Also notice how the addition of spaces around the operators and after the comma also increases the readability of the code. Small things, yes, but they can still make a big difference.

```
BankAccount newPersonalAccount = AccountFactory.
    createBankAccountFor(currentCustomer, startDate,
    initialDeposit, branch);
  int counter;
```

FIGURE **13.3. Paragraphing a multiline statement.**

```
counter=1;
grandTotal=invoice.total()+getAmountDue();
grandTotal=Discounter.discount(grandTotal,this);
```

FIGURE 13.4. Source code without whitespace.

```
counter = 1;

grandTotal = invoice.total() + getAmountDue();
grandTotal = Discounter.discount(grandTotal, this);
```

FIGURE 13.5. Source code with whitespace.

4. **Your code should do one thing per line.** Back in the days of punch cards, it made sense to try to get as much functionality as possible on a single line of code because the speed of program execution was partially determined by the number of cards you had. Considering it has been over 20 years since I have even seen a punch card, I think we can safely rethink this approach to writing code. Whenever you attempt to do more than one thing on a single line of code, you make your code harder to understand. Why do this? You want to make your code easier to understand so it is easier to maintain and enhance. Just like a method should do one thing and one thing only, you should only do one thing on a single line of code. Furthermore, you should write code that remains visible on the screen. My general rule of thumb is you should not have to scroll your editing window to the right to read the entire line of code.

5. **Document why something is being done.** Fundamentally, you can always look at a piece of code and figure out what it does. For example, you can look at the code in Fig. 13.6 and determine that a 5 percent discount is being given on orders of $1,000 dollars or more. Why is this being done? Is there a business rule that says large orders get a discount? Is there a limited-time special on large orders or is it a permanent rule? Was the original programmer just being generous? You do not know unless it is documented somewhere, either in the source code itself or in an external document.

```
if (grandTotal >= 1000.00)
{
   grandTotal = grandTotal * 0.95;
}
```

FIGURE **13.6. Undocumented source code.**

13.3 TEST-DRIVEN DEVELOPMENT (TDD)

Test-driven development (TDD), also known as test-first programming or test-first development, is an approach where you identify and write your tests before your write your code. Although it is not obvious from the name, TDD is actually a programming technique and not a validation technique (Martin, Newkirk, and Koss 2002). TDD is one way to think through the detailed design of your code before you actually write it.

As you can see in Fig. 13.7 there are four basic steps to TDD. First, you quickly add a test (just enough code to fail). The idea is that a programmer refuses to write new code, even one single line, unless there is a test that fails without it. The second step is to run your tests, either all or a portion of them, to see the new test fail. Third, you make a little change to your code, just barely enough to make your code pass the tests. Next you run the tests and hopefully see them all succeed—if not you need to repeat step 3.

Kent Beck, who popularized TDD in XP, defines two simple rules for TDD (Beck 2003). First, you should write new business code only when an automated test has failed. Second, you should eliminate any duplication that you find. Beck explains how these two simple rules generate complex individual and group behavior:

- You design organically, with the running code providing feedback between decisions.
- You write your own tests because you cannot wait 20 times per day for someone else to write them for you.
- Your development environment must provide rapid response to small changes (e.g., you need a fast compiler and regression test suite).
- Your designs must consist of highly cohesive, loosely coupled components (e.g., your design is highly normalized) to make testing easier (this also makes evolution and maintenance of your system easier, too).

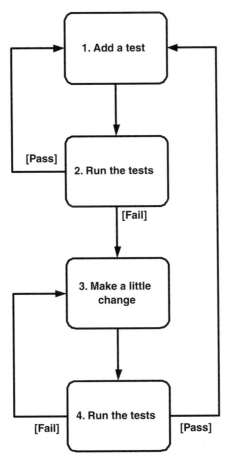

FIGURE **13.7. The steps of TDD.**

The focus of TDD is code-level testing, something that I like to refer to as "testing in the small," and in many ways TDD is simply an extreme form of unit testing. You will still need to consider traditional testing techniques such as functional testing, user-acceptance testing, system integration testing, and so on as the full lifecycle object-oriented test (FLOOT) methodology aptly points out (Chapter 3).

With traditional testing a successful test finds one or more defects. It is the same with TDD; when a test fails you have made progress because you now know that you need to resolve the problem. More importantly, you have a clear measure of success when the test no longer fails. TDD increases your confidence that your system actually meets the requirements defined for it,

TABLE 13.1. Comparing TDD and AMDD	
Test-Driven Development	Agile Modeling–Driven Development
• Nonvisually oriented • Rapidly provides feedback as to whether your software works • Helps to ensure that your design is clean by focusing on creation of operations that are callable and testable • New to traditional developers, including data professionals • Growing tool support for data-oriented TDD • Does not directly provide traditional data-oriented documentation (e.g., logical or physical data models) • Promotes the development of high-quality, working code • Supports communication with stakeholders via acceptance tests, but for the most part needs something else (e.g., sketches)	• Visually oriented • Can lead to excessive documentation if agile documentation-oriented practices are not adopted • *Prove it with code* practice provides concrete feedback, although TDD takes it one step further • Data professionals prefer an MDD approach, although many currently struggle with AMDD • Models often make it easier to look at the bigger picture (potentially a bad thing if taken too far) • Provides direct mechanisms to communicate with stakeholders

that your system actually works, and therefore that you can proceed with confidence.

13.3.1 TDD and AMDD

Table 13.1 compares TDD and AMDD. An important observation is that both TDD and AMDD are based on the idea that you should think through your design before you code. With TDD you do so by writing tests, whereas with AMDD you do so by creating diagrams or other types of models such as class responsibility collaborator (CRC) cards.

Which approach is better? The answer is that it depends on you and your teammates' cognitive preferences. Some people are dominantly "visual thinkers," also called spatial thinkers, who prefer to think things through drawing. Other people are dominantly text-oriented, nonvisual or nonspatial thinkers, who do not work well with drawings. Most people are somewhere in-between. The point is that the composition of your team will determine whether TDD or AMDD will work best for you.

Can you combine the two approaches? Absolutely. My experience is that you can enhance TDD with modeling; it is quite common to create models with your project stakeholders to help explore their requirements and then take a test-driven approach to implementation. You can also enhance AMDD with testing—as you know agile modeling includes integration points such as *consider testability* and *prove it with code* that enable you to dovetail TDD right into AMDD.

13.3.2 Why TDD?

There are several reasons why you should consider taking a TDD approach to programming:

1. **It ensures that your code is sufficiently unit tested.** By writing your tests before your code you know that your code actually works, dramatically reducing the risk to your project.

2. **Unit tests serve as detailed documentation for your code.** Like it or not, most programmers do not read the written documentation for a system; instead they prefer to work with the code. When trying to understand a class or operation most programmers will look for sample code that already invokes it. Well-written unit tests do exactly this. Therefore, unit tests are effectively documentation for your code because they provide real-world examples of how to work with it.

TIP

Recommended Reading

I highly suggest Kent Beck's book *Test-Driven Development* (Beck 2003) as well as Dave Astels' book by the same title (Astels 2003).

3. **It enables you to take small steps when writing software.** As I demon-
strated in Section 13.1, you are much more effective writing the code a few
lines at a time instead of in large chunks.

13.4 FROM OBJECT DESIGN TO JAVA CODE

In this section I show how to translate your object-oriented design into Java
source code. The basic concepts are the very similar for other object-oriented
languages, such as C#, although the syntax changes. Object-based languages,
such as Visual Basic, may not support all the concepts described in this section.
It is important to understand that the goal of this section is to introduce you
to the fundamental techniques for translating your models into source code.
The goal is not to teach you the nuances of the Java programming language.

In previous chapters you learned how to create a wide variety of design
models—UML class models, physical data models, UML sequence diagrams,
UML timing diagrams, and so on—but how do you convert them to code?
I have found UML sequence diagrams and UML class diagrams to be the
two most useful design models to base my object programming on. Sequence
diagrams convert almost directly to code, whereas class diagrams take a little
more skill to convert (a skill you can quickly gain). It is clearly possible to
iterate to programming from other design diagrams—experienced developers
do it all the time—although it is easiest to start with sequence diagrams and
class diagrams.

13.4.1 From UML Sequence Diagrams to Code

Figure 13.8 depicts a simple UML sequence diagram (taken from Chapter 11)
for the *enrollInSeminar()* method of the student class. Figure 13.9 presents
the corresponding Java source code that would appear in the *Student* class
and Fig. 13.10 the source code that would appear in *Seminar*. The code for
the *Course* class is not presented, as it requires relatively complex logic that
is not germane to this discussion. However, it is interesting to note that this
complex logic is not modeled in Fig. 13.8, implying that you either need to
model it or simply start coding it—this choice would depend on your skills
and preferences as a developer. Personally, I would write the code.

There are several interesting things to note about the two source code
examples:

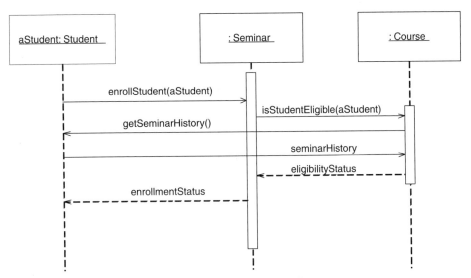

FIGURE 13.8. A UML sequence diagram.

1. **The methods need header documentation.** I left the header documentation, discussed in detail in Section 13.4.7, out in order to save space.

2. **The methods do not require a lot of internal documentation.** Because I have followed good naming conventions for both the methods and the data attributes, and because I have paragraphed it and used whitespace effectively, it is very easy to understand. Remember that you should add documentation only when it adds value.

3. **Some code is not implied in the diagrams.** Notice how the addition of a student to the waiting list in Fig. 13.10 is not modeled on the sequence diagram of Fig. 13.8. This is why the AM practice of *active stakeholder participation* is so important—because models will never be perfect, developers

```
public void enrollInSeminar(Seminar seminar) throws
    EnrollmentException
{
    seminar.enrollStudent(this);
}
```

FIGURE 13.9. Source code in the *Student* class.

```
public void enrollStudent(Student student)
    throws NotEligibleException, WaitingListException
{
  if (!(getCourse().isStudentEligible(student)))
      throw new NotEligibleExcpetion(this,student);
  if (isSeatAvailable()) {
    addStudent(student);
  } else {                           // automatically add to
                                     //    waiting list as a
    addToWaitingList(student); // courtesy if eligible
                                     //    but no seats are left
    throw new WaitingListException(this,student);
  }
}
```

FIGURE **13.10. Source code in the *Seminar* class.**

need access to someone who understands the domain, like a stakeholder, who can explain what should happen.

Although converting the UML sequence diagram of Fig. 13.8 into the source code in Fig. 13.9 and Fig. 13.10 may seem daunting at first it really is straightforward after you have done it a few times. The secret is to become comfortable with both sequence diagrams and the programming language—once you have done these two things, iterating back and forth between them will become very easy for you.

13.4.2 From UML Class Diagrams to Code

Now let us explore how to evolve a UML class diagram into source code. Figure 13.11 depicts a simple class diagram for the university system; it is based on the combination of several class diagrams presented in Chapter 12. I present a modified version because I want to depict the major object-oriented concepts you need to understand how to translate into code. As you can see in the diagram, however, I have not strayed far from our initial design; instead, I have simplified it, so I could focus on just what I need and no more.

The following sections describe how to translate individual aspects of a class diagram into Java source code as well as provide advice for effective object programming.

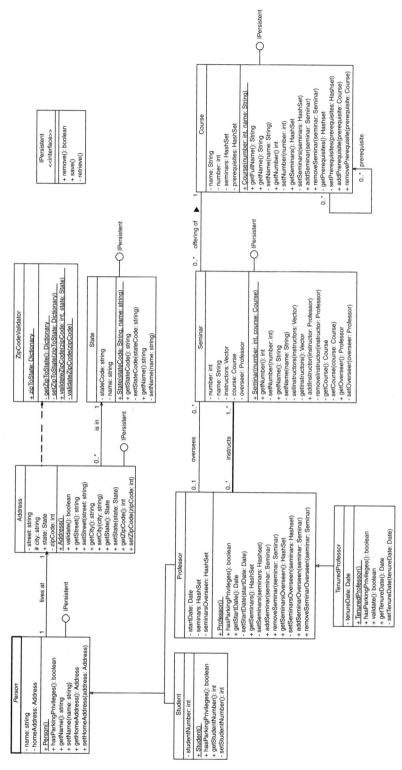

FIGURE 13.11. A simple class diagram for the university system.

```
/**
 * Person encapsulates basic behavior required of
 * employees and students of the University.
 *
 * @author John Nalbone, Scott Ambler
 * @version 3.0 April 22, 2004 JDK 1.4.2
 **/
abstract public class Person implements IPersistent
```

FIGURE **13.12. Declaring the *Person* class.**

13.4.3 Implementing a Class in Java

Figure 13.12 presents the beginning of source code to declare of the *Person* class in Java. The class itself is declared on the bottom line of Fig. 13.12 and the meaning of each word is described in Table 13.2. At the top is the header documentation for the class, using Java's documentation comment style, describing the class, and indicating its author and version number. The text *@author* and *@version* are Javadoc tags, predefined strings parsed by Java's

TIP

Set Commenting Style Guidelines

It is important that your organization set style guidelines for use of comments in Java or in any language. Java has three styles of comments:

1. **Documentation comments.** These start with /** and end with */ characters. I prefer to use documentation comments immediately before declarations of interfaces, classes, methods, and attributes to document them because they are processed by Javadoc to produce external source code documentation.
2. **C-style comments.** These comments start with /* and end with */ characters. I use C-style comments to document out lines of code no longer applicable, but that I want to keep in case my users change their minds or because I want to turn it off temporarily while debugging.
3. **Single-line comments.** These comments start with // and go until the end of the source-code line. I use single-line comments internally within methods to document business logic, sections of code, and declarations of temporary variables.

TABLE 13.2. The Meaning of Each Word in the Declaration of the *Person* Class	
Word	Meaning
Abstract	Indicates the class has no instances. If this keyword were not indicated, the class would have been assumed concrete.
Public	Indicates the class is accessible to every other class in your system. If this keyword were not indicated, the class would have assumed to be concrete.
Class	Indicates a class is being declared, the other option being an interface. Interface declarations are covered in Section 13.4.11.
Person	The name of the class being declared.
Implements	An optional keyword, which indicates a list of interfaces the class (or, optionally, its subclasses in the case of an abstract) must implement.
IPersistent	An interface the class implements. Could have been a list of several interface names separated by commas. Notice how the class diagram in Fig. 13.11 indicates the *Person* class implements the *IPersistent* interface.

Javadoc utility to generate external documentation for your code (Vermeulen et al. 2000). The documentation is fairly sparse because there is not much to this class. It is common to document a brief description of the class, any applicable invariants of the class, the author(s) of the class, and its version.

To implement a class in Java, you must first declare it, then declare its attributes, and then define its methods.

13.4.4 Declaring Instance Attributes in Java

The declarations for the instance attributes of the *Person* class are depicted in Fig. 13.13. The *name* attribute is a simple string, one of Java's primitive types, whereas the *homeAddress* attribute is a full-fledged object, in this case, an instance of the *Address* class depicted in Fig. 13.11. Each attribute is assigned

```
/**
 * The person's name.
 *
 * @example Ambler, Scott
 */
private string name;

/**
 * The person's home address.
 *
 * @see Address#Address(Person person)
 */
private Address homeAddress;
```

FIGURE **13.13. Declaring the attributes of the *Person* class.**

private visibility. The type of an attribute is declared immediately following the visibility, in this case, string for the *name* attribute and *Address* for the *homeAddress* attribute. Finally, the name of each attribute is indicated and the statement ends with a semicolon (Java statements end in semicolons).

To show you how to implement attributes with different visibilities, I present the declarations for the attributes of the *Address* class in Fig. 13.14. You can declare nonprivate attributes, but that is rarely a good idea.

In both Fig. 13.13 and Fig. 13.14, I have used documentation comments to describe each attribute, enabling Javadoc to recognize that I want to include it in my external documentation. I use Javadoc tags in the documentation, the *@example* is one of my own devising and *@see* is one of the standard Javadoc tags. The book *The Elements of Java Style* (Vermeulen et al. 2000) provides an excellent discussion of how to document attributes effectively.

13.4.5 Implementing Instance Methods in Java

Instance methods are implemented exactly as you would expect: there should be header documentation describing the method, the method signature is declared, and the Java statements that implement the code for the method are declared. Figure 13.15 depicts the implementation of the *hasParkingPrivileges()* method of the *Person* class. The declaration of the method signature is similar to the declaration of the class and attributes you saw earlier. First, the visibility of the method is declared; in this case, the method is public

```
/**
 * The city street of the address
 *
 * @example 1701 Enterprise Way
 */
private String street;

/**
 * The name of the city
 *
 * @example Toronto
 */
protected String city;

/**
 * The state that the address is in
 */
public State state;

/**
 * The ZIP code that the address is in
 *
 * @example 90210
 */
private String zipCode;
```

FIGURE 13.14. **Declaring the attributes of the *Address* class.**

(you saw in Chapter 12 that methods can also have protected, private, and default visibility in Java). Next, the optional keyword *abstract* appears, which in Java implies this class will merely define a method signature that must be implemented by its concrete subclasses. Only abstract classes—you saw in Fig. 13.11 that the *Person* class is abstract—may declare abstract methods. The return type of the method then appears, in this case *boolean*. Finally, the method name, an open parenthesis, a list of parameter declarations (if any), and a closing parenthesis are indicated. In this case, the name of the method is *hasParkingPrivileges* and there are no parameters.

Figure 13.16 shows the implementation of the *hasParkingPrivileges()* method of the *Professor* class, an example of how a method in a subclass can override (redefine) one in its parent class. Because *Professor* is a concrete class, it must have (or inherit) an implementation of any abstract methods

```
/**
  * Indicates whether a person is allowed to park his or
    her vehicle
  * at the university.
  *
  * @return true if allowed to park, false otherwise
  */
public abstract boolean hasParkingPrivileges();
```

FIGURE 13.15. The *hasParkingPrivileges()* method in the *Person* class.

defined in its superclasses. You see in the class diagram of Fig. 13.11 that the *Student* class also implements its own version of this method. In this case, it returns false because students are not allowed to park their cars on university grounds because of a lack of parking spaces. Interesting to note is the documentation for this method is similar to that of Fig. 13.15, the main difference being that the documentation is now more specific.

13.4.6 Implementing Static Methods and Attributes in Java

Static methods potentially operate on all instances of a single class. Similarly, static attributes are applicable to all instances of a single class. In the class

```
/**
  * Indicates that a professor is allowed to park his or
    her vehicle
  * at the university.
  *
  * @return true
  */
public boolean hasParkingPrivileges()
{
  return true;
}
```

FIGURE 13.16. The *hasParkingPrivileges()* method of the *Professor* class.

diagram of Fig. 13.11, static methods and attributes are underlined, the UML standard, whereas instance methods and attributes are not.

In Fig. 13.17, you see the implementation of the two validation methods of the *ZipCodeValidator* class, both static methods (note the use of the Java keyword *static* in its declarations). You see that parameters are declared type first, followed by the name, which is opposite of the UML approach to declare the name first, followed by the type. Compare the source code of Fig. 13.15 with the class diagram of Fig. 13.11 to see what I mean. In fact, the ordering of a method declaration in Java is significantly different from that of the UML, something you will easily get used to. Like attributes, the types of parameters may be Java primitive types or full-fledged objects.

The source code of Fig. 13.17 is interesting for several reasons:

1. **The source code presents an example of overloaded methods.** The methods *validateZipCode(zipCode, State)* and *validateZipCode(zipCode)* are overloaded. An overloaded method is one where one or more methods exist (within the same class, within its superclasses, or within its subclasses) that have the same name, but different parameters. This is allowed in Java, enabling you to define families of methods similar to each other, but that have different implementations.

2. **Overloading might not have been appropriate here.** I specifically named the methods the way I did so I could have a simple example of overloading. The reality is the second method could have been named something like *validateZipCodeFormat(zipCode)* to make its purpose more obvious.

3. **Each method has several return statements.** Note that each of the statements provides an answer of the type defined in the declaration of the methods (in both cases Boolean).

4. **Each method presents an example of Java's exception-handling approach in the form of a "try/catch" structure.** The method invocations and statements within the scope of the try, anything between the opening and closing curly braces, are attempted. If any of them throw an exception, via Java's *throw* statement (see Fig. 13.21 for an example), then processing ends at that point and the catch clauses are invoked. In this case, it is possible the conversion of a string to an integer may fail—the *Integer.parseInt()* method throws an exception if a string containing nondigit characters is passed to it, something you can look up in the documentation for the Java Development Kit (JDK).

> **TIP**
>
> **Do Not Gold Plate**
>
> The addition of requirements by developers is often referred to as "gold plating"—the addition of "really cool" features that you are convinced your users need is conceptually equivalent to putting a layer of gold on top of an otherwise functional item. In short, it is the role of project stakeholders to provide requirements; it is the role of developers to understand and implement them.

5. **The methods have different visibilities.** In my design, I want the *validateZipCode(zipCode, state)* method to be invoked by other objects—in this case address objects—so they can validate their zip codes effectively. Therefore, this method was declared public. However, the behavior to validate the format of zip code, although normalized (Ambler 2003b) into its own method, does not need to be available to external objects in my design. Therefore, the *validateZipCode(zipCode)* method was declared private.

6. **The internal documentation is good.** I also believe in writing documentation only when it adds value, which is why both methods in Fig. 13.17 include just enough internal documentation to make obvious what is happening. Notice how the documentation is written in straightforward business terms such as "Ensure that a hyphen exists in the sixth position" and not "Invoke charAt() with 5 as a parameter and compare it to a hyphen," which is merely an English wording of the statement. Internally within a method you should document any control structures, what and why the code does something, local variables, difficult or complex code, and the applicable processing order if applicable.

7. **The *validateZipCode(zipCode)* method likely has bugs.** Although I have not built a test case to validate this, I suspect I can pass the string "–1701," which is an invalid zip code, although a valid integer as a string of length five, so it would likely get through my existing code. Had I taken a TDD approach to writing this code I would not be in this position.

Figure 13.18 depicts the declaration of the static attribute *stateZips* of *ZipCodeValidator*. It is declared to be static; therefore, it is accessible by the methods of the class in which it is declared. It is also assigned a value of *null* to initiate its value.

```
/**
 * Verify that the ZIP code is valid.
 * The ZIP code should be in a valid format and should be
 * a valid ZIP code for the given state.
 *
 * @return true if valid, false otherwise
 */
public static boolean validateZipCode(String zipCode,
  State state)
{
  // Check that the ZIP code only is in the proper format
    if (! validateZipCode(zipCode)) {
      return false;
  }
  // Verify that the ZIP code corresponds to the state
  try {
    String stateCode = zipCode.substring(0,2);
    int number = Integer.parseInt(stateCode);
    return isValidState(number, state);
  } catch (Exception e) {
  }
  return false;
}

/**
 * Validate the format of a ZIP code
 *
 * Valid ZIP codes are in the format NNNNN or NNNNN-NNNN,
 * for example 90210 and 74656-1701
 *
 * @return true if the format is valid, false otherwise
 */
private static boolean validateZipCode(String zipCode)
{
  if (zipCode == null)
    return false;

  // A valid ZIP code may be in the format NNNNN
    (5 digits)
  if (zipCode.length() == 5) {
    try {
        // Ensure that there is only digits
```

FIGURE 13.17. Implementing the *validateZipCode()* methods in the *ZipCodeValidator* class.

```
        Integer.parseInt(zipCode);
        return true;
      } catch (Exception e) {
        return false;
      }
    } else {
      // A valid ZIP code may be in the format NNNNN-NNNN
      if (zipCode.length() == 10) {
        // Ensure that a hyphen is in the sixth position
        if (! (zipCode.charAt(5) == `-'))
          return false;

        // Get the first five characters of the ZIP code
        String str1 = zipCode.substring(0,5);
        // Get the last four characters of the ZIP code
        String str2 = zipCode.substring(6);

        try {
          // Ensure that the strings only hold digits
          Integer.parseInt(str1);
          Integer.parseInt(str2);
          return true;
        } catch (Exception e) {
          return false;
        }
      }
    }
    return false;
}
```

FIGURE 13.17 (*continued*)

```
/**
 * Maps the first two digits of a ZIP code to the state
 * that the ZIP code is in.
 */
static Vector stateZips = null;
```

FIGURE 13.18. The *zipToState* attribute of the *ZipCodeValidator* class.

13.4.7 Documenting Methods

Every method should include some sort of documentation at the top of the source code that documents all (but no more) of the information critical to understanding it. This information potentially includes, but is not limited to, the following:

1. **What and why the method does what it does**. By documenting what a method does, you make it easier for others to determine whether they can reuse your code. Documenting why it does something makes it easier for others to put your code into context. You also make it easier for others to determine whether a new change should actually be made to a piece of code (perhaps the reason for the new change conflicts with the reason the code was written in the first place).

2. **Known bugs**. Any outstanding problems with a method should be documented so other developers understand the weaknesses/difficulties with the method. If a given bug is applicable to more than one method within a class, then it should be documented for the class instead. Better yet, fix the bug!

3. **Any error conditions or exceptions that a method throws**. You should document any and all error conditions and/or exceptions a method throws, so other programmers know what their code will need to catch.

4. **Visibility decisions**. If you feel other developers will question your choice of visibility for a method—perhaps you have made a method public even though no other objects invoke the method yet—then you should document your decision. This will help to make your thinking clear to other developers, so they do not waste time worrying about why you did something questionable.

5. **How a method changes the object**. If a method changes an object, for example the *withdraw()* method of a bank account modifies the account balance, then this fact needs to be indicated if it is not obvious from the name of the method (which in this case it is). This information is needed so other Java programmers know exactly how a method invocation will affect the target object.

6. **Examples of how to invoke the method, if appropriate**. One of the easiest ways to determine how a piece of code works is to look at an example. Consider including an example or two of how to invoke a method.

TIP

Nothing Should Be Built That Does Not Satisfy a Requirement

Your system should be based on the requirements, the whole requirements, and nothing but the requirements.

---

7. **Applicable preconditions and postconditions.** A precondition is a constraint under which a method will function properly. A postcondition is a property or assertion that will be true after a method is finished running (Meyer 1997). In many ways, preconditions and postconditions describe the assumptions you have made when writing a method (Ambler 1998a), defining exactly the boundaries of how a method is used.

Internally within a method you should consider documenting these items:

1. **Control structures.** Describe what each control structure, such as comparison statements and loops, does and why it does it. You should not have to read all the code in a control structure to determine what it does. Instead, you should only have to look at a one- or two-line comment immediately preceding it.

2. **Why, as well as what, the code does.** You can always look at a piece of code and figure out what it does, but for code that is not obvious, you can rarely determine why it is done that way. The description could be as something simple as a reference to a business rule definition, or as complex as several paragraphs of prose.

3. **Local variables.** Each local variable defined in a method should be declared on its own line of code and should include an endline comment describing its use if it is not apparent from the variable name (it is far better to simply use descriptive variable names).

4. **Difficult or complex code.** If you find you cannot refactor code to make it easier to understand then you should add documentation to improve its understandability.

5. **The processing order.** If statements in your code must be executed in a defined order, then you should ensure this fact gets documented. There is nothing worse than making a simple modification to a piece of code only to find it no longer works, and then spending hours looking for the problem, only to find you have things out of order.

```
/**
 * Public constructor
 */
public Seminar()
{
  super();

  instructors = new Vector();
}
/**
 * Public constructor
 *
 * @param The course which describes this seminar
 */
public Seminar(Course course)
{
  this();

  this.course = course;
  course.addSeminar(this);
}
```

FIGURE **13.19. Two constructor methods of the *Seminar* class.**

In Fig. 13.17 it is important to note that I only wrote a small sub-set of the documentation described above. That is because I only write documentation that adds value—it would be a serious mistake to blindly write all this documentation for each method.

13.4.8 Implementing Constructors

Figure 13.19 depicts two constructors for the *Seminar* class. The Java convention is that the constructor for a class must have the same name as the class itself. The first method is an example of an "empty" constructor because it takes no parameters. The second method takes as a parameter the course object of which the object is a seminar and assigns it to the object's *course* attribute. I am not invoking the getter method for *course* to show you an example of how to do this because invoking getters within a constructor can be dangerous. The problem is if the getter method checks the value it is passed against that of another attribute of the class, and if that attribute is not yet set by the constructor, then an error results. The constructor invokes a method on the course object to maintain the association between the two objects (the implementation of associations is discussed in detail in Section 13.4.12). The empty constructor typically takes care of basic housekeeping. In this instance, the constructor explicitly calls the constructor of its superclass via *super*(). The *instructors* attribute is also set to an instance of a new vector that will be used to maintain the association to the *Professor* objects that teach it. Subsequent nonempty constructors invoke the empty constructer via a call to *this*() so that they do not each have to perform the same housekeeping.

The constructor takes a parameter identical in name to one of its instance attributes. Because instance attributes are accessible by the constructor method of a class, there is a name-hiding problem with this parameter. To resolve it, the method must refer to the attribute using its fully qualified name, in this case *this.course*, to differentiate it from the parameter.

Notice the use of whitespace in Fig. 13.19, spaces and blank lines within the source code. Whitespace improves the readability of your code. The spaces between the equal signs make it easier to distinguish where the names of the attributes end on the left and where the new value starts on the right-hand side. More important, the blank line before the statement where the *instructors* attribute is set helps to separate it from the statements that focus on working with the course object.

13.4.9 Encapsulating Attributes with Accessors

Accessor methods come in two flavors: setters and getters. A setter modifies the value of an attribute, whereas a getter obtains its value. Although accessors add minimal overhead to your code, the reality is the loss in performance is often trivial compared to other performance detractors such as questionable database designs. Accessors help to hide the implementation details of your classes and, thus, increase the robustness of your code. By having, at most, two control points from which an attribute is accessed, one setter and one getter, you are able to increase the maintainability of your classes by minimizing the points at which changes need to be made. Accessors also provide the debugging benefit of being able to determine exactly when an attribute is accessed or changed.

Figure 13.20 depicts the implementation of the getter and setter methods for the *homeAddress* attribute of the *Person* class. Both methods do exactly as you would expect. Getters and setters are useful because they enable you to encapsulate important business rules, transformation logic, and/or validation

```
/**
 * Gets the person's home address
 *
 * @return homeAddress
 */
public Address getHomeAddress()
{
  return homeAddress;
  }
/**
 * Sets the person's home address
 *
 * @param homeAddress
 */
public void setHomeAddress(Address homeAddress)
{
  this.homeAddress = homeAddress;
}
```

FIGURE **13.20.** **The getter and setter for the *homeAddress* attribute of the *Person* class.**

logic applicable to your data attributes. For example, Fig. 13.21 presents an alternative implementation of the setter method. See how it first verifies the address object that it has been passed is valid by invoking its *validate()* method and, if it is, then it sets the value of the *homeAddress* attribute. If the address is not valid, then it throws an exception (as you saw in Fig. 13.17 exceptions are handled by the invoker of a method via Java's try/catch statement).

One of the most important standards your organization can enforce is the use of accessors. Some developers do not want to use accessor methods because they do not want to type the few extra keystrokes required (for example, for a getter, you need to type in "get" and "()" above and beyond the name of the attribute). The bottom line is the increased maintainability and extensibility from using accessors more than justifies their use.

13.4.9.1 Naming Accessors

Getter methods should be given the name *get + attribute name*, unless the attribute represents a Boolean (true or false), and then the getter is given

```
/**
 * Sets the person's home address
 *
 * @param homeAddress
 * @return homeAddress
 */
public Address setHomeAddress(Address homeAddress) throws
  InvalidDataException
{
  // Only set the address if it is valid
  if (homeAddress.validate()) {
    this.homeAddress = homeAddress;
  }
  else {
    throw new InvalidDataException();
  }
}
```

FIGURE **13.21. Alternative implementation of the *setHomeAddress()* method.**

the name *is + attribute name*. Setter methods should be given the name *set + attribute name*, regardless of the attribute type (Gosling, Joy, and Steele 1996). As you see in Table 13.3, the attribute name is always in mixed case with the first letter of all words capitalized. This naming convention is used consistently within the JDK and is what is required for JavaBeans development.

TABLE 13.3. Example Accessor Names			
Attribute	Type	Getter Name	Setter Name
name	String	getName()	SetName()
homeAddress	Address object	getHomeAddress()	SetHomeAddress()
persistent	Boolean	isPersistent()	SetPersistent()
zipCode	Int	getZipCode()	SetZipCode()
instructors	Vector of Professor objects	getInstructors()	SetInstructors()

TIP

Accessors Are the Only Place to Access Attributes

An essential concept with the appropriate use of accessor methods is the *only* methods allowed to work directly with an attribute are the accessors themselves. Yes, it is possible to directly access a private attribute within the methods of the class in which the attribute is defined, but you do not want to do so because you would increase the coupling within your class.

13.4.9.2 Visibility of Accessors

You should always strive to make accessors protected, so only subclasses can access the attributes. You should try to make accessors private if subclasses do not need access to the attribute. Only when an external class or object needs to access an attribute should you make the appropriate getter or setter public. As you see in Fig. 13.11, it is quite common for the visibility of corresponding getter and setter methods to be different: in the class *Seminar*, you see the *getName()* method has public visibility, yet *setName()* has private visibility. Figure 13.22 reveals the only place the setter method is called is in the getter to formulate the name of the seminar, a combination of the course number, seminar number, and course name.

13.4.9.3 Lazy Initialization

The implementation of the *getInstructors()* method in Fig. 13.23 is an example of lazy initialization, an approach where the value of an attribute is initialized (set) when it is first accessed. The advantage of this approach is you only incur the expense of obtaining the value when and if you need it. The main disadvantage of lazy initialization is your code becomes more complex because you need to check to see whether the attribute has been defined yet and, if not, obtain its value. Lazy initialization is typically used when an attribute is expensive to calculate or obtain (perhaps it is very large and would take significant time to transmit across the network) and when it is not always required each time the object is brought into memory.

13.4.9.4 Why Use Accessors?

Accessors improve the maintainability of your classes in the following ways:

```
/**
 * Returns the name of the seminar.
 * The seminar name is the concatenation of the
   course number (CCC),
 * the seminar number (SSS), and the name of the
   course (NNN) in the
 * format "CCC-SSS NNN"
 *
 * @return String Name of the seminar
 * @example "CSC 158-2 Introduction to Java Programming"
 */
public String getName()
{

  If (name == null) {
    // Build the name
    String newName = new String();
    newName += course.getNumber() + "";
    newName += getNumber();
    newName += "" + course.getName();
    setName (newName);
  }
  return name;
}

private void setName(String newName) {
  name = newName;
}
```

FIGURE 13.22. The getter and setter methods for the *name* attribute of the *Seminar* class.

1. **Updating attributes.** You have single points of update for each attribute, making it easier to modify and to test. In other words, your attributes are encapsulated.

2. **Obtaining the values of attributes.** You have complete control over how attributes are accessed and by whom.

3. **Obtaining the values of constants.** By encapsulating the value of constants in getters when those values change, you only need to update the value in the getter and not every line of code where the constant is used. Constants are often implemented as static attributes of Java interfaces; therefore, I

```
public Vector getInstructors()
{
   if (instructors == null)
     instructors = new Vector();
   return instructors;
}
```

FIGURE **13.23. Lazy instantiation within a getter method.**

avoid the inclusion of static attributes in interface definitions in favor of static getter methods.

4. **Initializing attributes.** The use of lazy initialization ensures attributes are always initialized and are initialized only if they are needed.

5. **Reduction of the coupling between a subclass and its superclass(es).** When subclasses access inherited attributes only through their corresponding accessor methods, this makes it possible to change the implementation of attributes in the superclass without affecting any of its subclasses, effectively reducing coupling between them. Accessors reduce the risk of the "fragile base class problem" where changes in a superclass ripple throughout its subclasses.

6. **Encapsulating changes to attributes.** If the business rules pertaining to one or more attributes change, you can potentially modify your accessors to provide the same capability as before the change, making it easier for you to respond to the new business rules.

7. **Name hiding becomes less of an issue.** Although you should avoid name hiding (giving local variables the same names as attributes), the use of accessors to always access attributes means you can give local variables any name you want. You need not worry about hiding attribute names because you never access them directly anyway.

8. **Provide debugging support.** By having all accesses and changes happen in one place, it is relatively easy to determine exactly when (and by whom) an attribute is accessed or changed.

13.4.9.5 Why Shouldn't You Use Accessors?

The only time you might not want tot use accessors is when execution time is of the utmost importance, but it is a rare case, indeed, that the increased

---

TIP

Requirements Come from Stakeholders, Not Developers

Project stakeholders are the only official source of requirements. Yes, developers can suggest requirements but stakeholders need to adopt the suggestions.

---

coupling within your application justifies this action. Lea (1997) makes a case for minimizing the use of accessors on the grounds that it is often the case that the values of attributes in combination must be consistent and it is not wise to provide access to attributes singly. He is right, so don't! I think Lea has missed the point that you do not need to make all accessor methods public. When you are in the situation where the values of some attributes depend on one another, then you should introduce methods that do the "right thing" and make the appropriate accessor methods protected or private as needed.

13.4.10 Implementing Inheritance In Java

Figure 13.24 depicts how to have a class inherit from another in Java: with the *extends* keyword when a class is declared. Java only supports single inheritance, the capability of a class to inherit from zero or one classes, as opposed to C++, which supports multiple inheritance, the capability to inherit from zero or more classes (except for Interfaces, which can extend multiple other interfaces). Because *Student* inherits from *Person*, we say *Student* is the subclass of *Person* and *Person* is the superclass of the *Student* class.

13.4.11 Implementing Interfaces in Java

Two aspects of implementing interfaces are in Java: the actual definition of the interface itself and the definition of the code for a class to implement that interface.

```
public class Student extends Person
```

FIGURE **13.24.** Indicating the *Student* class inherits from the *Person* class.

```
/**
 * Interface for persistent objects
 *
 * Objects that are persisted must implement
   this interface
 *
 * @author Chris Roffler, Scott Ambler
 * @version 5.0 November 28, 2003
 */
public interface IPersistent
{
/**
 * Remove the object from permanent storage
 *
 * @postcondition This object will no longer be
   available to other objects
 *
 * Note: Removal does not necessarily mean deletion,
   it may simply mean the archival
 * of the object.
 */
void remove();

/**
 * Write the object to permanent storage
 *
 * @postcondition This object is written to
   permanent storage
 */
void save();

/**
 * Retrieve the object from permanent storage
 *
 * @precondition None. The object does not need to
   exist in permanent storage.
 * @postcondition If the object exists in storage it will
   be brought into memory.
 */
void retrieve();
}
```

FIGURE 13.25. Defining the *IPersistent* interface.

13.4.11.1 Defining an Interface

In Fig. 13.11 you see an interface called *IPersistent*. Interface definitions are indicated on UML class diagrams using a class box with the *interface* stereotype. In the diagram, I deviated from the common UML notation by indicating the *interface* stereotype below the name of the interface, instead of above it. I do this throughout this book because my experience is the name of the element, be it a class, an interface, or an object, is more important to most developers than its stereotype. Figure 13.25 depicts the code for the complete definition of the *IPrsistent* interface.

Interesting things to note about Fig. 13.25:

1. **Interfaces are declared in the same manner as classes**. The only difference is the use of the *interface* keyword instead of the *class* keyword. Although not indicated here, interfaces can inherit from zero or more other interfaces via the *extends* keyword, just like a class. This feature leads many people to claim that Java does, in fact, support multiple inheritance. My opinion is this is wishful thinking at best.

2. **Interfaces are documented similarly to classes**. Notice how header documentation exists for the interface as for the method definitions.

3. **Method definitions do not include a body of source code**. The purpose of a Java interface is to define a collection of signatures that a class must implement, not to provide the actual implementation.

4. **The methods all return void, accept no parameters, and do not throw any exceptions**. It is possible to indicate these just as you would for a method declaration in a class. The reality is these methods should throw exceptions because it is possible for errors to occur within the permanent storage mechanism or anywhere along the communication chain to it. As indicated at the beginning of the chapter, I wanted to keep this as simple as possible.

It is possible to declare static attributes in Java interfaces, although only for named constants (you cannot update them). As indicated in my discussion in Section 13.4.9.4 of why you should use accessors, I prefer to use a getter method to return constants (hence, making my code more flexible). However, everyone else seems to do this without accessors, including Sun, so take this advice with a grain of salt.

The documentation of the methods in Fig. 13.25 is interesting because they use two more of my suggested Javadoc tags: *@precondition* and *@postcondition*.

These tags are important because they provide a minimal support for design by contract (Meyer 1997). Actual support can be implemented via the *assert* statement in Java, added in JDK 1.3. Because these tags are not yet standard in the Java world, and I do not know when they will be, you need to write a Java doclet to support them if you want to include them in your documentation. I would also use these tags to document the methods implemented in classes.

13.4.11.2 Implementing an Interface in a Class

It is fairly straightforward to implement an interface in a class. You must declare that the class implements the interface, as you saw in Fig. 13.11, and then you must implement methods in the class which conform to the method signature definitions defined by the interface, as you see in Fig. 13.26. Notice the similarity of the method documentation to the original documentation defined within the interface; it is almost identical. Second, notice how the *remove()* method traverses the associations the seminar object has with Instructor objects and the course object it represents. It does this to ensure the referential integrity of your objects (a topic discussed in detail in Section 13.4.12). For the actual code to persist seminar objects, I have merely written comments in their place because database coding is covered in detail in Chapter 14.

13.4.12 Implementing Relationships in Java

Relationships—in this section, when I use the term relationship, I mean association and composition—are implemented via the combination of attributes and methods. The attributes describe the relationship, and the methods define and update the relationship. To understand this topic fully, you need to understand how to implement

- Unidirectional and bi-directional relationships;
- One-to-one relationships;
- One-to-many relationships;
- Many-to-many relationships;
- Recursive relationships;
- Several relationships between the same classes; and
- Aggregation and composition.

```java
/**
 *
 * Remove the seminar from permanent storage
 *
 * @postcondition This seminar will no longer be available
   to other objects
 *
 */
public void remove()
{
  if (instructors != null) {
    // Each instructor of this seminar must have
    // it removed from their list of seminars.
    Enumeration instructorList = instructors.elements();

    while (instructorList.hasMoreElements()) {
      Professor professor =
        (Professor)instructorList.nextElement();
      professor.removeSeminar(this);
    }
  }

  //
  // Disassociate the Course from this seminar
  //
  if (getCourse() != null) {
    getCourse.removeSeminar(this);
    setCourse(null);
  }

  // Specific code to remove the seminar from permanent
     storage
}

/**
 * Write the seminar to permanent storage
 *
 * @postcondition This seminar is written to permanent
   storage
 */
public void save()
{
  // Specific code for to save this seminar
}
```

FIGURE 13.26. Implementing the methods of the *IPersistent* interface in the *Student* class.

```
/**
 * Retrieve the seminar from permanent storage
 *
 * @precondition None. The seminar does not need to exist
   in permanent storage.
 * @postcondition If the seminar exists in storage it will
   be brought into memory.
 */
public void retrieve()
{
   // Specific code to retrieve this seminar from
   // permanent storage
}
```

FIGURE 13.26 (*continued*)

13.4.12.1 Implementing Unidirectional and Bi-directional Relationships

A unidirectional relationship is one that may be traversed in one direction only. For example, in Fig. 13.11, you see a unidirectional association from *Person* to *Address*. You know it is unidirectional because the association line has an arrowhead pointing from *Person* to *Address*. The implication is that person objects know about their address objects, but address objects do not know about the person objects that live there. In the diagram, you see that *Person* has scaffolding code to maintain the association, in this case the *home-Address* attribute and its corresponding getter and setter method. This code is sufficient to manage the association between the two objects, maintaining the fact that a person lives at one and only one address (one-to-many association management is discussed in the following).

Bidirectional relationships are naturally harder to manage than unidirectional ones because they can be traversed in both directions. Here is a little secret: maintaining a bi-directional association is just like maintaining two unidirectional associations. The only added complication is you need to maintain them both in tandem. In Section 13.4.12.3, I discuss how to implement a bi-directional one-to-many association between *Seminar* and *Course*, and I discuss a bidirectional many-to-many association between *Seminar* and *Instructor* in Section 13.4.12.4.

13.4.12.2 Implementing One-to-One Relationships

One-to-one relationships are the easiest to maintain because you only need to have an instance attribute in either one or both classes. For example, in Fig. 13.20, you see the code needed to maintain the one-to-one unidirectional association from *Person* to *Address*. Had this association been bi-directional similar code, and an attribute, it would have been needed in the *Address* class as well. One-to-one associations are always implemented as the combination of a simple attribute, such as an instance of *Address* in the case of the *Person* class, and a getter and setter method to manipulate that attribute.

One-to-one associations can also be implemented in a manner similar to how you would in a relational database, using a foreign key and methods to manipulate the key. The basic idea is the unique identifier, the key, for the other object knows the associated object. This value is then used to retrieve the associated object when it is needed, effectively a use of lazy initialization described in Section 13.4.9.2. Using this approach to maintain the association from *Person* to *Address*, you would first need to add an attribute to *Address* to be used to identify it—ideally an object ID (OID) as described in Chapter 14, along with its corresponding getter and setter. This attribute would also be added to *Person*, perhaps called *homeAddressOID*, along with a getter and setter to manipulate it. The *getHomeAddress()* method of Fig. 13.20 must be updated to check whether *homeAddress* has been set and, if not, then use the value of *homeAddressOID* to retrieve the appropriate address object.

13.4.12.3 Implementing One-to-Many Relationships

One-to-many relationships, also called many-to-one relationships, are a little more difficult to implement. Actually, it is the "many" aspect of the relationship that is the problem, because it cannot be implemented simply as the combination of an attribute, a getter, and a setter. Instead, to manage the "many" part of a relationship, you must use a collection object such as an instance of Java's *Vector* or *Hashset* classes to track the relationship to potentially several other objects. Collection classes enable you to keep track of zero or more items by adding and removing them from the collection as needed. Each type of collection class works differently; for example, an instance of *Hashset* only lets you add one reference to any given object, whereas an instance of *Vector* lets you add as many references as you want to the same object. The *Hashset* class is good to use if you need a unique collection of objects, whereas the *Vector* class is good to use if speed is of the essence. Each collection class has different strengths and weaknesses.

```
/**
 * Add a seminar to the course
 */
public void addSeminar(Seminar seminar)
{
   getSeminars().add(seminar);
}

/**
 * Remove a course from the seminar
 */
public void removeSeminar(Seminar seminar)
{
   getSeminars().remove(seminar);
}
```

FIGURE **13.27. Managing the association from a course to its seminars.**

In Fig. 13.11, you see a one-to-many bi-directional association between the *Course* and *Seminar* class. The *Seminar* class includes scaffolding to maintain the association to course objects. It has a course attribute and a getter and setter for the attribute, and even takes a course object as a parameter to its constructor, the *Seminar(number, course)* method, as you saw in Fig. 13.19. To manage the association in the other direction, the *Course* class has the instance attribute *seminars*, which is a hashset, and a corresponding getter and setter called *getSeminars()* and *setSeminars()*, which work exactly as you would expect. However, because *seminars* is a collection, I also needed to add methods to add and remove objects to/from it, in this case the methods *addSeminar()* and *removeSeminar()* as depicted in Fig. 13.27.

Notice the consistency of the names of the collection attribute, its "add" and "remove" methods, and the role of the objects stored in the collection. I follow this naming convention for all the scaffolding attributes and methods to maintain the "many" portion of an association. The more consistent your code is, the easier it is to understand and to enhance.

Also notice the *addSeminar()* and *removeSeminar()* methods both use the getter method to access the collection and do not directly access the attribute itself. For example, instead of writing *getSeminars().remove(seminar)* I could just as easily written *seminars.remove(seminar)*. Although this code would run slightly faster, it would also lose the information-hiding benefits enabled by

```
    private HashSet seminars;

    public void addSeminar(Seminar seminar)
    {
      // If the seminar is not already in the collection
         add it
      // The if statement avoids an infinite loop managing
         the association
      if (! getSeminars().contains(seminar)) {
        getSeminars().add(seminar);
        // The Seminar should know who instructs it
        seminar.addInstructor(this);
      }
    }

    public void removeSeminar(Seminar seminar)
    {
      // Only perform the removal of the seminar if it is in
         the collection
      // The if statement avoids an infinite loop managing the
         association
      if (getSeminars().contains(seminar)) {
        getSeminars().remove(seminar);

        // Update the seminar so that it knows that the
           professor no longer instructs it
        seminar.removeInstructor(this);
      }
    }
```

FIGURE 13.28. The scaffolding code in the *Professor* class.

accessor methods. This is a trade-off I chose not to make, however. I prefer to optimize code as a last resort, not as a first resort.

13.4.12.4 Implementing Many-to-Many Relationships

Many-to-many relationships require the most amount of work to implement because each object involved in the relationship must maintain a collection of references to the other objects to which it is related. You saw in the previous section how to implement the "many" sides of an association. When using a many-to-many association, you merely need to do this on both sides. Figure

```
private Vector instructors;

public void addInstructor(Professor professor)
{
   // If the professor does not exist in the collection
      add it
   // The if statement avoids an infinite loop managing
      the association
   if (! getInstructors().contains(professor)) {
     getInstructors().add(professor);

     // Update the other end of the association
     association
     professor.addSeminar(this);
   }
}

public void removeInstructor(Professor professor)
{
   if (getInstructors().contains(professor)) {
     getInstructors().remove(professor);

     // Update the other end of the association
     professor.removeSeminar(this);
   }
}
```

FIGURE **13.29. The scaffolding code in the *Seminar* class.**

13.28 presents the scaffolding code in the *Professor* class to manage its part of the *instructs* association with instances of *Seminar*. Figure 13.29 presents the similar code to manage its part of the association. I did not include the header documentation or the accessors for the sake of brevity.

Notice how, in Fig. 13.28, the *addSeminar(seminar)* method automatically invokes *addInstructor(professor)* in the *Seminar* class and, in Fig. 13.29; this method does the same thing in the other direction. This code is more robust than that presented in Fig. 13.27 because it automates the management of the association in both directions, reducing the chance of introducing a logic error in your code. Also notice the use of whitespace in the parameter list of method invocations in Fig. 13.29, as compared to Fig. 13.28. Both styles are fine; just pick one and follow it consistently in your code.

```
private HashSet prerequisites;

public void addPrerequisite(Course course)
{
   getPrerequisites().add(course);
}

public void removePrerequisite(Course course)
{
   getPrerequisites().remove(course);
}
```

FIGURE 13.30. The scaffolding code to manage the recursive association of the *Course* class.

13.4.12.5 Implementing Recursive/Self Relationships

Recursive relationships are implemented exactly as nonrecursive associations: that is, with attributes and methods. The only difference is all the scaffolding code is implemented in one class instead of two. In Fig. 13.11, you see a course knows its prerequisites, a unidirectional recursive association. Figure 13.30 presents code necessary to maintain this relationship, once again, not including the header documentation or the accessors for the sake of brevity.

13.4.12.6 Implementing Several Relationships between the Same Classes

To implement several relationships between the same two classes, you merely implement the appropriate scaffolding code to maintain the relationships. For example, in Fig. 13.11, you see two relationships exist between the *Professor* and the *Seminar* class: *instructs* and *oversees*. As you can see in the class diagram, each class has the appropriate scaffolding code to manage both of these associations.

13.4.12.7 Implementing Composition

As you might have guessed, aggregation and composition associations are handled exactly the same way as associations. The main difference, from a programming point-of-view, is aggregation implies a tighter relationship between the two classes than association does, and composition implies an even tighter relationship still. Although Fig. 13.11 does not include composition associations, the association between *Seminar* and *Course* is tight, in fact, at least as tight as you would see with composition (unfortunately the sentence

```
/**
 * Remove a course
 *
 * @postcondition The course and its seminars will be
   removed
 */
public void remove()
{
  if (getSeminars() != null) {
    // Clone the original set because we can't safely
       remove
    // the items from the set while we iterate over it
    HashSet set = (HashSet) getSeminars().clone();
    Iterator iterator = set.iterator();

    // Remove each seminar of this course
    while (iterator.hasNext()) {
      Seminar seminar = (Seminar) iterator.next();

      // Remove the seminar from the collection
      getSeminars().remove(seminar);
    }
  }

  // Remove the instance from permanent storage
  // Persistence code ...
  }
```

FIGURE **13.31. Implementing the *remove()* method in the *Course* class.**

rule does not make sense in this case). In Fig. 13.31, you see the result of this closeness in the implementation of the *remove()* method in the *Course* class—when a course is removed, its seminars are also removed. This type of lifecycle management code is typical within composition hierarchies.

Figure 13.31 is interesting because it implements the business rule that when a course is made unavailable, it is removed from the university catalog, and its seminars must also be made similarly unavailable (remember that removed does not necessarily mean deleted). This is effectively a referential integrity (RI) issue. In a relational database, this logic would be implemented as a trigger, discussed in Chapter 14. However, my philosophy is that business logic belongs in the business layer, which is implemented using object

```
/**
 * Validate the address
 *
 * @return true if the address is valid, false otherwise
 */
public boolean validate()
{
  // Code to validate the street, city, and state ...

  // Validate the ZIP code
  return ZipCodeValidator.validateZipCode(zipCode, state);
}
```

FIGURE 13.32. Implementing the *validate()* method in the *Address* class.

technology, not in the database. Therefore, I prefer to implement "triggers" in my business code, not in my persistence code.

Writing code to enforce RI in your business classes instead of your database only works when all your applications are written this way (and, one hopes, they share a common code base). This situation, however, is rarely the case. Instead, many organizations are in the position that some of their applications, often most, are written assuming the database(s) will handle referential integrity. Unfortunately a database-oriented solution works best when there is a single database, something that also is rarely the case. The implication is that you should decide where to implement your RI code wisely.

13.4.13 Implementing Dependencies

You do not really implement dependencies in Java; instead, dependencies are simply reflected in the code you write. For example, in Fig. 13.11, you see a dependency exists between the *Address* class and the *ZipCodeValidator* class. This dependency is a reflection of the fact that in the *validate()* method of *Address*, it invokes the *validateZipCode(zipCode, state)* method of the *Zip-CodeValidator* class, as seen in Fig. 13.32. The method is invoked on the class. As you see in the class diagram, it is a static method, so you invoke it on the class and not on an instance of the class, returning a Boolean indicating whether the zip code is valid.

```
/**
 * A tenured professor must have been given tenure on or
   after
 * the date that he or she started with the university.
 *
 * @return true if the attribute values are
   self-consistent, false otherwise
 */
public boolean validate()
{
   return getTenuredAnniversary().getTime() >=
      getStartDate().getTime();
}
```

FIGURE **13.33.** The *validate()* method in the *TenuredProfessor* class.

13.4.14 Implementing Collaborations in Java

Collaboration occurs for one of two reasons: either an object requests information from another object or it requests another object to do something for it. Collaboration is implemented as a method invocation on an object or class. In Fig. 13.11, you saw the implementation of the *getName()* method of *Seminar*–to formulate its name, a seminar object must collaborate with its corresponding course to get the base information it needs. Figure 13.32 presents an example of how an address object collaborates with the *ZipCodeValidator* class to determine whether a zip code is valid.

13.4.15 Implementing Business Rules

Business rules can be implemented using a variety of methods. For example, the business rules pertaining to the validation of a zip code are encapsulated by the *ZipCodeValidator* class. A business rule may also be implemented as a method. For example, Fig. 13.33 implements the business rule that a tenured professor must receive tenure on or after the day he or she starts with the university. Business rules may also be implemented using business rule engines, software products specifically designed to implement complex rules, a topic that is beyond the scope of this book.

13.4.16 Iterate, Iterate, Iterate

I cannot say this enough—successful developers iterate back and forth between various activities. They model a little, they test a little, they code a little, they test some more, code some more, model a bit, and so on.

13.5 What You Have Learned

This chapter began with a discussion of philosophies, tips, and techniques for effective object-oriented programming. It then described how to take a test-driven approach to development, arguing that this is the most effective way to program. The majority of the chapter focused on how to convert your primary object design models, UML sequence diagrams, and UML class diagrams, into Java source code. In effect you have learned the fundamental skills required to turn design models into object business code. In Chapter 10 you will learn the skills required to persist those business objects into a relational database.

13.6 Review Questions

1. In addition to the languages mentioned in this chapter—Java, Visual Basic, and C#–name five other object-oriented languages and provide at least two sources (vendors, open source Web sites, or freeware Web sites) from which you can obtain each language. List three strengths and weaknesses for each language and describe a use for which the language is well suited.

2. What changes would you need to make to the implementation of the *Course* class if its recursive association was bi-directional instead of uni-directional?

3. Develop a *DateRange* class in Java. It should have two attributes: *startDate* and *endDate*. Start by modeling this class. What invariants should it exhibit? What methods are needed to ensure these invariants? What visibilities should these methods be assigned? Write the source code for the *DateRange* class based on your model.

4. What did you learn modeling, and then coding, the *DateRange* class? How far did your source code stray from your initial design? What changes did you need to make to your model? How easy/difficult were the changes to make to your model? In hindsight, what could you have done when you were modeling to minimize the changes you needed to make?

5. Implement the *instructs* association between the *Professor* and *Seminar* classes as depicted in Fig. 13.11. Write three classes—*Professor, Seminar,* and *Instructs*—that include enough code to implement the association. The *Instructs* class should do the bulk of the work.

6. Compare and contrast your implementation in Question 5 and the code presented in Fig. 13.28 and Fig. 13.29. Which approach is easier to write and to maintain? Which is potentially more reusable? Why?

7. Regardless of your answer in Question 6, assume you have decided that the addition of the *Instructs* class to maintain the association between *Professor* and *Seminar* is your best implementation strategy. Should you update Fig. 13.11 to reflect this? Why? In what situations would you update the diagram, in what situations wouldn't you? What are the potential drawbacks of updating or not updating it?

8. Implement several classes for the bank case study, focusing on the classes pertaining to accounts, customers, and transactions. For the account classes, take a "test last" approach and write your business code first. For the customer classes take a "test first" approach (you may need to download a unit testing tool). You may want to review the code-testing techniques described in Chapter 2. Do not implement the code required to persist your business objects to permanent storage.

9. Compare and contrast a "test last" approach to development and a "test first" approach. What are the advantages and disadvantages of each?

10. What standard Javadoc tags are available to you? From what you have seen in this chapter and the previous one, what tags do you think are missing? Describe how each tag will be used and provide an example of its use.

CHAPTER 14

Agile Database Development

Data does not have to be a four-letter word anymore.

The predominant development technologies are object technology for implementing business logic and relational database (RDB) technology for storing information. You have other options—procedural technologies such as COBOL for implementing business logic and XML-based or object-oriented databases for storage, for instance. COBOL is beyond the scope of this book and XML databases and object databases are at best niche technologies (albeit very interesting ones). My focus is on mainstream, modern development, and that means objects on the front end and RDBs on the back end.

The fit between object technology and RDB technology is not perfect. In the early 1990s, the difference between the two approaches was labeled the *object/relational impedance mismatch*, also referred to as the *O/R impedance mismatch* or simply the *impedance mismatch*, terms still in common use today. Why does a technological impedance mismatch exist? The object-oriented paradigm is based on proven software engineering principles. The relational paradigm, however, is based on proven mathematical principles. Because the underlying paradigms are different, the two technologies do not work together seamlessly. The impedance mismatch becomes apparent when you look at the preferred approach to access: With the object paradigm you traverse objects via their relationships, whereas with the relational paradigm you join rows of tables. This fundamental difference results in a nonideal combination of the two technologies, although when have you ever used two different things together without a few hitches?

There is also a cultural impedance mismatch between developers in the object community and data professionals in the data community. Object developers have been taking an evolutionary (iterative and incremental) approach to development for years and are now quickly moving towards agile development methods such as extreme programming (Beck 2000), Scrum (Beedle and Schwaber 2001), feature-driven development (FDD) (Palmer and Felsing 2002), and agile modeling (Ambler 2002). Unfortunately many within the data community look upon evolutionary development as a questionable approach, and agile approaches (Ambler 2003b) are just now being considered. Object developers typically take an object-oriented approach to modeling using unified modeling language (UML) diagrams, whereas data professionals focus on data-oriented models such as logical data models (LDMs) and physical data models (PDMs). Furthermore, many object developers are not skilled at data modeling and data professionals are not skilled at object modeling. When it gets right down to it the real issue is that data professionals view the world as data to be manipulated, whereas object developers view it as objects to be combined to perform behavior.

Due to these two impedance mismatches, one technological and one cultural, it can be very difficult to succeed at object persistence. Unfortunately we have little choice in the matter: these are the two technologies that we typically have to work with, and so we need techniques to overcome the inherent challenges. The goal of this chapter is to describe how you can effectively develop the data aspects of your business software.

This chapter is organized into the following sections:

- Philosophies for effective data development;
- Mapping objects to relational databases;
- Strategies for implementing persistence code;
- From design to database code;
- Data-oriented implementation strategies;
- Database refactoring;
- Legacy analysis; and
- What you have learned.

> **TIP**
>
> **Essential Reading**
>
> For a more detailed discussion of effective data techniques, I highly suggest *Agile Database Techniques* (Ambler 2003b).

14.1 PHILOSOPHIES FOR EFFECTIVE DATA DEVELOPMENT

The following philosophies have helped me to succeed at object persistence over the years:

1. **Data are important.** Data are clearly an important issue that we as developers must deal with. We cannot successfully develop business software if we are unable to persist our business objects, so we must invest the time to learn the techniques required to do so.

2. **Data are one of many issues.** Although data are important, so is telecommunications, user interface development, working with stakeholders, business component architectures, frameworks, understanding the business domain, and so on. It is quite common for data professionals to overestimate the importance of data, which is unfortunate.

3. **You need to take an evolutionary approach.** As noted earlier, modern software development methods are evolutionary in nature. The implication is that the data-oriented aspects of development must also be evolutionary if it is to fit into your overall approach. Luckily these techniques exist; they include agile modeling–driven development (AMMD) described in Chapter 4, test-driven development (TDD) described in Chapter 13, and database refactoring described in this chapter.

4. **You always have options.** A recurring theme in this chapter is that there are always several implementation strategies available to you. Not everything belongs in your business objects, nor does it all belong in your database. Effective developers understand that they have options and then choose the best one for the situation. More on this in Section 14.5.

5. **You need to look at the enterprise picture.** Few systems work in isolation; instead they are one of many systems within your overall enterprise. Your system must fit in with the rest of your organization's environment;

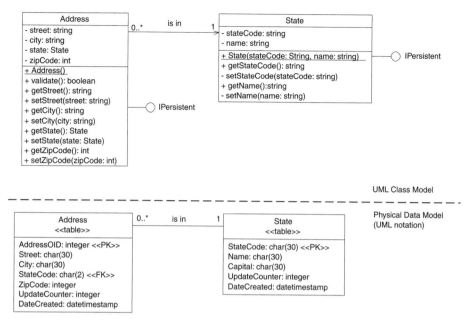

FIGURE 14.1. Mapping the *Address* and *State* classes into a relational database.

otherwise you will run into serious problems. Luckily data professionals are often very good at considering enterprise-level issues—yet another reason developers should work with them closely.

6. **Everyone needs to work together.** Everyone has their strengths and weaknesses, and everyone has something of value to add to a team, but everyone must be willing to work together to do so. The core values of agile software development focus on communication and teamwork—adopt those values.

14.2 MAPPING OBJECTS TO RELATIONAL DATABASES

The term "mapping" refers to how objects and their relationships are stored in a relational database. To overcome the O/R impedance mismatch you need to both understand the process of mapping objects to relational databases and how to implement those mappings. This section overviews the basics of mapping.

Let us start with some basics. First, an attribute of a class will map to zero or more columns in a relational database. Figure 14.1 depicts two diagrams, a simple UML class model and the physical data model that it maps to. To keep things simple I have used a similar naming convention in each model and have used a one-to-one mapping—the *street* attribute of the *Address* class maps to the *Street* column of the *Address* table. Throughout this chapter I will use the naming convention of *ClassName.attributeName* and *TableName.ColumnName* to indicate the *attributeName* attribute of *ClassName* and the *ColumnName* column of *TableName*. For example, *Address.street* maps to *Address.Street*.

Some attributes of an object are objects in their own right; in the class model *Address.state* is actually a *State* object. As you saw in Chapter 13 this really reflects an association between the two classes; association mapping is described in Section 14.2.3. For now trust me that the two models in Fig. 14.1 map to one another.

Remember that not all attributes are persistent; some are used for temporary calculations. For example, a *Student* object may have an *averageMark* attribute that is calculated by the object but is not saved into the database. Similarly, as you see in Fig. 14.1 not all table columns map back to your object schema—there is no corresponding attribute for the *State.Capital* column. The important thing to understand is that at some point each attribute of a class will be mapped to zero or more columns.

Mapping is only this clean when you have control over both your object and data schemas. In situations where you cannot easily change the database schema, which is typical when you are working with one or more legacy databases, you will find that the mappings are much more complex. In these situations mappings between classes and tables become many-to-many—the attributes of a class will map to the columns of several tables, and any given table will have several classes mapping to it. You may even have several attributes mapping into the same column (and worse yet vice versa). When you are working with a legacy database you may need to do significant legacy analysis (Section 14.7) if adequate documentation is not in place. You will also find that you need to write code to encapsulate these complex mappings, perhaps in the form of data access objects (DAOs) discussed in Section 14.3.

14.2.1 Shadow Information

Shadow information is any data that objects need to maintain, above and beyond their normal domain data, to persist themselves. This typically includes primary key information, particularly when the primary key is a surrogate key that has no business meaning, and concurrency control markings such as timestamps or incremental counters. For example, in Fig. 14.1 you can see that the *Address.AddressOID*, *Address.UpdateCounter*, and *Address.DateCreated*

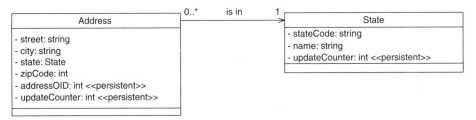

FIGURE **14.2. Including "shadow information" on a class diagram.**

columns have not been mapped into the *Address* class. *Address.AddressOID* is not mapped because it is a surrogate key, *Address.UpdateCounter* is used to support the concurrency control strategy of optimistic locking (see Section 14.5.1), and *Address.DateCreated* is used to record the first time the row was written into the table. Although these three columns are not pertinent to the business aspects of address objects they are still important and must potentially be mapped.

Figure 14.2 depicts an updated class model for the *Address* and *State* classes. There are several interesting things to note. First, I have simplified the diagram to only show the data-oriented aspects of the classes, an approach that I will take throughout the chapter. Second, shadow attributes have a private visibility and are assigned the stereotype *persistence* (this is not a UML standard although should be). Third, the shadow attributes that I needed to add were *Address.addressOID*, *Address.updateCounter*, and *State.updateCounter*. Business objects need to maintain the primary key value(s) used to identify them in the database, in this case *Address.addressOID* and *State.stateCode*. They also need to maintain any information used for concurrency control, in this case *Address.updateCounter*, and *State.updateCounter*. Fourth, I did not map the two *DateCreated* columns because the business objects do not need these values nor will they change while the business objects are in memory.

The accessor methods, not shown in Fig. 14.2, for shadow information are often more complicated than that for business attributes. Shadow attributes are often read-only—you set their values when you initially read the data from the database and that is it. Your setter methods will need to reflect this requirement with adequate documentation of why this is happening.

14.2.2 Mapping Inheritance Structures

Relational databases do not natively support inheritance, forcing you to map the inheritance structures within your object schema to your data schema.

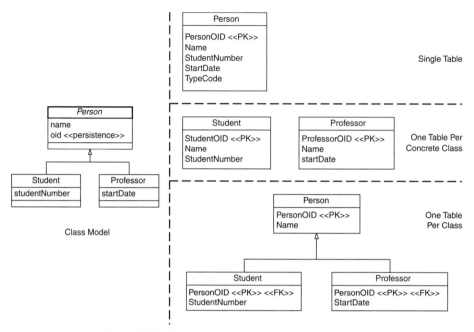

FIGURE 14.3. Mapping a simple inheritance structure.

There are three primary solutions for mapping inheritance into a relational database:

1. Map the entire class hierarchy to a single table.
2. Map each concrete class to its own table.
3. Map each class to its own table.

Figure 14.3 depicts a simple class hierarchy and the three ways it could be mapped into an RDB. A common approach to keys was used in all three PDMs, that of a surrogate object id (OID), all of which map to the *Person.oid* attribute. In the single table strategy the *Person* table includes *Person.TypeCode* to indicate which type of object (a student, a professor, etc.) is being stored in the individual row. The one table per class strategy applies an interesting key strategy—the *Student* and *Professor* tables each use *PersonOID* as their primary key as well as the foreign key to the *Person* table. Table 14.1 compares the three approaches. It is important to note that no single strategy is best for all situations and that for any given hierarchy you can mix and match the techniques if need be. Having said that, I have found that the single table per hierarchy approach is often your best option.

TABLE 14.1. Comparing the Three Techniques

Technique	Advantages	Disadvantages
Single table	<ul><li>Simple approach.</li><li>Easy to add new classes: you just need to add new columns for the additional data.</li><li>Supports object polymorphism by simply changing the type of the row.</li><li>Data access is fast because the data are in one table.</li><li>Ad hoc reporting (Section 14.5.6) is very easy because all of the data are found in one table.</li></ul>	<ul><li>Coupling within the class hierarchy is increased because all classes are directly coupled to the same table. A change in one class can affect the table, which can then affect the other classes in the hierarchy and their related mappings.</li><li>Potential space wasted in the database because many rows will have empty columns.</li><li>Indicating the type becomes complex when significant overlap between types exists (e.g., someone is both a professor and a student).</li><li>Table can grow quickly for large hierarchies.</li></ul>
One table per concrete class	<ul><li>Good performance to access a single object's data.</li><li>Ad hoc reporting simple because all of the data you need about a single class are stored in only one table.</li></ul>	<ul><li>Modifications to classes require you to modify its table and the table of any of its subclasses. For example if you were to add *birthDate* to the *Person* class you would need to add columns to the *Person*, *Student*, and *Professor* tables.</li></ul>

(continued)

TABLE 14.1 (*continued*)

Technique	Advantages	Disadvantages
		• Whenever an object changes its role, e.g., perhaps the university hires one of its students, you need to copy the data into the appropriate table. • It is difficult to support multiple roles and still maintain data integrity. For example, where would you store the name of someone who is both a professor and a student?
One table per class	• Simple mapping because it is one-to-one. • Easily supports object polymorphism because you merely have records in the appropriate tables for each type. • Very easy to modify superclasses and add new subclasses as you merely need to modify/add one table. • Data size grows in direct proportion to growth in the number of objects.	• There are many tables in the database, one for every class (plus tables to maintain relationships). • Potentially takes longer to read and write data because you need to access multiple tables. • Ad hoc reporting is difficult, unless you add views to simulate the desired tables.

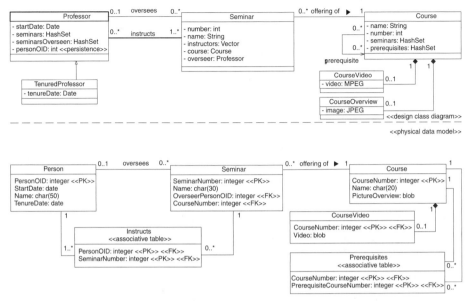

FIGURE 14.4. **Mapping associations.**

14.2.3 Mapping Relationships

For the purposes of our discussion the term relationship shall apply to either associations or composition associations as there is no significant difference between the two from a mapping point of view. Relationships in object schemas are implemented by a combination of references to objects and operations, whereas in RDBs they are maintained through the use of foreign keys. A foreign key is a data attribute(s) that appears in one table that may be part of or is coincidental with the key of another table.

The way that you map a relationship depends on its multiplicity:

1. **One-to-one relationships**. To map a one-to-one relationship you have two strategies. If each class corresponds to a table, which we see in Fig. 14.4 with the *Course* and *CourseVideo* classes, then a foreign key needs to be implemented in one of the two tables. In this case the *CourseVideo.CourseNumber* column acts as the foreign key to the *Course* table. From a data point of view it does not really matter which table the foreign key goes in, although if the relationship is unidirectional association then it makes sense to have the foreign key in the table corresponding to the class that maintains the relationship. For example, if there is a unidirectional

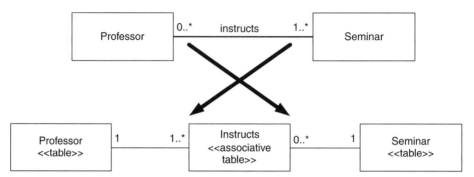

FIGURE 14.5. Resolving a many-to-many association.

association from *Person* to *Address* then add the foreign key into the *Person* table. The second mapping strategy is to simply store the data for both classes in a single table, the approach we took to map the relationship between the *Course* and *CourseOverview* classes.

2. **One-to-many relationships.** One-to-many relationships, such as *offering of* in Fig. 14.4, are implemented in classes via a collection such as a *Hashset* on the many side of the relationship and by an object reference on the one side of the relationship, in this case *Course.seminars* and *Seminar.course*, respectively. Within the database the relationship is implemented via a foreign key on the many side of the relationship, in this case *Seminar.CourseNumber.*

3. **Many-to-many relationships.** A many-to-many relationship between two classes is mapped to an associative table within a database. This table comprises the primary keys of the two business tables. In Fig. 14.4 the *instructs* relationship between the *Professor* and *Seminar* classes is mapped to the *Instructs* table within the database. By adding an associative table like this we say that we have resolved the many-to-many relationship by converting it into two one-to-many associations.

Notice how the multiplicities from the *instructs* association in the class diagram have crossed over into the physical data model as shown in Fig. 14.5. A multiplicity of 1 is always introduced on the outside edges of the relationship within the data schema to preserve overall multiplicity of the original relationship. The original relationship indicated that a professor *instructs* one or more seminars and that zero or more professors instruct a seminar. In the data schema you see that this is still true even with the associative table in place to maintain the relationship.

A general rule of thumb with relationship mapping is that you should keep the multiplicities the same; i.e., a one-to-one object relationship maps to a one-to-one data relationship, a one-to-many maps to a one-to-many, and a many-to-many maps to a many-to-many. The fact is that this does not have to be the case; you can implement a one-to-one object relationship with to a one-to-many or even a many-to-many data relationship. This is because a one-to-one data relationship is a subset of a one-to-many data relationship and a one-to-many relationship is a subset of a many-to-many relationship. However, implementing a one-to-one or a one-to-many as a many-to-many is an example of overbuilding your software so I discourage it.

A recursive relationship, also called self or reflexive relationships, is one where the same entity is involved with both ends of the relationship. For example, the *prerequisites* association in Fig. 14.4 is recursive, representing the concept that a course may be a prerequisite to other courses. There is nothing special about recursive relationships; you map them the exact same way that you would a nonrecursive relationship. For example, because the *prerequisites* association is many-to-many I simply map it to the *Prerequisites* associative table.

14.3 STRATEGIES FOR IMPLEMENTING PERSISTENCE CODE

There are three basic approaches, often referred to as encapsulation strategies, for implementing persistent business objects. They are

1. **Brute force.** Business objects access data sources directly by submitting structured query language (SQL) to the database. In Java applications this is usually done via the Java database connectivity (JDBC) protocol. The advantage of this approach is it enables you to write code quickly and it is a viable approach for small applications and/or prototypes; however, there are two main disadvantages. First, it directly couples your business classes with the schema of your relational database; a simple change in your database requires you to rework your source code and could force a recompile and redistribution of files. Second, it forces you to write significant amounts of SQL code, which must be tested and maintained.

2. **Data access objects (DAOs).** With this approach specialized data classes encapsulate the database access logic required of business objects. The typical approach is for there to be one data access object for each business

Seminar

SeminarNumber: integer <<PK>>
Name: char(30)
OverseerPersonOID: integer <<FK>>
CourseNumber: integer <<FK>>

0..*   offering of ▶   1

Course

CourseNumber: integer <<PK>>
Name: char(20)
PictureOverview: blob

FIGURE 14.6. A simple physical data model.

object; for example, the *Student* class would have a *StudentData* class, which then implements the SQL code. This strategy is suitable for prototypes, small systems of less than 40 to 50 business classes, or systems where the mappings are very complex (often there is a legacy database involved). The main advantage of DAOs over the brute force approach is that your business classes are no longer directly coupled to the database; instead the data access classes are. You can either write your own DAOs or follow an industry-standard approach such as Java data objects (JDOs), described at http://www.jdocentral.com. The main disadvantage is that this approach still results in a rework of the data classes when simple changes to the database are made.

3. **Persistence frameworks.** A persistence framework, often referred to as a persistence layer, fully encapsulates database access from your business objects. Instead of writing code you instead define metadata that represents your mappings. Based on this metadata the persistence framework generates the database access code it requires to persist business objects and the relationships between them. A list of persistence frameworks is maintained at http://www.ambysoft.com/persistenceLayer.html. The advantage of this approach is that application programmers do not need to know a thing about the schema of the relational database. In fact, they do not even need to know that their objects are being stored in a relational database. Instead of writing code that needs to be tested and maintained over time, someone uses an administration tool to define the mappings between your object schema and your data schema. Furthermore the overall performance of persistence layers is often better than SQL code written by developers because most developers do not know all the tricks and techniques that the experts writing the persistence framework understand. The main disadvantage is that developers now need to learn the persistence framework.

If you take either a brute force approach or a DAO approach you will likely need to learn the basics of SQL code, the subject of the next section. If your

```
CREATE TABLE Seminar (
    SeminarNumber          INTEGER NOT NULL,
    CourseNumber           INTEGER NOT NULL,
    OverseerPersonOID      INTEGER NULL
);
```

FIGURE 14.7. SQL statement to create the *Seminar* table.

team uses a persistence framework approach you should still learn the basics of SQL in order to understand what the framework is doing for you.

14.4 FROM DESIGN TO DATABASE CODE

The goal of this section is to give you a basic understanding of SQL code. Figure 14.6 presents a simple UML data model for an RDB consisting of two tables. The *Seminar* data entity has four columns, one of which is the primary key *SeminarNumber*, the value of which uniquely identifies each row of the table. The column *CourseNumber* is the primary key of the *Course* table and is a column of *Seminar* used as a foreign key to maintain the association between seminar rows and course rows. This database schema is used as the running example for this section.

14.4.1 Defining and Modifying Your Persistence Schema

To define, update, and remove tables in a relational database, you need to write data definition language (DDL) SQL statements. DDL is straightforward, as you see in Fig. 14.7, Fig. 14.8, and Fig. 14.9. Granted, there is a lot more to DDL than just this. You can use DDL to define database triggers and stored procedures (discussed below), add indexes on tables to speed data access, and

```
ALTER TABLE Seminar
        ADD Comments      CHAR(120) NULL
```

FIGURE 14.8. SQL statement to add a column to the *Seminar* table.

```
DROP TABLE Seminar;
```

FIGURE 14.9. SQL statement to remove the *Seminar* table.

add views on your database (think of views as virtual tables). I will typically use data-modeling tools to define and generate DDL—hand-coding DDL makes little sense to me these days.

DDL code is typically defined in a script and then run against a database in order to change the schema. Your database vendor will have tutorials, and most likely training classes and consultants, available from which you can learn.

14.4.2 Creating, Retrieving, Updating, and Deleting Data

To manipulate the data stored in a relational database, you issue data manipulation language (DML) SQL statements to the database. Figure 14.10 depicts a SQL *INSERT* statement to create a row in a table. You can see the columns of the table and the values to insert into those columns are listed–each value maps, in order, to one and only one column in the list. Notice how the *Comments* column has its value in quotes. This is because it is a character value, whereas the other columns are numeric, so there are no quotes around their values.

To retrieve data from a database, you can issue a SQL *SELECT* statement. Figure 14.11 presents a straightforward example of retrieving zero or one row from the database. Zero or one row will be returned because the *WHERE* class specifies an exact value for the primary key: the *SeminarNumber* column must have the value 1701. Either a row exists with this key value or it does not. There

```
INSERT INTO Seminar
   (SeminarNumber, CourseNumber, OverseerPersonOID,
     Comments)
VALUES
   (74656, 1234, 1138, 'Sign up now!')
```

FIGURE 14.10. SQL statement to insert a row into the *Seminar* table.

```
SELECT * FROM Seminar
WHERE SeminarNumber = 1701
```

FIGURE 14.11. SQL statement to retrieve a row from the *Seminar* table.

cannot be more than one row with this value by definition (remember that key values must be unique). If a row with that value already exists, and someone tries to insert another row with the same value into the table, the statement will result in an error. Figure 14.12 presents a more complex example, one that will result in zero or more rows being returned. The *WHERE* clause has two parts: one provides a value for the key (you do not always have to specify values for the key in the *WHERE* clause) and the other provides a wild-card search value for the *Comments* column—in SQL the % sign represents a multicharacter wild card and the underscore character a single-character wild card. The statement also includes an *ORDER BY* clause to specify the sort order of the data rows in the result set.

As an aside, *SeminarNumber* is an example of a natural key, one that has business meaning. Although I prefer to use surrogate keys that do not have business meaning I will still use natural keys if that makes the most sense for the situation. It is not a black and white issue.

Figure 14.13 presents an example of how to update data in a relational table via a SQL *UPDATE* statement. You simply specify the values of the columns you want to set and include an appropriate *WHERE* clause, so the right rows get updated. Updating several rows at once is possible simply by writing a *WHERE* clause that is less specific.

To delete data from a relational database, you need to issue a SQL *DELETE* statement, as depicted in Fig. 14.14. The syntax of the *DELETE* statement is similar to the syntax of the other types of SQL DML statements, as you can see.

```
SELECT * FROM Seminar
WHERE        SeminarNumber > 1701
AND          Comments LIKE 'Sign%'
ORDER BY     CourseNumber, OverseerPersonOID
```

FIGURE 14.12. SQL statement to retrieve several rows from the *Seminar* table.

```
UPDATE Seminar
   SET OverseerPersonOID = 1234,
      Comments = 'Professor now assigned'
WHERE SeminarNumber = 1701
```

FIGURE 14.13. SQL statement to update a row in a table in the *Seminar* table.

14.4.3 Interacting with a Database from Java

SQL statements run in your database, so you need a way to invoke them within your database, which is what the JDBC library is for. Assuming that your database is installed and configured properly, this is a two-step process:

1. **Open connection to your database.** Figure 14.15 presents Java code, which takes a lazy instantiation approach to setting up a database connection (for simplicity I left out the try/catch statement). This code is implemented by the *UniversityApplication* class, which manages the overall application. I have hard-coded the driver name and the database URL, something that you should obtain from a configuration file. Note also that I get the userID and password via getters; presumably the *UniversityApplication* class maintains this information after the user has logged on.

2. **Submit SQL statements.** Using the open connection you submit SQL statements as you see in Fig. 14.16. The first step is to define the statement, in this case an SQL INSERT statement. The next step is to fill the four values in the statement, something done positionally via the *setXXXX()* statements. Finally you execute and close the statement. It is interesting to note how your object schema, in this case the *Seminar* class, is coupled to your data schema through the need to positionally set the data values in the SQL statement.

```
DELETE FROM Seminar
   WHERE       SeminarNumber = 1701
   OR          SeminarNumber < 1000
```

FIGURE 14.14. SQL statement to delete data from the *Seminar* table.

```
/**
  * Get the connection to the database
  */
protected Connection getDatabaseConnection()
{
  if (connection == null)
  {
    Class.forName("jdbc.YourDriver"); // Load the
                                      database driver
    connection = DriverManager.getConnection
      ("jdbc:UniversityDB", getUserID(), getPassword());
  }
  return connection;
}
```

FIGURE 14.15. Connecting to a database in Java.

```
/**
  * Insert the seminar into the database
  */
  protected void insert() throws SQLException {
    PreparedStatement statement = null;
  Connection connection = UniversityApplication.
                      getConnection();
  statement = connection.prepareStatement("INSERT INTO
          Seminar VALUES(?,?,?,?)");
  statement.setInt(1, getNumber());
  statement.setString(2, getName());
  statement.setInt(3, getOverseerPersonOID());
  statement.setInt(4, getCourse().getNumber());

  statement.executeUpdate();

  connection.commit();
  statement.close();
}
```

FIGURE 14.16. Invoking SQL in Java code.

The code presented in Fig. 14.15 and Fig. 14.16 is just meant to be a brief example of how your business objects can include hard-coded SQL statements to interact with your database via JDBC. There is much more to JDBC than this, as the myriad of books on the subject attest to. If you are taking either a brute-force or DAO approach with Java you will need to learn more about JDBC. A good resource is the Sun Microsystems tutorial posted at http://java.sun.com/docs/books/tutorial/jdbc/.

14.4.4 Implementing Your Mappings

With brute-force and DAO approaches to persistence coding you need to write the code yourself to perform basic functionality. This includes code to traverse relationships between objects. For example, when you save a student object you should also automatically traverse the relationship it has with its Address object and save it too. An important issue that you need to take into consideration is referential integrity, discussed in Section 14.5.3.

Managing inheritance structures is also important. This is particularly true when an inheritance hierarchy is mapped to a single table. In particular each class in the hierarchy will need to write out an identifying code, such as the Person.TypeCode column in Fig. 18.3, to indicate the type of object being stored in the table row.

14.5 DATA-ORIENTED IMPLEMENTATION STRATEGIES

There is more to object persistence than the simple creation, retrieval, update, and/or deletion of objects and their relationships. You will need to do combinations of these things, you need to support business logic surrounding persistence-related activities, and you need to do it in a secure manner. Complicating manners is the fact that you are working in a multitier and multiplatform environment, as the high-level deployment diagram of Fig. 14.17 shows. Many traditional data-oriented techniques are geared towards a simpler mainframe-based environment where business logic ran on the mainframe and the data were all stored in a single database. Unfortunately many data professionals still want to follow these techniques, even though we are in an environment where business logic can be implemented in several locations

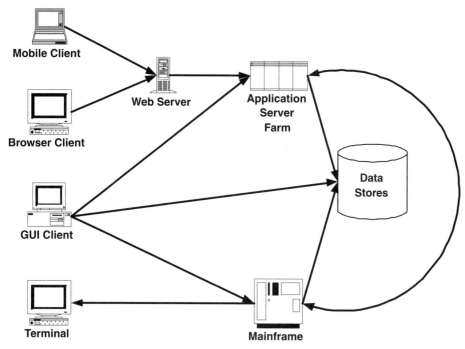

FIGURE 14.17. Potential deployment architecture for modern applications.

and data are stored in many sources. Because the software world has changed we need to change along with it.

A critical implication is that you need to look beyond the database, and beyond your business objects, to take the whole picture into account. Many of the issues covered in this section are traditionally thought of as database issues, which in fact they were back in the good old mainframe days. Yes, your database is often involved but it is not the only thing that you need to be concerned with. This section, which summarizes detailed material from *Agile Database Techniques* (Ambler 2003b), addresses issues that all software developers need to be familiar with:

- Concurrency control;
- Transaction control;
- Shared logic and referential integrity;
- Security access control;
- Search logic; and
- Reports.

14.5.1 Concurrency Control

Concurrency control deals with the issues involved in allowing multiple people simultaneous access to shared entities, such as objects or data records. The first step in understanding concurrency control is to start with the concept of collisions. A *collision* is said to occur when two activities attempt to change the same entity. There are three fundamental ways (Celko 1999) that two activities can interfere with one another:

1. **Dirty read.** The first activity, A1, reads an entity from the system of record and then updates the entity without but does not commit the change (e.g., make the change official). The second activity, A2, reads the entity, unknowingly making a copy of the uncommitted version. A1 aborts the changes and restores the entity to the original state. A2 now has an unofficial version of the entity that was never committed.

2. **Nonrepeatable read.** A1 reads an entity from the system of record and makes a copy of it. A2 deletes the entity from the system of record. A1 now has a copy of an entity that does not officially exist.

3. **Phantom read.** A1 retrieves a collection of entities from the system of record based on a given search criteria. A2 then creates a new entity that would have met the search criteria and saves it to the system of record. If A1 reapplies the search criteria it now gets a different result set.

So what can you do? When your database is the system of record, which it usually is, then database elements—the entire database, a table, a collection of rows, or a single row—need to be locked somehow. There are three fundamental locking strategies:

1. **Pessimistic locking.** Pessimistic locking is an approach where a database element is locked for the entire time that it is in application memory. A write lock indicates that the holder of the lock intends to update the entity and disallows anyone from reading, updating, or deleting the entity. A read lock indicates that the holder of the lock does not want the entity to change while it is holding the lock, allowing others to read the entity but not update or delete it. A significant problem occurs when someone reads record and then goes to lunch, home, or on vacation with it still open.

2. **Optimistic locking.** With this strategy you detect collisions and then resolve them later. The idea is that you accept the fact that collisions occur

infrequently so you should simply detect them and resolve them when they do occur. Elements are locked in the database only for the brief period of time required for updating them but are unlocked while being manipulated in memory.

3. **Overly optimistic locking.** With this strategy you assume that collisions will never occur and therefore do not try to detect them or even to bother locking database elements. This strategy is appropriate for single-user systems, systems where the system of record is guaranteed to be accessed by only one user or system process at a time.

Optimistic locking is the most common strategy, even though it is the most complex. Pessimistic locking typically results in poor performance and overly optimistic locking is only applicable for very simple systems. It is critical that developers understand how to handle database collisions. This is basically a two-step process—detect the collision and then resolve it.

There are two basic strategies to detect whether a collision has occurred:

1. **Mark the source with a unique identifier.** The source data are marked with a unique value each time they are updated. At the point of update, the mark is checked and if there is a different value than what you originally read in, then you know that there has been an update to the source. An example of this is the *UpdateCounter* columns in Fig. 14.1: each time a row is updated the value of this column is incremented by one. There are different types of concurrency marks—date/timestamps assigned by the database, incremental counters, user IDs, and even values generated by a globally unique surrogate key generator.

2. **Retain a copy of the original.** The source data are retrieved at the point of update and compared with the values that were originally retrieved. This strategy may be your only option if you are unable to make sufficient changes to your database schema to maintain the concurrency marks.

You have five strategies that you can apply to resolve collisions:

1. **Give up.** You detect that a collision has occurred, reject the change you were going to make, and throw an exception (or return an error) to inform the calling application.

2. **Display the problem and let the user decide.** The collision is reported and the problem is presented to the user for resolution. At a minimum, a description of the problem is displayed along with an option either to continue the update or to cancel it.

3. **Merge the changes.** You can try to determine which data attributes have been changed and then attempt to merge the two changes together. This can be done either automatically, a risky decision, or in combination with strategy 2.

4. **Log the problem so someone else can decide later.** This strategy is similar to displaying the problem; the only difference being that the calling application is running unattended, perhaps in batch, so no one is there to address the problem. This approach suffers from the problem that additional changes to the source data may occur during the period that the collision is initially logged and someone can attempt to resolve it if you do not lock the data until the collision is resolved.

5. **Ignore the collision and overwrite.** This is basically an overly optimistic locking approach with the added overhead of collision detection.

Every business application requires a concurrency control strategy, and because optimistic locking is the most common approach you soon discover that your "simple database code" isn't so simple any longer. This is another reason why persistence frameworks (Section 14.3) are so important because a good one will encapsulate most of this sort of functionality (although even if you are using a persistence framework you would better understand what kind of concurrency strategy is in use).

14.5.2 Transaction Control

A transaction is a collection of actions that potentially modify one or more entities. An important fundamental of transactions is the four "ACID" properties that they must exhibit. These properties are:

1. **Atomicity.** A transaction occurs or it does not; there is no in-between. For example, the transfer of funds between two accounts is a transaction. If we transfer $20 from account A to account B then at the end of the transaction A's balance will be $20 lower and B's balance will be $20 higher

(if the transaction is completed) or neither balance will have changed (if the transaction is aborted). In SQL, the changes become permanent when a COMMIT statement is issued and they are aborted when a ROLLBACK statement is issued.

2. **Consistency.** When the transaction starts the entities are in a consistent state and when the transaction ends the entities are once again in a consistent, albeit different, state. The implication is that the referential integrity rules and applicable business rules still apply after the transaction completes.

3. **Isolation.** All transactions work as if they alone were operating on the entities. For example, assume that a bank account contains $200 and each of us is trying to withdraw $50. Regardless of the order of the two transactions, at the end of them the account balance will be $100, assuming that both transactions work. Isolation is often referred to as serializability.

4. **Durability.** The entities are stored in a persistent media, such as a relational database or file, so that if the system crashes the transactions are still permanent.

For a transaction to work you still need to ensure that the four ACID properties hold. The most common way to do this is to implement the two-phase commit (2PC) protocol, composed of the attempt phase where each system tries its part of the transaction and the commit phase where the systems are told to execute the transaction. With the 2PC protocol a transaction manager will assign a unique transaction ID to the transaction to identify it. The transaction manager then sends the various transaction steps to each target system so they may attempt them, each system responding back to the transaction manager with the result of the attempt. If an attempted step succeeds then at this point the system of record must lock the appropriate entities and then persist the potential changes in some manner (to ensure durability) until the commit phase. Once the transaction manager hears back from all systems of record that the steps succeeded, or once it hears back that a step failed, then it sends out either a commit or abort request to every system involved.

Databases are not the only things that can be involved in transactions. The fact is that objects, services, components, legacy applications, and nonrelational data sources can all be included. When objects are involved in transactions it is possible to have both data- and behavioral-oriented steps within a transaction. Can you imagine using a code editor, word processor, or drawing program without an undo function? If not, then it becomes reasonable to expect both behavior invocation and data transformations as steps of a transaction. Unfortunately this strategy comes with a significant disadvantage: increased complexity. For this to work your business objects need to be transactionally aware, something that is very difficult to implement in practice because any behavior that can be invoked as a step in a transaction requires supporting attempt, commit, and abort/rollback operations.

At the time of this writing the Web services community is struggling with the issue of supporting transactions and the EJB community still only supports flat transactions but not nested transactions. A nested transaction may include other transactions as a transaction step.

14.5.3 Shared Logic and Referential Integrity

Modern deployment architectures are complex as Fig. 14.17 depicts. The components of a new application may be deployed across several types of machines, including various client machines, Web servers, application servers, and databases. The implication is that business logic could be deployed to a wide number of platforms, to any of the machines on your network. For example, a new browser-based application could have JavaScript embedded in the HTML code to perform simple data validation, the primary business objects could reside on the application servers, and these objects in turn invoke several Web services that wrap access to procedures deployed on the mainframe as well as several stored procedures implemented in your database.

A critical principle for deciding where to implement shared logic is the *lowest common denominator (LCD)* principle: implement shared logic in the most commonly accessible location. For example, when there are several applications accessing a single database it often makes sense to implement shared business logic in the database because all applications can access that logic. However, when there are several databases involved, a single database no longer becomes the LCD; instead a new option such as a reusable code library (unfortunately this requires a common development platform) or reusable services (this requires a common protocol, such as that defined by the Web services standards) must be found.

It is important to consider a specialized form of business logic—referential integrity (RI). RI refers to the concept that if one entity references another then that other entity actually exists. For example, if Professor Jones claims to teach the *Introduction to Canadian History* seminar in the autumn of 2004 then that seminar should actually be scheduled. RI is a well-known concept within both the data and development communities, although within the development community RI problems are often referred to as dangling pointers or dangling references.

An interesting implication of Fig. 14.17 is that an entity can be represented in different ways. For example a student is represented as data displayed on an HTML page, as a student object that resides on an application server, and as a table in a database. Keeping these various representations in sync is a concurrency control issue, discussed in Section 14.5.1. When you are using object technology and relational technology together you are in a situation where you are implementing structure in two places: In your object schema as classes that have interrelationships and in your data schema as tables with interrelationships. You will implement similar structures in each place. For example you will have a *Student* object that has a collection of *Enrollment* objects in your object schema and a *Student* table related to the *Enrollment* table. It should be obvious that you need to deal with referential integrity issues within each schema.

What is not so obvious is that because the same entities are represented in multiple schemas you have "cross schema" referential integrity issues to deal with as well. Let us work through an example using professors and seminars. To keep things simple, assume that there is a straight one-to-one mapping between the object and data schemas. I read an existing professor and the seminars he teaches into memory on my computer. The professor is *John* and the courses are *North American Birds* and *Introduction to U.S. History*. Shortly thereafter you read the exact same information into memory on your computer. You decide to assign John to teach another seminar, *Travel Planning 101*, and save it to the database. The professor–seminar structure is perfectly fine on each individual machine—my professor object references the two seminar objects that exist in its memory space, your professor object references the three seminar objects that exist in its memory space, and the three rows in the *Seminar* table all include a foreign key to the row in the *Professor* table indicating who teaches it. When you look at it from the point of view of the entities, the professor and the seminars, there is an RI problem because my professor object does not refer to the new travel planning seminar.

A similar situation would occur if you had deleted the U.S. history seminar object—now my professor object would refer to a seminar that no longer exists. This assumes of course that the database is the system of record for these entities. When something is changed in the system of record it is considered an "official" change. Without a defined system of record it becomes difficult to determine what changes are official and which are not (perhaps the deletion of B should be backed out).

The implication of this discussion is that you need to be both aware of this problem and that you need a strategy to address it (that strategy may be to just learn to live with some types of RI issues). Because RI is a cross-platform issue the business logic that you implement surrounding RI will very likely need to be cross-platform as well. The object purists may argue that RI logic should be implemented solely in your objects, the data purists may argue that it should only be implemented within your database (perhaps as a combination of triggers and database constraints), but what you really need is a holistic strategy that takes all of your needs into account. As you would expect your concurrency control strategy and your RI strategy go hand-in-hand.

An agile software developer realizes that there are several options available to him when it comes to implementing referential integrity. Table 14.2 compares and contrasts them from the point of view of each strategy being used in isolation. No option is perfect, each has its trade-offs, and you can mix and match these techniques as appropriate.

The following heuristics should help to guide your decisions as to where to implement business logic:

1. **Recognize that it is not a black-and-white decision.** Your technical environment is likely too complex to support a "one size fits all" strategy.

2. **Follow the lowest common denominator principle.** Implement shared logic in the most commonly accessible place.

3. **Implement unique logic in the most appropriate place.** If business logic is unique to an application then implement it in the most appropriate place.

4. **Implement logic where it is easiest.** You may have better development tools, or more experience, on one tier than another and therefore may choose that platform.

5. **Be prepared to implement the same logic in several places.** In a multi-database environment, you may discover that you are implementing the same logic in each database to ensure consistency. In a multitier environment you may discover that you need to implement most if not all of your referential integrity rules in both your business layer (so that RI rules are reflected in your object schema) and your database. These situations are not ideal but they are realistic.

TABLE 14.2. Referential Integrity Implementation Options

Option	Description	Advantages	Disadvantages
Business objects	RI is enforced by operations implemented by business objects within your application.	• Testing is simplified because all business logic is implemented in one place.	• Every application must be architected to reuse the same business objects. • Extra programming is required to support functionality natively supported by your database.
Database constraints (declarative referential integrity)	DDL-defined constraints to enforce RI. For example, adding a NOT NULL constraint to a foreign key column.	• Ensures referential integrity within the database • Constraints can be generated, and reverse engineered, by data-modeling tools.	• Every application must be architected to use the same database, or all constraints must be implemented in each database. • Performance inhibitor with large tables.
Database triggers	Programmatic approach where a procedure is "triggered" by an event, such as a deletion of a row, to perform required actions to ensure RI.	• Ensures referential integrity within the database. • Triggers can be generated, and reverse engineered, by data-modeling tools.	• Every application must be architected to use the same database, or all triggers must be implemented in each database.

(*continued*)

TABLE 14.2 (*continued*)

Option	Description	Advantages	Disadvantages
			• Proves to be a performance inhibitor in tables with large numbers of transactions.
Persistence framework	RI rules are defined as part of the relationship mappings. The multiplicity of relationships and rules indicating the need for cascading reads, updates, or deletions are defined in the mapping metadata.	• Referential integrity implemented as part of overall object persistence strategy. • Referential integrity rules can be centralized into a single metadata repository.	• Every application must be architected to use the same persistence framework, or at least work from the same relationship mappings. • Can be difficult to test metadata-driven rules.
Updateable views	Referential integrity rules are reflected in the definition of the view.	• Referential integrity is enforced within the database.	• Updateable views that update several tables may not be an option within your database. • All applications must use the views, not the source tables.

6. **Be prepared to evolve your strategy over time.** Some database refactorings, see Section 14.6, include moving functionality into or out of your database.

7. **Databases are often the best choice for implementing RI.** The growing importance of Web services and XML point to a trend where application logic is becoming less object-oriented, even though object technology is the primary underlying implementation technology for both, and more data-processing oriented. This leads towards databases being a good long-term architecture choice for RI logic.

14.5.4 Security Access Control

Security access control (SAC) is the act of ensuring that an authenticated user—or object—accesses only what they are authorized to access and no more. There are two critical issues addressed by SAC:

- **Authentication.** This is the act of determining the identity of a user and of the host that they are using. You must verify that the user, either a person or system, which is attempting to interact with your system, is allowed to do so. Optionally you may need to gather information regarding the way that the user is accessing your system. For example, a professor should not be able to input student marks during off hours from an Internet café, although they should be able to do so from their secured workstation at their office.

- **Authorization.** This is the act of determining the level of access that a user has to specific behaviors and/or data. Your stakeholder's requirements will determine who is authorized to access certain aspects of your application. Never forget that the granularity of access, and your ability to implement it effectively, is a significant constraint. For example, although you may be asked to control access to specific columns of specific rows within a database based on complex business rules you may not be able to implement this in a cost-effective manner that also conforms to performance constraints.

Authorization can be enforced within your database by a variety of means (which can be combined):

1. **Permissions.** A permission is a privilege, or authorization right, that a user or role has regarding a database element. A permission defines the type of

access permitted, such as the ability to update a table or to run a stored procedure.

2. **Views.** You can control, often to a very fine level, the data that a user can access via the use of views. You must define views that restrict the tables, columns, and rows within the tables that a role can access and then you define permissions on those views.

3. **Stored procedures.** Code within the stored procedure can be written to programmatically check security access rules.

4. **Proprietary approaches.** A new option being offered by some database vendors are proprietary security tools such as Oracle Label Security (http://www.oracle.com), an add-on that enables you to define and enforce row-level permissions.

Authorization can be implemented with your objects following a variety of strategies:

1. **Brute force.** Any operation that requires authorization must implement all of the logic itself.

2. **Business rules engine.** Authorization logic via invocations to a business rules engine, such as Blaze (http://www.blazesoft.com) or Quick-Rules (http://www.yasutech.com). Each operation that requires authorization simply needs to invoke the appropriate rule(s) in the business engine and act accordingly.

3. **Permissions.** The same strategy as permissions within a database, the only difference being that permissions are applied to the operations of classes instead of to database elements. This approach is taken by Enterprise JavaBean (EJB) servers (Roman et al. 2002).

4. **Security framework/component.** Authorization functionality encapsulated within a security framework. Examples of commercial security frameworks include the security aspects of the. Net framework and the Java Authentication and Authorization Service (JAAS).

5. **Security server.** Security access control rules invoked as required and implemented by a a specialized, external server(s).

6. **Aspect-oriented programming (AOP).** An emerging collection of technologies and techniques for separation of concerns in software development.

The techniques of AOP make it possible to modularize crosscutting aspects of a system. A good resource is the Aspect Oriented Software Development home page (http://www.aosd.net).

I would like to share some advice regarding security access control that I have found useful over the years. First, this is not a black-and-white issue; you clearly have implementation choices. Second, you must keep performance in mind. A good rule of thumb is to keep security checks as close to the user as possible; for example, a three-tier system should not rely on the database to determine authorization if the client or application server can do it so as to eliminate potentially slow interactions across the network. Third, take advantage of existing database authorization practices. Consider evolving it to meet your current security needs, but do so with the realization that the security needs of objects differ from that of data. Fourth, be prepared to evolve your strategy over time to reflect new security needs.

14.5.5 Searching for Objects

Most business applications need to support the ability to search for collections of objects. Perhaps you want to list all the students enrolled in a seminar or perhaps you want to define basic search criteria so you can display and then update student information. Perhaps you need to include basic reporting functionality within your application, such as producing a grading list for a specific seminar. There are two fundamental decisions that you need to consider when searching for objects—how do you intend to represent the search criteria and how do you intend to represent the search results?

For the sake of convenience I use the term *find strategy* to refer to your implementation strategy for finding the data representing objects within relational databases. The deciding factor in choosing a find strategy is the level of database encapsulation that you wish to have, discussed earlier in Section 14.3. There are different find strategies that you may choose from:

- **Brute force.** With this find strategy you simply embed database access code, such as SQL statements or EJB Query Language (EJB QL), in your business objects. The typical strategy is to write a single operation for each way you want to find objects, such as the SELECT statement presented in Fig. 14.12.

- **Query objects.** This is the find strategy version of DAOs (Brant and Yoder 2000). Instead of embedding SQL code in your business objects you instead encapsulate it in separate classes. There is one query object for each finder, each of which would build implement the same type of logic described for the brute force approach.

- **Metadata-driven.** This is the most sophisticated strategy available to you and is typically implemented as part of a persistence framework. The basic idea is that you want to decouple your object schema from your data schema and the only way to do this is to describe the mappings (Section 14.3) between them in metadata instead of in hard-coded SQL. Instead of defining a SQL SELECT statement that specifies the search in terms of database columns your application must instead define the search in terms of the object attributes. The business object submits the metadata for a query, perhaps represented as an XML document or as a full-fledged object (Ambler 2000), to a query processor. This metadata would represent concepts to perform tasks such as return all students whose name looks like 'Sc* A*', or all professors whose hire date is between March 1, 1995, and February 29, 2000, that teach in the computer science department. The query processor passes the query to a query builder that uses the mapping metadata to build a SELECT statement that can then be submitted to the database.

The results of a search can be represented in several ways. Your choice will depend on how you intend to use the results, the implication being that you do not always need full-fledged objects. For example, consider searching for students. The first five options listed below describe internal representations that you would use in your code, and the next three are external representations for transferring information between machines. The options are listed in my personal order of preference:

1. **Proxies.** The result set is marshaled into a collection of proxy objects that contain just enough information for both the system and your users to identify the object. The primary advantage is that there is reduced network traffic required to transmit the proxies. The disadvantages are the marshaling overhead to create the proxies and the increased complexity to retrieve the real objects from the database once they are required.

2. **Data set.** The result set from the database, as it is returned by your database access library (e.g., JDBC or ADO.NET). There is no marshaling overhead

and it is very flexible, although the receiver must be able to work with the data set, coupling your code to the database access library.

3. **Business objects.** The result set is marshaled into a collection of *Student* objects that your business code can work directly with. The primary disadvantage is the overhead to create the objects can be significant.

4. **Data transfer objects.** The result set is marshaled into a collection of serializable objects that can be transmitted across a network connection that just contains the data and the getters and setters to access the data. This approach is flexible although suffers from the marshaling overhead required to convert back and forth between data and objects.

5. **Data structure.** The result set is marshaled into a collection of data structures. Each customer data structure is typically just a collection of data values. The data are relatively easy to access and the approach is flexible, enabling you to include nonstudent data if needed. Unfortunately you still need to parse the structure to obtain individual student information.

6. **XML documents.** The result set is converted into a single XML document, which will contain zero or more student structures. This is a standards-based, platform-independent approach. The primary disadvantage is the marshaling overhead required to convert back and forth between XML, objects, and data structures.

7. **Comma separated value (CSV) file.** The result set is marshaled into a text file, with one row in the file for each student, with commas separating the column values (e.g., Scott,William,Ambler). This is a platform-independent approach to representation that is flexible and supports simple data archival. The primary disadvantage is that the file needs to be parsed to obtain individual student information. This approach is being superceded by XML.

8. **Flat file.** The result set is marshaled into a text file, with one row in the file for each student, with the data values written into known positions (e.g., the student's name is written into positions 21 through 50). This is a flexible, platform-independent approach to representation. Unfortunately the file needs to be parsed to object individual student data and the approach is being superceded by XML.

When searching for objects I typically use either a query object or a metadata-driven approach for representing the search query. My choice of result representation strategy will be driven by what I intend to do with the results. Given the choice, for internal representation I prefer to work with either proxy objects or data sets as the result of a search, and then when I need the full-fledged object(s) I will fetch them when I need them. For externalizing data I will default to XML unless I have a direct requirement to represent them in a different manner.

14.5.6 Reports

Reporting is a necessity within every organization and virtually within every business application. Your project stakeholders will define some requirements best implemented as operational functionality, such as the definition and maintenance of student information, and other requirements best implemented as reports. Reports can be rendered in a variety of manners—printed, displayed on a screen, or an electronic file. Reports can be created in batch or in real time. A student transcript is a report and so is a list of all the students enrolled in a given department.

The fundamental decision that you need to make is whether a report will run against your operational database, the database that the rest of your application works with, or against an external reporting database. Although it seems that you would want to build a report against your real-time operational data there are several problems with this approach. First, your database schema may be highly normalized, which is good for storing data but not very good for reporting it. Second, reports can dramatically affect the performance of operational applications—you often do not want complex search queries run against your operational database during main business hours.

External reporting databases, a strategy often referred to as business intelligence (BI) or Ianalytical reporting, is a common approach. Ad hoc reporting facilities are often used against data marts, small single-purpose databases, whereas predefined reports are often run against larger data warehouses. Ad hoc reporting is typically performed for the specific purposes of a small group of users where it is common that the users write the report(s) themselves. Predefined reports are typically developed by the IT department in response to user requests, sometimes within the scope of an application and sometimes as a small project in its own right. Why separate ad hoc reports from predefined reports? Data marts are designed to support flexible, unpredictable access to data whereas data warehouses are not designed this way.

When implementing reports there are several implementation strategies you should adopt:

1. **Follow report design guidelines.** Your organization may report design guidelines, a subset of your user-interface guidelines. These design guidelines will describe issues such as standard headers and footers to critical report layout conventions. If all reports within your organization follow the same set of conventions they will be easier for your stakeholders to work with.

2. **Follow data design standards for extracted data.** Your database naming conventions should also be applied to data files, and XML documents should apply human readable names for the XML tags.

3. **Add database views to support common reporting needs.** Reporting data can be easier to extract with the addition of database views that perform common joins and projections within your database.

4. **Be prepared to work with imperfect data.** There are many potential data quality problems, discussed in Section 14.7.2, a problem exacerbated by the fact that the data in data marts and data warehouses come from many sources.

5. **Treat report requests as new requirements.** When someone requests a new report it should be treated exactly like any other requirement—it should be estimated, prioritized, put on the stack, and eventually implemented.

6. **Investigate printing facilities and supplies.** The type of printer, paper, and envelopes available to you will affect your physical report design. For example, does your organization have a standard envelope that requires you to print the address in a specific spot so that it lines up with the envelope window? Folding and envelope capacity are issues that may you need to be aware of as well. The point is that you need to work closely with your operations staff, people who are also considered to be project stakeholders.

14.6 DATABASE REFACTORING

Refactoring (Fowler 1999) is a disciplined way to restructure code to improve its design. A code refactoring is a simple change to your code that improves its design but does not change its behavioral semantics. In other words a code refactoring does not add new functionality. A database refactoring (Ambler 2003b) is a simple change to a database schema that improves its design while retaining both its behavioral and informational semantics. As a result database refactoring is more difficult than code refactoring, something which Fowler points out. One way to look at database refactorings is that they are a way to normalize your physical database schema after the fact. Database refactoring supports evolutionary database design as well as the incremental improvement of existing legacy database schemas.

There are different types of database refactorings. Some focus on data quality (such as applying a consistent format to the values stored in a column), some focus on structural changes (such as renaming or splitting a column), whereas others focus on performance enhancements (such as introducing an index). Structural database refactorings are the most challenging because a change to the structure of your database could cause your application (or others) to crash.

Let us work through an example of a structural database refactoring. An application developer has a new requirement that requires us to work with students in either first name order or last name order. The database schema is not robust enough to support this new requirement; student names are currently stored in a single column and therefore difficult to sort. Before we can implement this new requirement we need to refactor our database schema. Figure 14.18 depicts how a schema will potentially evolve throughout the act of refactoring it. We are applying the *Split Column* database refactoring, see http://www.agiledata.org/essays/databaseRefactoringCatalog.html for a detailed list of database refactorings, to the *Person* table to evolve the *Name* column into the *FirstName, MiddleName, Surname* columns. The *Person* table has already been deployed into production and therefore a deprecation period in which both the original and the new schemas are supported is required. This deprecation period gives application developers sufficient time to update, test, and deploy their applications that access this table.

Let us work through the steps that the developers would follow to implement the database refactoring depicted in Fig. 14.18:

1. **Verify that a database refactoring is required.** Perhaps there is another way to implement this requirement that does not involve a database refactoring? For example, the required data may be stored elsewhere or a view that represents the data in the required manner may exist. You also need to assess the overall impact of the refactoring—if you are going to need to

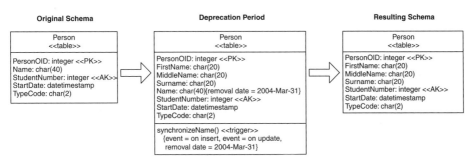

FIGURE **14.18. Refactoring the *Person* table.**

update, test, and redeploy twenty other applications to make this refactoring then it might not be viable for you to continue. For now, assume that the database refactoring is viable.

2. **Choose the most appropriate database refactoring.** You typically have several choices to improve the database design, but in this case *Split Column* seems the best option. The basic idea is that you will split the *Name* column into three smaller columns, one for each portion of a name.

3. **Determine data cleansing needs.** Taking a quick look at the values in the *Name* column you may discover the need to cleanse the source data, motivating you to apply one or more data-cleansing database refactorings before attempting this one. For example if some names are in the format *Ambler, Scott* whereas others are in the format *Scott Ambler* then you might want to choose a common format and refactor the *Name* column to store them all in one manner before applying *Split Column*. For the sake of simplicity, let us assume names are stored in one format.

4. **Write unit tests.** Like code refactoring, database refactoring is enabled by the existence of a comprehensive test suite—you know you can safely change your database schema if you can easily validate that the database still works after the change. Chapter 13 discussed the TDD approach to programming.

5. **Deprecate the original schema.** You cannot make database schema changes instantly; instead you must work with both the old and the new schema in parallel for a time to provide time for other application teams to refactor and redeploy their systems. This parallel running time is referred to as the deprecation period, a period that must reflect the realities of the sandboxes that you are working in. When the deprecation

period has expired, the original schema, plus any scaffolding code that you needed to write, needs to be removed and retested. Once that is done your database refactoring is truly complete. Figure 14.18 shows how this idea would work when we apply the *Split Column* database refactoring to *Name*. Notice the changes between the original schema and the schema during the deprecation period. The three new columns have been added, exactly what you would expect. The *Name* column has been marked as deprecated—you know this because a removal date has been assigned to it using a UML-named variable. A trigger was also introduced; triggers are modeled as methods of the table, and to keep the values contained in the four columns synchronized. The assumption being that new application code will work with the new columns but should not be expect to keep *Name* column up to date, and that older application code that has not yet been refactored to use the new schema will not know to keep the new columns up to date. This trigger is an example of database scaffolding code, a simple and common code required to keep your database "glued together." This code has been assigned the same removal date as the *Name* column.

6. **Implement the change**. You naturally need to refactor your application code to work with the new version of the database schema. An important part of implementing the change is ensuring that the changed portion of your database schema follows your corporate database development guidelines.

7. **Update your database management scripts**. At the present moment database refactoring has scant tool support—this will change in time—so scripts (Sadalage and Schuh 2002) are used to modify your database schema and should be written so that they can be applied in any of your sandboxes. A *database change log* implements all database schema changes in the order that they were applied throughout the course of a project. When you are implementing a database refactoring you include only the immediate changes in this log. When applying the *Split Column* database refactoring we would include the DDL for adding the new columns and the DDL to implement the trigger(s). The *update log* contains the source code for future changes to the database schema that are to be run after the deprecation period for database refactorings. In our example this would be the source code required to remove the *Name* column and the trigger we introduced. Finally, the *data migration log* contains the DML to reformat or cleanse the source data throughout the course of your project. In

our example this would include any code to improve the quality of the values in the *Name* column if required.

8. **Run your regression tests**. Once you have refactored your application code and database schema you must run your regression test suite. This effort should be as automated as much as possible. Testing activities include the installation or generation of test data, running of the tests themselves, comparison of the actual test results with the expected results, and resetting the database back the way you found it. Because successful tests find problems you will need to rework your code and schema.

9. **Document the refactoring**. Databases are shared resources, minimally within your application development team and typically by several application teams; therefore someone will need to communicate and often negotiate the changes with all interested parties.

10. **Version control your work**. A critical skill for agile developers is the habit of putting all of their work under configuration management (CM) control by checking it into a version control tool. This includes any DDL that you have created, change scripts, data migration scripts, test data, test cases, test data generation code, documentation, and models.

11. **Remove the deprecated schema**. At some point, you should remove the deprecated schema. How long you wait before doing so will determine how widely used the schema is and how fast your organization reacts to changes.

Database refactoring is an important skill that all agile software developers should have. Ideally you should try to get your database schema right to begin with and that very often involves doing some modeling first; in this case you would want to take an AMDD approach over a BDUF one. You should try to get your design as good as possible in the beginning, but you must recognize that you are not going to always get it right. Database refactoring enables you to improve your database schema after the fact, and thus reflects the practical realities that agile developers face every day.

14.7 LEGACY ANALYSIS

Sometimes you are in a position to develop a completely new, stand-alone system. If this is the case you should consider yourself amongst the lucky few because the vast majority of developers must often integrate/interface to existing legacy information resources. This could include anything from existing databases or files, existing systems, or even brand new reusable Web services. This section presents a brief overview of legacy system analysis as well as the common problems that you may encounter.

The need to work with legacy systems constrains a development team. It reduces your flexibility because you often cannot easily change the legacy systems to reflect the needs of your system. For example, legacy data often do not provide the full range of information required by your system because the existing data do not reflect your new requirements. Similarly, legacy systems that implement functionality that you would like to reuse can often be "almost good enough," but not quite.

14.7.1 Formalizing Contract Models

Agile modeling (AM) (Chapter 4) includes the *formalize contract models* practice, which is directly related to legacy system analysis. The basic idea is that when you discover that your system requires access to an information resource then you need to put a "contract model" (often called an external interface specification) in place between your group and the external one. Examples of contract models include the detailed documentation of an application programming interface (API), a file layout description, an XML DTD, or a physical data model describing a shared database. I call them contract models because they effectively form a contract between the owner of an information resource and the owners of other systems that use it—the owner cannot change the system without at least informing everyone else ahead of time or better yet negotiating any changes with them. As with a legal contract, a contract model often requires you to invest significant resources to develop and maintain the contract to ensure that it is accurate and sufficiently detailed. Your goal is to minimize the number of contract models for your system to conform to the AM principle of traveling light.

You often identify potentially legacy information sources that you need to work with as part of your deployment modeling efforts (Chapter 10). For each information source that your system must work with you will need to perform some form of legacy system analysis. If you are lucky accurate documentation already exists for the information resource, and if this is the case your entire analysis effort might be to talk to the system owners and read through the documentation to determine whether the information source meets your needs.

In many cases you will discover that little or no documentation exists or it is badly out of date. When this is the case either you or the system owner, or both of you, will need to invest the time to analyze and sufficiently document the legacy information source. This activity will often involve working closely with the owners to understand the legacy asset, poring through any pertinent source code, working with modeling tools that support reverse engineering documentation based on the existing source code, or simply working with the legacy information source to determine how it works. This often proves to be a long and arduous process.

14.7.2 Common Legacy Challenges

There are many common problems that you are likely to run into with respect to legacy data, including both data quality and database design issues. Common data quality problems include the following:

- A single data field is used for several purposes.
- The purpose of a data field is determined by the value of one or more other columns.
- Inconsistent values are stored in a single data field.
- There is inconsistent/incorrect data formatting within a column.
- Some data values are missing within a data field.
- One or more data fields that you require do not exist.
- Additional data fields that your application will need to support if it uses the legacy data exist.
- Multiple sources exist for the same data and it is not clear which one(s) to use.
- Important entities, attributes, and relationships are hidden and floating in text fields.
- Data values can stray from their field descriptions and business rules.
- Various key strategies are used to identify the same type of entity.
- You require a relationship between data records that is not supported by the legacy data.
- One attribute is stored in several fields.
- Special characters within a data field are Inconsistently used.
- Different data types are used for similar columns.
- The legacy data do not contain sufficient detail.
- The legacy data contain too much data.

- The legacy data are read-only, yet you require update access.
- The timeliness of data varies from what you require; for example it is updated by a nightly batch job but you need up-to-date data.
- The default value used by a legacy application does not reflect the default value required by your system.
- Different representations of the data exist.

You may also run into common database design problems, such as the following:

- A database encapsulation scheme exists but it is difficult to use.
- The naming conventions used are difficult to understand.
- The original design goals are at odds with current project needs.
- An inconsistent key strategy is used throughout the database, increasing the difficulty of supporting them.

When you are analyzing a legacy system or database you may also discover one or more architectural problems, such as the following:

- Individual applications are responsible for data cleansing instead of a single source or clean data to begin with.
- There are different implementation paradigms (e.g., the legacy system is built using structured technology and you are using object technology).
- There are different hardware, middleware, or software platforms.
- Fragmented data sources require you to access several sources.
- You require one or more information sources that are effectively inaccessible to you.
- Inflexible architectures do not allow for easy integration.
- Lack of event notification makes it difficult to detect data changes in legacy applications.
- Redundant data sources make it difficult to identify the true/best source of information.
- The approach to security is inefficient, if one exists at all.

14.7.3 Creating Contract Models

The most common style of contract model is an external interface (EI) specification, which describes how to access an external system. When I am creating an external interface specification I like to capture the following information:

- **Identifier.** A unique identifier, for example, EI-1701.

- **Description.** A couple of sentences or a paragraph describing the external system interface.

- **System owner.** The name(s) and contact information of the people who own the system. Include both the project manager and the technical contact.

- **Type.** The type of interface, for example, XML, JMS, Java API, and flat file transfer.

- **Direction.** The direction of the transfer—outwards, inwards, or bi-directional.

- **Frequency.** Approximately how often this interface is exercised, e.g., once a week, or 500 times a day.

- **Timing.** When the interface is used, for example, 24/7, or once a night at 2 AM.

- **Transfer rate.** Known or required transfer rates; for example, the file will be 50 megabytes on average or the records will be 125 bytes each.

- **Security.** Known security issues, for example, whether a log-in is required, whether the source system is protected by a firewall, or whether a secure socket layer is used.

- **Format.** The format of any data transfer. You may simply reference an XML schema definition, describe a file record layout, or describe a C API. The information in this section will vary depending on the interface specifics.

- **Issues.** Any "to dos," concerns to be addressed, and so on.

- **Decisions.** Any important decisions made during the development of this interface.

You can download an example EI specification at http://www.ronin-intl.com/downloads/index.html.

14.8 WHAT YOU HAVE LEARNED

This chapter overviewed the fundamental skills required to persist objects in relational databases. You need to start with an understanding of how to map objects into relational databases and the basics of how to implement basic persistence code in your object code. Once you understand these things the next step is to learn how to implement critical persistence aspects such as concurrency control, transaction control, referential integrity, and reports. Finally, an important skill, particularly for anyone interested in becoming a database administrator, is database refactoring.

Effective developers work side-by-side with data professionals, working together to ensure the success of their project. Not-so-effective developers get into political fights with the data professionals in their organization, putting their project at risk. It is far better to work together effectively.

14.9 REVIEW QUESTIONS

1. In addition to relational databases, identify four other categories of databases. Compare and contrast them, discussing both technical and business issues. Indicate situations where each one would be appropriate.
2. Write the DDL to create the database schema presented in Fig. 14.6. Implement it in a database; you may need to download and install an open source database such as MySql (http://www.mysql.com).
3. Write the code to persist the *Seminar* class, using the database schema presented in Fig. 14.6. You should be able to retrieve, update, insert, and delete *Seminar* objects. Do not worry about traversing any relationships that *Seminar* is involved with nor concurrency control issues.
4. Extend the code from Question 3 to traverse the relationship that it has with the *Enrollment* class.
5. Extend the *Seminar* code to take an optimistic locking approach to concurrency control issues into account. Create two versions of your code, one which does not change the existing database schema and one which adds new column(s) to add concurrency control marks to table rows.
6. Based on your experiences in Question 5, compare and contrast the two strategies for detecting collisions.
7. Perform the database refactoring described in Section 14.6. Write the DDL needed to create the original *Person* schema. Then write the code required to create the deprecated schema, including the code needed to support both schemas. Assume that names are currently in formats such as Ambler, Scott; Scott Ambler; Scott W. Ambler; Scott William Ambler; and Ambler, Scott William.
8. Identify three different strategies for implementing reports. Compare and contrast them, indicating when you would use each one.

CHAPTER 15

Where to Go from Here

Worrying about the increasing rate of change in the IT industry is so
15 minutes ago.

Your skills, and how you apply them, are significant determinants of your success as a software professional. By reading this book, you have gained the fundamental knowledge required to begin learning object technology and agile techniques. The bottom line is that software development is hard; it takes skilled people to be successful at it. By making it to the end of this book you have learned the basics of modern software development; you have learned some useful concepts and techniques; you have started to get a handle on how they fit together; and you have applied them by working through the review questions and case studies. You are now in a good position to continue your learning process, a process that will last throughout your entire career. This chapter provides insight into where the software profession currently is, where it is going, what skills will be needed over the next few years, and how you can obtain those skills.

15.1 BECOME A GENERALIZING SPECIALIST

I believe that one of the biggest problems the IT industry faces is over specialization of skills. Many organizations have IT departments filled with Java specialists, database specialists, business analyst specialists, project management specialists, and so on. This approach is based on an organizational behavior paradigm called *Taylorism*, named after Frederick Taylor, who in his 1911 paper *The Principles of Scientific Management* set the stage for large-scale manufacturing. The basic idea was that instead of having individual craftsman build an item it was better to break the manufacturing process down into a series of distinct steps, then have each worker specialize on just one step. Taylorism may have been effective for use within a manufacturing process but it does not work too well for software development.

The problem with software development specialists is that they have difficulty working effectively with others, often specialists themselves, because they do not have the background to understand the issues that others are trying to deal with. Furthermore, they are often motivated to create far more documentation than is required. For example, when all you can do is write use cases then those use cases will end up including information that could be better recorded elsewhere. The implication is that several specialists will often capture the same piece of information because they are afraid that they will lose it. It is quite common on projects dominated by specialists to see a business rule captured in a user interface specification, in a business rule specification, in a logical data model (LDM), in a UML class diagram, in acceptance tests, and in source code. Clearly there is a chance that the business rule will be described inconsistently, let alone the obvious overhead involved with reviewing and maintaining each version of it. Worse yet you will be motivated to review the documents to ensure that everything is in sync and fully documented before providing it to other specialists.

My advice is that you need to move away from being a narrowly focused specialist to become what I call a *generalizing specialist* (Ambler 2003b). A generalizing specialist is someone with one or more technical specialties who actively seeks to gain new skills both in their existing specialties and in other areas. When you get your first job it is often in the role of a junior programmer or junior DBA. You will initially focus on becoming good at that role, and if you are lucky your organization will send you on training courses to pick up advanced skills in your specialty. After a couple of years, once you are adept at that specialty, or even when you have just reached the point of being comfortable at it, it is time to expand your horizons and learn new skills in different aspects of the software lifecycle. When you do this you evolve from being a specialist to being a generalizing specialist—and this creates value for you!

This book covered many of the development-oriented skills that a generalizing specialist should strive to gain, although it did not touch on management or business skills to any extent. They are all important.

My experience is that a generalizing specialist will write less documentation than a specialist because they have a greater range of options available to them. Instead of having a user-interface specialist capture the rule in a screen specification, the data specialist captures it in an LDM, the use case specialist in a use case, and so on; the generalizing specialist will instead capture it in the most appropriate place. In this case that could be in the form of one or more acceptance tests as well as in the source code. In short, a generalizing specialist can choose the right artifact to get the job done and will be able to capture the information in one and one only place. The implication is that generalizing specialists are more effective than specialists because they can do significantly less work yet still achieve the goal of building an existing system that meets the needs of their stakeholders.

Generalizing specialists also make forming a team considerably easier. Having to pick business analysts, architects, coders, and testers to form a team can be a frustrating exercise in resource management, especially if your team is just one of many competing for resources. Scheduling a bunch of specialists' time to perform narrowly focused tasks is difficult. Specialists are often either part-time on projects or assigned to them for a small period of time. Trying to arrange their schedule to maximize return on their time is an area of project management that most people will avoid at all costs. Forming a team consisting of generalizing specialists avoids this problem. If the same person can write use cases, design, code, and test a system, planning and scheduling becomes much easier.

The primary challenge with this concept is that it takes time, experience, and hard work to become a generalizing specialist. Another issue is the fact that much of the IT industry is geared towards rewarding specialists. For example companies want to hire people who have certified expertise in a given specialty, such as Java programming, UML modeling, or Oracle database administration. Anyone who has invested the time to gain this certification will very likely want to focus on that specialty.

Because a generalizing specialist is someone with a good grasp of how everything fits together they will typically have a greater understanding and appreciation of what their teammates are working on. This in turn leads to great cooperation and improved learning opportunities.

A generalizing specialist is more than just a generalist. A generalist is a jack-of-all-trades but a master of none, whereas a generalizing specialist is a jack-of-all-trades and master of a few. Big difference. A team of generalists can easily flounder because none of them have the skills to get anything done.

My experience is that the best developers are generalizing specialists, or are at least actively trying to become so. There is still room for specialists within your IT departments, they can often act as internal consultants to your development teams, but as IT departments become more agile we will see fewer specialists surviving over time.

15.2 CONTINUING YOUR LEARNING PROCESS

To become a generalizing specialist you need take advantage of every learning opportunity that you can. In this section, I discuss a collection of techniques you can use to continue your learning process:

1. **Work closely with others.** One of the best ways to learn a new skill is to work side-by-side with someone that already has that skill. One of the side benefits of agile practices such as pair programming and modeling with others (Chapter 4) is that you quickly learn new, practical skills.

2. **Take general introductory training.** A good place to start learning is an introductory course. Professional training companies, colleges, and even conferences are very good sources of introductory training. Let your manager know that you are interested in taking training courses; that way when the budget exists you may be given an opportunity to do so.

3. **Gain hands-on experience.** You can read all you want, and you should, and take lots of training courses, but you do not really learn something until you try it. If you currently are not on a software project using the techniques in which you want to gain experience, then you may need to transfer to another project within your organization, find employment at another firm, or work at home after hours on an open-source project.

4. **Obtain mentoring.** A mentor is someone experienced with a given technique or technology who guides novices through the learning process. The best mentors have several years of experience in the technologies and techniques, mentoring experience, and good communication skills. If your organization does not have a formal mentoring process, and few do, then consider identifying potential experts yourself, and either work closely with them or ask them for help learning the new skills you need.

Most people will be flattered that you asked and more than happy to help you.

5. **Work in a learning team.** An effective way to learn new skills is to work in a learning team, a small group of people given the task of working together to learn a particular subject. Learning teams are often asked to produce a small application for the company, perhaps something for the human resources or marketing departments. They are usually asked to spend between 20 and 50 percent of their working hours on the mini-project, devoting the rest of their time to their current responsibilities. The best learning teams are made up of people who have different skills and who are from separate areas in your systems department. Perhaps one is a manager, another a systems programmer, another an analyst, and so on. This wide range of skills and backgrounds enables the team to approach the learning process from several directions, increasing its learning opportunities.

6. **Read, read, read.** I cannot stress enough that for your learning efforts to be successful you must read, read, read. You should read a wide range of books. I suggest reading one book a month just to keep up with changes in the industry. I also suggest reading technical magazines such as *Software Development* (I write the agile column) and business magazines such as *Fortune* and *The Economist* (these magazines will help you to get a broad understanding of business issues). As you know the Web has a lot of great material available free of charge.

7. **Take advanced training.** After several months of hands-on experience under the tutelage of an experienced mentor, the next step is to return to the classroom for advanced training in specific skills. These courses will typically focus on specialized skills or technologies. For example, an advanced modeling course is likely to concentrate on analysis and design patterns, and an advanced programming course conveys a series of programming tips and tricks. The experience you have gained gives you the knowledge that you need to understand and absorb the material presented in the advanced courses.

8. **Challenge yourself.** If you find that you are bored, move onto something else. Boredom is a clear signal that you are not learning anything new. Challenge yourself to constantly learn new things. Do not be afraid of the unknown.

9. **Communicate, communicate, communicate.** Do not take for granted that people will know what you are doing—or what you want to do. Make

it known. This means marketing yourself internally and letting everyone around you know what you want out of the current—and future—positions.

The following tips should help you to improve your learning efforts:

1. **Read before attending training.** Have you ever noticed the people who come prepared to a course, who know something about the material before attending the class, tend to get a lot more out of it than people who go into it cold? My advice is to take advantage of this observation and prepare before taking any course. If possible, before you take a course ask the training instructor what they recommend you read.

2. **Recognize that you have not done it before.** It is quite common for experienced developers, especially the really good ones, to convince themselves initially that they have been doing this new stuff all along. This is because object-oriented software techniques include many important structured software-engineering principles that you likely already use. Familiarity with some of the underlying principles, those usually taught in the introductory classes and introductory books such as this one, make it easy to convince yourself that you have been doing this stuff all along.

3. **Constantly learn.** The rate of change in the IT industry is simply too fast to allow someone to train once, and then sit on his or her laurels. You should be constantly reading, taking courses, and upgrading your skills and experiences.

15.3 Parting Words

One of my fundamental beliefs is that choosing to succeed is one of the most difficult decisions you can make. For software professionals, you choose to succeed when you choose to become a generalizing specialist who continually strives to learn something new every day.

May you live long and prosper.

Glossary

Abstract class. A class that does not have objects instantiated from it.

Abstract use case. See *essential use case.*

Abstraction. The essential characteristics of an item, such as a class or operation.

Accessor. An operation used either to modify or to retrieve a single attribute. Also known as getter and setter operations.

Activity diagram. A UML diagram used to model high-level business processes, including data flow, or to model the logic of complex logic within a system.

Actor class. A representation of an actor that appears in your use case model.

Actor. A person, organization, or system external to the system you are developing.

Ad hoc reporting. Reporting performed for the specific purposes of a small group of users where it is common for the users to write the report(s) themselves.

Aggregation. The representation of "is part of" associations.

Agile model. A model that is just barely good enough.

Agile modeling. A chaordic, practices-based methodology that describes how to be effective at modeling and documentation.

Agile model-driven development. An iterative and incremental approach to development where you create agile models before you implement source code.

Agile software process. A software process that reflects the values and principles of the Agile Alliance (http://www.agilealliance.org).

Alpha testing. A testing period in which prerelease versions of software products, products that are often buggy, are released to users who need access to the product before it is officially deployed. In return, these users are willing to report any defects they uncover back to the software developers. Alpha testing is typically followed by a period of beta testing.

Alternate course of action. An infrequently used path of logic in a use case that is the result of an alternate way to work, an exception, or an error condition.

Alternate key. See *secondary key.*

AM. See *agile modeling.*

AMDD. See *agile model-driven development.*

Analysis error. An analysis error occurs when a requirement is missing, when a requirement is misunderstood, or when an unnecessary requirement is included.

Analysis pattern. A pattern that describes a solution to a common business/analysis issue.

Anonymous object. An object appearing on the diagram that has not been given a name; instead, the label is simply an indication of the class, such as: *Invoice.*

Antipattern. The description of a common approach to solving a common problem, an approach that in time proves to be wrong or highly ineffective.

Application backlog. The average amount of time it takes for the systems department to start the development of a system as measured from the time that the idea for the project was first conceived.

Application server. A server on which business logic is deployed. Application servers are key to an *n*-tier client/server architecture.

Artifact. A document, model, file, diagram, or other item produced, modified, or used during the development, operation, or support of a system.

ASD. Agile software development.

Associative table. A table in a relational database used to maintain a relationship between two or more other tables. Associative tables are typically used to resolve many-to-many relationships.

Attribute. Something that a class or object knows. An attribute is basically a single piece of data or information.

Audit logging. The recording of information to identify an action of interest to the system, when the action took place and whom/what took the action.

Baseline. A tested and certified version of a deliverable representing a conceptual milestone, which thereafter serves as the basis for further development, and that can be modified only through formal change control procedures. A particular version becomes a baseline when a responsible group decides to designate it as such.

Base use case. A use case extended by another via an extend association.

Basic course of action. The main path of logic that an actor will follow through a use case. Often referred to as the "happy path" because it describes how the use case works when everything works as it normally should.

BDUF. Big design up front.

Behavior diagram. A type of UML diagram that depicts behavioral features of a system or business process. This includes activity, state machine, and use case diagrams as well as the four interaction diagrams.

Behavioral requirement. The functional tasks your system must support.

Beta testing. Similar to alpha testing except the software product should be less buggy. This method is used by software development companies who want to ensure they meet as many of their clients' needs as possible.

BFC. Better, faster, cheaper.

Bi-directional association. An association that may be traversed in both directions.

Black-box testing. Testing that verifies the item being tested when given the appropriate input provides the expected results.

Bug. See *defect.*

Building. The process by which a software product is created from its base source code. This is the act of compiling and linking source code in compiled languages such as Java and C++, or packaging code in languages like Smalltalk.

Bulk setter. A setter method that updates several interdependent attributes as one transaction. Bulk setter methods will invoke the individual setter methods for each attribute as needed.

Business analyst. The person who works with the future users of a system to identify the fundamentals of their business problem, their requirements for the system, how they will likely work with the system, and how they will likely need the system to evolve over time.

Business class. Places, things, concepts, and events pertinent to your problem domain. Business classes implement the concepts pertinent to your business domain such as customer or account, and are usually found during the analysis process. Although business classes often focus on the data aspects of your business objects, they will also implement methods specific to the individual business concept.

Business rule. A definition or constraint intended to assert business structure or influence the behavior of one aspect of your business.

C++. A hybrid object-oriented programming language that adds object-oriented features to the C programming language.

C#. An object-oriented programming language based on C from Microsoft Corporation. Very similar to Java.

Callback. An approach where one object indicates that it wants to be sent a message once its request has finished processing; in effect it wants to be "called back."

Cardinality. The representation of the concept "how many?" in associations.

Change case. A potential requirement that your system may need to support in the future.

Change case model. The collection of change cases applicable to your system.

Class. A template from which objects are created (instantiated). Although in the real world Doug, Wayne, John, and Bill are all student objects; we would model the class *Student* instead.

Class diagram. A UML diagram that shows a collection of static model elements such as classes and types, their contents, and their relationships.

Class hierarchy. See *inheritance hierarchy.*

Classifier. A UML term that refers to a collection of instances that have something in common. This includes classes, components, data types, and use cases.

Class-integration testing. The act of ensuring that the classes, and their instances, which form a larger software entity, perform as defined.

Class model. A class diagram and its associated documentation.

Class normalization. The process by which you refactor the behavior within a class diagram in such a way as to increase the cohesion of classes while minimizing the coupling between them.

Class responsibility collaborator (CRC) card. A standard index card that has been divided into three sections, one indicating the name of the class the card represents, one listing the responsibilities of the class, and the third listing the names of the other classes that this one collaborates with to fulfill its responsibilities.

Class responsibility collaborator (CRC) model. A collection of CRC cards that model all or part of a system.

Class-type architecture. A defined approach to layering the classes that compose the software of a system. The interaction between classes is often restricted based on the layer to which they belong.

Clear-box testing. See *white-box testing.*

Client. A single-user PC or workstation that provides presentation services and appropriate computing, connectivity, and interfaces relevant to the business need. A client is also commonly referred to as a "front-end."

Client class. A class whose instances send messages to instances of other classes, but do not receive them.

Client/server (C/S) architecture. A computing environment that satisfies the business need by appropriately allocating the application processing between the client and the server processes.

Client/server class. A class whose instances both send and receive messages to and from instances of other classes.

Cohesion. The degree of relatedness within an encapsulated unit (such as a component or a class).

Collaboration diagram. See *communication diagram.*

Column. The relational database equivalent of an attribute of a data entity stored in a relational table.

Comment. Documentation in source code.

Commercial package. Software that is developed for sale.

Common gateway interface (CGI). A simple protocol used to communicate between Web forms and your program.

Common object request broker architecture (CORBA). An industry-standard, proven approach to distributed object computing, although in practice CORBA has also proven to be a significant force in the middleware arena.

The CORBA specification is defined and maintained by the Object Management Group (OMG).

Communication diagram. A UML diagram that shows instances of classes, their interrelationships, and the message flow between them. Communication diagrams typically focus on the structural organization of objects that send and receive messages. Formerly called collaboration diagrams in UML 1.x.

Component. A cohesive unit of functionality that can be independently developed, delivered, and composed with other components to build a larger unit.

Component-based development. An approach to development in which software is deployed as collections of interacting components, each of which encapsulate a defined set of behaviors.

Component diagram. A UML diagram that depicts the components that compose an application, system, or enterprise. The components, their interrelationships, interactions, and their public interfaces are depicted.

Component testing. See *class-integration testing.*

Composite structure diagram. A UML diagram that depicts the internal structure of a classifier (such as a class, component, or use case), including the interaction points of the classifier to other parts of the system. New to UML 2.

Composition. A strong form of aggregation in which the "whole" is completely responsible for its parts and each "part" object is only associated with the one "whole" object.

Computer-aided system engineering (CASE) tool. Software that supports the creation of models of software-oriented systems.

Conceptual modeling. The task of discovering the entity types that represent the things and concepts, and their relationships, pertinent to your problem space.

Concrete class. A class that has objects instantiated from it.

Concurrency. The issues involved with allowing multiple people simultaneous access to a shared resource, such as an object or persistent storage.

Connascence. Between two software elements, *A* and *B*, the property by which a change in *A* would require a change to *B* to preserve overall correctness within your system.

Constraint. A global requirement, such as limited development resources or a decision by senior management, that restricts the way you develop a system.

Constructor. A method, typically a static one, whose purpose is to instantiate and optionally initialize an object.

Contract. Any service/behavior of a class or component that is requested of it.

Controller class. A class that implements business logic that involves collaborating with several business/domain classes or even other controller/process classes.

Convenience inheritance. See *implementation inheritance.*

Coupling. The degree of dependence between two items. In general, it is better to reduce coupling wherever possible.

Coverage testing. The act of ensuring that each line of code is exercised at least once.

Creation state. See *initial state.*

CRUD. Create retrieve update delete. The basic functionality of a persistence mechanism.

C-style comment. A style of multiline comment in Java that begins with "/*" characters and ends with "*/" characters.

Database administrator (DBA). The person responsible for the care and support of your permanent storage mechanisms.

Database proxy. An object that represents a business object stored in a database. To every other object in the system, the database proxy appears to be the object it represents. When other objects send the proxy a message, it immediately fetches the object from the database and replaces itself with the fetched object, passing the message onto it.

Database server. A server that has a database installed on it.

Data definition language (DDL). Commands supported by a persistence mechanism that enable the creation, removal, or modification of structures (such as relational tables or classes) within it.

Data dictionary. A repository of information about the layout of a database, a flat file, and a class, and any mappings among the three.

Data entity. The representation of the data describing a person, place, thing, event, or concept.

Data-flow diagram (DFD). A diagram that shows the movement of data within a system between processes, entities, and data stores. Data-flow diagrams, also called process diagrams, are primary artifacts of structured/procedural modeling.

Data manipulation language (DML). Commands supported by a persistence mechanism that enables the access of data within it, including the creation, retrieval, update, and deletion of that data.

Data model. A model depicting data entities and the relationships between those entities.

Data modeler. The person responsible for the development and maintenance of data models.

Defect. Anything that detracts from your application's capability to completely and effectively meet your user's needs. Also known as a bug, fault, or feature.

Dependency relationship. A relationship that exists between class *A* and *B* when instances of class *A* interact with instances of class *B*. Dependency relationships are used when there is no direct relationship (inheritance, aggregation, or association) between the two classes.

Dependent class. A fine-grained class typically identified through the normalization of an attribute into a full-fledged class.

Deployment diagram. A UML diagram showing the execution architecture of systems. This includes nodes, either hardware or software execution environments, as well as the middleware connecting them.

Design pattern. A pattern that describes a solution to a common design issue.

Destructor. A method whose purpose is to remove an object completely from memory.

Development/maintenance trade-off. A trade-off between development techniques that speed the development process but often have a negative impact on your maintenance efforts and techniques that lead to greater maintainability but negatively impact your development efforts, at least in the short term.

Development process. A process that focuses on the development aspects of a system, including requirements definition, modeling, programming, testing, and delivery of the system.

Diagram. A visual representation of a problem or solution to a problem.

Disconnected usage. The potentially full use of an application when it is not connected to your organization's network.

Distributed objects. An object-oriented architecture in which objects running in separate memory spaces (that is, different computers) interact with one another transparently.

Documentation comment. A style of multiline comment in Java that begins with "/**" characters and ends with "*/" characters. Also known as a Javadoc comment.

Domain class. See *business class.*

Domain component. A large-scale component that encapsulates cohesive portions of your business domain.

Domain model. A representation of the business/domain concepts, and their interrelationships, applicable to your system. A domain model helps to establish the vocabulary for your project.

DTD. Document-type definition.

EAI. See *enterprise application integration.*

E-commerce. The use of technology to support the selling of products and services electronically. Also known as electronic-commerce or Internet-based commerce.

Education. The teaching of skills and knowledge typically applicable over the student's entire career.

Eiffel. A "pure" object-oriented programming language.

Electronic data interchange (EDI). An industry-standard approach to sharing data between two or more systems.

Encapsulation. The grouping of related concepts into one item, such as a class or component.

Endline comment. The use of a single-line comment to document a line of source code where the comment immediately follows the code on the same line as the code. Also known as an inline comment.

End-to-end prototyping. See *technical prototyping.*

Enterprise application integration (EAI). The integration of disparate software applications into a cohesive whole to support new and complex business processes.

Enterprise Java Beans (EJB). A component architecture, defined by Sun Microsystems, for the development and deployment of component-based distributed business applications.

Enterprise process. The overall process of a single organization, encompassing the processes of all aspects of the organization.

Enterprise software architect. The person responsible for the software architecture of your organization.

Enterprise unified process (EUP.) A six-phase prescriptive software process that extends the RUP with production and retirement phases as well as new disciplines for enterprise management and operations & support in order to cover the entire software lifecycle (not just development).

Entity type. The representation of the things and concepts pertinent to your problem space.

Essential model. A model intended to capture the essence of a problem through technology-free, idealized, and abstract descriptions.

Essential use case. A simplified, abstract, generalized use case that captures the intentions of a user in a technology- and implementation-independent manner.

Essential use case model. A use case model composed of essential use cases.

Essential user-interface prototype. A low-fidelity prototype of a system's user interface that models the fundamental, abstract characteristics of a user interface.

EUP. See *enterprise unified process.*

Evolutionary development. An iterative approach to software development that delivers working software in an incremental fashion.

Exception. An indication that an unexpected condition has occurred within some software. In Java, exceptions are "thrown" by methods to indicate potential problems.

Extend association. A generalization relationship where an extending use case continues the behavior of a base use case. The extending use case accomplishes this by inserting additional action sequences into the base use case sequence. This is modeled using a use case association with the <<extend>> stereotype.

Extending use case. A use case that extends another use case via an extend association.

Extensibility. A measure of how easy it is to add new features to, to extend, existing software. If item *A* is easier to change than item *B*, then we say that item *A* is more extensible than item *B*.

Extensible markup language (XML). A standardized approach to representing text-based data in a hierarchical manner and for defining metadata about the data. XML is a subset of standard generalized markup language (SGML), the same parent of hypertext markup language (HTML).

Extension point. A marker in a use case where extension is allowed.

Extreme programming (XP). A deliberate and disciplined approach to software development that stresses communication, simplicity, feedback, and confidence. XP focuses on working with users, on development that is simple and elegant, and on testing.

Facilitator. The person responsible for planning, running, and managing modeling sessions.

Fat-client. A two-tiered C/S architecture in which client machines implement both the user interface and the business logic of an application. Servers typically only supply data to client machines with little or no processing done to it.

Fault. See *defect.*

FDD. Feature-driven development.

Feature creep. The addition, as development proceeds on a nonagile project, of new features to a system beyond what the original specification called for. This is also called scope creep.

Feature. A small, client-valued function expressed in the form <action>the<result><of|for|the|. . .><object>.

Final state. A state from which no transitions lead out of. Objects will have zero or more final states.

Firewall. A set of security programs residing on a computer, often a gateway server into a network, that protect your resources.

Flow chart. A diagram depicting the logic flow of a single process or method. Flow charts were a primary artifact of structured/procedural modeling.

Foreign key. One or more attributes within a data entity that represent a primary or secondary key in another table. Foreign keys are used to maintain a relationship to a row in another table.

Framework. A reusable set of prefabricated software building blocks that programmers can use, extend, or customize for specific computing solutions.

Free-form diagram. A diagram that does not follow a defined notation, exactly as the name implies.

Full lifecycle object-oriented testing (FLOOT). A testing methodology for object-oriented development that comprises testing techniques that taken together provide methods to verify your application works correctly at each stage of development.

Functional cohesion. A measure of how well the behaviors of an item make sense when considered as a whole.

Function testing. A testing technique in which development staff confirms that their application meets the user requirements specified during analysis.

Galactically unique OID. A persistent OID with a value guaranteed to be unique across all organizations that follow the same value generation strategy.

Generalization set. A UML 2.0 approach for indicating taxonomical classifications.

Generalizing specialist. Someone with one or more specialized skills who also has a general knowledge of software development and ideally of the business domain as well.

Getter. A method to obtain the value of a data attribute, or to calculate the value, of an object or a class.

Globally unique OID. A persistent OID with a value guaranteed to be unique within the organization that generated it.

Gold-plating. The addition of extraneous features to a system.

Graphical user interface (GUI). A style of user interface composed of graphical components such as windows and buttons.

GUI testing. See *user-interface testing.*

Has-a relationship. See include association.

Human-factors engineer (HFE). A person who is an expert in the analysis and design of the user interface for an application and/or work environment for your users.

Hypertext markup language (HTML). Industry-standard definition of a platform-independent file formats for sharing information. HTML pages are the *de facto* standard approach for user interfaces on the World Wide Web (WWW).

Idiom. A description of how to implement a particular part of a pattern, the part's functionality, or the relationship to other parts in the design. Idioms are often specific to a particular programming language.

Implementation inheritance. An inheritance applied simply for convenience, even though it does not make sense to say that the subclass *is a* superclass.

Include association. A generalization relationship denoting the inclusion of the behavior described by a use case within another use case, modeled using a use case association with the <<include>> stereotype. Also known as a *uses* or a *has-a* relationship.

Incremental development. An approach to software development that organizes a project into several releases instead of one "big-bang" release.

Information hiding. The restriction of external access to attributes.

Inheritance. The representation of an *is a, is like,* or *is kind of* relationship between two classes. Inheritance promotes reuse by enabling a subclass to benefit automatically from the entire behavior that it inherits from its superclass(es).

Inheritance hierarchy. A set of classes related through inheritance. Also referred to as a class hierarchy.

Inheritance regression testing. The act of running the test cases of the superclasses, both direct and indirect, on a given subclass.

Initial state. The state an object is in when it is first created. All objects have an initial state. Often referred to as the creation state.

Inline comment. See *endline comment.*

Installation testing. The act of ensuring that your application can be installed successfully.

Instance. An object serving as an example of a particular class.

Instance attribute. An attribute applicable to a single instance (object) of a class. Each object will have its own value for an instance attribute.

Instance method. A method that operates on a single instance (object) of a class.

Instantiate. The creation of objects from class definitions.

Integration plan. A plan that describes the schedule, resources, and approach to integrating the elements of a system.

Integration testing. The act of ensuring that several portions of software work together.

Interaction diagram. A subset of UML behavior diagrams that emphasize object interactions. This includes communication, interaction overview, sequence, and timing diagrams.

Interaction overview diagram. A variant of an activity diagram that overviews the control flow within a system or business process. Each node/activity within the diagram can represent another interaction diagram.

Interface. A collection of one or more operation signatures, and optionally attribute definitions, that composes a cohesive set of behaviors. Some object languages support the capability for classes and/or components to implement interfaces.

Interface flow diagram. See *user-interface flow diagram.*

Interface navigation diagram. See *user-interface flow diagram.*

Interface testing. See *black-box testing.*

Internet-based commerce. See *e-commerce.*

Interprocess communication (IPC). The act of having software running on two separate pieces of hardware interact with one another.

Intuitable. The state of users' guesses and presuppositions being more likely right than wrong, and even when wrong, resulting in reasonable responses from the system that are readily understood by the users.

Invariant. A set of assertions about an instance or class that must be true at all "stable" times, where a stable time is the period before a method is invoked on the object/class and immediately after a method is invoked.

Invoke. The sending of message *X* from object *A* to object *B* by calling the *X* method implemented by object *B*.

Iterative development. A nonserial approach to software development where you are likely to do some requirements definition, some modeling, some programming, or some testing on any given day.

Java. An object-oriented programming language based on the concept of "write once, run anywhere."

Javadoc. A Java utility that parses Java source files for Javadoc comments to use as a basis from which to generate external code documentation.

Javadoc comment. See *documentation comment.*

Javadoc tag. A predefined string of text, beginning with the "@" symbol, that can be embedded in documentation comments for formatting purposes. Examples include the "@returns" and "@throws" tags.

Java virtual machine (JVM). An abstract computing machine that supports a defined set of instruction set. JVMs are what makes Java portable: Java code is compiled into standard byte-code that can be run on any platform with a JVM.

Joint application development (JAD). A structured, facilitated meeting in which modeling is performed by a group of people. JADs are often held for gathering user requirements or for developing system designs.

JVM. See *Java virtual machine.*

Key. A data attribute, or collection of data attributes, that uniquely describes a data entity. In a relational database a key is one or more columns in a table that when combined form a unique identifier for each record in the table.

Layering. The organization of software collections (layers) of classes or components that fulfill a common purpose.

Lazy initialization. An approach in which the initial value of an attribute is set in its corresponding getter method the first time the getter is invoked.

LDM. See *logical data model.*

Learning team. A small group of people given the task of working together to learn a particular subject.

Lifeline. The representation, in a sequence diagram, of the life span of an object during an interaction.

Load balancing. A technique where processing requests are distributed across several nodes so the overall processing burden is spread as evenly as possible across the nodes.

Lock. An indication that a table, record, class, or object is reserved so work can be performed on the item. Typically, a lock is established, the work is performed, and the lock is removed.

Logical data model. A data model used to explore domain concepts and their relationships.

Maintainability. A measure of how easy it is to add, remove, or modify existing features of a system. The easier a system is to change, the more maintainable we say that system is.

Maintenance burden. The need for software organizations to invest money in the support, operation, and enhancement of existing hardware.

Major user-interface element. A large-grained item such as a screen, HTML page, or report.

Many-to-many association. An association where the maximum of both multiplicities is greater than one.

Many-to-one association. An association where the maximum of one multiplicity is one and the other is more than one.

MDA. See *model-driven architecture.*

Mentoring. The processes of having an experienced professional impart his or her expertise to novices following a hands-on basis.

Message. A request from one object, the sender, to another, the target. Messages are implemented as a method invocation on the target object.

Message-invocation box. The long, thin, vertical boxes that appear on sequence diagrams, which represent invocation of an operation on an object or class.

Meta data. Data that describe other data or information.

Method. Something that a class or object does. A method is similar to a function or procedure in structured programming and is often referred to as an operation or member function in object development.

Methodology. See *process.*

Method response. A count of the total number of messages sent as a result of a method being invoked.

Microsoft solutions framework (MSF). A software process defined and promoted by Microsoft.

Middleware. Technology that enables software deployed on disparate computer hardware systems to communicate with one another.

Minor user-interface element. A small-grained item such as a user input field, menu item, list, or static text field.

Mirror hierarchies. Two or more class hierarchies that take on structures similar to one another, because they are highly related model concepts.

Model. An abstraction describing a problem domain and/or a solution to a problem domain. Traditionally, models are thought of as diagrams plus their corresponding documentation although nondiagrams, such as interview results and collections of CRC cards, are also considered to be models.

Model-driven architecture. A framework for software development, defined by the Object Management Group (OMG), where development efforts are driven by modeling.

Model review. A technical review in which an analysis and/or design model is inspected.

Model walkthrough. A less formal version of a model review.

MSF. See *Microsoft solutions framework.*

Multiple classification. The classification of an entity type into more than one generalization set.

Multiple inheritance. The direct inheritance of a class from more than one class.

Multiplicity. The combination of the concepts of cardinality and optionality into a single concept.

Mutator. See *setter.*

Name hiding. The practice of using the same, or at least similar, name of an attribute/variable/parameter for one of higher scope. The most common abuse of name hiding is to name a local variable the same as an instance attribute.

Network diagram. A diagram used to depict hardware nodes as well as the connections between them. Network diagrams are arguably a high-level form of UML deployment diagram with extensive use of visual stereotypes.

Node. A computer, switch, printer, or other hardware device.

Nonfunctional requirement. The standards, regulations, and contracts to which your system must conform; descriptions of interfaces to external systems that your system must interact with; performance requirements; design and implementation constraints; and the quality characteristics to which your system must conform.

Note. A modeling construct for adding free-form text to UML diagrams.

n-tier. An architectural approach where application logic is implemented on several (*n*) categories of computing device (tiers) such as Web, application, security, and database servers.

Object. A person, place, thing, concept, event, screen, or report. Objects both know things (that is, they have data) and they do things (that is, they have functionality).

Objectbase. See *object database*.

Object-based programming language. Any programming language that natively supports some, but not all, of the properties of an object-oriented language. Example: Visual Basic.

Object COBOL. A hybrid object-oriented programming language that extends COBOL with object-oriented concepts.

Object constraint language (OCL). A formal language, similar to structured English, to express side-effect-free constraints within UML models.

Object database (ODB). A permanent storage mechanism, also known as an objectbase or an object-oriented database management system (OODBMS), which natively supports the persistence of objects.

Object Database Management Group (ODMG). A standards body responsible for the standard definition for object-oriented databases and the object query language (OQL).

Object diagram. A UML diagram that depicts objects and their relationships at a point in time, typically a special case of either a class diagram or a communication diagram.

Object identifier (OID). A unique identifier assigned to objects, typically a large integer number. OIDs are the object-oriented equivalent of keys in the relational world.

Object Management Group (OMG). An industry-recognized standards body responsible for standards such as the unified modeling language (UML) and the common object request broker architecture (CORBA).

Object modeler. The person responsible for the analysis and design of object-oriented software.

Object modeling language (OML). An alternative to the unified modeling language (UML), promoted by the OPEN Consortium (http://www.open.org.au).

Object-oriented database management system (OODBMS). See *object database.*

Object-oriented paradigm. A development strategy based on the concept of building systems from reusable components called objects.

Object-oriented programming language. Any programming language that natively supports the object-oriented concepts of inheritance, classes, objects, polymorphism, and message passing. Examples: Java and C++.

Object-oriented software process (OOSP). A collection of process patterns that together describe a complete process for developing, maintaining, and supporting software. The OOSP is based on the concept that large-scale, mission-critical software development is serial in the large, iterative in the small, delivering incremental releases of software in Internet time.

Object Pascal. A hybrid object-oriented programming language that extends Pascal with object-oriented concepts.

Object programming language. Any programming language that is either object-oriented or object-based.

Object role model (ORM) diagram. A diagram that depicts objects (entity types), the relationships (fact types) between them, the roles that the objects play in those relationships, constraints within the problem domain, and optionally examples (called fact-type tables).

Object space. The memory space, including all accessible permanent storage, in which objects exist and interact with one another.

ODMG. See *Object Database Management Group.*

OML. See *object modeling language.*

One-to-many association. See *many-to-one association.*

One-to-one association. An association where the maximums of each of its multiplicities is one.

Ontology. The representation and communication of knowledge about a topic as well as a set of relationships and properties that hold for the entities included within that topic.

OO. Object-oriented, or object orientation. For example, OO programming refers to object-oriented programming, while a book that describes OO is describing object orientation.

OOA. Object-oriented analysis.

OOCRUD. Object-oriented create, retrieve, update, and delete.

OOD. Object-oriented design.

OPEN process. A mature software process defined and promoted by the OPEN Consortium (http://www.open.org.au).

Open-source software (OSS). Fully functioning software whose source code is available free of charge. Changes, either new features or bug fixes, are often made to open-source software by its users, and then made available (usually) free of charge to the entire user community.

Operations testing. The act of ensuring that the needs of operations personnel who have to support/operate the application are met.

Optimistic locking. An approach where an item is locked only for the time that it is accessed. For example, if a customer object is edited, a lock is placed on it in the persistence mechanism for the time that it takes to read it in memory, and then it is immediately removed. The object is edited, and then when it needs to be saved, it is locked again, written out, and then unlocked.

Optionality. The representation of the concept "do you need to have it?" in associations.

OQL. Object query language, a standard proposed by the ODMG for the selection of objects. This is basically SQL with object-oriented extensions that provide the capability to work with classes and objects, instead of tables and records.

ORM. Diagram. See *object role model (ORM) diagram.*

Overload. The defining of two methods with the same name, but with different parameters.

Override. The redefining of an attribute or method in a subclass.

Package. A UML construct that enables you to organize model elements into groups.

Package diagram. A UML diagram that shows how model elements are organized into packages as well as the dependencies between packages.

Paradigm. An overall strategy or viewpoint for doing things (pronounced *para-dime*). A paradigm is a specific mindset.

Paragraphing. A technique where you indent the code within the scope of a code block by one unit, usually a horizontal tab, to distinguish it from the code outside the code block. Paragraphing helps to increase the readability of your code.

Pattern. A solution to a common problem taking relevant forces into account, effectively supporting the reuse of proven techniques and approaches of other developers.

PDA. Personal digital assistant.

PDM. See *physical data model.*

Peer review. A style of technical review in which a project deliverable, or portion thereof, is inspected by a small group of people with expertise in the product being reviewed.

Perl (practical extraction and report language). A scripting language originally developed for the automation of UNIX system administration tasks, which are now commonly used for Web-based software development.

Permanent storage. Any physical medium to which data may be saved, retrieved, and deleted. Potential permanent storage mechanisms for objects include relational databases, files, and object databases.

Persistence. The issue of how objects are permanently stored.

Persistence administrator. See database administrators (DBAs).

Persistence class. A class that provides the capability to store objects permanently. By encapsulating the storage and retrieval of objects via persistence classes, you are able to use various storage technologies interchangeably without affecting your applications.

Persistence framework. See *persistence layer.*

Persistence layer. Software, also known as a persistence framework, which encapsulates permanent storage mechanisms, such as relational databases, so application developers do not have knowledge of how or where objects are stored. Persistence layers automate significant portions of the efforts required to persist objects.

Persistence mechanism. The permanent storage facility used to make objects persistent. Examples include relational databases, object databases, flat files, and object/relational databases.

Persistent association. An association that is permanent or at least semipermanent in nature, which must be saved as permanent storage (that is, it must be persisted).

Persistent object. An object saved to permanent storage.

Pessimistic locking. An approach where an item is locked for the entire time it is in memory. For example, when a customer object is edited, a lock is placed on the object in the persistence mechanism, the object is brought into memory and edited, and then eventually the object is written back to the persistence mechanism and the object is unlocked.

Physical data model. A model that describes the persistent data aspects of a software system.

Pilot testing. A testing process equivalent to beta testing used by organizations to test applications they have developed for their own internal use.

PIM. See *platform-independent model.*

Platform-independent model (PIM). An MDA model that is independent of implementation technology that is also at a high-level of complexity.

Platform-specific model (PSM). An MDA model created by transforming a PIM, which is tailored to specify your system in terms of implementation constructs available in one specific technology.

Polymorphism. The ability of different objects to respond to the same message in different ways, enabling objects to interact with one another without knowing their exact type.

Portability. A measure of how easy it is to move an application to another environment (which may vary by the configuration of either their software or hardware). The easier it is to move an application to another environment, the more portable we say that application is.

Postcondition. An expression of the properties of the state of an operation or use case after it has been invoked successfully.

Precondition. An expression of the constraints under which an operation or use case will operate properly.

Prescriptive process. A process where the activities are described in minute detail.

Primary key. The preferred key for a data entity.

Primitive type. A type of attribute built into a programming language. For example, Java includes primitive types such as int, string, and boolean.

Problem space. The scope of your business domain being addressed by your system.

Process. The definition of the steps to be taken, the roles of the people performing those steps, the artifacts being created, and the artifacts being used to fulfill a purpose that provides value to someone or some organization.

Process antipattern. An antipattern that describes an approach and/or series of actions for developing software proven ineffective and often detrimental to your organization.

Process class. See *controller class.*

Process diagram. See *data-flow diagram.*

Process pattern. A collection of general techniques, actions, and/or tasks (activities) that address specific software process problems considering the relevant forces/factors.

Programmer. The person who implements and initially tests source code based on the models for your system.

Project infrastructure. The tools, standards, guidelines, processes, and other supporting artifacts used by your project team.

Project manager. The person responsible for the organization and management of a software project.

Project scope. The definition of the functionality that will, and will not, be implemented by a project.

Project stakeholder. Any person who is a direct user, indirect user, manager of users, senior manager, operations staff member, support (help desk) staff member, developer working on other systems that integrate or interact with the one under development, or maintenance professional potentially affected by the development, upkeep, and/or deployment of a software project.

Project success. The state of a project when it is on time, is on budget, and meets the needs of its users.

Proof-of-concept prototyping. See *technical prototyping.*

Prototype. A simulation of an item, such as a user interface or a system architecture, the purpose of which is to communicate your approach to others before significant resources are invested in the approach.

Prototype walkthrough. A process by which your users work through a collection of use cases using a prototype as if it was the real system. The main goal is to test whether the design of the prototype meets their needs.

PSM. See *platform-specific model.*

Pure inheritance. Inheritance in which the subclass does not override any behavior implemented by its superclass(es). The subclass is free to add new behavior.

Quality assurance. The validation that something was built the right way.

Quality assurance engineer. The person responsible for ensuring that developers build software according to the accepted standards and processes within your organization.

Rational unified process. A four-phase prescriptive software process that is evolutionary in nature.

Read into memory. The obtaining of the data for an object from persistent storage, with no intention to update it.

Read lock. A type of lock indicating that a table, record, class, or object is currently being read by someone else. Other people may also obtain read locks on the item, but no one may obtain a write lock until all read locks are cleared.

Realizes relationship. A type of relationship where an item implements a concept or type, such as a standard or an interface.

Record. See *row.*

Recursive association. An association in which the objects involved in it are instances of the same class. For example, people marry people.

Reference manual. A document, either paper or electronic, aimed at experts who need quick access to information.

Referential integrity. The assurance that a reference from one entity to another entity is valid. If entity *A* references entity *B*, then entity *B* exists. If entity *B* is removed, then all references to entity *B* must also be removed.

Regression testing. The validation that existing software still works after changes have been made.

Relational database (RDB). A permanent storage mechanism in which data are stored as rows in tables. RDBs do not natively support the persistence of objects, requiring the additional work on the part of developers and/or the use of a persistence layer.

Relational table. The physical implementation of a data entity within a relational database.

Requirement review. A technical review in which a requirements model is inspected.

Requirements model. The collection of artifacts, including your use case model, user-interface model, domain model, change-case model, and supplementary specification that describes the requirements for your system.

Responsibility. An obligation that a class must fulfill, such as knowing something or doing something.

Retrieve into memory. The obtaining of the data for an object from persistent storage with the intention to update it.

Robustness diagram. A simplified UML communication diagram that uses graphical symbols to represent boundary/interface, control/process, and domain/entity classes.

Role. The context that an object takes within an association. For example, a person can have the role of "husband" within a family.

Root class. The topmost class in an inheritance hierarchy.

Row. The relational database equivalent of an instance of a data entity stored in a relational table. Also called a record or tuple.

Rule engine. Software, typically based on artificial intelligence (AI) techniques, used specifically for the purpose of implementing complex logic in the form of rules.

RUP. See *rational unified process.*

Scaffolding. Additional code, often complete methods and attributes, required to make your design work. Programmers often introduce scaffolding; it is not modeled as part of analysis and often not even as part of design.

Scope creep. See *feature creep.*

Scribe. A person responsible for recording information as it is identified.

SDLC. Software development lifecycle.

Secondary key. A key that is an alternative to the primary key for a data entity. Also known as an alternate key.

Security access control. The act of ensuring that users of a system may only invoke the behaviors they are entitled to, including, but not limited to, the manipulation of components, objects, and data.

Semantics. The meaning, or definition, of something.

Sequence diagram. A UML diagram that models the sequential logic, in effect the time ordering of messages between classifiers.

Server. One or more multiuser processors with shared memory that provide computing connectivity, database services, and interfaces relevant to the business need. A server is also commonly referred to as a "back-end."

Server class. A class whose instances receive messages, but does not send them to instances of other classes.

Service. A function that is well-defined, is self-contained, and does not depend on the context or state of other services.

Service-oriented architecture (SOA). A collection of services.

Setter. A method that sets the value of a data attribute of an object or class. Also known as a mutator.

Signature. The combination of the name, parameter names (in order), and name of the return value (if any) of a method.

Simple network management protocol (SNMP). A standard protocol that specifies how to simply communicate status, often in near real time, of system services. SNMP is used to monitor the status of the various software and hardware components of a system.

Single classification. The existence of an entity type in only one generalization set.

Single inheritance. When a class directly inherits from only one class.

Single-line comment. A style of Java comment that begins with the characters "//" anything and runs to the end of the current line.

Smalltalk. A pure object-oriented programming language.

SOA. See *service-oriented architecture*.

Software architecture. The set of significant decisions about the organization of a software system, the selection of the system's structural elements, and their interfaces; the definition of the behavior, structure of those elements, the definition of the associations, and interactions between those elements; the composition of the elements into progressively larger subsystems;

and the definition of the architectural style that guides the efforts of software architects.

Software configuration management (SCM). A collection of engineering procedures for tracking and documenting software and its related artifacts throughout their lifecycles to ensure that all changes are recorded and the current state of the software is known and reproducible.

Software port. The migration of software from one platform to another. You will often need to port software to other operating systems, other database systems, and even other hardware platforms.

Software process. A process that describes how to develop, operate, and support one or more systems.

Solution space. The problem space being addressed by your system plus the non-domain functionality required to implement your system.

SQL. Structured query language.

SQL statement. A piece of SQL code used to retrieve, update, insert, or delete data, or to manipulate the schema of a relational database.

State. The representation of a stage in the behavior pattern of an object. A state can also be said to represent a condition of an object to which a defined set of policies, regulations, and physical laws apply.

State machine diagram. A UML diagram that describes the states an object or interaction may be in, as well as the transitions between states. Formerly referred to as a state diagram, state chart diagram, or a state-transition diagram.

Static attribute. An attribute whose value is all instances of a class. Each instance of a class shares the single value of a static attribute.

Static method. A method that operates at the class level, potentially on all instances of that class.

Stereotype. A common use of a modeling element. Stereotypes are used to extend the UML in a consistent manner.

Sticky note. A small piece of paper, often a few inches on a side, that has glue on one side so it can be stuck easily onto things. Sticky notes are produced by several manufacturers and come in a variety of sizes and colors.

Stored procedure. An operation that runs in a persistence mechanism.

Stress testing. The act of ensuring that the system performs as expected under high volumes of transactions, high numbers of users, and so on.

Structure diagram. A category of UML diagram that depicts the elements of a specification that are irrespective of time. This includes class, composite structure, component, deployment, object, and package diagrams.

Subclass. A class that inherits from another class.

Subject matter expert (SME). A person responsible for providing pertinent information about the problem and/or technical domain either from personal knowledge or from research.

Substate. A specific state that is part of a more generalized superstate.

Superclass. A class that is inherited from by another class.

Superstate. A general state that is decomposed into several substates.

Supplementary specification. An artifact where all requirements not contained in your use case model, user-interface model, or domain model are documented.

Support testing. The act of ensuring that the needs of support personnel who have to support the application are met.

Support user's guide. A brief document, usually a single page, that describes the support services for your application that are available to your user community. This guide includes support phone numbers, fax numbers, and Web site locations, as well as hours of operations and tips for obtaining the best services.

Surrogate key. A key without a business meaning.

System boundary box. A rectangle optionally included on a use case diagram that depicts the scope of your system.

System class. A class that provides operating-system-specific functionality for your applications or that wraps functionality provided by other tool/application vendors. System classes isolate your software from the operating system (OS), making your application portable between environments, by wrapping OS-specific features.

System layer. The collection of classes that provide operating-system-specific functionality for your applications or that wrap functionality provided by non-OO applications, hardware devices, and/or non-OO code libraries.

System testing. A process in which any known problems are found and fixed in order to prepare your application for user testing.

System use case. A detailed use case that describes how your system will fulfill the requirements of a corresponding essential use case, often referring to implementation-specific features, such as aspects of your user-interface design.

System use case model. A use case model comprising system use cases.

Task case. See *essential use case.*

Taxonomy. A classification hierarchy.

TDD. See *test-driven development.*

Technical prototyping. The act of creating a prototype to validate that your proposed solution works. Often called "proof-of-concept" prototyping or "end-to-end" prototyping.

Technical review. A testing technique in which one or more development artifacts are examined critically by a group of your peers. A review typically focuses on accuracy, quality, usability, and completeness. Less formal versions of this process are often referred to as walkthroughs or peer reviews.

Temporal cohesion. A measure of whether the behaviors of an item occur during the relatively same time period.

Ternary relationship. A relationship involving three entity types.

Test case. A description—including the setup, series of actions, and expected results—of a situation that software item must support.

Test-driven development. An iterative development technique where you write a test and then write the functional code required for that test to pass.

Test engineer. The person responsible for verifying that software fulfills the requirements from which it was built.

Test harness. The portion of the code of a test suite that aggregates the test scripts.

Testing. The validation that the right thing was built.

Test script. The steps to be performed to run a test case. Test scripts will be implemented using a variety of techniques, from source code for code tests to written steps for function testing.

Test suite. A collection of test scripts.

Test target. An item, such as a model, document, or portion of software, to be tested.

Thin client. A two-tiered client/server architecture in which client machines implement only the user interface of an application.

Three-tier client/server. A client/server architecture that is separated into three layers: a client layer that implements the user interface, an application server layer that implements business logic, and a database server layer that implements persistence.

Tier. A layer within a deployment architecture.

Timing diagram. A UML diagram that depicts the change in state or condition of a classifier instance or role over time. Typically used to show the change in state of an object over time in response to external events. New to UML 2.

Top-down design. The breaking down of a problem that is not easy to deal with into a collection of smaller problems that can be dealt with one at a time.

Traceability. The ease with which the features of one artifact—perhaps a document, model, or source code—may be related to the features of another.

Training. The teaching of specific, narrowly focused skills that are often immediately applicable to the current position of the student.

Transaction. A single unit of work that either completely succeeds or completely fails. A transaction may be one or more updates to an object, one or more reads, one or more deletes, or any combination thereof.

Transition. A progression from one state to another triggered by an event (either internal or external to the object).

Transitory association. An association that is not permanent and not saved to permanent storage. Transitory associations are modeled in the UML as dependency relationships.

Transitory object. An object not saved to permanent storage.

Trigger. An operation automatically invoked as the result of data manipulation language activity within a persistence mechanism.

Tuple. See *row.*

Tutorial. A document, either paper or electronic, aimed at novice users who need to learn the fundamentals of an application.

Two-tier client/server. A client/server architecture that is separated into two layers, an application layer (the client) and a server layer.

UCDD. Use case-driven development.

UDDI. Universal description, discovery, and integration.

UML. See *unified modeling language.*

Unidirectional association. An association that may be traversed in only one direction.

Unified modeling language (UML). The definition of a standard modeling language for object-oriented software, including the definition of a modeling notation and the semantics for applying it, as defined by the Object Management Group (OMG).

Unified process (UP). A framework from which a software development process may be instantiated. Examples: the rational unified process (RUP) and the enterprise unified process (EUP).

UP. See *unified process.*

URI. Uniform resource identifier.

Usability. The ease with which people are able to learn how to use and use productively highly usable systems. Such systems make it easy to remember from one use to another how to use them, and they help people to make fewer mistakes.

Usage centered design. A modeling methodology that focuses on the work that users are trying to accomplish and on what the software needs to supply via the user interface to help users accomplish their goals.

Usage scenario. See *use case scenario.*

Use case. A sequence of actions that provide a measurable value to an actor.

Use case diagram. A UML diagram that shows use cases, actors, and their interrelationships.

Use case model. A model comprised of a use case diagram, use case definitions, and actor definitions. Use case models are used to document the behavioral requirements of a system.

Use case scenario. The basic course of action through a single use case, a combination of portions of the basic course replaced by the steps of one or more alternate paths through a single use case, or a logic path spanning several use cases. Use case scenarios are also called usage scenarios.

Use case scenario testing. A testing technique in which one or more person(s) validate your domain model (typically a CRC model) by acting through the logic of use case scenarios.

User-acceptance testing (UAT). A testing technique in which users verify that an application meets their needs by working with the software.

User interface (UI). The user interface of software is the portion the user directly interacts with, including the screens, reports, documentation, and software support (via telephone, electronic mail, and so on).

User-interface class. A class that provides the ability for users to interact with the system. User-interface classes typically define a graphical user interface for an application, although other interface styles, such as voice command or HTML, are also implemented via user-interface classes.

User-interface event. An occurrence, often initiated by a user, such as keyboard input, a mouse action, or spoken input captured by a microphone, that causes action within your application.

User-interface flow diagram. A diagram that models the interface objects of your system and the relationships between them; also known as an interface-flow diagram, a windows navigation diagram, or an interface navigation diagram.

User-interface model. A model comprising your user-interface prototype, user-interface flow diagram, and any corresponding documentation regarding your user interface.

User-interface prototype. A prototype of the user interface of a system that could be as simple as a hand-drawn picture or a collection of programmed screens, pages, or reports.

User-interface testing. The testing of the user interface (UI) to ensure that it follows accepted UI standards and meets the requirements defined for it. Often referred to as graphical user-interface (GUI) testing.

User manual. A document, either paper or electronic, aimed at intermediate users who understand the basics of an application, but who may not know how to perform all applicable work tasks with the application.

User story. A very-high-level definition of a requirement, containing just enough information so that the developers can produce a reasonable estimate of the effort to implement it. A good way to think about a user story is that it is a reminder to have a conversation with your project stakeholder(s).

User testing. Testing processes in which the user community, as opposed to developers, performs the tests. User testing techniques include user-acceptance testing, alpha testing, beta testing, and pilot testing.

Uses relationship. See *include association.*

Utility. The condition of a system that does something of sufficient value to justify the investment in it.

Utility computing. An approach where the use of a computing service is charged for by the vendor on a usage basis, much as electricity or water is charged for.

Version control tool. A software tool used to check in/out, define, and manage versions of project artifacts.

Visibility. The level of access that external objects have to an item, such as an object's attributes or methods, or even to a class itself.

Visual Basic. An object-based programming language developed by Microsoft Corporation that extends Basic with several object-oriented concepts.

Volume testing. A subset of stress testing that deals specifically with determining how many transactions or database accesses an application can handle during a defined period of time.

Waterfall approach. An approach to building applications where development efforts proceed in a serial manner from one project stage to another.

Web service. A function that is accessible using standard Web technologies in accordance with common standards.

White-box testing. Testing to verify that specific lines of code work as defined. Also referred to as clear-box testing.

Whitespace. Blanks, such as blank lines or spaces, in source code.

Windows navigation diagram. See *user-interface flow diagram.*

Wrapper. A collection of one or more classes that encapsulates access to non-OO technology to make it appear as if it is OO.

Wrapping. The act of encapsulating non-OO functionality within a class, making it look and feel like any other object within the system.

Write lock. A type of lock indicating that a table, record, class, or object is currently being written to by another source. No one may obtain either a read or a write lock until this lock is cleared.

Write once, run anywhere (WORA). A marketing pitch for the Java language that points out Java's cross-platform nature.

WYSIWYG. What you see is what you get.

WYSIWYN. What you see is what you need.

XML. See *extensible markup language.*

XOR. Exclusive or.

XP. See *extreme programming.*

XSL-T. Extensible stylesheet language transformations.

References and Recommended Reading

Agile Alliance (2001a). *Manifesto for Agile Software Development*. Retrieved November 12, 2003 from http://www.agilemanifesto.org

Agile Alliance (2001b). *Principles behind the the Agile Manifesto*. Retrieved November 12, 2003 from http://www.agilemanifesto.org/principles.html

Alur, D., Crupi, J., and Malks, D. (2003). *Core J2EE Patterns: Best Practices and Design Strategies* (2nd ed.). Upper Saddle River, NJ: Prentice Hall PTR.

Ambler, S. W. (1995). *The Object Primer: Application Developer's Guide to Object Orientation*. New York: Cambridge University Press.

Ambler, S. W. (1998a). *Building Object Applications That Work: Your Step-By-Step Handbook for Developing Robust Systems with Object Technology*. New York: Cambridge University Press.

Ambler, S. W. (1998b). *Process Patterns—Building Large-Scale Systems Using Object Technology*. New York: Cambridge University Press.

Ambler, S. W. (1999). *More Process Patterns—Delivering Large-Scale Systems Using Object Technology*. New York: Cambridge University Press.

Ambler, S. W. (2000). *The Design of a Robust Persistence Layer for Relational Databases*. Retrieved November 12, 2003 from http://www.ambysoft.com/persistenceLayer.html.

Ambler, S. W. (2001). *The Object Primer: The Application Developer's Guide to Object Orientation* (2nd ed.). New York: Cambridge University Press.

Ambler, S. W. (2002). *Agile Modeling: Effective Practices for Extreme Programming and the Unified Process*. New York: Wiley.

Ambler, S. W. (2003a). *Active Stakeholder Participation*. Retrieved November 12, 2003 from http://www.agilemodeling.com/essays/activeStakeholder Participation.htm

Ambler, S. W. (2003b). *Agile Database Techniques: Effective Strategies for the Agile Software Developer*. New York: Wiley.

Ambler, S. W. (2003c). *The Elements of UML Style*. New York: Cambridge University Press.

Ambler, S. W., and Constantine, L. L. (2000a). *The Unified Process Inception Phase*. Gilroy, CA: CMP Books.

Ambler, S. W., and Constantine, L. L. (2000b). *The Unified Process Elaboration Phase*. Gilroy, CA: CMP Books.

Ambler, S. W., and Constantine, L. L. (2000c). *The Unified Process Construction Phase*. Gilroy, CA: CMP Books.

Ambler, S. W., and Constantine, L. L. (2002). *The Unified Process Transition and Production Phases*. Gilroy, CA: CMP Books.

Armour, F., and Miller, G. (2001). *Advanced Use Case Modeling: Software Systems*. Reading, MA: Addison Wesley Longman.

Arranga, E. C., and Coyle, P. C. (1996). *Object-Oriented COBOL*. New York: Cambridge University Press.

Astels, D. (2003). *Test Driven Development: A Practical Guide*. Upper Saddle River, NJ: Prentice Hall.

Atkinson, C., Bayer, J., Bunse, C., Kamsties, E., Laitenberger, O., Laqua, R., et al. (2002). *Component-Based Product Line Engineering with UML*. London: Pearson Education.

Beck, K. (2000). *Extreme Programming Explained—Embrace Change*. Reading, MA: Addison Wesley Longman.

Beck, K. (2003). *Test Driven Development: By Example*. Boston, MA: Addison Wesley.

Beck, K., and Cunningham, W. (1989). A laboratory for teaching object-oriented thinking. In *Proceedings of OOPSLA'89*, pp. 1–6.

Beedle, M., and Schwaber, K. (2001). *Agile Software Development with SCRUM*. Upper Saddle River, NJ: Prentice Hall.

Bennett, D. (1997). *Designing Hard Software: The Essential Tasks*. Greenwich, CT: Manning.

Binder, R. (1999). *Testing Object-Oriented Systems: Models, Patterns, and Tools*. Reading, MA: Addison Wesley Longman.

Boehm, B. W. (1988). A spiral model of software development and enhancement. *IEEE Computer, 21(5)*, 61–72.

Booch, G., Rumbaugh, J., and Jacobson, I. (1999). *The Unified Modeling Language User Guide*. Reading, MA: Addison Wesley Longman

Brant, J., and Yoder, J. (2000). Creating reports with query objects. In N. Harrison, B. Foote, and H. Rohnert (Eds.), *Pattern Languages of Program Design, Vol. 4* (pp. 375–390). Reading, MA: Addison Wesley.

Buschmann, F., Meunier, R., Rohnert, H., Sommerlad, P., and Stal, M. (1996). *A Systems of Patterns: Pattern-Oriented Software Architecture*. New York: Wiley.

Celko, J. (1999). *Joe Celko's Data & Databases: Concepts in Practice*. San Francisco: Morgan Kaufmann Publishers.

Coad, P. (1992). Object-oriented patterns. *Communications of the ACM, 35(9)*, 152–159.

Coad, P., Lefebvre, E., & DeLuca, J. (1999). *Java Modeling in Color with UML: Enterprise Components and Process*. Upper Saddle River, NJ: Prentice Hall, Inc.

Coad, P., and Mayfield, M. (1997). *Java Design: Building Better Apps and Applets*. Englewood Cliff, NJ: Prentice Hall.

Cockburn, A. (2001a). *Writing Effective Use Cases*. Boston: Addison Wesley.

Cockburn, A. (2001b). *Crystal "Clear": A Human-Powered Software Development Methodology for Small Teams*. Retrieved November 12, 2003, from http://members.aol.com/humansandt/crystal/clear/

Cockburn, A. (2002). *Agile Software Development*. Reading, MA: Addison Wesley Longman.

Constantine, L. L., and Lockwood, L. A. D. (1999). *Software for Use: A Practical Guide to the Models and Methods of Usage-Centered Design*. New York: ACM Press.

Coplien, J. O. (1995). A generative development-process pattern language. In J. O. Coplien and D. C. Schmidt (Eds.), *Pattern Languages of Program Design* (pp. 183–237). Reading, MA: Addison Wesley Longman.

Date, C. J. (2001). *An Introduction to Database System* (7th ed.). Reading, MA: Addison Wesley Longman.

DeMarco, T. (1997). *The Deadline: A Novel about Project Management.* New York: Dorset House.

Douglass, B. P. (1999). *Doing Hard Time: Developing Real-Time Systems with UML, Objects, Frameworks, and Patterns.* Reading, MA: Addison Wesley Longman.

Evans, E. (2004). *Domain Driven Design: Tackling Complexity in the Heart of Software.* Reading, MA: Addison Wesley Longman.

Fowler, M. (1997). *Analysis Patterns: Reusable Object Models.* Menlo Park, CA: Addison Wesley Longman.

Fowler, M. (1999). *Refactoring: Improving the Design of Existing Code.* Menlo Park, CA: Addison Wesley Longman.

Fowler, M. (2001). *The New Methodology.* Retrieved November 12, 2003, from http://www.martinfowler.com/articles/newMethodology.html

Fowler, M. (2004). *UML Distilled* (3rd ed.). Reading, MA: Addison Wesley Longman.

Fowler, M., Rice D., Foemmel, M., Hieatt, E., Mee, R., and Stafford, R. (2003). *Patterns of Enterprise Application Architecture.* Boston: Addison Wesley Longman.

Gane, C., and Sarson, T. (1979). *Structured Systems Analysis: Tools and Techniques.* Englewood Cliffs, NJ: Prentice Hall.

Gamma, E., Helm, R., Johnson, R., and Vlissides, J. (1995). *Design Patterns: Elements of Reusable Object-Oriented Software.* Reading, MA: Addison-Wesley.

Gosling, J., Joy, B., and Steele, G. (1996). *The Java Language Specification.* Reading, MA: Addison Wesley Longman.

Grady, R. B. (1992). *Practical Software Metrics for Project Management and Process Improvement.* Englewood Cliffs, NJ: Prentice-Hall.

Halpin, T. A. (2001). *Information Modeling and Relational Databases: From Conceptual Analysis to Logical Design.* San Francisco: Morgan Kaufmann.

Hay, D. C. (1996). *Data Model Patterns: Conventions of Thought.* New York: Dorset House.

Hay, D. C. (2003). *Requirements Analysis: From Business Views to Architecture.* Upper Saddle River, NJ: Prentice Hall.

Hock, D. W. (2000). *Birth of the Chaordic Age.* San Francisco: Berrett-Koehler.

Hunt, A. & Thomas, D. (2000). *The Pragmatic Programmer: From Journeyman to Master*. Reading, MA: Addison Wesley Longman, Inc.

IBM (2003). *Rational Unified Process Home Page*. Retrieved November 12, 2003, from http://www.rational.com/products/rup/index.jsp.

Jacobson, I., Booch, G., and Rumbaugh, J. (1999). *The Unified Software Development Process*. Reading, MA: Addison Wesley Longman.

Jacobson, I., Christerson, M., Jonsson, P., and Overgaard, G. (1992). *Object-Oriented Software Engineering—A Use Case Driven Approach*. Wokingham, UK: ACM Press.

Jeffries, R., Anderson, A., and Hendrickson, C. (2001). *Extreme Programming Installed*. Boston: Addison-Wesley.

Jones, C. (1996). *Patterns of Software Systems Failure and Success*. Boston, MA: International Thomson Computer Press.

Kerievsky, J. (2001). Patterns and XP. In G. Succi & M. Marchesi (Eds.), *Extreme Programming Examined*. (pp. 207–220). Boston, MA: Addison Wesley.

Kleppe, A., Warmer, J., and Bast, W. (2003). *MDA Explained: The Model Driven Architecture, Practice and Promise*. Boston, MA: Pearson Education.

Kruchten, P. (2000). *The Rational Unified Process: An Introduction* (2nd ed.). Reading, MA: Addison Wesley Longman.

Larman, C. (2002). *Applying UML and Patterns: An Introduction to Object-Oriented Analysis and Design and the Unified Process*. Upper Saddle River, NJ: Prentice Hall PTR.

Lea, D. (1997). *Concurrent Programming in Java: Design Principles and Patterns*. Reading, MA: Addison Wesley Longman.

Leffingwell, D., and Widrig, D. (2000). *Managing Software Requirements: A Unified Approach*. Reading, MA: Addison Wesley Longman.

Lieberherr, K., Holland, I., and Riel, A. (1988). Object-oriented programming: An objective sense of style. In *OOPSLA'88 Conference Proceedings* (pp. 91–102). New York: ACM Press.

Linthicum, D. S. (2000). *Enterprise Application Integration*. Reading, MA: Addison Wesley Longman.

Lorenz, M., and Kidd, J. (1994). *Object-Oriented Software Metrics*. Englewood Cliffs, NJ: Prentice-Hall.

Maguire, S. (1994). *Debugging the Development Process*. Redmond, WA: Microsoft Press.

Marick, B. (1995). *The Craft of Software Testing: Subsystems Testing Including Object-Based and Object-Oriented Testing.* Upper Saddle River, NJ: Prentice Hall PTR.

Marick, B. (2002). *Agile Testing Home Page.* Retrieved November 12, 2003, from http://www.testing.com/agile/

Martin, R. C., Newkirk, J. W., and Koss, R. S. (2003). *Agile Software Development: Principles, Patterns, and Practices.* Upper Saddle River, NJ: Prentice Hall.

Mayhew, D. J. (1992). *Principles and Guidelines in Software User Interface Design.* Englewood Cliffs, NJ: Prentice Hall.

McConnell, S. (1996). *Rapid Development: Taming Wild Software Schedules.* Redmond, WA: Microsoft Press.

McGovern, J., Tyagi, S., Stevens, M. E., and Mathew, S. (2003). *Java Web Services Architecture.* San Francisco: Morgan Kaufman.

McGregor, J. D. (1997, February). Quality assurance: Planning for testing. *Journal of Object-Oriented Programming, 9(9),* 8–12.

Meyer, B. (1997). *Object-Oriented Software Construction* (2nd ed.). Upper Saddle River, NJ: Prentice-Hall PTR.

Moriarty, T. (2001, April 16). To unify architecture with methodology: The rational unified process meets the zachman information systems architecture. *Intelligent Enterprise, April 16, 2001.*

Nagler, J. (1995). *Coding Style and Good Computing Practices.* Retrieved November 12, 2003 from http://wizard.ucr.edu/~nagler/coding_style.html

Nalbone, J., Vizdos, M., and Ambler, S. (2003). *The Enterprise Management Discipline: Extending the RUP for Multi-system Environments.* Retrieved November 12, 2003, from http://www.enterpriseunifiedprocess.info/essays/enterpriseManagement.html

Object Management Group (2003). *Unified Modeling Language: Superstructure version 2.0.* OMG document ad/2003–04–01. Retrieved November 12, 2003, from http://www.omg.org.

Page-Jones, M. (1995). *What Every Programmer Should Know About Object-Oriented Design.* New York: Dorset-House.

Page-Jones, M. (2000). *Fundamentals of Object-Oriented Design in UML.* New York: Dorset-House.

Palmer, S. R., and Felsing, J. M. (2002). *A Practical Guide to Feature-Driven Development*. Upper Saddle River, NJ: Prentice Hall PTR.

Raskin, J. (1994). Intuitive equals familiar. *Communications of the ACM, 37(9)*, 17–18.

Riel, A. J. (1996). *Object-Oriented Design Heuristics*. Reading, MA: Addison Wesley Longman Inc.

Roman, E., Ambler, S. W., and Jewell, T. (2002). *Mastering Enterprise Java Beans* (2nd ed.). New York: Wiley.

Rosenberg, D., and Scott, K. (1999). *Use Case Driven Object Modeling with UML : A Practical Approach*. Reading, MA: Addison Wesley Longman.

Ross, R. G. (2003). *Principles of the Business Rule Approach*. Reading, MA: Addison Wesley Longman.

Royce, W. (1998). *Software Project Management: A Unified Framework*. Reading, MA: Addison Wesley Longman.

Rumbaugh, J., Jacobson, I., and Booch, G. (1999). *The Unified Modeling Language Reference Manual*. Reading, MA: Addison Wesley Longman.

Sadalage, P., and Schuh, P. (2002). *The Agile Database: Tutorial Notes*. Paper presented at XP/Agile Universe 2002. Retrieved November 12, 2003, from http://www.xpuniverse.com

Schneider, G., and Winters, J. P. (2001). *Applying Use Cases: A Practical Guide* (2nd ed.). Reading, MA: Addison Wesley Longman.

Shalloway, A. (2000). *A Lightweight Methodology for Design and Code Reviews*. Retrieved from http://www.netobjectives.com/download/designreviews.pdf

Software Engineering Institute (1995). *The Capability Maturity Model: Guidelines for Improving the Software Process*. Reading, MA: Addison-Wesley Publishing Company.

Stapleton, J. (2003). *DSDM: Business Focused Development* (2nd ed.). Harlow, UK: Addison Wesley.

Tourniaire, F., and Farrell, R. (1997). *The Art of Software Support: Design and Operation of Support Centers and Help Desks*. Upper Saddle River, NJ: Prentice Hall PTR.

Vermeulen, A., Ambler, S. W., Bumgardner, G., Metz, E., Misfeldt, T., Shur, J., et al. (2000). *The Elements of Java Style*. New York: Cambridge University Press.

Warner, J., and Kleppe, A. (1999). *The Object Constraint Language: Precise Modeling with UML*. Reading, MA: Addison Wesley Longman.

Weiss, E. H. (1991). *How to Write Usable User Documentation*. Phoenix, AZ: Oryx Press.

Wiegers, K. (1996). *Creating a Software Engineering Culture*. New York: Dorset House.

Wiegers, K. (1999). *Software Requirements*. Redmond, WA: Microsoft Press.

Wilkinson, N. M. (1995). *Using CRC Cards: An Informal Approach to Object-Oriented Development*. New York: Cambridge University Press.

Williams, L., and Kessler, R. (2002). *Pair Programming Illuminated*. Boston, MA: Addison Wesley.

Wirfs-Brock, R., Wilkerson, B., and Wiener, L. (1990). *Designing Object-Oriented Software*. Englewood Cliffs, NJ: Prentice-Hall.

Yourdon, E. (1997). *Death March: The Complete Software Developer's Guide to Surviving "Mission Impossible" Projects*. Upper Saddle River, NJ: Prentice-Hall.

ZIFA (2002). *The Zachman Institute for Framework Advancement*. Retrieved November 12, 2003 from http://www.zifa.com

WEB-BASED RESOURCES

Agile Database Techniques: http://www.agiledata.org

Agile Modeling: http://www.agilemodeling.com

Enterprise Unified Process: http://www.enterpriseunifiedprocess.com

Modeling Style Guidelines: http://www.modelingstyle.info

The Process Patterns Resource Page: http://www.ambysoft.com/ processPatternsPage.html

Scott Ambler's Online Writings: http://www.ambysoft.com/ onlineWritings.html

Index